THE BRITISH COMMONWEALTH

THE DEVELOPMENT OF ITS LAWS AND CONSTITUTIONS

General Editor

George W. Keeton

Volume 4

NEW ZEALAND

N.Z

a

AUSTRALIA
The Law Book Co. of Australasia Pty Ltd.
Sydney : Melbourne : Brisbane

CANADA AND U.S.A.
The Carswell Company Ltd.
Toronto

INDIA
N. M. Tripathi Ltd.
Bombay

NEW ZEALAND
Legal Publications Ltd.
Wellington

PAKISTAN
Pakistan Law House
Karachi

NEW ZEALAND

The Development of its Laws and Constitution

UNDER THE GENERAL EDITORSHIP OF

J. L. ROBSON

LL.M., Ph.D.

WITH

SPECIALIST CONTRIBUTORS

LONDON

STEVENS & SONS LIMITED

1954

N.Z.

a*

*First published in 1954 by
Stevens & Sons Limited
of 119 & 120 Chancery Lane
London – Law Publishers
and printed in Great Britain
by The Eastern Press, Ltd.
of London and Reading*

124701

GENERAL EDITOR

J. L. ROBSON, LL.M., PH.D.,
    Assistant Secretary (Administrative), Department for Justice, Wellington.

CONTRIBUTORS

J. W. BAIN, LL.B.,
    Assistant Crown Solicitor, Crown Law Office, Wellington.

I. D. CAMPBELL, LL.M.,
    Professor of English and New Zealand Law, Victoria University College, Wellington.

E. J. HAUGHEY, M.A., LL.M., B.COM.,
    Assistant Crown Solicitor, Crown Law Office, Wellington.

K. J. SCOTT, M.A., LL.B., D.P.A.,
    Senior Lecturer, School of Political Science and Public Administration, Victoria University College, Wellington.

PREFACE

Sir Joshua Williams, a famous New Zealand Judge, said in 1903[1]:

> "Fifty years in New Zealand mean much more than fifty years in England. The changes, political, social and material that have taken place in New Zealand during the latter half of the nineteenth century are greater than those that have taken place in England from the time of the Tudors to the present day."

These changes had a profound influence on constitutional, judicial, legislative, and administrative developments. Although Sir Joshua was referring to the latter half of the nineteenth century, the first half of this century has produced its full share of changes, although relatively less rapid and less original.

The aim of this book is to discuss how the law has responded to these changes and an endeavour has been made to relate legal development to the social forces behind it. The book is not an exhaustive treatise on every branch of the law ; emphasis has been placed on those branches which have had to make a substantial response to social conditions. It is inevitable that the great bulk of the book should be a discussion of legislation, for it is there that New Zealand has made its contribution rather than in the field of judicial creativeness. The text includes significant legislation to the end of 1953.

The prime responsibility for each chapter rests with the person or persons named in the Table of Contents, but we have gained from mutual criticism and from the advice of others who have kindly read the manuscript.

Although some of us hold official positions, the views expressed in this work are those of individuals and are devoid of any official significance.

We express our thanks to Mr. G. J. Grace, Department for Justice, Wellington, for his valuable assistance in the checking of the proofs and the preparation of the indices.

J.L.R.

January, 1954

[1] N.Z. P.C. Cases, 1840-1932, Appendix p. 752.

CONTENTS

Preface .. .. *page* vii

Chronological Table xv

1. INTRODUCTION .. .. *J. L. Robson and K. J. Scott* 1

  Early Constitutional Developments 1
  The Personal Discretion of the Governor-General in the Exercise
    of his Executive Powers 8
  The Problems Facing Justice 16
  Legislation and its Background 21

2. PARLIAMENT .. .. *K. J. Scott* 30

  The Franchise 30
  Electoral Boundaries 31
  Elections 33
  Size of House of Representatives 35
  Life of Parliament 35
  The Legislative Council 37
  Privilege and Procedure 39
  Assent to Bills 40
  Legislative and Constituent Powers 41
  The Entrenched Sections 41
  Extraterritorial Legislation 44
  Repugnancy 45
  Reservation 47
  Disallowance 49
  Flexibility of the Constitution 50

3. THE JUDICIAL SYSTEM .. .. *J. W. Bain* 52

  The Courts of Civil and Criminal Jurisdiction 52
    The Magistrates' Courts 53
    The Supreme Court 60
    The Court of Appeal 67
    Children's Courts 69
  Courts of Special Jurisdiction 69
    The Maori Appellate Court and Maori Land Court 69
    The Coroners' Courts 71
    The Court of Arbitration and the Compensation Court 72
    The Land Valuation Tribunals 72
    The Court of Review 72
    The Wardens' Courts 73
    Other Judicial Tribunals 74
  Constitutional Position and Duties of Judiciary and Magistracy .. 76
  The Legal Profession 79
  The Council of Law Reporting 82

4. PUBLIC ADMINISTRATION AND ADMINISTRATIVE LAW
J. L. Robson and K. J. Scott 84

    Administrative Law 89
    Subordinate Legislation.. 91
    Administrative Tribunals 103
        Functions 105
        Numerical Strength of Tribunals 108
        Tenure of Office 108
        Qualifications for Appointment 109
        Procedure 110
        Quorum and Decision making 111
        Extent of Independence 112
        The Lewis Case 114
        Contribution to Legal Development 117
        Judicial Control 118
        General Observations 126
    Proceedings Against the Crown 129

5. SOCIAL LEGISLATION .. .. *J. L. Robson* 135

    Health 137
        General Local Authorities 138
        Hospital Boards 140
        The Department of Health 141
        Tuberculosis 142
        Infirm and Neglected Persons 143
        Professional, Vocational and Technical Standards 143
        Medical Advertisements 144
        Other Regulatory Functions 145
        Health Education and Other Services 146
        Health Benefits 146
    Education 147
        School Committees 147
        Education Boards 148
        Post-Primary Schools 149
        The Department of Education 149
        Appeal Tribunals for Teachers 150
        Judicial Control 151
    Child Welfare 152
        Private or Public Institutions 155
        Infants' Homes 156
        Illegitimate Births 157
        Children's Courts 157
    Social Security 159
        Residential Qualifications 162
        Character Provisions 163
        Rates of Benefits 163
        Means Test 164
        Reciprocity with Other Countries 164
        Financing of Scheme 165
    Maori Welfare 165
    Reform in Social Legislation 169

6. INDUSTRIAL RELATIONS .. .. *J. L. Robson* 172

 Conciliation and Arbitration 173
  Conciliation Procedure 175
  Court of Arbitration 177
  An Award 178
  Evidence and Procedure 180
  Penal Provisions 181
 Labour Disputes Investigation Act, 1913 185
 The Court of Arbitration 187
  Compulsory Unionism 190
  Problems Facing the Court of Arbitration 191
  The Attitude of the Ordinary Courts 191
  The Health of Unions 193
 Strikes 195

7. MONOPOLY AND PRICE CONTROL .. .. *J. L. Robson* 197

 Monopolies 197
  The Crown Milling Case 202
  Export Control and Internal Prices 209
  Subsequent Trends 213
  Profiteering 213
 Price Control 215
  Industrial Efficiency 219
  Scheme of the Act 219
  Registration and Licensing 220
  The Policy of the Appeal Authority 222

8. MARKETING AND THE PRIMARY PRODUCER .. *J. L. Robson* 225

 The Meat Producers' Board 225
 The Dairy-Produce Control Board 228
 Marketing Boards and the Courts 229
 Further Marketing Legislation 231
 Internal Marketing 236
 Further Recent Legislation 238

9. EXCHANGE CONTROL AND BANKING .. .. *J. L. Robson* 240

 Export Control and Overseas Funds 240
 Import Control 242
 Banking 247
 Reserve Bank 250

10. CRIMINAL LAW .. .. *I. D. Campbell* 257

 Transition to a New World 257
 Adoption of English Criminal Law 259
 Early Penal System 260
 Progress of Reform 262
 Codification 264
 Capital Punishment 268
 General Principles of Liability 269
 Trial by Jury 272
 Criminal Law and Individual Liberty 272
 The Maori People 274
 Current Trends 274

11. THE HISTORICAL DEVELOPMENT OF THE CIVIL LAW

                                              E. J. Haughey   276

    Property 276
        Statutory Simplification of Real Property Law 276
        Registration of Deeds 278
        Land Transfer System 279
        Crown Land Tenures 280
        The Right of Eminent Domain and the Control and Conservation
            of Land and Natural Resources 282
        Married Women's Property Legislation 285
        Tenancy Law 287
        Fencing Legislation 289
        Chattels Securities 289
        Succession on Intestacy 290
        The Taxation of Property and Incomes 291
    Contracts and Commercial Law 292
        Codification of Commercial Law 293
        Mercantile Law Legislation 294
        The Carriage of Goods and Passengers 295
        Secret Commissions 295
        Contracts Protecting Workers and the Weaker Party to Transactions 296
        Protection of Workmen's Wages and Contractors' Liens 297
        Statutory Interference with Contractual Relationships in Times of
            War and Economic Depression 299
        Law Reform Legislation 302
        Third Party Motor Insurance 303
        Company Law 304
        Co-operative Companies for Processing and Marketing of Primary
            Products 305
        Restrictions on the Raising of Capital 305
        Incorporated Societies 306
        Bankruptcy 306
    Torts 306
        Damage Caused by Dogs 307
        Statutory Modification of Law of Defamation 307
        Death in Relation to Torts 308
        Contributory Negligence 311
        Injuries Arising from Mental or Nervous Shock 311
        Injury to Employees and Workers' Compensation 312
    Conclusion 315

12. FAMILY LAW .. ..   *I. D. Campbell*   317

    Marriage 317
    Divorce 322
        Grounds 322
        Domicile 324
    Other Matrimonial Causes 326
        Judicial Interpretation 327
    Summary Proceedings 328
    Custody of Children 330
    Illegitimate Children 331
        Legitimation 331
        Statutory Provisions for Illegitimate Children 333
    Adoption 334
    Family Protection Act 335
    Family Homes 338

13. LEGAL TRENDS WITHIN NEW ZEALAND

J. L. Robson and J. W. Bain 339

The Growth of Status	340
Legislation and the Common Law	341
Legislation and Limiting Factors	344
Betting	344
The Sale of Liquor	345
Illegal Abortions	345
Industrial Relations	346
Regulation of Sales of Land	347
Tax Evasion	347
Administrative Difficulties	347
The Respect of the Executive for the Law	348
Remission of Penalties	349
Retrospective and Validating Legislation	350
Law Reform	352

Bibliography 359

Table of Statutes 363

Table of Cases 375

Index 377

CHRONOLOGICAL TABLE

1642—New Zealand discovered by Tasman.

1769—Captain James Cook landed in New Zealand.

1814—Arrival of Rev. Samuel Marsden as missionary.
Marsden commissioned as Magistrate.

1817—Act of Imperial Parliament that New Zealand was not within His Majesty's dominions.

1823-28—Jurisdiction of Courts of Justice in New South Wales extended to British subjects in New Zealand.

1825—First attempt at colonisation by an expedition under Captain Herd.

1833—James Busby appointed as British Resident at Bay of Islands.

1839—Governor-in-Chief of New South Wales authorised to include within the limits of that colony any territory that might be acquired in sovereignty by Her Majesty in New Zealand.

1840—Arrival of New Zealand Company's settlers at Port Nicholson.
Treaty of Waitangi signed.
British sovereignty proclaimed.
Captain Hobson assumed office as Lieutenant-Governor with residence at Auckland.

1841—New Zealand Company incorporated by Charter.
New Zealand separated from New South Wales and proclaimed a separate colony.
Courts of Law established.

1842—Conveyancing simplified by ordinance.

1843—Members of a European party slain by Maoris at Wairau.

1844—Royal flagstaff at Kororareka cut down by Maoris.

1845—Kororareka destroyed by Maoris.

1846—Maori hostilities near Wellington.
Provision made for the division of New Zealand into two provinces—New Munster and New Ulster—and representative institutions conferred by Act of Imperial Parliament.

1847—Wanganui attacked by Maoris.

1848—Imperial Parliament suspended that portion of the 1846 constitution that gave representative institutions.

1850—New Zealand Company surrendered its Charter to Imperial Government.
State Bank created.

1852—Constitution Act passed by Imperial Parliament establishing representative institutions and dividing New Zealand into six provinces.
Gold discovered at Coromandel.

1854—Opening at Auckland of first session of the General Assembly.

1856—First ministry appointed under system of responsible government.

1857—Goldfield opened at Collingwood.
Constitution Amendment Act (Imp.).

1858—District Courts established.
English Laws Act.

1860—Fighting with Maoris in Waitara district.
Land Registry Act.

1861—Gold discovered in Otago.

1862—Court of Appeal created by Act of Parliament.
Maori Land Court established.

1863—Waikato war began and spread.
Partial control of Maori affairs assumed by New Zealand Cabinet.

1864—Severe fighting in Waikato and elsewhere.
Gold discovered on West Coast of South Island.
1865—Seat of Government transferred from Auckland to Wellington.
Proclamation of peace issued but fighting continued in some areas.
Colonial Laws Validity Act (Imp.).
1866—Crown Debts Act ; simplified procedure for recovery of Crown debts.
1867—Provision made for admission of four Maori members to House of Repre-
sentatives as direct representatives of Maori people.
Opening of Thames goldfield.
Legislation passed to deal with neglected and delinquent children.
1869—Government Life Insurance Department established.
New Zealand Law Society constituted by statute.
1870—Further fighting with Maori rebels.
Last Imperial troops withdrawn from New Zealand.
Plans laid for a vigorous public works and immigration policy.
Land Transfer Act—effectively established land transfer system in New
Zealand.
1871—Crown Redress Act.
1872—Two Maori Chiefs appointed to Legislative Council.
Public Trust Office created.
First comprehensive measure dealing with public health was passed.
1876—Legislation came into force abolishing provincial government and dividing
the country into counties and boroughs.
1877—Provision under Education Act for free and compulsory education.
1878—Trade Union Act.
1879—Law altered to provide that, upon a grant of administration by the Court,
the real estate of a deceased person was vested in his executor or administrator instead of passing to the heir-at-law.
Triennial Parliaments Act.
Adult male suffrage introduced.
Tax on land introduced.
1881—Statutory provision made for the adoption of children.
Crown Suits Act.
1882—Refrigeration ; first shipment of frozen meat from New Zealand.
Pleading was simplified by Supreme Court Act.
Industrial Schools Act.
1884—Married Women's Property Act.
1885—Scheme enacted for the creation of boards to administer public hospitals
which were to assume the function of granting charitable aid.
1887—Mother's position in relation to the custody and guardianship of infants
strengthened by statute.
1890—Children's Protection Act.
Great maritime strike.
First election of House of Representatives under one-man-one-vote
principle.
1891—Liberal or Liberal-Labour Party took office under Ballance.
Factories Act passed as a result of the recommendations of the commission
which investigated " sweating ".
Employers' Liability Act.
Truck Act.
Income tax introduced.
1892—Lease-in-perpetuity system of land tenure introduced.
Dispute between Governor and his Ministers settled by a ruling of Secretary of State that Governor should, as a general rule, accept the advice of
his Ministers when Imperial interests were not affected.
1893—Seddon became Prime Minister on death of Ballance.
Franchise extended to women.

1894—System of industrial conciliation and arbitration introduced with provision for a Court of Arbitration.

Provision made for the legitimation of illegitimate children by the subsequent marriage of parents.

1896—Abolition of property qualifications in national voting.

1898—Old-age Pensions Act.

1900—Testator's Family Maintenance Act.

Workers' Compensation for Accident Act : jurisdiction of Court of Arbitration extended to embrace claims under that Act.

1903—State Fire Insurance Act.

New Zealand Judges severely criticised by Privy Council in Wallis case.

1905—Legislation passed to deal with unfair competition from abroad in the sale of agricultural implements.

1906—Death of Seddon, Prime Minister, and Ward ultimately became Prime Minister.

1907—New Zealand constituted a Dominion.

Legislation passed to deal with the problem of monopoly in flour and other products.

1908—Monopoly Prevention Act.

1910—More stringent legislation enacted to repress monopolies.

1911—Widows' Pensions Act.

1912—Reform Party (Conservative) under Massey takes office.

Public Service placed under Commissioner control.

Land Laws amended.

1913—Extensive strikes.

Labour Disputes Investigation Act.

1914—The Regulation of Trade and Commerce Act passed shortly after the outbreak of the First World War.

1915—National Government formed under Massey.

1916—Rent restriction legislation enacted.

1919—Women made eligible for seats in Parliament.

National Government broke up and Reform Party under Massey took office again.

1920—Mandate from League of Nations to administer Western Samoa.

1922—The era of Marketing Boards began with the formation of the Meat Producers' Board.

1924—Land Transfer (Compulsory Registration of Titles) Act.

1925—Death of Massey, and Coates later became Prime Minister.

Child Welfare Act.

1926—Family Allowances Act.

1928—Compulsory insurance of motor-vehicles provided for by Motor-Vehicles Insurance (Third-Party Risks) Act.

United Party under Ward assumed office.

1931—Council of Legal Education created.

Coalition Government took office under Forbes as Prime Minister.

Parliament approved draft Statute of Westminster.

To meet adverse economic conditions, legislation passed providing for reduction of wages and salaries and for the relief of mortgagors.

1932—Access to the Court of Arbitration restricted by legislation.

Provision made for reductions in pensions, in salaries of public servants, and in rents, interest rates and other fixed charges.

Public Safety Conservation Act.

1933—Interest reduced on public internal debt. Provision made for a reduction in the interest payable by local authorities on loans, and for conversion of loans.

1934—Reserve Bank began business.

Executive Commission of Agriculture established.

1935—Labour Party under Savage assumed office.

1936—Reserve Bank nationalised.
Change in marketing structure.   (Primary Produce).
System of guaranteed prices for butter and cheese.
Forty-hour week.
Compulsory unionism.
Prevention of Profiteering Act.
Industrial Efficiency Act.
Fair Rents Act.

1937—Government assumed control of the internal marketing of some items of primary produce.

1938—Import, export and exchange control introduced.
Social Security Act.

1939—First British High Commissioner took up his duties in New Zealand.
Declaration of war with Germany.
Emergency war legislation.
Price Investigation Tribunal, later styled Price Tribunal, was formed.

1940—Special Compensation Court established to administer Workers' Compensation Act, 1922.
First High Commissioner for Canada took up his office in New Zealand.
Fraser became Prime Minister on the death of Savage.
Universal superannuation came into force.
Special War Cabinet of five members formed.

1941—Pharmacy benefits introduced under the Social Security Scheme.
Death penalty for murder abolished, also flogging and whipping.

1942—Control of industrial manpower.
Economic Stabilisation Emergency Regulations.

1944—Australian-New Zealand Agreement 1944, providing for collaboration on matters of mutual interest.
Mutual-Aid Agreement between Canada and New Zealand signed.

1945—" Country quota " (electoral) abolished.
New Zealand National Airways Act.
Criminal jurisdiction of the Court of Appeal substantially enlarged.
Housing Improvement Act.
Maori Social and Economic Advancement Act.

1946—First appointment of women to Legislative Council.
Family benefit (Social Security) made universal.
No-confidence debate in Parliament on question whether Lewis, a member of a Land Sales Committee, should have been removed from office.

1947—Local Government Commission appointed.
First woman Cabinet Minister in New Zealand appointed.
Dairy Products Marketing Commission.
Statute of Westminster adopted.
New Zealand Constitution (Amendment) Act (Imp.).
Civil Jurisdiction of Stipendiary Magistrates enlarged by the Magistrates' Courts Act.
Contributory Negligence Act.
Supply Regulations Act.

1948—Legislation passed providing for the replacement of Land Sales Court and Land Sales Committees by a Land Valuation Court and Land Valuation Committees with wider functions.

1949—Maori electors given the right to vote in general licensing polls.
National Party, under Holland as Prime Minister, assumed office.

1950—Control of land sales, except of farm land, removed.
Easing of price control.
Legislative Council abolished.
Death penalty for murder restored.

1951—Easing of import control.
Waterfront strike : Public Safety Conservation Act invoked.

1951—Police Offences Amendment Act.
    Industrial Conciliation and Arbitration Amendment Act.
    United States of America, Australia and New Zealand sign Pacific Security
      Treaty.
1952—Population of New Zealand, exclusive of Island Territories:

Europeans	1,886,403
Maoris	121,105
Total	2,007,508

    Criminal jurisdiction of Stipendiary Magistrates substantially enlarged by
      Summary Jurisdiction Act, 1952.
    Crown Proceedings Act, 1950, came into force on January 1, 1952
1953—Primary Products Marketing Act.

CHAPTER I

INTRODUCTION

NEW ZEALAND is young historically, yet it has had a variety of fruitful experience. The development of its Constitution and laws reflects that experience and cannot be understood except in the light of that experience. In this chapter we shall deal with three subjects : we shall trace the evolution of the New Zealand Constitution and show how the centre of power moved from the Governors to the democratic institutions that exist today ; we shall discuss the problems that have faced the administration of justice and have coloured and retarded legal development ; and we shall sketch in broad outline the contribution that has been made by legislation.

EARLY CONSTITUTIONAL DEVELOPMENTS

When the New Zealand Parliament acquired plenary powers in 1947, the New Zealand Constitution became in all essential respects the same in content as the British. Since 1947, however, one important difference in content has been created—by the abolition of the New Zealand Second Chamber in 1950. There is also one important difference in form : the core of the New Zealand Constitution is found in a single statute—the ' Act to Grant a Representative Constitution to the Colony of New Zealand ' passed by the Parliament of the United Kingdom in 1852.[1] Before considering the Constitution granted by this statute it is necessary to review the constitutional history of New Zealand up to 1852. Undoubtedly the event with the most important enduring legal consequences was the extension of British sovereignty to New Zealand in 1840. The interpretation of the legal effect of the various steps taken by various British authorities at that time constitutes one of the most interesting legal problems that have arisen in New Zealand.

Previously more than one European State had moved in the direction of annexing New Zealand, but none had completed a series of actions adequate to establish sovereignty. The first European expedition to make a landing was that of Captain James Cook, in 1769. Captain Cook took possession in the name of George III, but this inchoate title was not completed by any act of occupation. From about 1800 onwards the Governors of New South Wales were impelled by the anarchical conditions in the Pacific to seek to extend their jurisdiction even as far as Tahiti. Thus in 1814 and again in 1819 a New Zealand missionary

[1] 15 & 16 Vict. c. 72.

1

was commissioned as a magistrate.   The only legal justification for this
Pacific policy was a strained interpretation of the 1786 Order-in-Council
which had annexed for the Colony of New South Wales a defined part
of the Australian continent and also ' all the islands adjacent '.   The
attitude of the British Government was equivocal until 1817, when an
Act [2] was passed which explicitly treated New Zealand as being ' not
within His Majesty's dominions '.   In the succeeding years similar
references were made in other Acts, and the denial of sovereignty formed
the basis of numerous administrative decisions.   James Busby, the
British Resident in New Zealand from 1833 to 1840, was not a Governor
but a British agent in non-British territory.

During the thirties the number of Europeans living in lawless conditions in New Zealand was steadily growing (by the opening of 1840 it
had reached about 2,000), and there was a progressive weakening of tribal
authority among the Maoris living near to the harbours that were
frequented by Europeans.   Moreover, New Zealand was becoming
commercially important to New South Wales.   Humanitarian and
commercial considerations alike pointed to the need for fuller British
intervention.   In January 1839 the Colonial Office decided to establish
sovereignty over at least part of New Zealand.   It used in part the forms
of acquiring sovereignty by cession from the Maori chiefs ; but whether
these forms were effective in transferring sovereignty, or whether New
Zealand became British territory through annexation coupled with
settlement, has been a matter of considerable debate.   Before considering which of these views is correct, we shall briefly narrate the most
important of the relevant events.

Letters Patent were issued by the Crown on June 15, 1839, extending
the limits of the Colony of New South Wales to include any New Zealand
territory ' which is or may be acquired in sovereignty by Her Majesty '.
The task of acquiring sovereignty was entrusted to Captain William
Hobson, R.N., who had previously led an expedition to New Zealand,
and was then in England.   He was instructed ' to treat with the Aborigines
of New Zealand for the recognition of Her Majesty's sovereign authority
over the whole or any parts of those islands which they may be willing
to place under Her Majesty's dominion ' ; and to assert sovereignty over
the South Island on the ground of discovery if he found it ' uninhabited,
except but by a very small number of persons in a savage state, incapable
from their ignorance of entering intelligently into any treaties with the
Crown '.

Hobson arrived in New Zealand on January 29, 1840, and between
then and the following October secured execution of a treaty of cession
by about five hundred Maori chiefs.   The first signatures, about eighty

[2]   57 Geo. 3, c. 53.

in all, were appended at Waitangi in the North Island on February 6, and the treaty is known to history as the Treaty of Waitangi. On May 21 Hobson proclaimed sovereignty over the North Island on the ground of cession and over the South Island on the ground of discovery. In the same year the United Kingdom Parliament provided in the New South Wales Continuance Act, 1840, that New Zealand might be constituted a separate Colony by Letters Patent, and Letters Patent were issued on November 16. On May 3, 1841, Hobson proclaimed New Zealand a separate Colony. By that time the New Zealand Company had established organised settlements at Wellington (January, 1840), Wanganui (September, 1840) and New Plymouth (March, 1841).

Although a good deal of contemporary opinion was that New Zealand had been acquired by annexation associated with settlement, it was not long before the Treaty came to play a central part in New Zealand's political mythology, and the accepted view became, and till recent times remained, that New Zealand had been acquired by cession from the Maoris under the Treaty. This could not, however, have been true of the South Island, as Hobson's ground in respect of the South Island was discovery. Moreover, it is now agreed that in 1839-40 international law deemed, as it still does, that savage tribes are incapable of exercising sovereignty. The so-called Treaty could therefore not properly be considered a treaty, and could not be valid as an instrument of cession.

Moreover, various actions by the British authorities can be explained only on the assumption that they were treating New Zealand as being in the process of acquisition by annexation and settlement. Englishmen carried their political rights into a settled colony, and only a constitution established under the authority of the United Kingdom Parliament could withhold from them the right to representation in the legislature.[3] In a ceded colony, on the other hand, prerogative powers could be used to create an appointive legislature. New Zealand when it became a separate Colony in 1841 was clearly not ripe for a representative legislature, and in fact was given an appointive one. This is no doubt the reason why the Colonial Office, though it had been content to rely on prerogative powers for the 1839 Letters Patent extending the boundaries of New South Wales, obtained statutory powers for the 1840 Letters Patent creating New Zealand a separate Colony. That the Colonial Office believed that at law the separate colony of New Zealand would be a settled Colony seems also to be demonstrated by James Stephen's statement in a minute of July 21, 1840, that ' without the authority of Parliament the Crown can create no legislature in New Zealand except by

---

[3] A. B. Keith, *Responsible Government in the Dominions*, 2nd ed. (1928), Vol. I, pp. 3-4.

establishing there a Representative Assembly which I suppose everyone would agree in pronouncing an absurdity '.[4]

Also, the temporary inclusion of New Zealand within the boundaries of New South Wales is hard to explain on any other assumption, except possibly that this would make it easier for Hobson to obtain backing from New South Wales while he was establishing sovereignty. It was a short-lived arrangement. Within six months of Hobson's arrival in New Zealand the United Kingdom Parliament was considering the Bill that authorised the establishment of a separate colony ; and within another four months the Letters Patent of November, 1840, were issued. New Zealand's elevation from a Dependency after so short a time was not attributable to a change of government or of Colonial Office policy, nor to any unexpected happening in New Zealand, nor to a belief that administration as a Dependency was an experiment that had failed. The Colonial Office had all along intended to create New Zealand a separate Colony, and had included it in New South Wales only as a temporary expedient to cover the interval while it obtained statutory authority under which it could constitute an appointive legislature. The inclusion of New Zealand within New South Wales facilitated the obtaining of this statutory authority. In 1839 a Bill authorising the future establishment of a separate Colony of New Zealand would possibly have been thrown out, just as a private member's Bill for granting a charter to the New Zealand Association had been the previous year ; but in 1840 parliamentary opposition was faced by the accomplished fact that a British Lieutenant-Governor already administered New Zealand. Thus New Zealand's initial inclusion in New South Wales was dictated by a political difficulty superimposed on a legal necessity. The legal necessity that underlay Colonial Office policy was the fact that at law New Zealand would be a settled Colony, not a Colony obtained by cession under the Treaty of Waitangi.

But though the legal process by which New Zealand was acquired was annexation, and the Colonial Office knew it, that does not make the Treaty of Waitangi a farce. The Treaty was more even than a concession to humanitarian opinion in England and a bid for co-operation from the Maoris in New Zealand. Hobson was not authorised to proceed

---

[4] Quoted in N. A. Foden, *The Constitutional Development of New Zealand in the First Decade (1839–1849)* (1938), p. 50. Stephen had long held this view about the location of the legislative power in a settled colony. *Historical Records of Australia*, Series IV, Vol. I, pp. 412–7, 432–5 and 525–6. Dr. Foden has revived the view that the legal process by which New Zealand became British was annexation. The only full treatment of the legal significance of the Treaty of Waitangi to appear since Dr. Foden's book is Professor J. Rutherford's bulletin, *The Treaty of Waitangi and the Acquisition of British Sovereignty in New Zealand, 1840* (1949). Professor Rutherford is critical of some of Dr. Foden's statements, but accepts his central thesis that the legal process was annexation, saying that ' the Treaty cannot be the legal means whereby Great Britain acquired sovereignty in New Zealand ' (p. 47).

unless he could procure at least a substantial measure of Maori consent, and there is no evidence that if he had reported opposition from the Maoris the Colonial Office would have instructed him to use the forms of annexation. As Dr. Foden puts it, cession ' was a matter of domestic and internal policy '.[5] As Professor Rutherford puts it : ' It was British policy to treat the obtaining of native consent to British sovereignty as the essential condition that had to be fulfilled to the satisfaction of H.M. Government before the annexation of New Zealand was recognised.'[6]

Although the Treaty of Waitangi is not itself part of the domestic law of New Zealand, the rights of land ownership that the Treaty purported to guarantee to the Maoris were promptly incorporated in domestic law by the Land Claims Ordinance, 1841, the relevant provisions of which were re-enacted and extended in scope by the Native Rights Act, 1865.

When British sovereignty was proclaimed, New Zealand became subject to the laws of England in so far as they were reasonably applicable to the circumstances of the Dependency. In addition, an Ordinance of the Legislative Council of New South Wales provided that the laws of New South Wales, so far as they could be made applicable to the conditions of the Dependency, were to be in force in New Zealand. When New Zealand became a separate Colony many Ordinances were passed modelled on Ordinances in force in Australian colonies. In 1858 the New Zealand Parliament removed doubts regarding what law had been inherited by providing in the English Laws Act that the laws of England, so far as they were applicable to the circumstances of the Colony, should be deemed to have been in force in the Colony since January 14, 1840 (the date on which the Governor-in-Chief of New South Wales had proclaimed the extension of the boundaries of New South Wales to include New Zealand).

Little need be said of the governmental institutions of the period before the 1852 Constitution Act came into force. The Constitution granted by the Letters Patent of November 16, 1840 (the ' Charter of 1840 ') was similar to the Constitution then existing in New South Wales. Some constitutional development had already taken place in that Colony, so New Zealand began its separate career several rungs up the ladder of constitutional development. The Legislative Council under this Constitution was an appointive one with a majority of official members. Dissatisfaction with this Constitution was almost universal in the Colony ; and in London the New Zealand Company maintained pressure for the creation of a representative legislature.

[5] N. A. Foden, *op. cit.*, p. 56.
[6] J. Rutherford, *op. cit.*, p. 47.

A new Constitution on a representative basis was provided by Statute in 1846, but it was never brought fully into force. It was characterised by changes in political geography and by the establishment of a complicated system of indirect election. The Colony was divided into two Provinces, New Ulster and New Munster, and provision was made for the establishment of municipal corporations which were to be not only local bodies but also parts of the machinery of indirect election. The burgesses were to elect councillors ; the councillors were to elect mayor and aldermen ; the mayors, aldermen and councillors of the municipal corporations in each province were to elect the lower houses of the provincial legislatures ; and these in turn were to elect from their own number the lower house of the General Assembly. The upper houses were to be appointive.

The Lieutenant-Governor, Captain (later Sir) George Grey, was given a discretion in deciding when the Constitution was to come into operation. Late in 1847 he issued a Proclamation bringing it into force on January 1, 1848 ; but he did nothing to constitute the General Assembly and Provincial Assemblies provided by the Constitution. His principal objection to the Constitution was that he preferred to retain power in his own hands. He had, however, another weighty objection : that the Maoris were disfranchised by an English literacy qualification. The Maoris posed a dilemma to any draftsman of a New Zealand Constitution : if they were enfranchised, their want of political experience and of sophistication would endanger the Colony; if they were not, they would promptly suspect that their rights under the Treaty of Waitangi were of little value, and they would in fact very likely be dispossessed of their lands by the enfranchised settlers. The second horn of this dilemma formed the substance of representations that Grey made to Earl Grey, the Secretary of State, during 1847. Earl Grey was persuaded, and a further Act was passed in 1848 suspending for five years the 1846 provisions regarding the three legislatures, and reviving the Legislative Council constituted under the Charter of 1840. Sir George Grey's procrastination was thus vindicated. The Suspension Act gave the Governor-in-Chief power to appoint additional members to the Legislative Council, and gave the Legislative Council power to constitute a local Legislative Council in each province. Some use was made of these powers, and finally provision was made for partly elective local Legislative Councils, but while the first elections were in progress news was received of the passing of the 1852 Act.

The novel feature of the 1852 Act was not that it sanctioned the establishment of representative institutions—the 1846 Act had done that —but that it provided institutions suitable for the scattered settlements of that time. The form of the institutions was not, except in detail, a matter of dispute between the parties in Britain ; the Act as passed under a Conservative Government was an amplification of proposals that had been approved by the Secretary of State under the previous Liberal Government. The most striking feature of the Act was that it divided New Zealand into provinces, originally six in number, and established provincial governments that were clearly expected to exercise wide powers. Each province was to have an elected Superintendent and an elected Council. The system has often been described as federal, but it was not genuinely federal as the provincial governments had no sphere of exclusive jurisdiction. The central government had a sphere of exclusive jurisdiction, and the Act provided that in the sphere of concurrent jurisdiction central enactments were to control and supersede provincial enactments. This alone meant that the system was not federal. In addition, the central government had other powers of interfering in the management of provincial affairs ; and in the process of amending the Constitution no part was played by the provincial governments or the provincial electorates or by any ' provinces' house ' in the central legislature.

The governments of the six original provinces were set up in 1853, and were already firmly established when the first Parliament met in the following year. The provincial governments at first enjoyed high prestige, and most of the colonists at that time felt that their primary duty was to their provinces. The powers exercised by the provincial governments at first were wide, but financial difficulties in one province after another made it politically feasible for the central government to assume increasing powers of control. The process of centralisation, however, was not unopposed, and ministerial legislation was sometimes mutilated by back-benchers in provincial interests. It was ministerial exasperation at such frustration that ultimately led to the abolition of the provinces in 1876. New local bodies were created, and as provincial legislation was superseded by central legislation the old provincial boundaries as such ceased to have any political or administrative meaning. The provincial system had been necessary so long as internal transport had been undeveloped ; and it had familiarised the colonists with representative institutions and equipped them to operate the more difficult but more efficient machinery of centralised government.

The most important constitutional development in the early years of the 1852 Constitution was the establishment of responsible government. The whole question of the executive powers of the Governor (and the Governor-General) is primarily historical in content, so it is included in this Chapter, as the next section. Other historical developments are postponed for mention where they are relevant by reason of their bearing on current law. Thus some constitutional history and history of administrative law are found in the Chapters on Parliament, the Judicial System, and Public Administration and Administrative Law.

The Personal Discretion of the Governor-General in the Exercise of his Executive Powers

While New Zealand was a Crown Colony the Governor (as the Queen's representative was designated by the documents creating the Constitution of 1840) or Governor-in-Chief (as he was designated by the documents creating the Constitution of 1846) was responsible only to the Colonial Office. He was provided with an Executive Council to assist him in the exercise of his executive powers, but it consisted, apart from himself, only of officials who were subordinate to him and whom he could suspend from office. Moreover his Instructions directed him in certain situations not to consult the Executive Council; and empowered him in all situations to reject any advice it might offer him, provided he reported the facts to the Colonial Office without delay. Usually he accepted its advice, but this was merely an administrative practice that he could abandon on appropriate occasions, not a constitutional convention that he needed to observe to avoid adverse legal or political consequences.

No change was effected by the 1852 Constitution Act: it contained no provision regarding the Executive Council, and no provision limiting the executive discretion of the Governor (as the Queen's representative was now once more designated). The most important provision, apart perhaps from the division of New Zealand into six provinces, was the establishment of a new legislature, the General Assembly, consisting of the Governor, an appointed Legislative Council and an elected House of Representatives. The Act contained detailed provisions on the constitution of the two Houses and on the Governor's legislative powers, but otherwise said nothing on the relations between the Governor and the two Houses except that the Governor might summon, prorogue and dissolve the General Assembly [*sic*]. In short, the Act established a representative legislature but not a responsible executive. Neither did the Despatch forwarding a copy of the Act to the Governor mention responsible government. This was more significant than the Act's silence on the question, for responsible government had been granted by Despatch to every one of the Colonies in which it had so far been introduced (Canada, Nova Scotia and Prince Edward Island), and it had no statutory authorisation either in the United Kingdom or in any of these Colonies. In 1852 the Colonial Office did not intend the Governor to introduce responsible government in New Zealand.

When the first Parliament met in 1854 the House of Representatives passed a motion praying for ' the establishment of ministerial responsibility in the conduct of Legislative and Executive proceedings by the Government '. The Administrator who temporarily filled the Governor's position believed (probably rightly) that he had no authority to grant the request, but appointed three Members of Parliament (and later a fourth) to be additional members of the Executive Council without portfolio, and on the resignation of one of these members he filled the vacancy from Parliament.   Within two months the compromise proved to be unworkable and the new members resigned.   A second mixed Ministry was defeated within two days of its formation.   The Administrator had by now written to the Colonial Office seeking approval for the introduction of responsible government, and after the defeat of the second Ministry the House moved an Address to the Queen praying similarly. Colonial Office policy towards the four Australian Colonies and New Zealand had been developing rapidly, and the second Secretary of State replied to the Administrator that there was no objection to the introduction of responsible government.   In 1855 the Administrator summoned Parliament for the expressed purpose of dissolving it so that a further general election could be held before the introduction of responsible government.   The terms of the notice discouraged many Members from attending, and those who did attend agreed that as their numbers were so small they could not object to the postponement or to the dissolution. During the 1855 session the new Governor, Sir Thomas Gore Browne, arrived, and just over a week later he dissolved Parliament.   It was not till the second Parliament assembled in 1856 that the civil servants who sat with the Governor in the Executive Council were replaced by Ministers supported by a majority in the House of Representatives.

But the Governor's official actions did not all result from ministerial advice.   In matters involving Imperial interests, and in some purely domestic matters, the Colonial Office either laid down the policy he was to follow or else required him to be guided by his personal judgment. His Instructions still provided in general terms that he was empowered to act in certain situations without consulting the Executive Council, and that he could reject advice, provided he reported the facts promptly to the Colonial Office.   From 1856 the constitutional history of the Governorship becomes the history of the successive steps by which the Governor's responsibility to the Colonial Office was reduced in scope and finally abolished, and of the successive steps by which his power to reject advice has been reduced in scope.   The changes have been in constitutional conventions, and not all have been even reflected by amendments to the prerogative instruments concerning the Governorship.   The Instructions are much the most important of these documen s as a source of information about the Governor's personal discretion.

The only change in the Instructions necessitated by the introduction of responsible government was the omission of a provision requiring the Governor to appoint the senior military officer in the Colony to the Executive Council.   Another amendment to the Instructions indirectly reflects the introduction of responsible government.   The Colonial Office believed that the exercise of the prerogative of pardon should not be influenced by political considerations, and consequently required the Governor to exercise this prerogative according to his personal discretion. There was no need to provide specially for this in the Instructions so long as there was no convention that in all normal circumstances the Governor would accept the advice of the Executive Council. But when this convention was adopted an express provision excepting the prerogative of mercy became desirable. In 1867 an amendment was accordingly made to the Instructions requiring the Governor in the exercise of this prerogative to act on his 'own deliberate judgment', recording his reasons at length in any case where he rejected advice. Thus the adoption of the convention that the Governor would accept advice was reflected in the Instructions only by the insertion of a provision that he might reject advice. It was not till the 1892 revision of the Instructions that the members of the Executive Council were first described as being the Governor's responsible advisers; and not till the enactment of the Civil List Act, 1950, that there was any provision that only a Member of Parliament could be appointed a Minister of the Crown.

Native affairs and internal defence did not come under formal ministerial control till 1864. Sir George Grey, who had returned to New Zealand in 1861 to begin a second term as Governor, in fact continued to exercise considerable personal control after 1864, particularly in the conduct of the Maori Wars. His intervention in military affairs resulted in disputes with the generals commanding the Imperial forces and led to his recall, of which he received notice in 1867. When his successor arrived in 1868 he in turn found it impossible to play a passive role so long as Imperial forces remained in the country, but when the last Imperial forces were withdrawn in 1870 native affairs and internal defence came fully under normal ministerial control. These changes in the conventions were not reflected by any amendments in the Instructions.

The Governor's personal control over native affairs and internal defence was a special instance of his Imperial responsibilities. He was not only a representative of the Crown occupying the position of formal head of a parliamentary government; he was also an officer of the Imperial Government charged with the duty of protecting and promoting Imperial interests, and as such he was bound to reject any advice that he regarded as inimical to Imperial interests or as running counter to any specific directions that he might have received from the Colonial Office. This Imperial responsibility was referred to in a number of Dispatches: thus in 1856 the Colonial Office approved a minute from Gore Browne in which he had said that 'on matters affecting the Queen's prerogative and Imperial interests generally' he would feel himself free to reject advice. Till 1892 Imperial interests were not mentioned in any of the prerogative documents in connection with the Governor's executive powers, though the Instructions provided that Bills on certain subjects and Bills affecting certain specified kinds of Imperial interests were, unless they were urgent, to be reserved for the signification of the Royal pleasure. In 1892 a second reference to Imperial interests was included in the Instructions. In Canada the prerogative of pardon had been brought under ministerial control except where Imperial interests were concerned, and at the request of the New Zealand Government the Instructions were amended in 1892 to effect the same change in New Zealand. In 1892 the Governor's special responsibility for Imperial interests still existed, though by now it was somewhat attenuated. In that year, six months after the issue of the revised Instructions, the Secretary of State, when settling a dispute between the Governor and his Ministers over appointments to the Legislative Council, told the Governor that he should as a general rule accept the advice of his Ministers when Imperial interests were not affected; inferentially, if Imperial interests were affected the Governor still had a discretionary authority to reject advice. The 1907 Instructions contained no direction about reservation, but otherwise substantially repeated the provisions of the 1892 Instructions. The only material change in the 1917 Instructions was the substitution of the new designation of Governor-General for the old one of Governor. The 1917 Instructions are still in force, and the Governor-General is still formally required to consider Imperial interests when deciding whether to accept advice as to the exercise of the prerogative of pardon.

The erosion of the Governor's responsibility to the Colonial Office was a gradual process. In the nineteenth century Ministry after Ministry protested successfully against particular limitations on their authority, and the freedom of Ministries broadened down from precedent to precedent. In 1887 the first Colonial Conference met, and beginning with the meeting of the first Imperial Conference in 1907 the resolutions of Imperial Conferences granted further instalments of reform. The elevation of New Zealand to Dominion status in 1907 made no legal difference to the Governor's powers or to his responsibility to the Colonial Office, but the Governor's Imperial function was reduced to that of a channel of communication. In the 1907 revision of the Instructions the directions fettering his freedom to accept advice on reservation were omitted. From 1907 onwards where Imperial interests were affected the Government of the United Kingdom relied on persuasion instead of on the Governor's legal powers. But persuasion could be effective even when it failed to convince. Thus in September, 1914, the Governor met Cabinet on instructions from the Admiralty and persuaded it to dispatch troop transports with a naval escort that Cabinet considered inadequate. (A few hours after the transports sailed, a report was received that raiders were in the vicinity, and the transports were recalled safely; and when they were eventually dispatched they had an escort that Cabinet considered satisfactory.)[7] Cabinet is not entitled to object if a Governor gives advice when consulted, or chooses to encourage or to warn ; but if advice, encouragement or warning is offered at the behest of the Government of another country, albeit the Mother Country, an element extraneous to a parliamentary constitution is present. The anomaly was inherent in the system so long as the Government of the United Kingdom had no other political representative in New Zealand who could communicate its views to the New Zealand Government. The solution, found by the Imperial Conference of 1926, was to appoint such a representative. In future the Governor-General of a Dominion was to represent the Crown only, and the Government of the United Kingdom was to be represented by a High Commissioner. New Zealand, however, was not anxious to make the change, and the first High Commissioner for the United Kingdom did not take up his duties in Wellington till 1939.

The 1926 system in turn contained its own anomaly. In fact, in the Dominions to which High Commissioners were appointed promptly, but not in New Zealand, the appointment of Governors-General on the recommendation of the Government of the United Kingdom was now doubly anomalous : it was anomalous, firstly, because it constituted an inequality of status within the British Commonwealth of Nations that failed to accord with the convention of equality of status that the 1926 Conference had adopted in terms of the (Balfour) Report of the Inter-Imperial Relations Committee ; and it was anomalous, secondly, in the Dominions to which High Commissioners had been appointed, because Governors-General were appointed to those Dominions on the recommendation of a Government for which they no longer performed any services and to which they were no longer responsible. A mitigating factor was that since 1892 the New Zealand Government had been consulted by the Imperial Government before an appointment was made, and could presumably veto a particular nominee. The Imperial Conference of 1930 tidied up the question by adopting the convention that a Governor-General should in future be appointed on the advice of the Dominion Government concerned, to be tendered after informal consultation with the Crown. The only connection that now remains between the Governor-General of New Zealand and the Government of the United Kingdom is that there is an anachronistic provision that only the Crown and the Secretary of State may grant the Governor-General leave of absence additional to the leave for which approval is granted in the Instructions.

It remains to consider whether the Governor-General may still reject the advice of his Ministers. Here again, the power of Ministries broadened down from precedent to precedent during the nineteenth century. In

[7] W. Downie Stewart, *Sir Francis H. D. Bell, His Life and Times* (1937), pp. 110–15.

1892 the Secretary of State, when he was settling the dispute between the Governor and his Ministers over the appointment of Legislative Councillors, said that the Governor would be justified in rejecting advice only when Imperial interests are affected or when he ' is satisfied that the policy recommended to him is not only erroneous in itself, but such that he has solid grounds for believing, from his local knowledge, would not be endorsed by the legislature or by the constituents '. This was the last time that a dispute was referred to the Secretary of State ; and, so far as is publicly known, no Governor or Governor General has rejected advice since then, though in 1895 and again in 1897 the Governor protested when acting on advice to make appointments to the Legislative Council. In the 1892 revision of the Instructions the Governor lost the power to act without consulting the Executive Council, but the 1917 Instructions still provide that he may reject advice. ' In the execution of the powers and authorities vested in him, the Governor General shall be guided by the advice of the Executive Council, but if in any case he shall see sufficient cause to dissent from the opinion of the said Council, he may act in the exercise of his said powers and authorities in opposition to the opinion of the Council, reporting the same to Us without delay, with the reasons for his so acting.' The 1917 Instructions thus appear to allow broader scope for personal discretion than the Secretary of State had been prepared to allow in 1892. The convention adopted by the 1926 Imperial Conference is that the Governor-General of a Dominion holds ' in all essential respects the same position in relation to the administration of public affairs in the Dominion as is held by His Majesty the King in Great Britain '. This formula remedied the mischief of regarding the Governor-General as having the backing of the Government of the United Kingdom, but failed to recognise what a difference it makes politically that the Governor-General has less prestige and less security of tenure than a hereditary monarch. Today it is almost inconceivable that the Governor-General of New Zealand would reject the advice of Ministers (except perhaps a request for a dissolution, which is discussed in the second paragraph after this) unless the Ministry is opposed by a majority in the House. If the Ministry is opposed by a majority in the House, the Governor-General could reject its advice merely because, to quote the 1892 ruling, its advice ' would not be endorsed by the legislature '. He would not also need to be ' satisfied that the policy recommended to him is not only erroneous in itself, but such that he has solid grounds for believing, from his local knowledge, would not be endorsed . . . by the constituents '. The rejection of advice by the Governor-General would probably lead to the resignation of his Ministers, and resignation as a protest against his own action is a contingency that the Governor-General must avoid unless he can see a virtual certainty of obtaining alternative advisers with a majority who will endorse his action

A Governor-General who rejected advice and failed to obtain alternative advisers with a majority would be inviting his own recall. The New Zealand Cabinet now has plenary executive powers.

But this sanction compelling the Governor-General to accept advice exists only when the Ministry is not opposed by a majority in the House. The argument so far advanced does not demonstrate that the Governor-General is bound to accept the advice of a Ministry that is opposed by a majority in the House ; or that he cannot dismiss such a Ministry ; or that when a new Ministry is to be formed and is possibly to be granted a dissolution there is only one Member of Parliament who can succeed in forming a Ministry supported by a majority. Moreover, as will be seen in the next paragraph, the Governor-General could sometimes reject a request for a dissolution from a Ministry whose majority is not clear. The crucial question in all these cases is whether the Governor-General will finally have a Ministry that endorses his actions. The crucial distinction is not, as is sometimes supposed, the distinction between statutory powers and prerogative powers ; in fact the illustration of prerogative powers that is usually offered when this distinction is drawn, the power of dissolving Parliament, is a statutory power, having been withdrawn from the prerogative by the 1852 Constitution Act. It is now necessary to examine the various cases in which the Governor-General may have some personal discretion in the exercise of his executive powers.

It is not usually appreciated that the Governor-General's need for advisers who will endorse his actions prevents him from refusing a request for a dissolution from a united Ministry with a clear majority. Persistence in refusing a dissolution in such a case would not only be ruled out because of the necessities of the case, but would also be without precedent in the Commonwealth, including the United Kingdom.[8] If the Ministry's majority is not clear, or if the Opposition has a majority, the Governor-General could in some circumstances refuse a request for a dissolution. As to what these circumstances are, New Zealand precedents are not helpful : they amount only to three refusals to Ministries with doubtful majorities, three grants of dissolution to Ministries that had lost their majorities, and one grant of dissolution to a united Ministry with a clear majority. The conclusions that Dr. Forsey bases on his detailed analysis of Commonwealth precedents [9] appear to be applicable to New Zealand : while they cannot be accurately summarised in brief, they suggest that the chance that a dissolution will be granted on request is greatest when the Ministry has more support in the House than any alternative Ministry would have ; when the Ministry, though it has no

[8] E. A. Forsey, *The Royal Power of Dissolution of Parliament in the British Commonwealth* (1943), pp. 11, 107 and 284–6 (and consequential references).
[9] *Ibid.*, pp. 260–70.

majority, formerly had a majority in the existing Parliament ; when an important new issue has arisen on which it is desirable to consult the electorate ; and when the life of the existing Parliament has not been short.

The Governor-General could dismiss a Ministry that has clearly lost its majority and declines either to resign or to request a dissolution. He would need first to make certain that he would be supported by the incoming Ministry. Sir Philip Game's dismissal of Mr. Lang in New South Wales in 1932 is, however, a precedent that has only very limited applicability to New Zealand, since Mr. Lang was dismissed for failure to comply with a federal statute that the legislature of New South Wales was not competent to amend or repeal, and, now that the New Zealand Parliament has plenary powers, any Ministry with a majority in the House would probably prefer amending or repealing a statute to acting illegally. Short of dismissing a Ministry that is opposed by a majority in the House, and declines to resign or to request a dissolution, the Governor-General could safely reject its advice.

Finally, the Governor-General may sometimes have some discretion in deciding whom to commission to form a new Ministry. He is not likely to have any personal discretion when a Prime Minister has died or has tendered his own resignation unaccompanied by the resignation of the other members of the Ministry. (In such a case the Ministry does not at law cease to exist, but as all the offices will be at the disposal of the new Prime Minister the Ministry is regarded as ceasing to exist, and in practice does cease to exist on the date of the funeral or of the resignation.) The constitutional convention that has evolved is that the caucus of the Government party will elect a new leader and will thus indicate to the Governor-General whom he should commission to form a new Ministry ; and that if a Ministry is formed before the election in caucus it will be formed as a provisional Ministry only. All the twentieth-century precedents have been in accordance with this convention. Of the four precedents, three occurred with majority governments, and the other one with a minority government ; and presumably the convention would also be observed in the case of a coalition government, unless of course the coalition is disrupted at the time of the death or resignation.

If the Ministry as a whole has resigned because of defeat, and there is more than one opposition party, no one of them with a majority, the Governor-General may have some discretion in deciding which party's leader he should commission to form a Ministry. The only twentieth-century precedent occurred in 1928, when the leader of one opposition party moved a vote of no-confidence which was supported by both opposition parties, and was carried ; the mover of the motion was commissioned to form a Ministry, and was successful in forming a minority Ministry. It is likely that the course of Parliamentary proceedings or

the relative strengths of the parties will usually indicate to the Governoi-
General which party's leader he should commission to form a Ministry.
It is likely also that that party will already have chosen its leader in caucus.

If the Prime Minister and some or all of the other Ministers have
resigned because of dissension in the Ministry, there are the further
possibilities that the Governor-General may commission the retiring
Prime Minister to form a new Ministry on a different basis, and that he
may commission another member of the Prime Minister's party to form
a Ministry. There has been no precedent in New Zealand similar to the
British precedent of 1931. In a case of dissension leading to the Prime
Minister's resignation, the Governor-General may have some discretion.
Here, as in all other cases of the formation of a new Ministry, the Governor-
General's actions will be ineffective unless they result, either immediately
or after a general election, in the formation of a new Ministry with a
majority. The importance of the Governor-General's discretion in the
case of dissension is that, even if the Member of Parliament whom he
commissions to form a Ministry and to whom he possibly grants a
dissolution does succeed in forming a Ministry with a majority, the
possibility exists that some other Member could have been equally
successful if he had been commissioned to form a Ministry and, in the
event of his not having a majority in the existing Parliament, been granted
a dissolution.

THE PROBLEMS FACING JUSTICE

In the early life of the Colony the administration of justice faced serious
difficulties and at times reached a low ebb. The population in 1840
could be divided into three broad groups. First there were the settlers
brought out by the New Zealand Company under an organised colonisation scheme. They were carefully selected and carried with them the
traditions, customs and law-abiding instincts of British people. Second
there were the independent settlers who had arrived prior to 1840—they
were a mixed lot including missionaries, who wanted to protect the
interests of the Maoris, as well as whalers, and criminals who had escaped
from Australia or emigrated after serving their sentences. Third, there
were the Maoris, intelligent and considerably out-numbering the Europeans. These three groups with differing standards and outlooks posed
a social problem that was to exercise the Government for a long period.
The settlements were separated by long distances—not easily traversed
because of difficult terrain, thus leaving sea transport as the means of
occasional contact. On top of this were the troubles between the early
Governors and the New Zealand Company, in part due to the desire of
the former to assert their supremacy.

In the forties the administration of the law was an uneasy compromise
between principle and expediency owing to fear of the Maoris. On the

one hand there were instances of Maoris who were hanged for the murder of Europeans. On the other hand the courts were occasionally chary of action to restrain Maoris from obstructing Europeans in the use of land the latter had purchased, and sought escape through procrastination. This imported into the administration of the law an unsatisfactory element, but there is little doubt that it was the wiser course in the light of the dangers which faced the young Colony. In 1843 a party of Europeans who were taking premature and illegal action against Maoris arising out of a land dispute were attacked at Wairau and most of them slaughtered. In the following year war began in the north and it was waged until 1846. In the same decade there were isolated outbreaks in other areas. For the most part the causes had their roots in friction over land. In the midst of all this the young Colony was beset with serious economic difficulties.

The reception of English law could be little more than a gesture until such time as there was an adequate judicial system coupled with the means of enforcing the law. The problem was a physical and administrative one and included the question of gaining the respect of the Maoris for the way in which justice was administered. In an endeavour to obtain this respect, it was found necessary in 1844 to exempt in certain cases the aboriginal population from the ordinary process and operation of the law. For instance, in cases where natives were concerned, the Protector of the Aborigines was to direct a warrant to two principal chiefs, who were to apprehend the accused. Except in cases of murder and rape, the accused on making a deposit might be allowed to go at large until trial, the deposit to be forfeited upon his non-appearance. Furthermore, if a native were convicted of theft he was, in place of other punishment, to pay four times the value of the property stolen, the value to be determined by the jury, and in some cases to be awarded to the prosecutor.[10]

There was provision for natives to sit on mixed juries in trials affecting the property or person of a native. For civil disputes between persons wholly of native race, there were set up Courts of Arbitration consisting of a resident magistrate or any other person appointed by the Governor, assisted by native assessors. In 1846 and 1847 ordinances were made with the object of preserving peace among the Maoris themselves by means of an armed constabulary and by the prohibition of trading in guns and powder. Maori native constables were employed and native magistrates appointed.[11]

Although these provisions were constructive ones they could accomplish little in the absence of the wholehearted support of the Maoris.

[10] Hight and Bamford, *The Constitutional History and Law of New Zealand*, p. 178.
[11] *Ibid.*, pp. 181, 189, 191.

Maoris charged with crimes against Europeans were sometimes brought
to trial because members of their race had co-operated to this end, but
there were many areas where this co-operation did not exist and the
prospects of gaining it diminished with the growing hostility of the
Maoris towards the European. This, of course, extended to crimes
committed by one Maori on another.

In the fifties the settlers were living on the edge of a volcano, which
was to erupt in the next decade. The difficulty of maintaining law and
order was obvious when the Maoris were not willing to respond to
persuasion. In 1854 a chief named Rawiri was murdered in Taranaki
when he was proceeding to cut a boundary line on land about to be
taken over by the Government. The crime was committed by a party
of another chief, Katatore. Henry Sewell, an English lawyer who had
been sent out from England to represent the Canterbury Association
and who was Premier for a few days in 1856, records that a tribesman
of Rawiri's intended to put the matter to the Governor thus :—

> ' Was Rawiri a British subject ? If he was, punish his murderers.
> If he was not, don't interfere with me whilst I avenge him.'[12]

Rawiri was avenged : the Government was not strong enough to impose
its will on the warring tribes. In 1856 Henry Sewell summed up the
situation in these words :—

> ' What are we to say to a Government with 50,000 subjects over
> whom it exercises and can exercise not the slightest practical control ?
> We talk of their civilisation and respect for British law and so forth.
> It is a delusion and a sham. We profess to govern them, and are
> only able to do so just so long and so far as they choose to let us.'[13]

A magistrate named Fenton was sent to the Waikato in the late fifties,
but accomplished little in the way of encouraging the Maoris to use his
court. Several years later John Gorst, who was to become prominent
in English politics, went to the Waikato as a magistrate and while there
adopted the course, scarcely to be emulated by any judicial officer, of
publishing a newspaper for propaganda purposes. He withdrew in
1863 when war in that area seemed inevitable. In Hawke's Bay Maoris
were taking the law into their own hands to deal with the straying cattle
of settlers. They had been baffled in their efforts to secure redress in
the ordinary courts because of technical difficulties in determining their
status as owners of native land.[14]

In 1859 the Governor agreed to purchase land in Taranaki from a
Maori chief. The Governor was advised at the time that this chief had
the legal power to sell the land in question and the sale took place. It

[12] *Journal of Henry Sewell*, Vol. 1, Part 3, p. 1018. (Deposited in Turnbull Library,
Wellington.)
[13] *Ibid.*, Vol. 1, Part 3, p. 1165.
[14] *Ibid.*, Vol. 2, Part 2, p. 3.

was subsequently established that the chief had not the power to sell, but this came too late to prevent the outbreak of war. It is not proposed to recount the fighting that took place in various parts of the North Island during the next decade, but to avoid another blunder of this kind Parliament set up the Native Land Court with the function of investigating and determining the title to Maori land.

The early judges had to labour under severe difficulties. In 1857, for instance, there were only two judges of the Supreme Court for a Colony about the size of the United Kingdom. In the words of one of the judges of this period, Mr. Justice Gresson, a judge had to administer the law in nearly all its branches without the advice of brother judges, who were beyond his reach, without access to legal decisions or even textbooks, save a few of those most commonly used, and unaided or slightly aided by a Bar which at that time scarcely existed in the Colony.[15] The hope was sometimes expressed that the court would become more concentrated in one centre as in London and that as a result the New Zealand Bar would develop into a powerful and influential body in the State. There was no system of law reporting in operation and the decisions of the court in one province were little known in another. In these circumstances, the quality of justice had to suffer. A further adverse factor was the great difficulty in finding persons equipped to hold office. This was still more true of the subordinate judicial system. Persons appointed as Resident Magistrates were often not qualified in the law. At the same time any further expenditure on a better system would have strained the financial resources of the country. The cost of the subordinate judicial system was the subject of adverse comment by commissions which sat in 1866 and 1880.[16]

The Court of Appeal came under criticism in the seventies because it was practically nothing more than the Supreme Court under another name. There was also criticism of its delays in the hearing of cases and of the expense involved in appeals. It was cheaper for parties in Dunedin to appeal direct from the Supreme Court to the Privy Council in London rather than to the Court of Appeal in Wellington.[17]

It is not to be expected that the institutions of a young colony would command the respect generally accorded to similar institutions in older countries, and sometimes in the early history of New Zealand the institutions became almost submerged in the personalities playing upon the scene. We have the bizarre spectacle of the Superintendent for Otago who, when committed to gaol for debt, uses his legal powers as a public officer to declare his own private residence to be a common gaol

[15] N.Z.Jur. (1876), Vol. II, iv (supplement).
[16] D.–7, para 37, Appendix to Journals H. of R., 1866.
H.–2, p. 14, Appendix to Journals H. of R., 1880.
[17] N.Z.Jur. (1876), Vol. II, Part 3, p. 44 ; see also Vol. I, Part 4, p. 30.

for the reception of debtors and then orders his own removal to that residence.[18]

Towards the end of the Crown Colony period there was some lack of confidence in the administration of justice. This is reflected in the journal of Henry Sewell. He remarks that the Executive Council is defying the Supreme Court and setting at naught all law.[19] Again he says : 'The law power of the settlement is at the lowest possible ebb'.[20] Still again : 'The help which I might get from law in England is wholly wanting here'.[21] He records that Mr. Justice Stephen had complained that the Executive was attempting to overbear him and to destroy his independence.[22] Some of these remarks, however, should be discounted, because they were made when Sewell and others were strongly opposing the Governor's land policy.

There was no lack of vitriol within the Colony. Parliamentary debates were fierce, descending on at least one occasion into a donnybrook.[23] Politicians criticised judges, who reciprocated in like fashion. The Press criticised judges in strong terms. Judges on occasion publicly disagreed among themselves. Relations between Bench and Bar were sometimes acrimonious. The words 'contempt of court' were more on the lips of judges than now. There was a natural tendency for the judges to expand the scope of 'contempt' and to seek to enlarge the range of penalties that could be imposed.

By the turn of the century the public had acquired confidence in the administration of justice, but a rude shock was to come in 1903. In that year the Privy Council reversed a decision of the Court of Appeal with startling criticism of New Zealand judges and of the Solicitor-General.[24] In their view the judges of the Court of Appeal had deferred without justification to the wishes of the Executive, and the Solicitor-General had departed from the traditions of his high office. The judgment created a furore in legal circles in the Colony, and Bench and Bar united to protest vigorously against the attack.[25]

The case concerned land which had been granted to Bishop Selwyn in 1850 for the purposes of a college. The vital question was whether the Maoris or the Crown were the donors of the land and the founders of the charity.

It is beyond our scope to examine the legal issues that were involved in this case, but some of the findings and remarks in the judgment of

[18] *Journal of Henry Sewell*, Vol. 2, Part 1, p. 213.
[19] *Ibid.*, Vol. 1, Part 1, p. 325.
[20] *Ibid.*, Vol. 1, Part 2, p. 598.
[21] *Ibid.*, Vol. 1, Part 2, p. 639.
[22] *Ibid.*, Vol. 1, Part 1, p. 213.
[23] Hight and Bamford, *The Constitutional History and Law of New Zealand*, p. 282.
[24] *Wallis* v. *Solicitor-General* [1903] A.C. 173.
[25] See Protest of Judges in appendix, N.Z.P.C. Cases 1840–1932, 730 *et seq.*

the Privy Council make curious reading and would not have been made by any lawyer with a working knowledge of New Zealand conditions and case law. The course of early legislation was not studied in order to understand the setting of the trust. There was a misconception as to the educational system then in force, which was to encourage the heads of churches to establish and manage schools in return for grants of land and money from the Crown. The Privy Council spoke of the Treaty of Waitangi as a law, a view which was inconsistent with the flow of authority and with at least one earlier decision of the Privy Council. It was well settled that whatever demands the Treaty made on the conscience of the Crown it did not confer any legal rights on the Maoris. The Rules of Procedure applying in New Zealand were also overlooked.

To sum up, the Privy Council was astray in its grasp of some of the facts and it made a serious mistake in its view of the Treaty of Waitangi. However, it would be wrong to suggest that the Privy Council had no grounds for its criticism. There are passages in the New Zealand Reports of this case which can convey the impression of subservience to the Executive, although in fact there was none. Whatever may be thought of episodes in the early life of the Colony, it was clear that the New Zealand Bench had long acquired independence of the Executive. Several years before, Sir Joshua Williams had not minced words in chastising a Minister of the Crown, Sir Joseph Ward, for his part in an unsavoury company insolvency.[26] The strong character of the Chief Justice, Sir Robert Stout, does not suggest that he would have suffered dictation from the Executive. Because of dissatisfaction with the work of the Privy Council expressed in New Zealand and also in Canada the practice was adopted, whenever practicable, of adding to the Judicial Committee a judge from the Dominion from which the appeal had come. In the course of time both Sir Joshua Williams and Sir Robert Stout served in this way on the Judicial Committee.

LEGISLATION AND ITS BACKGROUND

After the first decade the Colony entered into what has been termed the ' pastoral age '—a period running from about 1850 to 1880. During most of this period conditions were prosperous except for those areas affected by the Maori wars. Gold was also discovered. By the seventies considerable progress had been made in the settlement of rural areas, although there remained large areas to be opened up and also areas in the interior in which the Maoris were hostile to the advance of the white man and where it could not be said that the Queen's Writ ran. It was urged that the making of roads was ' the true form of aggression upon native territory '.[27] The pastoral age is said to have ended with the

---

[26] W. Downie Stewart, *Portrait of a Judge*, p. 61.
[27] *Journal of Henry Sewell*, Vol. 2, Part 2, p. 276.

coming of refrigeration in the early eighties, but the effect of refrigeration
was to give encouragement to dairy farming as well as to sheep farming,
and it tended to lessen the size of the pastoral unit. It changed the
export picture to the extent that meat and dairy produce were added to
wool but New Zealand remained a pastoral country.

The economic trends in the thirty years from 1850 are reflected in
the type of legislation enacted and the cases heard by the courts. The
opening up of land for settlement was frequently the subject of legislation
and a substantial portion of the cases heard by the courts related to
land. At a sitting of the Court of Appeal in Canterbury in 1863 the few
cases heard were all ' connected with runs and squatting questions '.[28]

It was not long before New Zealand law in some sectors began to
diverge from English law. By the end of thirty years there had, of
course, been a good deal of legislation dealing with the opening up and
settlement of the waste lands of the Crown. Conveyancing had been
simplified to a great extent as early as 1842, and the disposal of land
was still more to be simplified by the land transfer system introduced in
1860, from South Australia. Special legislation was passed to deal
with mines and mining. English law relating to highways, water courses,
riparian rights and easements was not adaptable to the conditions existing
in a new country, and was amended by legislation. On the other hand
in the seventies we find at least one judge, Sir Joshua Williams, pointing
out the advantages of adopting Imperial Acts when legislating on commercial matters.[29] This, he pointed out, gave New Zealand the benefit
of English decisions on points of construction.

Where, however, legislation adapted to the needs of a new country
had been passed, English case law in the related fields tended to become
less in point. Some help, however, was derived from the decisions of
courts in other common law countries which were in a similar stage of
development to New Zealand. For instance, some help was obtained
from the decisions of the courts in Victoria. Analogies drawn from
American law were also fruitful : American judges had to face similar
problems. There was also a growing recognition in English courts of
the comparative value of American decisions. It was said by Lord
Cockburn in 1876, perhaps with some exaggeration, that there was
scarcely a discussion of any importance in which American decisions and
American authors were not cited ; the judgments and dicta of a Marshall
or a Story were as familiar to English lawyers as those of a Mansfield or an
Ellenborough.[30] It was natural that this favourable attitude towards
American case law should be reflected in New Zealand. In the seventies
American textbooks, American editions of English textbooks, and

[28] *Ibid.*, Vol. 2, Part 2, p. 143.
[29] N.Z.Jur. (1876), Vol. II, Part 3, p. 44.
[30] *Ibid.*, (1877), Vol. II, Part 7, p. 124.

American legal periodicals were circulating in the Colony. It was not uncommon for the New Zealand jurist to quote from American legal periodicals ; American decisions whether civil or criminal were discussed.

American influence was felt throughout the early years of the Colony. Trade brought contact, there were American whalers on the coast and some American capital was invested within the Colony. It was alleged that American whalers were encouraging the Maoris to adopt an unco-operative attitude towards British efforts at colonisation. Some of the colonists themselves, in the sixties, when there was heavy criticism of the Imperial Government, were contemplating the advantages of allegiance to the United States. As late as the eighties a group of unemployed in New Zealand were so dissatisfied with their lot that they implored the President of the United States to help them to enter his country. These political and economic manifestations of dissatisfaction, however, did not account for the whole of the favourable sentiment ; American experience in coping with the problems of development was found of value. Even one of Bishop Selwyn's schemes for the organisation of the Anglican Church was based on American ideas.[31] The Act of 1881 relating to the adoption of children appears to have been based in part on similar legislation in Massachusetts.

The practice of citing American decisions was popular for many years beyond the turn of the century. In a 1914 case dealing with monopoly Sir Robert Stout discussed the American cases under the Sherman Act.[32] A little later Mr. Justice Chapman was saying :[33]

> ' American authorities on constitutional questions can only be applied to questions arising under our constitutional system with great caution, but I cannot but recall the greatest constitutional cases decided by the Supreme Court of the United States.'

The Crown Milling case of 1925 is an illustration of the use of American material, although in the same case we find Mr. Justice McGregor protesting at the extensive use of the comparative method to arrive at the meaning and effect of ' plain words used in a New Zealand statute '.[34] Sir Robert Stout as Chief Justice habitually adopted a wide canvas and frequently supported his reasoning by illustrations from other parts of the common law world. The citation of American decisions however is not now as frequent as it was.

New Zealand has shown a readiness from early days to use the legislative weapon to deal with social and economic questions. As will be seen in the question of monopolies, there has been less readiness to rely on judicial creativeness in the evolution of case law. The ease with which

---

[31] *Journal of Henry Sewell*, Vol. 1, Part 1, p. 278.
[32] *Fairbairn Wright & Co.* v. *Levin & Co.* (1915) 34 N.Z.L.R. 1, 23.
[33] *Taratahi Dairy Co. and Mangorei Dairy Co.* v. *Att.-Gen.* [1917] N.Z.L.R. 1, 35.
[34] *The King* v. *Crown Milling Co. Ltd.* [1925] N.Z.L.R. 753, 816.

legislation is passed or amended lessens the role of the court, but as the courts in New Zealand are generally bound to follow the decisions of superior courts in England we have gained from the present positive trend of English decisions in adapting the common law to changing needs.

Ordinances were freely made in the Crown Colony days and the advantage of the legislative instrument was readily apparent to the colonists when they were given representative institutions. When the provinces were established Provincial Councils were not slow to exercise their legislative powers. The Provincial Council for Canterbury alarmed Henry Sewell at the way it confidently prescribed legislative remedies for social evils. He thought that law-making in Provincial Councils should be confined to objects of the most obvious necessity and he deprecated one measure which sought to embody the whole law of trespass in one compendious Ordinance and which contemplated that the bare fact of trespass was to be a ground for awarding damages even though the province was then virtually ' open unenclosed country '.[35]

It is true that the first session of Parliament distinguished itself by passing no legislation except an Act authorising the sale of liquor within the precincts of the House for the benefit of honourable members.[36] Once its comfort had been assured and the struggle of the early years for responsible government had been won, Parliament settled down, in earnest, to legislative programmes which expanded in scope and volume at a pace dictated by the philosophy of the dominant group. It was not the quantum of legislation that was so significant as the selection of subject-matter for legislation and the method of treatment. Although there were restrictions on the legislative powers of the General Assembly, these did not constitute a serious obstacle to the flow of novel and far-reaching legislation on internal affairs. The orthodoxy of the old world, although it had its champions in New Zealand, was no match for those who wanted to avoid the evils of the old world as they saw them. There was little reluctance to invade the realm of private enterprise, which as yet was not buttressed by tradition and was ill organised to withstand legislative attacks. A Government Life Insurance Department was launched in 1869 to compete with private insurance concerns and the Public Trustee was established in 1872 to administer trusts and the estates of deceased persons.

The motives behind the legislation establishing the Public Trustee throw some light on the conditions prevailing in the Colony in the early seventies. Testators and settlors had great difficulty in finding suitable persons willing to act as executors and trustees. During the

[35] *Journal of Henry Sewell*, Vol. 1, Part 2, pp. 597, 634.
[36] Hight and Bamford, *The Constitutional History and Law of New Zealand*, p. 283.

parliamentary debates it was stressed that in a new country such as New Zealand the number of persons who remained solvent amid the fluctuating conditions was limited. Misappropriations by trustees were not uncommon. Moreover, colonial property fluctuated very much in value and required close supervision. Many of the colonists had left relatives overseas who in other circumstances would have been available for selection. Another point urged in favour of the Bill was that the provision of such services would encourage wealthy people to remain in the Colony and would also tend to quicken the flow of English capital into the country for investment. The fact that the colonists were migratory in habit added to the difficulties of finding suitable persons to act as executors or trustees. Incidentally this same feature was to postpone the introduction of a system of taxation on income ; it also retarded the growth of labour unionism.

The seventies saw extensive plans adopted and carried into effect for public works and for immigration—all calculated to stimulate further development. There were also a number of administrative measures flowing from the abolition of the provinces in 1876. We have already seen that a new system of local government was established. For the purposes of education the country was divided into a number of districts, each of which had an Education Board. In 1879 Parliament turned to private law and passed an important measure affecting the administration of the estates of deceased persons. It was provided that upon a grant of administration by the court the real estate of a deceased person vested in the executor or administrator as from the death of the testator or intestate in the same manner as personal estate. Hitherto real estate had automatically passed to the heir-at-law on the death of the testator or intestate. This measure was well in advance of similar legislation to be passed in Great Britain in 1925. In a series of measures culminating in the Supreme Court Act, 1882, the cumbersome method of pleading inherited from English law was substantially simplified.

Amongst the early pieces of social legislation was the system of charitable aid introduced by the Stout-Vogel Ministry (1884–87). The humanitarian outlook reflected in this legislation may be contrasted with a view of an earlier politician who said that the gold-diggers ' must take their chance, and the privations they will probably have to endure are in reality Nature's corrective of a social disease '.[37] This humanitarian trend expressed itself in legislation in the interests of children. Statutory provision for the adoption of children was made in 1881. In 1887 the mother's position in relation to the custody and guardianship of infants was strengthened. The protection of infant life was the driving force behind the Children's Protection Act, 1890. In its legislation New Zealand has been solicitous for the interests of the illegitimate

[37] *Journal of Henry Sewell*, Vol. 2, Part 1, p. 311.

child. At first sight it might seem that Maori custom might have had
some effect, because for the purposes of Maori succession no child is
treated as illegitimate. ' Any child proved to be the offspring of a male
native who has died intestate is, according to native custom as laid down
by the Native Land Court, entitled to succeed to the interests in the
native land of the deceased.'[38] However, it is more likely that the
example of Scottish law has served to soften the traditional approach of
English law. A Scotch settler, John MacGregor, was the moving force
behind legislation in 1894, which provided that an illegitimate child could
be legitimated on the subsequent marriage of its father and mother.

It is in the early years of the Liberal-Labour Government, which
came to power in 1891, that we see a rapid increase in social legislation.
Workers and land were the subject of special treatment. An Employers'
Liability Act and a Truck Act were passed. A factory code was also
established. The State took the initiative in finding employment for
surplus labour. Freedom of contract was restricted by the creation of a
form of status to govern relations between employer and employee. The
Court of Arbitration emerged as a tribunal for dealing with industrial
disputes, and it is now a central wage-fixing authority proceeding
judicially.

It was the policy of the Liberal Government to attack the aggregation
and monopoly of farming land. In the pastoral age, the holding of large
areas of land was not necessarily inimical to the productive interests of
the country, but refrigeration, for instance, made smaller units an economic proposition and this, together with the land hunger of a growing
population, produced a powerful demand for a new land policy. A tax
on land, first initiated in 1879 by Grey as Premier, was developed as a
social instrument to break up monopoly, but its effect was nullified in part
by the rising price level. Land was also purchased by the State for
closer settlement and there was provision for compulsory acquisition.
The State lent money on easy terms to those who wanted to settle on the
land.

The Liberal Government competed against private enterprise in the
mining and sale of coal and also entered the fire insurance business. It
made special provision for the poor in the way of old-age pensions.
Nursing services were provided for the working classes. The legislative
programmes of the Liberal Government were wide in scope and much
was achieved, but in the closing years of the régime the tempo became
much slower.

Land was prominent in the platform of the Massey Government
that took office in 1912. Those Crown tenants who had been placed on
the land as the result of the Liberal Government's legislation were now
agitating for the option to purchase on favourable conditions the freehold

[38] XVII, N.Z.L.J., p. 173.

of their land. Their desires were satisfied in legislation introduced by Massey. In the period of the First Great War Massey's Coalition Government found itself obliged to intervene in many phases of the economic life of the country. The Regulation of Trade and Commerce Act, 1914, interfered with the operation of the ordinary law of supply and demand. It empowered the Governor to fix, at the cost of a class and for the benefit of the people at large, the price of any class of goods. The court, in discussing legislation of this type, had this to say :—[39]

> ' That the Order in Council controls the trade in the products of butter-fat in a manner which would be impossible apart from the special legislation is plain. Opinions may differ as to the wisdom of such legislation, for it no doubt does interfere with the liberty of the subject to trade as he pleases. This, however, is by no means without precedent, even with regard to legislation of a permanent character, such as the Acts which have created the Arbitration Court and have given to that court immense powers of control over all traders and manufacturers and over many others who are neither traders nor manufacturers. With regard to the legislation with which we have to deal in the present case, it is to be observed that it is emergency legislation which takes effect only in the time of war, when the public safety and the public good supersede for the time being all other considerations. It can therefore have no lasting ill effect either upon liberty or upon trade.'

In the twenties the Massey Government was putting through legislation for the setting up of marketing boards to regulate the marketing of primary produce. Whatever the colour of the Government in power, the State has never been able to take merely a passive interest in industries upon which the prosperity of the country depends. The Liberal-Labour Government, in an endeavour to improve the quality of primary produce for sale overseas, had made provision before the turn of the century for a system of compulsory inspection, branding and grading. The subsequent creation of statutory marketing boards was a further expression of the national interest in the economic condition of the primary industries but it has to be remembered that the initiative came from the producers themselves. The State was destined to play a more positive role in the early thirties, a period of intense depression with severe ramifications. This period was productive of much economic legislation.

Shortly after the end of the depression, in 1935, the Labour Government came to power and there began a still heavier programme of economic regulation, much of which was designed to improve the lot of the worker. The legislation resulting from this programme will be discussed in other portions of this book, and reference will be made to the changes since made by the National Government which succeeded the Labour Government in 1949.

[39] *Taratahi Dairy Co. and Mangorei Dairy Co.* v. *Att.-Gen.* [1917] N.Z.L.R. 1, 31.

Meantime, we recall the remarks of Sir Joshua Williams, quoted in the Preface, on the rapid developments that took place in New Zealand in the last fifty years of the nineteenth century. The question arises whether the picture is similar for the first fifty years of this century. There is a difference but not so much in kind as in degree. There has been a more intensive development of areas opened up by legislation in the preceding period. It has been a process of closer tilling. There has been less of originality in the latter period and many developments have been paralleled by similar developments overseas. In the latter age can be found broad counterparts of the other, particularly in economic and social areas. The movement started by the Liberal Government in the nineties to improve the lot of the worker was accelerated by the Labour Government. The industrial code introduced by the early Liberal Government became more restrictive for the employer. Secondary industry was given modest encouragement by the Liberal Government; it was given greater encouragement by the Labour Government but with provision for an examination of its efficiency. Old-age pensions granted in 1898 were the prelude to the comprehensive social security legislation of 1938. If there is a substantial difference between the two eras, it is in the extent and variety of the economic controls introduced in the later period. We have already mentioned these controls in relation to the First World War, the economic depression of the early thirties, and the advent of the Labour Government in 1935. The trend was still further accelerated by the demands of the Second World War and of the years immediately following it.

In the legislative sphere, New Zealand has borrowed not only from Great Britain, but from other countries. The Land Transfer system was copied from South Australia. Australia also provided a precedent for the marketing board legislation of the twenties. New Zealand legislation dealing with the introduction of the forty-hour week is similar to earlier legislation on the same subject enacted in Queensland. Clauses have been borrowed from English Acts and this has been particularly so in the realm of private law. It does not follow that such clauses are construed as they are construed by the English courts. The New Zealand Court of Appeal has held that their construction must be determined according to their meaning in the Act adopting them. The interpretation of words and phrases has been in the light of the New Zealand scene. For instance, the words ' benevolent institution ' and ' benevolent association ' have acquired a meaning in New Zealand which has been judicially noticed ; they are public institutions legislatively associated with such institutions as hospitals.[40]

The Public Trust Office, already discussed, was the first institution of its kind within the British Empire. India, however, does furnish

[40] *Clarke* v. *Att.-Gen. & Pritchard* (1914) 33 N.Z.L.R. 963.

illustrations of somewhat similar institutions, although much more limited in scope, which were established earlier. Denmark has had a Public Trustee system for at least 300 years and Norway since 1687,[41] but it is not known whether those who framed the New Zealand legislation were aware of these institutions. An illustration of original legislation was that creating the Court of Arbitration, but the idea of compulsion embodied in the legislation had already been advanced in Australia. The Testator's Family Maintenance Act of 1900 was an original piece of legislation.

Over a long period Parliament has shown a growing tendency to avoid minute detailed provisions in legislation. In many instances this has been done on the assumption that regulations will be made to fill in the picture, but apart from this aspect there has been a turning away from rigid legal rules to a system which confers a discretion with the object of meeting more effectively the circumstances of individual cases. The Testator's Family Maintenance Act, 1900, gave the Supreme Court a discretion to override the operation of a will in order to make provision for the proper maintenance and support of a member of the testator's family. The court has to discover all the relevant circumstances of the testator and of his family and the family history and then to consider moral as distinct from legal claims.

Although flexibility has become common in New Zealand legislation, the practice has grown of entrusting the exercise of discretion to specially created tribunals or to public servants rather than to the ordinary courts. This is more fully discussed in Chapter 4. The climax to a line of legislation dealing with a particular problem has often been the creation of a central agency to provide the initiative and drive for the execution of policy. Many illustrations of this trend will be seen in those portions of this book dealing with social and economic questions.

[41] Stephenson, *Studies in Trust Business*, pp. 240, 241.

CHAPTER 2

PARLIAMENT

The Franchise

THE Constitution Act of 1852 enfranchised most householders: the qualification was occupation of a dwelling with an annual value of £10 if in a town or £5 if in the country, or possession of a freehold estate with an annual value of £50 or a leasehold estate with an annual value of £10. Plural voting by owners and lessees of land was neither prohibited nor limited. In 1853, when the first election was held, for every hundred of population there were twenty names on the electoral rolls; in the United Kingdom in the eighteen-fifties for every hundred of population there were only four names on the electoral rolls. In each case the figure included plural registrations, and the registered electors would constitute fewer than 20 per cent. and 4 per cent. of the respective populations.

Before the end of the century regular instalments of reform of the franchise had reached their logical culmination in the adoption of the principle of one adult, one vote. In 1879 manhood franchise was introduced for all who could comply with the requirements of a residential qualification calling for twelve months' residence in the Colony and six months' residence in the electorate, and the occupiers' qualification was abolished as now being superfluous. The requirement of six months' residence in the electorate disfranchised many unmarried workers who travelled from job to job; in 1893 the Liberal Government reduced the period to three months, at which it still remains. The substitution of the residential qualification for the occupiers increased the number of names on the rolls per hundred of population from eighteen for the 1879 election (held before the enactment of the reform measure of that year) to twenty-four for the 1881 election.

In 1870 it was provided that no elector might exercise more than one vote in any one electorate; in 1879 the leasehold qualification was abolished, but the freehold qualification was extended by being reduced from £50 to £25; in 1889 plural voting was abolished. But new registrations under the freehold qualification were permitted till 1896 and registration on more than one electoral roll was permitted till 1902.

The Maoris have had four separate members since 1868, when the first elections were held under an Act passed the previous year which divided New Zealand into four Maori electorates and provided manhood franchise for Maoris. The reason why they were given manhood franchise so early was that their communal system of ownership of land prevented the vast majority of them from qualifying under the 1852 Act. In 1879 they were given a ratepayers' qualification for European electorates in addition to the freehold qualification; but it was provided that no Maori might vote in both Maori and European electorates. The ratepayers' qualification was abolished with the freehold qualification in 1896.

In 1893 New Zealand became the first British country to give the vote to women. A Bill to that effect had also been introduced the previous year but had been dropped because of a disagreement between the two Houses. The Legislative Council had insisted on an amendment that gave all women the right of postal voting; and the supporters of the Bill in the House had felt that a husband's directions might convert this right into a duty and thus destroy the secrecy of the ballot and open the way for the exercise of undue influence. The enfranchisement of women has probably had a negligible effect on the results of elections; but it has given government an additional inducement to enact and retain humanitarian legislation and legislation providing for referenda on prohibition. By 1893 the principle of one adult, one vote, was in force. Aliens, mentally defective persons and prisoners are disqualified.

Electoral Boundaries

The original division of the country into electorates was made by the Governor under a direction contained in the Constitution Act. Subsequent re-divisions were made by statute till 1887, when Parliament delegated responsibility to a non-partisan Representation Commission which was required to re-divide the country after every census. A census is held normally every five years. The tradition is well established that the Government of the day does not attempt to influence the Commission.

Till 1881 the division of the country into electorates was on the basis of the number of electors in each electorate. In 1881 total population (excluding Maoris) became the basis. In 1945 adult population (excluding Maoris) was substituted, and in 1950 total population (excluding Maoris) was reinstated. The use of total population as the basis has strengthened the electoral importance of country voters, because adults are a lower proportion of total population in the country than they are in the towns. The drift of population from the country to the towns between census and election has the same effect.

During the earlier period that total population was the basis, 1881 to 1945, the electoral importance of country voters was strengthened even more by the so-called country quota. The abolition of the provinces in 1876 had thrown the developing social conflict into the central arena, and in 1881 the Conservatives decided to strengthen their position by giving this additional weight to country votes. The re-division into electorates in 1881 gave town electorates 33⅓ per cent. more population than country electorates. The 1887 Act (which established the Representation Commission) instructed the Commission to add on to the country population a fictitious quota (the country quota), which the Liberals in office fixed at the reduced figure of 18 per cent. In 1889 the quota was increased to 28 per cent. under a Conservative Government, and it remained at this figure till 1945, when it was abolished. Under this system a town electorate would have 28 per cent. more population than a country electorate (hence a country electorate would have 22 per cent. less population than a town electorate). In an electorate that was partly town and partly country the quota would be correspondingly smaller, and would benefit town voters as well as country voters. The arguments in favour of the country quota were : that the British Constitution has traditionally given representation to communities and to interests rather than to numbers (but this tradition has now been departed from in the United Kingdom itself); that a country electorate drawn on a basis of equal numbers would be too difficult to canvass (but with improvements in transport and communications this point carries much less weight now than it did in the eighteen-eighties); latterly, that without the country quota Labour would be sure of electoral victory, and would consequently be virtually irresponsible (but this was disproved by Labour's defeat in the 1949 election); and, more cogently, that the whole country is so closely dependent on the prosperity of the primary industries that farmers should be given a sufficiently strong electoral voice to ensure that they will be fairly treated even by a townsmen's government. New Zealand was not alone in giving added weight to country votes, but the method chosen was probably unique. In other countries similar results have been achieved by delaying the revision of electoral boundaries ; or by defining unequal electorates in schedules to Acts ; or by appointing partisan representation commissions ; or by providing that electoral boundaries should not cross boundaries fixed for purposes of local government ; or by giving equal representation in a second chamber to states of unequal population. Under systems like these the weighting of country votes either has the appearance of justification by the federal principle or else it has the appearance of mere anomaly. But in New Zealand the country quota was unambiguous in purpose ; it was an overt breach of democratic principle that no self-respecting democracy could permanently endure. In 1945, when the tide of opinion in the electorate was running against the Labour Government, the country quota was abolished. The principle of one vote, one value, was adopted fifty-two years after the principle of one adult, one vote.

The Representation Commission's jurisdiction does not extend to the four Maori electorates. Ever since these electorates were established in 1867 the Executive has had the power to revise their boundaries by

Proclamation. This power was first used in 1952. The average population in the Maori electorates was originally higher than in the European
electorates, but the Maori population was falling during the second half
of the nineteenth century, and by the end of the century the Maoris
were clearly over-represented. More recently the rate of increase of
population has been higher among the Maoris than among the European
population, and on a basis of comparative numbers of voters the Maoris
are once more entitled to four seats in Parliament. The Maori boundaries
were seriously overdue for revision by 1952. Even originally the electorates varied greatly in population, the three electorates that were
established in the North Island each having more population than
Southern Maori, which comprised the South Island. With the passage of
time the disparities increased, and Southern Maori became little more
than a rotten borough. In 1952 part of the North Island was included
in Southern Maori, and other changes were made in the North Island.

Elections

For over a generation Members of Parliament have been elected by
the top-of-the-poll system in single-member electorates, but multi-
number electorates were used in all but three of the elections down to
1902, and the second ballot was used in the elections of 1908 and 1911.
The Constitution Act contemplated the establishment of multi-member
electorates ; it empowered the Governor to fix the number of members
to be returned by each electorate. Multi-member electorates were
constituted in 1853 and in all the re-divisions prior to 1881, but the
1881 re-division made the single-member electorate universal. In 1889
three-member electorates were constituted in each of the four main
cities, and this system operated in the five general elections from 1890 to
1902. The 1889 Bill in its original form provided for proportional
representation in the cities, but the Bill as enacted did not depart from
the top-of-the-poll system with each elector voting for three candidates.
These three-member electorates were only a by-product of the contemporary desire to secure more adequate representation for minorities. If
party organisation had been more effective, the system would have had
the very opposite result of enabling the majority party to capture all
three seats. But party organisation was not sufficiently effective to
enable this to be done, and there was not much to be said either for or
against the three-member electorates.

The legislation providing for the second ballot was passed in 1908 and
repealed in 1912. Where no candidate received a majority on the first
ballot a second ballot was to be held between the two leading candidates.
The interval between the two ballots was to be seven days in most
electorates and fourteen days in a few specified electorates covering wide
areas that could not conveniently be canvassed in seven days. Both the

introduction and the repeal of this system were motivated by partisan considerations. During the first decade of the century the Liberal-Labour alliance was splitting up, and the conservative Reform Party was likely to benefit from vote-splitting under the top-of-the-poll system. The second ballot was introduced under the Liberal Government, and was repealed as soon as the Reform Party took office in 1912. The top-of-the-poll system has been the subject of considerable criticism at times. Towards the end of the nineteenth century, when proportional representation was one of the latest devices for democratic reform, it attracted widespread interest. Proportional representation was again discussed widely in the nineteen-twenties, which were a period of three-party politics. In the 1928 election three-party politics produced the curious result that fewer votes were cast for successful candidates than for defeated ones. The two-party system is now firmly re-established —in fact, the elections of 1946, 1949 and 1951 produced Parliaments composed entirely of members of the Labour and National Parties— and the top-of-the-poll system is widely accepted as desirable.

Legislation on elections is very similar to British legislation. The Constitution Act required the Governor to establish electoral rolls, and in 1858 this provision was superseded by a local statute. Registration has been compulsory since 1924, but only in the early years were prosecutions instituted for failure to register. These provisions did not originally apply to the Maori electorates, and till 1946 the Maoris voted by declaration, but Maori electoral rolls were prepared in time to be used in the 1949 election. Voting has never been compulsory, but an extraordinarily high proportion of the registered electors cast their votes in most general elections—over 95 per cent. in the elections of 1946 and 1949. A partial explanation is that a licensing referendum is held in conjunction with a general election. A Corrupt Practices Prevention Act was passed in 1858 and a Secret Ballot Act in 1869. A Secret Ballot Bill had been thrown out by the Legislative Council the previous year.

Any registered elector of either sex may be a candidate. Women have been eligible for membership since 1919, and the first woman was elected to Parliament in 1933 in a by-election necessitated by the death of her husband. The Constitution Act gave the House of Representatives the responsibility for determining disputed elections ; the Electoral Petitions Act of 1880 provided for the establishment of Electoral Courts. The present procedure, which is substantially the same as that enacted in 1880, is that a petition is addressed to the Chief Justice, a trial is held before two judges of the Supreme Court appointed by the Chief Justice, the court determines whether the member whose return is complained of was duly returned or whether the election was void and certifies accordingly to the Speaker, and the House on being informed by the Speaker gives the necessary directions for confirming or altering the return or for issuing a writ for a new election as circumstances require. The provision that the House ' shall give the necessary directions ' makes the House's part in the proceedings purely ministerial so long as the statutory direction is not contested on the ground that no Parliament can bind succeeding Parliaments. Meantime the determination on disputed elections is non-political.

Size of House of Representatives

The lower house originally had thirty-seven members. Numerous small increases in membership were made in the early years, culminating in an Act of 1881 which fixed a total of ninety-five, including the four Maori members. The only changes since then have been a reduction to seventy-four under an Act of 1887 (an economy measure) and an increase in 1900 to the present figure of eighty. The House is frequently criticised as being too large for so small a country ; there is one member to every 25,000 population as against one to 80,000 in the United Kingdom. As a forum for debate, however, the House is not too large. Moreover, as a pool of ministerial talent it is definitely too small, especially when the government party has only a small majority. This can be seen from the case of the Fraser Labour Government in its last three years in office (1946–49), when it had a majority of forty-two to thirty-eight. From its members in the lower house it provided fourteen of the fifteen Cabinet Ministers, four Parliamentary Under-Secretaries, the Speaker, the Chairman of Committees and two Whips—*i.e.*, twenty-two of its forty-two members were required for various offices. A higher administrative standard could no doubt be obtained if the pool were bigger, enabling a higher proportion to be passed over. The problem did not exist when the present membership of eighty was established, as the Cabinet then was only half the size of the present Cabinet and there were no Parliamentary Under-Secretaries.

Life of Parliament

The maximum life of Parliament was fixed in the Constitution Act at five years, and was reduced in 1879 to three years. In 1879 a conflict between Government and Parliament led to a premature dissolution in August. When the new Parliament met, the Triennial Act of 1879 was passed. This Act specially provided that the Parliament of 1879 was to have a maximum life of only approximately two and a half years ; the reason was that the spring had been found to be the most convenient time to hold elections, and the Parliament of 1879, if it were given a three-year life, would expire in the winter. The succeeding election was held towards the end of 1881, and since then elections have normally been held every third year, usually towards the end of the year, and only once, when the election was necessitated by a premature dissolution, earlier than September. The only Parliaments prematurely dissolved since the Triennial Act was passed have been the Parliaments of 1881 and 1884 (when in each case the resulting election was held late in the calendar year in which an election was due to be held in the normal course of events), and the Parliament of 1949 (which was dissolved after less than two years to enable the Government to hold a snap election following a bitter industrial dispute in which drastic powers were taken). The life of the 1914 Parliament was extended till 1919, and the life of the 1938 Parliament till 1943 ; the 1931 Parliament passed a quadrennial Act, but the new Government elected in 1935 promptly restored the triennial system; the only other Parliament to extend its life has been the 1951 Parliament, which extended its life by 52 days to avoid holding the 1954 election unusually early in the year.

Till 1893 there was no statutory requirement that the expiration or prior dissolution of a Parliament should be followed within a specified period by a general election. The Constitution Act, however, though it fixed no time limit, implicitly forbade any hiatus by providing that on the expiration or prior dissolution of a Parliament the Governor was to cause writs to be issued for a general election. There was of course a constitutional convention that a general election would be held promptly and the convention was invariably observed. In 1893 the requirement that elections be held promptly became a statutory one : provision was made that within seven days of expiration or prior dissolution the Governor was to instruct the Clerk of the Writs to issue writs for a general election, that the Clerk of the Writs was to issue writs accordingly within three days, and that the date fixed for the return of the writs was to be not more than twenty-one days after the date of issue. This last period was extended in 1910 to 28 days, in 1927 to 40 days, and in 1953 to 50 days.

The quinquennial and triennial provisions have been to the effect that a Parliament should continue only for a period of five or three years computed from the day fixed for the return of the writs for a general election. The practice has always been not to allow a Parliament to expire, but to have it dissolved shortly before the date on which it would expire. Only one Parliament has expired under this legislation, the Parliament of 1943. It was elected on September 25, 1943, the writs being made returnable by October 11, 1943. This Parliament expired on October 11, 1946. Presumably in 1946 the responsible authorities overlooked the fact that in 1943 the elections had been held unusually early in the year. However that may be, the 1946 session of the 1943 Parliament lasted till October 12, 1946, but fortunately the invalid proceedings of the final day were confined to formal and valedictory business. On November 4, 1946, a Proclamation was issued purporting to dissolve Parliament.

Three years is a short life. Usually the first session is occupied largely with settling down after the elections, and the third session largely with preparations for the coming elections. Substitution of a quadrennial system, by increasing the proportion of working sessions from one in three to two in four, would materially increase the effectiveness of Parliament without materially decreasing Parliament's responsibility and responsiveness to its masters the electors.

The Legislative Council

The Upper House, the Legislative Council, which was abolished in 1950, was an appointive body. Earl Grey, the Colonial Secretary in Lord John Russell's Government of 1846–52, intended to establish an indirectly elected Legislative Council to which each Provincial Council would elect three members, but on the change of government in 1852 Sir John Pakington substituted the appointive body. This was the only important change the Conservatives made in the course of amplifying the 'heads of a bill' that they inherited from their Liberal predecessors. The Constitution Act placed control over appointments in the hands of the Colonial Office by providing that Her Majesty was empowered to authorise the Governor to make such appointments as she thought fit. Such a provision proved most inconvenient in the case of so distant a colony, and in fact the Governor was authorised by his Instructions to make appointments without specific prior approval. An 1868 Imperial Act [1] confirmed all previous appointments and gave the appointing power for the future to the Governor. Appointments were already being made on ministerial advice, though it was not till the last decade of the century that the principle was established that the Governor must always accept such advice.[2] Appointment was originally for life, but the Legislative Council Act of 1891 provided that future appointments were to be for seven years only, with eligibility for re-appointment.

The Constitution Bill provided that the Council was to consist of from ten to fifteen members, but the upper limit was removed by the House of Commons. An upper limit of fifteen was fixed by Governor's Instructions in 1855 ; the limit was raised to twenty in 1861 and was removed altogether in 1862. Till the end of the century the membership of the Council was usually about half the membership of the House. The highest membership the Council ever had was fifty-four, in 1885, when the House had ninety-five members. From about 1900 the number of councillors was usually between thirty and forty, *i.e.*, rather less than half the number in the House. In March, 1950, the number fell to twenty-five, but it was increased to fifty-three before the passing of the Legislative Council Abolition Bill later in the year. Statutory provision

---

[1]   31 & 32 Vict. c. 57.
[2]   See p. 13.

was made in 1941 for the appointment of women to the Council, and the first two women councillors were appointed in 1946.

Down to 1893 important measures sent up from the House were frequently rejected, shelved or radically amended by the Council. To give only one instance, in 1882 the House passed a Bill establishing a new system of perpetual leases of Crown lands, the rent to be fixed afresh every thirty years; the Council inserted a clause, which the House ultimately accepted, giving the tenant the right to purchase, thereby converting the leasehold scheme into a scheme for deferred purchase of the freehold. The Council in this period was Conservative in general, and in particular protected the interests of the large landowners. Down till 1890 conservatism called for only spasmodic conflicts with the House, but after the election of a determined Liberal-Labour Government in 1890 came three sessions of consistent opposition to the House. Three events made the Council more conciliatory from 1894 onwards: the reduction in term to seven years in 1891 (creating in some councillors a desire to court re-appointment); the Colonial Secretary's ruling in 1892 that the Governor should make appointments to the Council as his Ministers recommended (creating a fear of swamping); and the overwhelming popular support for Liberal policy in the 1893 election. Thenceforth the Council resisted very few important measures apart from measures for its own reform. Probably the most important instance is the Old-age Pensions Bill of 1897, which the Council rejected; but it passed a similar Bill in 1898. In 1916 the Leader of the Council, Sir Francis Bell, though himself a member of Cabinet, persuaded the Council to insist on amending a Government Bill, the Military Service Bill, by inserting a clause exempting religious objectors. Apart from that single incident it is doubtful whether the Council performed any useful function in its last fifty years. It was not an effective revising body; it did not prevent the passing of hasty and ill-considered legislation; it did not relieve the members of the lower House from the ardours of committee work; and it did not represent a distinct interest in the community.

The question of ending or mending the Council had cropped up throughout New Zealand history. The first motion that came before the Council in 1854 was one that it be made elective. Until recent years outright abolition had not found many supporters in either House, but the substitution of election for appointment had appealed to many—to conservatives because it would strengthen the Council and to progressives because it would make it more democratic. A Legislative Council Act providing for a Council of forty elected European members and three appointed Maori members was passed in 1914 and was to come into force on a date to be notified by Proclamation. The Act remained inoperative until it was repealed in 1950 when the Legislative Council was abolished. During this period the Council was probably the only second chamber in the world whose constitution was capable of being changed without further expression of its own consent. The reason why the Act was never brought into force was that conservative governments were uncertain whether it would be wise to establish a stronger Council that might be captured by a radical electorate and the Labour Government of 1935-49 found the Council a convenient field for patronage.

In 1947 the Leader of the National Opposition introduced a Bill for the abolition of the Council, apparently believing that of all possible measures this was the one on which Labour back-benchers were most likely to disobey the Whips. The Bill was, however, defeated on the second reading, on the understandings that Parliament would seek plenary powers to enact constitutional legislation and that the whole question of the second chamber would be considered by a joint Constitutional Reform Committee. Plenary powers were obtained later in the year,[3] and in 1948 the Committee reported that it was unable to agree upon a recommendation. In the 1949 election campaign the Leader of the Opposition committed his party to the abolition of the Council as then constituted ; the National Party won the election, and in 1950 the Council was abolished. At the same time a Constitutional Reform Committee was set up to consider possible alternatives to the Council. It reported in 1952 recommending the establishment of a Senate of thirty-two with power to delay legislation for two months ; after every general election senators were to be nominated by the Prime Minister and the Leader of the Opposition and any other party leaders in proportion to party strengths in the House. When the Report was debated in the House the Government gave no indication of its intentions ; and, at the time of going to press (December, 1953), there the matter rests.

Privilege and Procedure

New Zealand's inherited law consists only of common law and statute, and does not include the *lex et consuetudo Parliamenti*. Consequently the New Zealand Parliament is not a High Court, and it has no inherent power to commit for contempt. Parliamentary privileges and Parliament's power to commit depend upon express enactment. The first Act on these subjects was passed in 1856 ; a fuller Act was passed in 1865 giving the two Houses the same privileges as were enjoyed on January 1, 1865, by the House of Commons in so far as these privileges were consistent with the Constitution Act. The Legislative Council was thus apparently given the right to initiate and amend Money Bills, but this was due to an error in drafting, and in 1872 the Council accepted an opinion that had been obtained from the Law Officers of the Crown in England that it did not possess these rights. The Council never

[3] See p. 41.

initiated or rejected Money Bills, but it amended many Bills that were certainly or possibly Money Bills. In some cases it did not insist on its amendments; in other cases the House waived its privilege; and in most of the remaining cases the Bills did not deal with taxation, supply or appropriation but made financial provision for State business undertakings, and it was doubtful whether the House of Commons would have regarded them as Money Bills.

In organisation, ceremonial and procedure the House of Representatives closely follows the House of Commons. The Speaker is strictly non-partisan in the discharge of his duties, but is usually opposed in a general election, and a Speaker was defeated in a general election as early as 1871 and as recently as 1946. On a change of government it has been usual for the Speaker, if still a member, to remain in office, but in 1950 a new precedent was established by the use of the new Government party's majority to elect a new Speaker although the retiring Speaker was a member. Till 1891 the Speaker of the Legislative Council was appointed by the Governor, but under the Legislative Council Act, 1891, the Council was given power to elect its Speaker for five-year terms.

Time limits on speeches in the House date from 1895. ' Urgency ' dates from 1929; when a Minister moves for urgency for Government business no debate is allowed on that particular motion beyond the mover's speech, and if urgency is granted no other business is considered and the House does not rise until the business in hand is disposed of. The closure dates from 1931. The kangaroo closure and guillotine are not used. There are no standing committees, but some Bills are referred to *ad hoc* or sessional select committees either immediately before or immediately after the second reading. Belated amendments are sometimes inserted under a provision in the Constitution Act that authorises the Governor-General, when a Bill is forwarded to him for his assent, to refer it back to one of the Houses and request that a particular amendment be made. Since 1936 the proceedings of the House have been broadcast, and Parliament has been able to perform its educative function more effectively; but many listeners have been appalled at the standard of debate. Caucus (a meeting of the parliamentary members of a party) has much more power than in the United Kingdom. The crucial debate on legislative proposals usually takes place behind the locked doors of the Government party's caucus; the function of debate in the House is educative rather than legislative. Since 1950 an explanatory memorandum has been printed with every Bill.

Assent to Bills

No Bill has ever been vetoed by the Governor, though in 1877 a new Premier (Sir George Grey, himself formerly twice Governor of the Colony) recommended the Governor to veto a Bill introduced while the previous Government had been in office and finally passed in a form of which the new Government did not approve. The Constitution Act, in addition to providing that the Governor might assent to a Bill, and might refuse to assent, provided that he might reserve a Bill for the signification of the Royal pleasure, and also provided for disallowance by Her Majesty of a Bill to which the Governor had assented. Reservation and disallowance are treated in the following sections of this chapter.

Legislative and Constituent Powers

Until 1947 there were five limitations on the legislative and constituent powers of the New Zealand Parliament. First, it could not alter, suspend or repeal the entrenched clauses of the Constitution Act; second, it could not legislate with extraterritorial effect; third, it could not legislate repugnantly to the law of England; fourth, the Governor-General could reserve Bills for the signification of the Royal pleasure; fifth, the Crown could disallow Acts to which the Governor-General had assented. The New Zealand Constitution (Amendment) Act, 1947, enacted by the United Kingdom Parliament, removed the first of the limitations; the Statute of Westminster Adoption Act, 1947, enacted by the New Zealand Parliament, removed the second and third of the limitations; and these two Acts between them gave the New Zealand Parliament power to remove the fourth and fifth of the limitations. Since 1947 the New Zealand Parliament has had plenary powers, save for unimportant exceptions which are considered later in this chapter under the headings of reservation and disallowance.

The Entrenched Sections

Parliament derives its principal constituent powers from the Constitution Act and its amendments and the Statute of Westminster, 1931. Section 53 of the Constitution Act provided inter alia: ' It shall be competent to the said General Assembly . . . to make laws for the peace, order and good government of New Zealand, provided that no such laws be repugnant to the law of England '. The power given by section 53 has been used to enact constitutional legislation supplementary to the Constitution Act, for instance on the privileges of Parliament. Section 67 specifically authorised supplementary constitutional legislation dealing with electoral machinery. Neither of these sections required the reservation of Bills for the signification of the Royal pleasure.

Sections 68 and 69 authorised amendments to the Constitution Act itself on the subjects respectively of elections and the powers of the provinces, subject to reservation. The Constitution Amendment Act, 1857 (Imperial), gave power, subject to reservation, to alter, suspend or repeal all but twenty-one sections of the 1852 Act. Power to repeal one of those entrenched sections was given by Imperial Act[4] in 1862, and was exercised by the Native Land Act, 1873. When power to abolish the provinces was exercised by the Abolition of Provinces Act, 1875, five entrenched sections ceased to be operative, and these sections were repealed by the Repeals Act, 1878. Of the remaining fifteen entrenched sections the most important were : section 32, which established a General Assembly, to consist of the Governor, a Legislative Council and a House of Representatives ; section 53, mentioned in the preceding paragraph, which conferred a legislative power ; and sections 56–59, which provided for assent, refusal of assent, and reservation, by the Governor, and for disallowance by Her Majesty. So long as the New Zealand Parliament was unable to alter, suspend or repeal the entrenched sections, its constituent powers were limited by these sections ; thus, section 32 would have prevented Parliament from abolishing the Legislative Council. Even outside the entrenched sections, Parliament's constituent powers were limited by the requirement of reservation.

The powers granted by the 1857 Act have several times been used. The current (1932) Reprint of New Zealand Statutes contains notes to the effect that various sections were repealed by the Regulation of Elections Act, 1881, the Legislative Council Act, 1891, and the Electoral Act, 1902, and that all the other repealed sections were repealed by Imperial legislation. Actually some of these other sections were repealed by the New Zealand Parliament before being repealed by the Imperial Parliament ; thus sections 2 and 17 were repealed by a New Zealand Act, the Abolition of Provinces Act, 1875, but are shown in the Reprint as having been repealed by an Imperial Act, the Statute Law Revision Act, 1892.

Of the original eighty-two sections of the 1852 Act nineteen remain in force, including the fifteen entrenched sections. One amendment, however, has been made to the entrenched sections since the New Zealand Parliament was granted plenary powers in 1947 : the Legislative Council Abolition Act, 1950 deleted the reference to the Legislative Council from section 32, which now provides that the General Assembly is to consist of the Governor and a House of Representatives.

It was formerly sometimes contended that full constituent powers were given to the New Zealand Parliament by sections 3 and 5 of the Colonial Laws Validity Act, 1865, but today all authorities agree in rejecting this view. Section 3 provided that a Colonial law should not be void on account of repugnancy unless the English law to which it was repugnant extended to the Colony in question. This section had the limited purpose of remedying the mischief caused in South Australia by Mr. Justice Boothby's propensity for declaring local legislation void for repugnancy to the law of England even though the English law to which

4   25 & 26 Vict. c. 48.

it might be repugnant did not extend to South Australia. This section gave the New Zealand Parliament no power to amend the Constitution Act, for an amendment would be repugnant to the Constitution Act, and the Constitution Act extended to New Zealand. Section 5 empowered a Colonial legislature to legislate on the subjects of the Colonial judiciary and legislature ; but there was a doubt whether a constituent power given to Colonial legislatures generally in 1865 should be interpreted as having been given to a particular Colonial legislature which had been specially given specified constituent powers in 1857 (*generalia specialibus non derogant*) ; and, moreover, as section 5 dealt only with legislation concerning the judiciary and the legislature, it could not give the New Zealand Parliament power to legislate on any of the other subjects covered in the Constitution Act. In 1868 the New Zealand Government showed that it was not prepared to rely on the Colonial Laws Validity Act as an authority for enacting either legislation relating to the judiciary and the legislature or legislation relating to other subjects covered in the Constitution Act : in that year the Imperial Parliament, on representations from the New Zealand Government, passed an Act [5] to amend the Constitution Act to give the Governor, retrospectively, the power to make appointments to the Legislative Council, and a further Act [6] to clarify the meaning of the 1857 Amendment Act and declare that the New Zealand Parliament had power to amend the Constitution Act to abolish provinces. But, though the Colonial Laws Validity Act did not give full constituent powers to the New Zealand Parliament, and the applicability of section 5 to New Zealand was questionable, there was the possibility that the Act gave the New Zealand Parliament power to legislate on the judiciary and the legislature.

The only Imperial Acts enlarging the constituent powers of the New Zealand Parliament between 1857 and 1947 were, apart from the doubtful case of the Colonial Laws Validity Act, the 1862 Act conferring power to repeal one of the entrenched sections, and the 1868 Act clarifying the powers given by the 1857 Act. In 1947, during the debate on the Opposition Bill for the abolition of the Legislative Council, the Prime Minister proposed that, before proceeding further with the Bill, Parliament should obtain full legislative powers including constituent powers. It would not be sufficient to adopt sections 2–6 of the Statute of Westminster, 1931,[7] since section 8 provided that the Statute did not confer on the New Zealand Parliament any power to amend the Constitution Act otherwise than in accordance with the law existing before the commencement of the Statute. Section 8 applied also to Australia, and a similar provision in section 7 applied to Canada. The denial of full constituent

[5]   31 & 32 Vict. c. 57.
[6]   31 & 32 Vict. c. 92.
[7]   The leading authority is K. C. Wheare, *The Statute of Westminster and Dominion Status*, 5th ed. (1953).

powers to the central legislatures of the federal Dominions clearly had its
constitutional justification. In the case of the New Zealand legislature,
the reason for the inclusion of this provision had been political: the
Government that was in office when the Statute of Westminster Bill
was drafted did not want to smooth the path of any later Government that
might be bent on constitutional reform. Not only did section 8 provide
that the Statute give the New Zealand Parliament no new powers in
respect of the Constitution Act; section 2 (1) provided that the Colonial
Laws Validity Act should not apply to any law made after the commencement of the Statute by the Parliament of a Dominion. If the New Zealand
Parliament possessed any constituent powers under the Colonial Laws
Validity Act, section 2 (1) withdrew them; though possibly section 8
revived them by necessary intendment. Section 2 (2) abolished repugnancy in respect of any law made by the Parliament of a Dominion after
the commencement of the Statute, but so far as the New Zealand Constitution Act was concerned the general provisions of section 2 (2) were
overridden by the special provisions of section 8. If the New Zealand
Parliament were to obtain plenary powers, the United Kingdom Parliament would need either to repeal section 8 so far as it concerned New
Zealand or to enact an amendment to the Constitution Act empowering
the New Zealand Parliament to alter, suspend or repeal the entrenched
sections. The latter course was adopted. The New Zealand Parliament
passed the New Zealand Constitution (Request and Consent) Act, 1947,
and in accordance with the request contained in it the United Kingdom
Parliament passed the New Zealand Constitution (Amendment) Act,
1947, repealing the 1857 Act and giving the New Zealand Parliament
power to alter, suspend or repeal all or any of the provisions of the
Constitution Act. At the same time the New Zealand Parliament passed
the Statute of Westminster Adoption Act, 1947, adopting sections 2–6 of
the Statute of Westminster. Unlike the Australian Adoption Act, the
New Zealand Adoption Act did not provide that the adoption of sections
2–6 was to date back from the date of commencement of the Adoption
Act to the date of commencement of the Statute itself.

Extraterritorial Legislation

Extraterritorial powers were not expressly withheld by the Constitution Act, but neither were they granted. The power to legislate for the
peace, order and good government of New Zealand has been construed
as a power relating to New Zealand only. Formerly the New Zealand
courts put a narrow construction on the New Zealand Parliament's
territorial powers,[8] but recently the Court of Appeal has followed the
more generous interpretation of territorial powers approved by the Judicial

[8] *R.* v. *Lander* [1919] N.Z.L.R. 305.
     Tagaloa v. *Inspector of Police* [1927] N.Z.L.R. 883.

Committee in a Canadian case in 1932[9] and applied and developed in later cases.[10] The recent cases have decided that territorial powers extend to the control of events outside the territory that bear on peace, order and good government within the territory.

Sometimes when extraterritorial powers were required they were granted by Imperial statute. Thus section 15 of the Whaling Industry (Regulation) Act, 1934 (Imperial), granted extraterritorial powers which were used by the New Zealand Parliament in the Whaling Industry Act, 1935. Power to legislate for the mandated territory of Western Samoa was expressly given by an Imperial Order in Council of March 11, 1920, which provided that the New Zealand Parliament should ' have full power to make laws for the peace, order and good government of the territory of Western Samoa subject to and in accordance with the provisions of the said Treaty of Peace '. But these special grants of extraterritorial powers were always limited in their scope, and their scope was not always as wide as could have been desired. This applies particularly to the power to control shipping given by section 5 of the Emergency Powers (Defence) Act, 1939 (Imperial). It took a Pacific war to persuade the Australian Government to secure adoption of the Statute of Westminster in 1942 ; and war-time experience was one reason for adoption by New Zealand in 1947. Under section 3 of the Statute of Westminster the New Zealand Parliament now has full power to legislate with extraterritorial effect. Unlike section 2 (which abolished repugnancy), section 3 is not expressly limited in its operation to laws ' made after the commencement of this Act '. Whether it should be construed as being retrospective in its operation is doubtful.[11] If it is so construed, that solves all problems of extraterritoriality ; but if it is not so construed, then any possibly extraterritorial provision in an earlier Act can be saved only by demonstrating that the extraterritorial events concerned have bearing on the peace, order and good government of New Zealand, and persuading the Court to follow the recent line of decisions.

Repugnancy

The third limitation was prohibition of legislation repugnant to the law of England. This prohibition was contained in section 53 of the Constitution Act, the section which gave power to legislate for the peace, order and good government of New Zealand. The Colonial Laws Validity Act reduced the scope of repugnancy by providing that Colonial legislation was not to be considered repugnant unless it was repugnant to

[9] *Croft* v. *Dunphy* [1933] A.C. 156.
[10] *Woolworths (New Zealand) Ltd.* v. *Wynne* [1952] N.Z.L.R. 496.
[11] *Ibid., per* F. B. Adams J., pp. 518, 519.

Imperial legislation that extended to the Colony. Presumably, however,
Imperial legislation could extend to a Colony by necessary intendment
as well as by express provision. It was the prohibition of repugnancy
that guarded the entrenched sections of the Constitution Act by preventing the New Zealand Parliament from arrogating to itself a power of
amendment. Probably only two other Acts that extended to New Zealand
had a fettering rather than a liberating effect; the Colonial Courts of
Admiralty Act, 1890 (in two unimportant provisions), and the Merchant
Shipping Act, 1894, and Regulations thereunder (in many important
provisions). The category of Imperial Statutes thus fettering the New
Zealand Parliament was long ago closed by convention, but the three
Imperial Statutes mentioned still extended to New Zealand, and the
New Zealand Parliament was incompetent to legislate repugnantly to
them until power to amend the Constitution Act was granted by the New
Zealand Constitution (Amendment) Act, 1947, and repugnancy was
abolished by section 2 of the Statute of Westminster.

In a discussion of the legislative competence of the New Zealand
Parliament repugnancy has called for separate treatment, but it was
itself an expression of a broader principle: the legislative supremacy
of the United Kingdom Parliament. The prohibition of repugnancy was
the only respect in which the legislative supremacy of the United Kingdom Parliament actually limited the legislative competence of the New
Zealand Parliament, but prior to the Statute of Westminster the United
Kingdom Parliament also had the power, limited only by convention, to
enact statutes extending to New Zealand without consulting the New
Zealand Government and even in opposition to the wishes of the New
Zealand Government or Parliament. This power can be said to have
been abolished (if we assume that the United Kingdom Parliament will
continue to be unwilling to enact amending legislation)[12] by section 4
of the Statute of Westminster, which provided: ' No Act of Parliament
of the United Kingdom passed after the commencement of this Act
shall extend, or be deemed to extend, to a Dominion as part of the law
of that Dominion, unless it is expressly declared in that Act that that
Dominion has requested, and consented to, the enactment thereof '.
Section 3 (1) of the Statute of Westminster Adoption Act, 1947, purported
to amend this section by providing: ' For the purposes of section 4 of
the said Statute of Westminster the request and consent of New Zealand
to the enactment of any Act of the Parliament of the United Kingdom
shall be made and given by the Parliament of New Zealand, and not
otherwise '.

---

[12] Possibly s. 4 is binding on the United Kingdom Parliament. Zelman Cowen,
' Parliamentary Sovereignty and the Limits of Legal Change', *Australian Law
Journal*, September 22, 1952, pp. 237, 240.

Reservation

Provisions for reservation were of two kinds : discretionary and obligatory. Discretionary reservation was provided for in section 56 of the Constitution Act, which gave the Governor the power, subject to the provisions of the Act and of his Instructions, to decide at his discretion whether to assent to a Bill or to refuse his assent or to reserve the Bill for the signification of the Royal pleasure. Reservation was obligatory in four cases. First, section 57 of the Constitution Act provided that the Governor must act in obedience to any Instructions issued to him regarding reservation, and till 1907 his Instructions required him to reserve bills on certain subjects. Second, amendments to the unentrenched sections of the Constitution Act passed under the powers given by the 1857 Act were required to be reserved. Third, much merchant shipping legislation was required to be reserved under sections 735 and 736 of the Merchant Shipping Act, 1894. Fourth, a similar provision existed in section 4 of the Colonial Courts of Admiralty Act, 1890.

After 1892, when the Governor was instructed that save in the most exceptional circumstances he must accept the advice of his Ministers unless Imperial interests were affected,[13] discretionary reservation of Bills not affecting Imperial interests was made only on the advice of Ministers. Where Imperial interests were affected, it is probable that Ministers were always willing to recommend reservation in what the Governor or the Imperial Government considered appropriate cases. New Zealand Ministers were sensitive to the wishes of the Imperial Government, and were also prepared to amend Bills to which the Imperial Government objected. The negotiations over the Shipping and Seamen Amendment Bill, 1909, were typical : the Imperial Government objected to several sections but pressed its objections to only one section ; the New Zealand Government undertook to secure the repeal of the offending section ; the Royal assent to the whole Bill was then granted ; and in the next ensuing session of the New Zealand Parliament the section was repealed by the Shipping and Seamen Amendment Act, 1911. Only one reserved Bill failed to secure the Royal assent after 1900. This was the Shipping and Seamen Amendment Bill, 1910, containing a proposal to levy a heavy tax on any ships trading to New Zealand which employed lascars. The Secretary of State for the Colonies forwarded a Dispatch observing that the Bill went beyond the limits of the legislative power laid down at the Imperial Conference of 1907 with the consent of the Prime Minister of New Zealand, and that as one subject that the New Zealand Government had placed on the agenda for the Imperial Conference of 1911 was merchant shipping he had no doubt that the Prime Minister would wish to discuss the provisions of the Bill at the Conference and pending that

[13] See p. 13.

discussion he did not propose to tender any advice to His Majesty with respect to the Bill. The Bill was not heard of again. The effective reason for amending the 1909 Act and dropping the 1910 Bill was the desire to meet the legitimate objections raised by a partner in the Empire ; and this reason would have operated just as effectively without the requirement for reservation.

When finally a convention was established in 1930 that reserved Bills would receive the Royal assent whenever Dominion Ministers so advised, reservation ceased to be any greater limitation on the legal powers of the New Zealand Parliament than the Governor's power of veto. At least, in normal circumstances that was the case ; but the remote possibility remained that the Crown, departing from constitutional convention perhaps on the advice of Imperial Ministers, would fail to follow the advice of New Zealand Ministers on a reserved Bill. A further disadvantage was that a reserved Bill could not come into force until it had received the Royal assent, and the delay might be inconvenient.

The provision regarding discretionary reservation in section 56 of the Constitution Act was not repealed in 1947, but the New Zealand Parliament was given power to repeal it by the New Zealand Constitution (Amendment) Act, 1947. The first case of obligatory reservation had disappeared in 1907 when the Imperial Government withdrew the Instructions requiring the Governor to reserve Bills on certain subjects ; and in 1947 the New Zealand Parliament was given power to repeal section 57 by the New Zealand Constitution (Amendment) Act, 1947. The second case disappeared when the same Act provided full power to alter, suspend or repeal the four unentrenched sections of the Constitution Act. Section 5 of the Statute of Westminster disposed of the third case by exempting the Dominions from sections 735 and 736 of the Merchant Shipping Act. Section 6 of the Statute of Westminster disposed of the fourth case by exempting the Dominions from section 4 of the Colonial Courts of Admiralty Act. (Section 6 also removed a related anachronism by exempting the Dominions from so much of section 7 of the Colonial Courts of Admiralty Act as required the approval of His Majesty to any rules of court for regulating the practice and procedure of Colonial Courts of Admiralty.) Thus the 1947 legislation did not entirely dispose of the statutory provision for reservation, since sections 56 and 57 of the Constitution Act remain on the Statute-book; but the New Zealand Parliament now has power to repeal them.

Reservation has been treated in this discussion as having constituted a limitation on the legislative competence of the New Zealand Parliament. Discretionary reservation, however, was not a limitation on the competence of the General Assembly or legislature in the same way as obligatory reservation, entrenchment, want of extraterritorial powers, repugnancy and disallowance were. Discretionary reservation did not limit the legislative competence of the General Assembly, for the Governor was himself part of the General Assembly, and, if he decided to reserve a Bill to which he had power to assent, the competence of the General Assembly was no more limited than it would have been if one House had declined to pass a Bill that had already been passed by the other House or if the Governor had refused his assent to a Bill that had been passed by both Houses. In strict law, this applied even when discretionary reservation was exercised pursuant to obligatory Instructions, for section 4 of the Colonial Laws Validity Act provided that a Colonial law to which a Governor had assented would not be void or inoperative by reason only of any Instructions that might have been given to the Governor. But, where an instruction to the Governor-General to reserve a Bill was completely contained in a statute, he had no power to assent to it, and the competence of the General Assembly was limited. Even so, if Royal assent was forthcoming the limitation on the competence of the General Assembly that resulted from the limitation on powers of the Governor-General made no difference to the content of legislation ; it was only if Royal assent was not forthcoming that the limitation on the competence of the General Assembly could affect the content of legislation. Only eight reserved Bills failed to secure the Royal assent.

Disallowance

The fifth limitation on the powers of the New Zealand Parliament before 1947 comes under the head of disallowance. Section 58 of the Constitution Act required the Governor to transmit to the Secretary of State a copy of every Act he had assented to, and permitted disallowance of an Act by the Crown within two years of receipt of the copy by the Secretary of State. The power was only twice used, in respect of Acts passed and assented to in 1856 and 1867. The Imperial Government preferred to transmit its objections to the New Zealand Government and give the New Zealand Parliament an opportunity to meet these objections by passing amending legislation. By the end of the nineteenth century disallowance was clearly obsolete, at least as far as domestic matters were concerned. It was revived in 1900 by the Colonial Stock Act, 1900 (Imperial), which provided that a Colonial legislature must formally recognise the propriety of disallowance if its stocks were to rank as trustee securities in the United Kingdom. The New Zealand Parliament accordingly passed the British Investors in New Zealand Government Securities Act, 1900, declaring in section 4 that any Act affecting the rights of holders of New Zealand Government securities might properly be disallowed. In 1934 a new Colonial Stock Act, 1934 (Imperial), offered a new formula that made no mention of disallowance, and the New Zealand Parliament adopted this formula in the New

Zealand Loans Amendment Act, 1947. This Act confirmed an under-taking given by the New Zealand Government to the Imperial Government that legislation that appears to the Imperial Government to affect the rights of stock-holders detrimentally will not be submitted for assent without the consent of the Imperial Government, and that, if any such legislation does receive assent before the Imperial Government raises objections to it, the New Zealand Parliament will amend it in accordance with the wishes of the Imperial Government. This undertaking and statutory confirmation qualify New Zealand Government securities to rank as trustee securities in the United Kingdom.

The statutory provisions regarding disallowance before 1947 were section 58 of the Constitution Act and section 32 of the New Zealand Loans Act, 1932, which re-enacted section 4 of the 1900 Act. Section 32 of the New Zealand Loans Act was repealed in 1947 by the New Zealand Loans Amendment Act ; the former section is still on the Statute-book. The Statute of Westminster and the Constitution (Amendment) Act of 1947 made no reference to disallowance. The innovation made in respect of section 58 in 1947 was not a legislative one but an administrative one : a decision to disregard the statutory duty to transmit to the Secretary of State a copy of every Act assented to by the Governor-General. Before 1947 convention forbade the disallowance of New Zealand Acts ; now disallowance is rendered more difficult or perhaps even prevented by the fact that the Secretary of State does not receive the official copy to dis-allow. It is unsatisfactory that this step in New Zealand's constitutional development should have taken an unlawful form. The New Zealand Parliament will have to repeal section 58 of the Constitution Act as well as sections 56 and 57 if it wishes properly to lay the ghost of its original subordinate status.

Flexibility of the Constitution

In 1950 the Cabinet considered the adoption of a written Constitution by the enactment of a constitutional statute containing an entrenching provision to the effect that its terms might not be altered, suspended or repealed except by a special procedure. After consideration, the Cabinet dropped the proposal on the grounds that the New Zealand Parliament probably has no power to bind itself in this way. It is possible that the courts would decide that Parliament has this power [14] ; but the

---

[14] Judgment of Owen Dixon, J. in *Att.-Gen. for New South Wales* v. *Trethowan*, 44 C.L.R. 394. W. I. Jennings, *The Law and the Constitution*, 3rd ed. (1943), 143–5. W. Friedmann, ' Trethowan's Case, Parliamentary Sovereignty and the Limits of Legal Change ', *Australian Law Journal*, July 20th, 1950.

law on the subject is nebulous, as it cannot be laid down authoritatively by statute, and has not been decided by the courts. Somewhat similar cases that have arisen in New South Wales [15] and the Union of South Africa [16] were decided on grounds that would not exist in a New Zealand case.

[15] *Att.-Gen. for New South Wales* v. *Trethowan* [1932] A.C. 526.
[16] *Harris* v. *Minister of the Interior* [1952] (2) S.A. 428 [1952] 1 T.L.R. 1245.

CHAPTER 3

THE JUDICIAL SYSTEM

THE COURTS OF CIVIL AND CRIMINAL JURISDICTION

THE administration of justice is the modern and civilised substitute for the primitive practices of private vengeance and violent self-help. In the beginning a man redressed his wrongs and avenged himself upon his enemies by his own hand, aided, if need be, by the hands of his friends and kinsmen ; but at the present day he is defended by the sword of the State.[1] So far as New Zealand is concerned, the substitution of the rule of law for other means of suppression of wrongs may be said to have begun in the year 1841. That year, for the purposes of this chapter, marks the beginning of the evolution of New Zealand's judicial system as it exists today.

In 1840 about one-half of the white inhabitants were concentrated in the Bay of Islands locality, where the most advanced methods of maintaining law and order of the times had become developed. It was there that the Kororareka Vigilants' Association came into being. To protect society from its enemies in the locality, this band of early inhabitants imposed and administered such salutary sanctions as tarring and feathering, and, in the absence of a more spacious prison, confinement in an old sea chest.

The power to establish courts of judicature in New Zealand and to provide for the administration of justice therein was conferred by Royal Charter of November 16, 1840, in the following terms :

> ' And we do hereby authorise and empower the Governor of our said Colony of New Zealand for the time being, to constitute and appoint Judges, and, in cases requisite, Commissioners of Oyer and Terminer, Justice of the Peace, and other necessary Officers and Ministers in our said Colony, for the due and impartial administration of Justice, and for putting the Laws into execution, and to administer or cause to be administered unto them such oath or oaths as are usually given for the due execution and performance of these offices and places, and for the clearing of truth in judicial matters.'

The legislature which was established under the authority of the Letters Patent of November 16, 1840, proceeded with commendable promptitude to implement this power, and the earliest courts were established under Ordinance No. IV of the first session held in 1841. Not unnaturally the contemporary English courts were taken as models, the same names even being used to identify them.

[1] *Salmond on Jurisprudence*, 10th ed., p. 103.

The Magistrates' Courts

This enactment repealed certain New South Wales legislation relating to the administration of justice which was theoretically in force in New Zealand, and proceeded to ordain that courts of general and quarter sessions for the Colony of New Zealand should be held at Auckland, Port Nicholson, Russell, and at such other places as the Governor might proclaim. These courts were to exercise jurisdiction equivalent to that of the courts of the same name in England. After making provision for jury trial in general and quarter sessions, the Ordinance went on to empower the Governor to proclaim places at which petty sessions might be held, and to authorise the appointment of two or more visiting justices whose function it was to peregrinate to those whaling stations and other places of business where petty sessions were not authorised to be held. Jurisdiction to sit in petty sessions or as visiting justices was vested in two or more justices of the peace. These courts were the earliest criminal courts.

The next courts to be established by the legislature were the courts of requests, the constitution of which was prescribed in Ordinance No. VI of the first session. These courts were also designated to sit at Auckland, Port Nicholson and Russell, and were to be presided over by Commissioners to be appointed by the Governor. The jurisdiction conferred upon them was in respect of civil claims where the amount in dispute did not exceed £50.

By the second Ordinance passed during its second session (1841–42) the legislature set up county courts of civil and criminal jurisdiction. These courts had exclusive jurisdiction in all civil cases where the debt or damages did not exceed £20. Their criminal jurisdiction extended to all crimes (except perjury) punishable by fine or imprisonment or both or by transportation for any period not exceeding seven years. In addition, the county courts were clothed with jurisdiction to grant probate and administration, and certain equitable remedies. The courts of requests established in the previous session were abolished, but were reinstated in 1844 by Ordinance No. VIII of that year. The county courts assumed the judicial functions of the courts of general and quarter sessions which were shorn of all jurisdiction save in relation to the formation of jury lists.

The preamble to Ordinance No. IV of the second session of the legislature (1842) recites that ' great evils have been found to arise from the imprisonment of persons before trial, and it is desirable to diminish as far as may be safely done the number of cases in which such imprisonment may by law be required '. This Ordinance sought to mitigate the evils by providing that a police magistrate should have the power of two justices in relation to minor charges of larceny committed by juveniles, in relation to assaults, in relation to larceny by adults where the property stolen did not exceed £5 in value and where the person charged confessed to the offence. In addition a police magistrate was given the power of two justices to admit a person charged with a felony to bail. This Ordinance was short-lived, its repeal being enacted in 1846.

The procedure now contained in Parts II and X of the Justices of the Peace Act, 1927 (as to summary hearings and general appeals respectively) can be traced directly to Ordinance No. V of the second session. This enactment regulated the conduct of criminal proceedings before justices in summary cases, and provided a limited right of appeal from the determination of the justices to a district court or county court.

It is recited in the preamble of Ordinance No. VIII of the third session of the legislature, held in the year 1844, that it had become practicable by the appointment of an additional judge of the Supreme Court to have all crimes and offences tried before a judge of the Supreme Court, and that it was desirable to make provision for the more speedy recovery of small debts. This Ordinance abolished the county courts, and reconstituted the courts of requests. The courts of requests were to be presided over by commissioners who, to qualify for appointment, were required to be barristers or solicitors. The jurisdiction of the courts of requests was limited to £20, except where the parties agreed to an extension beyond that limit.

Resident magistrates' courts were created in 1846 by Ordinance No. XVI of the seventh session of the Lieutenant-Governor and the Legislative Council. Although by this legislation it was provided that the jurisdiction of these courts in civil cases concerning Europeans was to be in respect of ' every claim or demand [2] of a civil nature . . . where the parties shall reside beyond a distance of ten miles from the office of any court of requests . . . up to £20 ', they survived the courts of requests, and were indeed the embryos of the magistrates' courts of the present day. Their jurisdiction was extended to £100 in 1856, reduced to £20 when district courts were established, and again extended, this time to £50, in 1862. But it was not until the year 1913 that all magistrates, to be eligible for appointment, had to be qualified as barristers or solicitors. The resident magistrates' courts also fell heir to the jurisdiction of the police magistrates whose courts were abolished by the immediately preceding Ordinance.

The confidence which was implicit in the preamble to Ordinance No. IV of the second session that the additional judge of the Supreme Court would be able to deal with all crimes and offences was apparently

[2] Jurisdiction in relation to certain causes of action, *e.g.*, in relation to devises and bequests, malicious prosecutions, libel and slander, breach of promise of marriage, criminal conversation, seduction, and where title to land in dispute, was withdrawn from resident magistrates' courts in 1856. The magistrates' courts are still without jurisdiction in proceedings in which the validity of a devise or bequest is in question : Magistrates' Courts Act, 1947, s. 35 (1).

misconceived, for only five years later, in 1846, we find Courts of Sessions of the Peace established. Within the limits of their jurisdiction these courts functioned concurrently with the Supreme Court. They were to be presided over by two or more justices of the peace, one of whom was to be chairman or deputy chairman. They were to function with juries, and their jurisdiction extended, with several exceptions, to crimes (other than capital offences) and felonies which when committed by persons not previously convicted of felony, were punishable by transportation for life.

The year 1858 marked the advent of the district courts. These courts were established by the District Courts Act, 1858, as a kind of intermediate tribunal between the resident magistrates' courts and the Supreme Court, whose development will be briefly traced later in this chapter. The district courts were to be presided over by judges, who, to qualify for appointment, had to be barristers or solicitors of the Supreme Court. The civil jurisdiction of the district courts extended to claims between £20 and £100 (later increased to £200 and, in 1893, to £500) and to the granting of representation in the estates of deceased persons. Their criminal jurisdiction (subsequently—in 1870—enlarged to include, if so proclaimed, non-capital offences, with some exceptions, punishable by more than seven years' penal servitude) embraced felonies and indictable misdemeanours (except perjury) punishable by fine or imprisonment not exceeding seven years or by penal servitude not exceeding four years. Trial by jury was provided for, and the district courts were given concurrent jurisdiction with the Supreme Court in relation to appeals against summary convictions. Successive extensions of the jurisdiction of the magistrates' courts were made at the expense of the business of the district courts, until they eventually became completely redundant. Their *raison d'être* finally disappeared when legal qualifications became essential for appointees to the magistrates' court bench. But, although these tribunals had ceased to function many years previously, it was not until 1925 that they were formally abolished by the District Courts Abolition Act of that year.

The district courts displaced the courts of general and quarter sessions, courts of requests, county courts and courts of sessions of the peace which were all abolished by the statute (the District Courts Act, 1858) by which the district courts were created.

In the same year, every resident magistrate had conferred on him the powers exercisable by two justices of the peace, and this jurisdiction is retained by the stipendiary magistrates of the present day. It is from this source that they derive their general summary jurisdiction in criminal cases. In fact, however, as will be shown in a description of their functions, their powers in criminal proceedings, and certain other proceedings where the procedure as for the prosecution of criminal matters is capable of being used, now considerably exceed those exercisable by justices. This is due to the reservation frequently included in penal legislation to the effect that the jurisdiction therein conferred to try summary cases, pass certain types or quantum of sentence, or make certain kinds of order, is exclusive to stipendiary magistrates.

Courts of petty sessions were constituted anew in 1865 by the Petty Sessions Act of that year. A quorum of this court, which exercised concurrently some of the civil and all of the criminal jurisdiction of the resident magistrates' courts, was the chairman and one justice or, in the absence of the chairman, three justices. Justices of the peace retained jurisdiction to try civil claims up to £20 until the end of the year 1948. Courts of petty sessions fell into disuse, and eventually, in 1891, in a general statute repealing a considerable number of redundant laws, the Petty Sessions Act, 1865, was repealed.

Technically speaking, this repeal left justices of the peace and magistrates in their criminal jurisdiction without any statutory court over which to preside and adjudicate. Their jurisdiction and judicial powers were, however, left unimpaired and they continued to function as ' police courts ', by which term they were then and still are colloquially known. All the ministerial offices connected with their administration remained with magistrates' courts, whose clerks were custodians of their records and receiving officers of fees and fines payable and imposed. This curious consequence was corrected by the Magistrates' Courts Act, 1947, which provided that the criminal jurisdiction conferred on magistrates and justices by the Justices of the Peace Act, 1927, was to be exercised in magistrates' courts.

The source of the present criminal jurisdiction, functions and powers of justices of the peace and magistrates is the Justices of the Peace Act, 1927. This Act is the direct descendant of the Justices of the Peace Act, 1866, which was described by its title as ' An Act to facilitate the performance of the duties of Justices of the Peace '. The first Act contained 132 sections, dealing mainly with the procedure to be followed in summary cases and in the preliminary investigation of indictable offences. Under certain conditions, a limited jurisdiction to hear and determine venial charges of assault and larceny was also conferred. The Act of 1866 was considerably amended and supplemented in the immediately succeeding years, and was eventually consolidated with further amendments in the Justices of the Peace Act, 1882. This Act, which comprised 327 sections, covered a wide range of topics relating to justices and their jurisdiction, including the mode of appointment to the Commission of the Peace, the powers and duties of justices, the procedure to be followed in summary and indictable cases, the rules governing appeals to the Supreme Court, and the protection of justices in relation to their judicial functions. It also considerably extended the summary jurisdiction of justices and magistrates. and declared a number of rules of criminal law. The 1882 Act was consolidated in 1908, and the consolidating Act was again consolidated, with some amendment, in 1927. The Justices of the Peace Act, 1927, contains 390 sections, and, notwithstanding several subsequent refinements, is substantially the same as the 1882 measure. This legislation is long overdue for a complete overhaul to rid it of its many anachronisms and faults of draftsmanship. Considerable advances in this direction had already been made when this book went to press.

It is to be remembered that in New Zealand all offences are statutory. Broadly, the jurisdiction of two justices of the peace sitting together,[3] or of a stipendiary magistrate sitting alone, in criminal proceedings and proceedings conducted according to the procedure as for criminal matters. extends to the following :

(a) the summary trial of offences where the punishment prescribed does not exceed three months' imprisonment ;

(b) the summary trial, unless the accused elects jury trial, of offences where the punishment prescribed is expressed to be in excess of three months' imprisonment ' on summary conviction ' ;

(c) the summary trial, with the consent of the accused (where such is required), of certain specified indictable offences ;

(d) the conducting of preliminary hearings in other indictable cases.

In indictable cases not tried summarily, it has first to be decided by the justices or the magistrate whether the evidence is sufficient to put the accused upon his trial for any indictable offence. Where not so satisfied, the justices or magistrate may discharge the accused. Where on the other hand they are satisfied that a prima facie case for an indictable offence is disclosed by the evidence, they must warn the accused that it is proposed to commit him for trial and inform him that he may plead guilty and be committed for sentence. If he pleads guilty, he is committed for sentence accordingly, and he will be brought as soon as possible before a judge of the Supreme Court to be sentenced. If he pleads not guilty, he is committed for trial at the next ensuing sittings of the Supreme Court in the judicial district.

The summary trial of indictable offences (with the consent of the accused) extends, in the case of courts presided over by justices of the peace, to thefts, attempted stealing, and receiving anything stolen, in each case where the value of the property does not exceed £20. Where a stipendiary magistrate presides, however, his summary jurisdiction to try (with the consent of the accused) extends to such a large list of indictable offences, that only the most serious crimes are left to the exclusive jurisdiction of the Supreme Court. The power of punishment in relation to such cases is limited, in the case of justices, to the statutory penalty provided for the particular offence, but not in any case exceeding six

---

[3]　See, however, the Police Offences Act, 1927, which prescribes a few offences which are justiciable by one Justice.

months' imprisonment or a fine of £50. A magistrate, if otherwise permitted by statute, may however inflict up to three years' imprisonment, or a fine not exceeding £200, and he has in addition the power to impose certain other punishments, e.g., reformative detention and borstal detention which are not within the province of lay justices. This latest extension of the jurisdiction of stipendiary magistrates was effected by the Summary Jurisdiction Act, 1952, and has already had a marked effect on the criminal business of the Supreme Court. The procedure as for criminal cases is used in the magistrates' courts for the hearing and determining of affiliation, maintenance, separation and guardianship applications, but here again magistrates have exclusive jurisdiction. The widest rights of appeal are given to the Supreme Court against summary convictions, orders and sentences, but it says much for the efficiency of the magistrates' courts that the proportion of cases in which the appeal rights are availed of is very small, and the proportion of successes in appeals still smaller.

The years 1866 and 1867 are important landmarks in New Zealand's judicial history, for the administration had by then reached the close of the experimental stages in its quest for a 'people's court' to serve the ordinary everyday needs of the community. Having in 1866 completed the task of providing for the dispensation of summary justice in criminal matters, it then set about establishing a court to secure the just, speedy and inexpensive determination of the more commonplace civil litigation of the Colony. The Ordinances and Statutes relating to the resident magistrates' courts were repealed by the amending and consolidating Resident Magistrates' Act, 1867, the framework of this statute being also retained in all subsequent revisions. The Act provided for the appointment of resident magistrates (not necessarily qualified in law) and for their court to have jurisdiction up to a value of £20. This Act, and a number of amendments, were in turn repealed in 1893, the Magistrates' Courts Act of that year effecting the change of names to magistrates' courts and stipendiary magistrates by which the courts and their presiding officers respectively are still known. At the date last mentioned, resident magistrates, or stipendiary magistrates as they were then to be called, still did not require to be qualified lawyers—a situation which caused much dissatisfaction—but the trend towards appointing qualified persons had begun. To meet to some extent the prevalent objection against unqualified persons acting judicially in relation to fairly substantial civil claims, a curious differentiation of jurisdiction was evolved. So we find in the Act of 1893 three types of jurisdiction provided for : (a) ordinary jurisdiction, which went to £100 ; (b) extended jurisdiction, which went to £200 ; and (c) special jurisdiction relating to partnership accounts, compensation for false imprisonment, illegal arrest, malicious prosecution, libel or slander, breach of promise of marriage or seduction, the recovery of pecuniary legacies, in each case up to £500, and the granting of injunctions to prevent irreparable damage to property valued up to £500, or in the case of land, £210 a year rental value. No person was to be appointed to exercise the extended or special jurisdiction unless he was a barrister or solicitor, or unless he had for at least five years been exercising the extended jurisdiction under the Acts repealed, or the ordinary jurisdiction under the 1893 Act. The Magistrates' Courts Amendment Act, 1913, saw the end of the appointment of unqualified stipendiary magistrates and, as a consequence, the end of the distinctions in jurisdiction. Henceforward, the jurisdiction was standardised at claims for £200, excluding causes of action for libel and slander, false imprisonment, etc., and where the title to land was in dispute. The monetary limit of jurisdiction was increased to £300 in 1927, and, with effect from the beginning of 1949, it was further enlarged by the Magistrates' Courts Act, 1947, to £500, with provision for further extension by consent of the parties. All restrictions against hearing particular causes of action have now been removed, except where the validity of any devise or bequest is in question or the limitations under any will or settlement are in dispute. At the same time, the court was empowered by the 1947 Act, in proceedings within its jurisdiction, to grant equitable remedies heretofore to be sought only in the Supreme Court. In general, the jurisdiction of the magistrates' courts is concurrent with and not in derogation from that of the Supreme Court. The persons eligible for appointment to the magisterial bench are barristers or solicitors of seven years' standing or persons who have been registrars of the court for seven years, and who have been qualified for admission, or admitted, as barristers or solicitors for not less than seven years. The court is not empowered to sit with a jury, though it is of historical interest that jury trials of civil actions in the magistrates' courts were authorised in 1856 but were abolished in 1858 when the district courts were established.

So far, we have traversed only the history of the magistrates' courts both in their civil and criminal jurisdiction. These are the real people's courts, whose scope has increased over the short period of New Zealand's history as the needs of the general public have required. They deal with an overwhelming proportion of the judicial business of the country, and the policy of successive Governments has been to maintain for them a high standard of efficiency at the least possible cost and inconvenience to all who have to seek their shelter or who are brought into their shadow. Such public confidence is reposed in the stipendiary magistrates who preside in these courts that the tendency is to enlist their services in an ever-increasing amount of the judicial work of the country. Thus, in addition to the civil and criminal business mentioned, magistrates are vested with authority to grant orders of adoption of children, consents for minors to marry, land agents' and auctioneers' licences, exemptions from observing statutory closing hours for shops, orders as to fair rents of premises under rent restriction legislation, and a multifarious collection of other applications and contentious business requiring the exercise of judicial discretion.

The Supreme Court [4]

The Supreme Court of New Zealand was created by Ordinance No. I of the second session of the Governor and Legislative Council held in 1841. That Ordinance was, however, superseded by Ordinance No. I of the third session (January, 1844), which was amended by Ordinance No. III of the seventh session (November, 1848). By the Ordinance of 1844 it was enacted that there should be within the Colony of New Zealand a court of record for the administration of justice throughout the Colony, to be called the Supreme Court of New Zealand. The Ordinances of 1841 and 1844 were repealed by the Supreme Court Act, 1860, and that Act by the Supreme Court Act, 1882, which in turn was repealed by the Judicature Act, 1908. All the repealing Acts continued the court in being.

It is provided in the Judicature Act, 1908, that the Supreme Court shall continue to have all the jurisdiction which may be necessary to administer the laws of New Zealand. It thus repeats substantially the wording of the Supreme Court Act, 1882. By virtue of the Ordinances of 1841 and 1844 already referred to, the court had a legal jurisdiction similar to that of the Courts of Queen's Bench, Common Pleas and Exchequer in England, and an equitable jurisdiction similar to that of the Court of Chancery, and also a jurisdiction similar to that of the Ecclesiastical Courts of England so far as it related to testacy and intestacy.[5] The jurisdiction given by the 1841 and 1844 Ordinances was substantially the same, so far as jurisdiction at law and equity was concerned, and as to infants and lunatics, but the latter Ordinance was more extensive as to probate and administration. It also created a Vice-Admiralty Court and gave certain criminal jurisdiction. With the exception of the Vice-Admiralty and criminal jurisdiction, the Supreme Court Act, 1860, adopted, but in fuller and more precise manner, the jurisdiction contained in the Ordinance of 1844.

The Act of 1860 provided that the Supreme Court of New Zealand should be a court of record for the administration of justice throughout the Colony. It vested in the court:

(a) Jurisdiction within the Colony ' in all cases whatsoever as fully as Her Majesty's Courts of Queen's Bench, Common Pleas and Exchequer at Westminster, and each of such Courts have or hath in England at the time of the passing of this Act '.

(b) All such equitable and common law jurisdiction ' as the Lord

---

[4] With acknowledgment to the late learned author of Stephens, Supreme Court Forms.

[5] Supreme Court Procedure Act, 1856.

High Chancellor of England, the Court of Chancery or any other Superior Court of Equity hath in England '.

(c) All such jurisdiction and control within the Colony ' over the persons and estates of infants, idiots, lunatics and persons of unsound mind, and over the guardians and committees of such persons and estates respectively, as the Lord High Chancellor of England hath under or by virtue of the Royal Sign Manual or otherwise, so far as the same shall be applicable to the circumstances of the Colony '.

(d) Jurisdiction and authority within the Colony ' in relation to granting and revoking probate of wills and letters of administration of the effects of deceased persons and in regard to the hearing and determining of all questions relating to actions testamentary depending, or which shall or may arise or be depending, within the Colony, as fully as the Court of Probate now hath in England in relation to those matters and causes testamentary and those effects of deceased persons which are within the jurisdiction of such Court of Probate, or as any Ecclesiastical Court had in England previously to the coming into operation of the Act 20 & 21 Vict. c. 77, commonly called the Court of Probate Act, 1857 '.

There have been slight extensions of civil jurisdiction but in the main the Act of 1860 describes the basis of the Supreme Court's jurisdiction as it exists today.

New Zealand has had no other superior court exercising jurisdiction at law or in equity. In the words of the New Zealand Procedure Commissioners in their report of 1849–52, ' The [Supreme] Court combined in itself the jurisdiction of a Court of Equity with that of a Court of Law '. The union of the two jurisdictions has spared New Zealand the great inconvenience which existed in England at the time when the Colony was founded whereby there could be an action founded on a legal right in one of the courts of common law, and a suit in the Chancery, founded on an equitable right, to restrain the common law action. The rules of court, from the beginning, have enabled the so-called equitable defence to be pleaded in the original action. Thus, in the Supreme Court, law and equity have always been administered so far as may be concurrently, and the particular form of proceeding as to claim and defence has been of little importance so long as it indicated with sufficient certainty and precision the grounds on which the parties relied.[6] This may be contrasted with the position in England prior to the fusion in 1873 of all the superior courts into the High Court of Judicature.[7] In 1841, when the Colony was established, England was still labouring under the

[6] *Per* Johnston J. in *Sheehan* v. *Russell* (1883) 2 N.Z.L.R., C.A. 139, 154.
[7] See Holdsworth, *History of English Law*, Vol. I, pp. 634 *et seq.* ; Jenks, *Short History of English Law*, p. 357.

inconveniences which resulted from having the ill-defined and clashing jurisdictions of the courts of common law, equity and admiralty, and the ecclesiastical courts, each administering separate bodies of the law, and each having divergent procedures, language and technical terms. The early New Zealand judges had the difficult task of applying the practice of the several English courts to that of the one court of New Zealand. So successful were they that the 1849–52 New Zealand Procedure Commissioners were able to say that, in the reports of the contemporary English Commissioners on Procedure, and the evidence on which they were founded, there was to be found no slight confirmation of the fundamental principles upon which the judicial system of the Colony was founded. That the courts should not escape some misunderstandings was, however, to be expected, and that they did not do so entirely is suggested in a few judicial utterances,[8] and by the fact that it was found necessary in 1878 to pass a Law Amendment Act, the object of which was to prevent a multiplicity of proceedings.

In the year 1880, a comprehensive revision of the rules of procedure of the Supreme Court was undertaken, and a sub-committee of the revising Committee was appointed to draft a new set of procedure rules. This sub-committee reported that it had appeared necessary to devote special and careful attention to secure amongst other things ' that the laws of the Colony should be administered as one organic whole irrespective of any division into law and equity '. The sub-committee, which consisted of Mr. Justice Williams, Mr. Allan Holmes and Sir Robert Stout, went on to say : ' The desirability of bringing about a fusion of the systems of law and equity is now admitted to be the chief object that ought to be kept in view in any attempt to reform civil procedure. The framers [9] of the existing rules of procedure and practice in the Supreme Court seem to have recognised the importance of this, and have, indeed, done so much towards bringing about the desired result, that your Sub-Committee can only be considered as following in their footsteps. . . . All that seems necessary to complete the work is an Act providing for the cases in which there is any conflict between the rules of the two systems, and section 5 of the Law Amendment Act, 1878 appears to your Sub-Committee to be sufficient for that purpose.' That section was accordingly re-enacted in the Law Amendment Act, 1882, as sections 2 to 11. Some of the provisions of those sections have found places in other enactments, but the general provisions with which we are here concerned are contained in sections 98 and 99 of the Judicature Act, 1908. Section 98 provides that in questions relating to the custody and education of infants the rules of equity shall prevail ; and section 99 provides that in all matters

---

[8]   *Gillies* v. *Davidson* (1875) 1 N.Z.J.R. (N.S.) 102 ; *Chapman* v. *Tooth* (1867) 1 N.Z., C.A. 34 ; *Eagle* v. *Booth* (1883) 2 N.Z.L.R., S.C. 165.
[9]   *Viz.* the 1849–52 New Zealand Procedure Commissioners previously referred to.

in which there is any conflict or variance between the rules of equity and the rules of common law with reference to the same matter the rules of equity shall prevail.

We have seen that for a brief period in New Zealand's early history there existed courts of general and quarter sessions, and that these courts were abolished on the establishment of the district courts. We have also seen that the latter court exercised jurisdiction concurrent with that of the Supreme Court in relation to certain crimes. The Criminal Code Act, 1893, abolished the terms ' felony ' and ' misdemeanour ' and the distinctions they implied. Henceforward all indictable offences not triable summarily were to be tried exclusively in the Supreme Court, or, if within its jurisdiction, in a district court. The eventual redundancy and ultimate abolition of the district courts left the Supreme Court exclusive original jurisdiction[9a] in respect of all crimes listed in the Crimes Act, 1908, which is the existing consolidation of the Criminal Code Act, 1893. It is to be remembered, however, that this is not the only criminal jurisdiction possessed by the Supreme Court. Having regard to its appellate functions, and its general overriding authority over courts of inferior jurisdiction, it can truthfully be said of the Supreme Court that it casts its shadow over every type of punishable crime or delinquency, be it a capital charge or a mere breach for which a fine of a few shillings would be an adequate penalty.

Trials in the Supreme Court in civil actions may be (*a*) before a judge sitting alone, or a bench of judges (two or more constituting the ' full court ') or (*b*) before a judge and jury, either special or common, of twelve or of four, depending on the class of action, the wishes of the parties, and, as to the number of jurymen, upon the sum or value involved. In criminal trials, the proceedings always commence with the presentation of a bill of indictment to a Grand Jury of not less than twelve nor more than twenty-three. The presentment may be made by the Attorney-General, or by order of the Supreme Court, but such cases are very rare. Except in such cases, no bill of indictment may be presented to a Grand Jury unless there has been a preliminary investigation by and committal for trial from a magistrates' court. If the Grand Jury presents a true bill, the trial of the prisoner before the judge and a common jury or, in certain circumstances, special jury, takes place. Where an accused person has pleaded guilty in the lower court, or before being given in charge of a jury for trial, he may be forthwith convicted by a judge sitting without a jury.

In 1867 the Supreme Court inherited the jurisdiction of the ecclesiastical courts in relation to matrimonial causes such as divorce (divorce

---

[9a] This jurisdiction is no longer exclusive. The Summary Jurisdiction Act, 1952 now confers jurisdiction on stipendiary magistrates to try summarily most of the indictable crimes in the criminal calendar if the accused elects summary trial.

a vinculo matrimonii), judicial separation (divorce *a mensa et thoro*), restitution of conjugal rights, nullity of marriage, and jactitation of marriage, and this jurisdiction has continued to exist and, indeed, to thrive, the present-day law and practice being governed by the Divorce and Matrimonial Causes Act, 1928. In addition, the court has jurisdiction conferred upon it by many other statutes, *e.g.*, the Bankruptcy Act, 1908 ; the Companies Act, 1933 ; the Administration Act, 1952 ; the Trustee Act, 1908 ; the Aged and Infirm Persons' Protection Act, 1912 ; and the Family Protection Act, 1908, to name but a few.

Besides being a court of first instance, the Supreme Court functions as an appeal court from the decisions of the inferior courts in both their civil and criminal jurisdiction. As we shall later see, it has also a limited appellate jurisdiction from certain of the courts of special jurisdiction.

The persons who are eligible for appointment as judges are barristers or solicitors of the Supreme Court of New Zealand of seven years' standing, or barristers or advocates of the United Kingdom, also of seven years' standing, and the number of judges who may be appointed to the Supreme Court is eleven, of whom one is the Chief Justice. In addition to attending to the judicial work in the centres where they are resident—there being normally one or more judges resident in each of the four main centres—these judges divide between them the judicial work of all the other judicial districts in which the Supreme Court regularly sits. For the purpose of administration, the Dominion is divided into ten such judicial districts, each having one or more places where sittings of the court are held, there being four regular sittings a year at each such place, except in three instances where three sittings are held each year. The dates when sessions are to be held are fixed annually by the judges themselves, but are subject to the approval of the Governor-General in Council.

Jury lists are compiled annually for each place in which the Supreme Court holds a session. Subject to certain statutory exemptions, all men between the ages of twenty-one and sixty-five living within a radius of fifteen miles from the Supreme Courthouses of Auckland, Wellington, Christchurch and Dunedin respectively, and ten miles from other Supreme Courthouses where sessions are held are eligible to serve on juries ; women may also serve if they apply to be included in the lists. Supervision of the preparation of jury lists is delegated to justices of the peace, but the selection from the jury lists of persons to serve on Grand and Special Juries is the function of the sheriff of each place where the Supreme Court sits. His selections are made from the Common Jury roll, with the result that a person selected to serve if ballotted as a grand juror or special juror is also eligible for ballot as a common juror, though he will not be called upon to serve in two capacities at any one session of the court. By the system of ballot in use, a common juror serves only once in each year for which the common jury list is in existence ; but if his name is also included in the Grand Jury list he is capable of being drawn once in his capacity as a grand juror and once in his capacity as a common juror in the same jury year.

It is questionable whether the Grand Jury has any useful place in the modern judicial system. This institution was originally established to multiply accusations of crime, but by a curious transmutation, its present function, being revisory, is actually to reduce the number of indictments presented. The Grand Jury comprises any number of persons from twelve to twenty-three, but twelve must agree in a decision. It does not usually hear all the evidence for the prosecution, and it functions without the presence of judge, counsel or the prisoner. The depositions are not usually before it, and except to the extent to which they have been directed by the judge in his charge, the grand jurymen have no inkling of what the proceedings are about when their examination is conducted. The examination is held in private without any record of what has taken place beyond the initials of the foreman against the names of witnesses examined. There is thus no check upon the accuracy of the testimony of any witness examined. In the result the sole purpose of the Grand Jury is to repeat badly a function which has already been done well ; it hears in secret and in the absence of the accused part only of one side of the case after both sides have already been heard fully in accordance with regular judicial procedure in the preliminary investigation before the magistrate or justices. An unsatisfactory and cumbersome tribunal is laboriously brought together to revise the work of a better one. In his *Speeches* (pp. 184, 191) Sir Henry Maine thought the Grand Jury ' secret, one-sided, irresponsible and an obstruction to justice '.

In defence of the retention of the Grand Jury, it is claimed that it affords the judge his only opportunity of making public pronouncements and observations unconnected with litigation actually before him, and that the Grand Jury gives a more emphatic assurance of innocence if an accusation is rejected before anything beyond the prosecution is heard. The second argument assumes somewhat questionably that innocence is more clearly demonstrated by acquittal upon a secret and imperfect hearing of the case against the accused than by acquittal upon a public hearing of the accused's vindication of himself. ' I should have directed you to ignore the bill, as there is no evidence to sustain it ; but, that the defendant may clear his character, I recommend you to return a true bill ', said Mr. Justice Bailhache in his charge to the Grand Jury at the Oxford Assizes (England) in October, 1915. In the words of Lord Denman, ' If the Grand Jury agree with the committing magistrate, they are useless ; if they differ from him, they may defeat justice irreparably, and yet they do not clear the character of the accused effectually '.[10]

[10] See Kenny's *Outlines of the Criminal Law*, 13th ed., pp. 462, 463.

The history of the Special Jury is somewhat obscure, but it seems clear that the practice of selecting special jurymen to try important civil cases developed without legislative enactment in the procedure of the courts. Until 1898, the Supreme Court exercised a general discretion in applications for trials by Special Jury, there being then no express limitations as to the classes of cases for which Special Juries could be ordered. In the year mentioned, however, a Bill was introduced to abolish both Grand and Special Juries, but the clause to dispense with the Grand Jury was dropped and the proposed abolition of the Special Jury was changed to a provision that no case or inquiry should be heard by a Special Jury unless by consent or unless in the opinion of the judge expert knowledge was required. At that time, Special Jury lists were required to comprise ' esquires, gentlemen, merchants, managers of banks, civil engineers, architects and such other persons as [were] known to be in the best condition '. The Labour administration thought in 1936 that these qualifications savoured of class distinction, and they amended the legislation to provide that except with the consent of all parties, no application for trial by Special Jury was to be granted unless in the judge's opinion a knowledge of business, mercantile or banking matters was required on the part of the jury. At the same time, the constitution of Special Jury lists was altered so that such juries would in future comprise persons acquainted with business, mercantile or banking matters. This was found unsatisfactory, and in 1939 a further amendment provided for the formation of Special Jury lists from ' men who are qualified, whether by reason of their education, training or occupation or otherwise, to determine difficult questions in relation to scientific, technical, business or professional matters '. Special Jury trials were by the same enactment limited to cases where the parties consent to trial by Special Jury, or where difficult questions in relation to scientific, technical, business or professional matters are likely to arise.

It does not follow in relation to trial by Special Jury that a case requiring expert knowledge on the part of the jurymen is tried by a panel of persons all possessing that particular expert knowledge. Fundamentally, the Special Jury panel is a panel drawn indiscriminately by ballot from the Special Jury list. A jury comprised largely of accountants and other men of business might thus be drawn to adjudicate upon the facts applicable to issues of engineering or science, while a Special Jury comprising no knowledgeable man of business might conceivably be empanelled to try a business or commercial question. The predominant criticism of the abolitionists is that the natural leanings of special jurymen are towards the class in society from which they are largely drawn. These views are not shared by the judges. Nevertheless, the fact remains that the power to order trials by Special Juries, selected as they are not because of any special qualification or training in relation to the issue to be tried, but because of some standing in the community given them by virtue of their callings, is in itself to some degree a reflection on the intelligence and education of the rank and file of those comprising the Common Jury roll. If it were not for the habit inherited by New Zealand of clinging tenaciously to old and well-tried institutions in the administration of justice, there would be little justification for the continued existence of the Special Jury in a community enjoying the high standard of universal education that is enjoyed in the Dominion.

There has been no recent agitation for the abolition of the Grand Jury, but the Special Jury is subjected to criticism from time to time, mainly by organisations of workers. It may be that when the Juries Act, 1908, receives the comprehensive revision that is long overdue, these anachronisms will find little excuse for survival, and they may disappear as they have disappeared from the judicial systems of the United Kingdom and other countries of the Commonwealth.

The Court of Appeal

The Court of Appeal owes its origin to the Court of Appeal Act, 1862, though the functions and jurisdiction therein prescribed bear little resemblance to those which are provided by the Judicature Act, 1908, as amended from time to time. The Court of Appeal Act, 1862, was superseded by the Court of Appeal Act, 1882, which was consolidated in Part II of the 1908 Act cited.

The judges of the Supreme Court for the time being comprise the Court of Appeal, and the court consists of two Divisions. Each Division consists of five judges appointed by the Governor-General in Council on the recommendation of not less than three judges, of whom the Chief Justice is one. Six judges can be appointed to any one Division when all the judges are present in New Zealand, and any one judge can be a member of both Divisions. The court sits three times a year, the two Divisions sitting alternately, except when, on account of the special difficulty or importance of the litigation, both Divisions may be called upon to sit together. The presence of three judges is necessary to form the Court of Appeal, and, if present, the Chief Justice presides. In his absence the senior puisne judge presides. The opinions of the majority of the judges present is the judgment of the court, but, in the event of the court being equally divided, the decision of the court appealed from is deemed to be affirmed.

In its civil capacity the Court of Appeal exercises original jurisdiction in the following matters when ordered by the Supreme Court to be removed into the Court of Appeal :

(*a*) any rule *nisi* granted [11] ;

(*b*) any notice of motion made [12] ;

(*c*) any petition presented ;

(*d*) any special case stated ;

(*e*) any question of law ordered to be argued ;

(*f*) facts stated by a jury that has not found for either party.

In addition, the Court of Appeal has jurisdiction and power to hear and determine appeals from any judgments, decrees or orders of the Supreme Court, subject to the rules governing the terms and conditions on which appeals may be made. The determination of the Supreme Court on appeals from inferior courts is final unless leave to appeal to the Court of Appeals is given, but in certain circumstances appeals may be made directly from an inferior court into the Court of Appeal. The decision of the Court of Appeal is final as regards the tribunals of New Zealand, except that leave to appeal to the Judicial Committee of the Privy Council may be given.

Until 1945, when the Criminal Appeal Act was passed, the criminal jurisdiction of the Court of Appeal was very limited. By virtue of the Judicature Act, 1908, it has jurisdiction to conduct a trial at Bar of any indictment in any case of extraordinary importance and difficulty, but this jurisdiction has never been invoked in this country. It has appellate jurisdiction in respect of the judgment of the Supreme Court on any conviction or order removed into such court or taken there on appeal from an inferior court, but by far its most important function in criminal matters is derived from the Criminal Appeal Act, 1945 and, to a less extent, the Crimes Act, 1908. Prior to 1945, the Court of Appeal's functions in criminal matters were similar to those of the English Court of Crown Cases Reserved, its appellate jurisdiction from Supreme Court convictions being invoked by way of case stated by the judge of the Supreme Court, or by way of leave granted by the trial judge on application made on the ground that the verdict was against the weight of evidence. Now it is provided that any person convicted on indictment or sentenced on committal to the Supreme Court for sentence, may appeal to the Court of Appeal :

(*a*) against his conviction on any ground of appeal which involves a question of law alone ;

(*b*) with leave of the Court of Appeal, or upon the certificate of the judge who tried him that it is a fit case for appeal, against his conviction on any ground of appeal which involves a question

---

[11] A ' rule *nisi* ' is a form of court order which affords to the party against whom it is made an opportunity of coming before the court within a specified time to show cause why it should not take effect, that is, by being made absolute.

[12] A ' notice of motion ' is the method of applying to the court where no other form of procedure is prescribed.

of fact alone, or a question of mixed law and fact, or on any other ground which appears to the Court of Appeal to be a sufficient ground of appeal ; and

(c) with leave of the Court of Appeal against the sentence passed on his conviction, unless the sentence is one fixed by law.

The grounds upon which a criminal appeal may be allowed against conviction are (a) unreasonable verdict, (b) error in law, and (c) miscarriage of justice ; and if it allows the appeal the Court of Appeal may quash the conviction and either direct a new trial or direct the entry of a verdict of acquittal.   On an appeal against sentence, the Court of Appeal may either dismiss the appeal or quash the sentence and pass another sentence warranted by law, whether more or less severe.   In addition to having these appellate functions in criminal matters, the Court of Appeal may be invoked to assist the Governor-General in his exercise of the prerogative of mercy.   On an application for the exercise of the mercy of the Crown having reference to the conviction on indictment or to the sentence (other than a sentence fixed by law) passed on a person convicted, the Governor-General may, if he thinks fit, at any time, by Order in Council, either (a) refer the whole case to the Court of Appeal, and the case shall then be heard and determined as in the case of an appeal by a person convicted, or (b) if he desires the assistance of the Court of Appeal on any point arising in the case with a view to the determination of the application, refer that point to the Court of Appeal for its opinion thereon.

The Court of Appeal also exercises appellate jurisdiction in relation to certain of the courts of special jurisdiction whose functions will later be discussed.   For example, the judges respectively of the Court of Arbitration and the Land Valuation Court may state a case to the Court of Appeal on any question of law arising in matters before them.

Children's Courts

These courts are discussed in Chapter 5.

COURTS OF SPECIAL JURISDICTION

So far in this chapter we have dealt only with the courts exercising ordinary jurisdiction within the Dominion.   There are, however, a number of other courts having special jurisdiction whose functions it will be necessary briefly to mention in order to present a complete survey of the machinery of justice operating within the community.

The Maori Appellate Court and Maori Land Court

The Treaty of Waitangi, signed on February 6, 1840, may be regarded as the foundation on which rests the whole of New Zealand's legislation with respect to Maoris. By the Treaty, Her Majesty Queen Victoria amongst other things declared that she confirmed and guaranteed to the chiefs and tribes of New Zealand and the respective families and individuals thereof the full exclusive and undisturbed possession of their lands and estates which they collectively or individually held so long as it should be their desire to retain the same. It was further declared that the chiefs yielded to Her Majesty the exclusive right of pre-emption over such lands as the proprietors thereof might be disposed to alienate.

It was recited in the preamble to the Native Lands Act, 1862, that ' it would greatly promote the peaceful settlement of the Colony and the advancement and civilisation of the Natives if their rights to land were ascertained, defined and declared and if the ownership of such lands as ascertained, defined and declared were assimilated as nearly as possible to the ownership of land according to British law '. Accordingly the Governor was authorised to constitute by Order in Council a court or courts for the purpose of ascertaining and declaring who according to Native Custom were the proprietors of any Native lands and the estate or interest held by them therein, and for the purpose of granting to such proprietors Certificates of Title to such lands. From this beginning there grew into being the Native Land Court and Native Appellate Court, administering both English law and Maori custom.

The present-day constitution and jurisdiction of the Maori Land Court and Maori Appellate Court (as they are now called) are contained in the Maori Affairs Act, 1953, a consolidating statute containing no fewer than 473 sections which comes into force on April 1, 1954.

The Maori Land Court comprises a chief judge, who, to be eligible, must be a barrister or solicitor of not less than seven years' standing, and such other judges, commissioners, assessors (being Maoris), and other officers as may be required. At the present time there are a chief judge and six judges of the court. All judges are judges of the Maori Appellate Court, any two judges having power to act as that court, the concurrence of a majority, and of at least two judges, being necessary for a decision of that court. The judges, with one exception, are also judges of the Cook Islands Native Appellate Court.

The Maori Appellate Court has exclusive jurisdiction in appeals from the Maori Land Court, there being no right of appeal to the Supreme Court. There is, however, a right of appeal from the Appellate Court to the Privy Council.

The exclusive jurisdiction of the Maori Land Court extends to the following in relation to Maoris :

(*a*) investigation of title to customary lands ;
(*b*) ascertainment of equitable ownership of Maori land ;
(*c*) claims to ownership and possession of land ;

(*d*) probate and administration in estates of Maoris ;

(*e*) assessment of compensation for Maori lands taken for public purposes ;

(*f*) adoption of Maori children by Maoris ;

(*g*) determination of succession to real and personal property ;

(*h*) partition of Maori land ;

(*i*) consolidation of land, including Crown and European land ;

(*j*) power to make provision out of the estate for a Maori testator's family when this is not sufficiently provided for in the deceased's will or on his intestacy ;

(*k*) power to restrain injury and waste to land ;

(*l*) power to appoint and remove trustees for persons under disability ;

(*m*) powers in respect of exchanges of land ;

(*n*) confirmation of all alienations of Maori lands by Maoris ;

(*o*) certain miscellaneous matters affecting land and money, *e.g.*, laying of tramways, roadlines and easements ; charging orders for rates ; declarations of trust in respect of land or money ; setting aside reservations and appointing trustees ; housing sites ;

(*p*) making recommendations to the Board of Maori Affairs with respect to land development ;

(*q*) claims under the Fencing Act, 1908.

Jurisdiction concurrent with that of the Supreme Court and inferior courts extends to the following :

(*r*) enforcement and administration of trusts ;

(*s*) power to restrain trespass and injury to land ;

(*t*) power to award damages, up to £200, for trespass ;

(*u*) powers in relation to settled land.

The Coroners' Courts

The statute law relating to the appointment, functions and powers of coroners is now contained in the Coroners Act, 1951, which came into force on April 1, 1952. This Act is a consolidation, with considerable amendment, of the previous statute law on the subject which was comprised in the Coroners Act, 1908, and a number of amending enactments.

It is the duty of a coroner to hold an inquest where he is informed that a person is dead and there is reasonable cause to suspect that the deceased has died a violent or unnatural death, or while detained in prison or in such a place or under such circumstances that it is required by statute that an inquest be held. Except in clear cases of natural death a coroner must also hold an inquest where the deceased has died a sudden death of which the cause is unknown.

The Act, in addition, confers on coroners a discretionary power to hold inquests into the deaths of inmates of certain institutions such as Borstal Institutions, Mental Hospitals, Inebriates' and Reformatory Homes, and Children's Homes functioning under the Child Welfare Act, 1925.

Coroners are especially appointed to office by the Governor-General, and hold office during pleasure until they reach the statutory retiring age of seventy-two years. All stipendiary magistrates are coroners *ex officio* by virtue of section 8 (*d*) of the Magistrates' Courts Act, 1947.

The Court of Arbitration and the Compensation Court

As part of the machinery prescribed for the settlement of industrial disputes between employers and employees, there was established in 1894 a Court of Arbitration. The jurisdiction of the court was then and still is expressed to be for the settlement of industrial disputes pursuant to the Industrial Conciliation and Arbitration Act, the provisions of which are now consolidated in the Act of 1925. The role of the court in relation to industrial disputes is fully discussed in Chapter 6.

The jurisdiction of the Court of Arbitration was extended in 1900 to embrace claims maintainable under the Workers' Compensation for Accident Act of that year, under which New Zealand adopted from England the principle of the liability of an employer to pay compensation to his servants for injuries suffered by them in the course of their employment. This added jurisdiction remained with the court until the year 1940, when a separate court, known as the Compensation Court, was established to exercise all the powers expressed to be conferred on the Court of Arbitration by the Workers' Compensation Act, 1922, by which workers' compensation claims are now regulated. The judge of the Compensation Court enjoys the same privileges and protection as a judge of the Supreme Court.

The Land Valuation Tribunals

These tribunals are discussed in Chapter 4.

The Court of Review

The Court of Review, which still retains a statutory identity, is a product of the depression and ensuing years. It was set up to adjust mortgages according to the values of land then prevailing. It virtually ceased to function in 1939, though until the end of 1950 it sat occasionally to interpret orders originally made by it. As it has now no active place in the judicial system of the Dominion, it needs no further mention in this chapter.

The Wardens' Courts

The Crown is at common law presumptively the owner of all gold and silver mines. In New Zealand, the Crown does not work the gold or metal mines itself, but, pursuant to legislation, grants rights to private individuals to do so. The policy of such legislation is, subject to certain limitations, to enable Crown lands and various easements connected therewith to be taken up, held and used for mining for gold or other metals or minerals. This legislation was originally modelled on an Act of the Parliament of the State of Victoria known as ' The Goldfields Act, 1874 ', and is now contained in the Mining Act, 1926. Under this Act, certain portions of New Zealand may be constituted mining districts, that is to say, districts where mining operations are carried on for gold or any other metals or minerals. The grant by the Crown, through the operation of the Mining Act, of mining privileges, of which there are several kinds, creates certain titles in respect of land and water. It is with such privileges that the wardens' courts are principally concerned.

For districts proclaimed mining districts, wardens' courts may be established, and fit persons may be appointed as wardens to hold office during the Governor-General's pleasure. The modern practice is to appoint such stipendiary magistrates as preside in mining districts to be also wardens in those districts.

The jurisdiction of the wardens' courts under the Mining Act extends to the hearing and determining of all such actions, suits and other proceedings cognisable by courts of civil or criminal jurisdiction as arise (either wholly or in some material part) within the district concerning the following :

(a) area, dimensions and boundaries of mining privileges ;

(b) forfeiture of mining privileges ;

(c) title to and ownership or possession of mining privileges or the products of mining operations ;

(d) questions or disputes relating to water or water rights ;

(e) encroachment upon, infringement of or injuries to mining privileges ;

(f) specific performance of contracts relating to mining privileges or operations ;

(g) transfers and other dispositions of mining privileges ;

(h) trusts relating to mining privileges or operations ;

(i) mining partnerships, the formation and dissolution thereof, the taking of accounts connected therewith, and the determination of all questions arising between the partners ;

(j) encroachment upon or injury to land by reason of mining operations, whether held under the provisions of the Mining Act or otherwise howsoever ;

(*k*) breaches of the Mining Act or of the regulations thereunder
punishable by summary conviction ;

(*l*) encroachment upon, injuries to and the determination of all
questions concerning roads, tramways, railroads, or fences
constructed, held or occupied under the Mining Act ;

(*m*) generally concerning all contracts, torts, questions or disputes of
any kind relating to mining privileges or operations, or to any
matter in respect whereof jurisdiction is conferred upon the court
or the warden, whether the parties thereto are or are not engaged
in mining operations ;

(*n*) all such matters as aforesaid or corresponding thereto arising in
respect of leases, licences, and coal-mining operations under the
Coal-mines Act, 1925, within a mining district.

In so far as insufficient provision has been conferred upon the warden
or the wardens' courts by the Mining Act, the court and the warden are
declared to have power to exercise the powers of the Supreme Court
or a judge. Generally speaking, an appeal lies to the Supreme Court
from the wardens' courts.

The warden's authority in relation to coal-mining extends, by virtue
of the Coal-mining Act, 1925, to performing in a mining district the
functions which a Commissioner of Crown Lands exercises in other parts
of the Dominion. That is to say, in such mining districts he is the
authority to grant on behalf of the Crown coal prospecting licences,
coal-mining leases, tramway licences, and way-leaves and other easements.

Other Judicial Tribunals

The Governor-General's authority now embodied in the seventh
clause of the Letters Patent of May 11, 1917,[12a] empowers him to appoint,
in the name of Her Majesty, all such judges, commissioners, justices of
the peace and other necessary officers and Ministers of the Dominion
as may be lawfully constituted or appointed by Her Majesty. This
clause, which is a delegation of the Royal Prerogative, is invoked when it
is desired to appoint what is known as a Royal Commission. The power
is frequently exercised for a variety of purposes, including investigations
conducted with the object of advising the Government on important
issues and inquiring into matters of public interest. In recent years,
Royal Commissions have been established to inquire into the sheep-
farming industry, Maori claims concerning certain lands, gaming and
racing, the licensing laws and system, trans-harbour facilities for the city
of Auckland, and a disastrous fire which occurred in business premises
with heavy loss of life. It has been held by the Court of Appeal,[13] however, that the power of appointment must be exercised in accordance with

---

[12a] Vide N.Z. Gazette, 1919, p. 1213.
[13] *Cock* v. *Att.-Gen.* (1910) 28 N.Z.L.R. 406.

the law and constitutional practice, and that it does not extend to the appointment of a Commission to inquire into a matter triable under the criminal law. The reason advanced by the Court of Appeal for this finding was that the statute 42 Edw. 3, c. 3 (which enacts that no man shall be put to answer for a crime unless in the manner prescribed by law) and the statute 10 Car. 1, c. 10 (abolishing the Star Chamber) are in force in New Zealand. The privileges, powers and immunities relating to Commissions of Inquiry (mentioned in the next paragraph) are made applicable, with necessary modifications, to Royal Commissions by the Commissions of Inquiry Act, 1908.

A second type of judicial tribunal may be set up under the Act last mentioned. This Act authorises the Governor-General to appoint a commission to inquire into and report upon any question arising out of the administration of the Government, or the working of any existing law, or regarding the necessity of legislation, or concerning the conduct of any officer of the public service, or concerning the proceedings of any court-martial. Such commissions are clothed with certain of the judicial powers of magistrates, including power to summon witnesses, administer oaths, hear evidence and maintain order. In addition the Act confers on witnesses and counsel the privileges they would enjoy in an ordinary court of law, enables disputed points of law to be referred to the Supreme Court, and provides for costs and the enforcement of orders for the payment of the same. The jurisdiction of both Royal Commissions and Commissions of Inquiry is circumscribed by the terms of their orders of reference as set out in the instruments by which they are appointed.

There are in existence a number of other bodies having either judicial, quasi-judicial, or administrative powers, or a combination of those powers. These bodies are set up by particular statutes for specific purposes as designated by those statutes. It is usual for such bodies to be vested with the powers of a Commission of Inquiry under the Commissions of Inquiry Act, 1908, or to be ' deemed to be ' such Commissions so as to clothe them with the powers contained in that Act. Included in this category are such bodies as the Social Security Commission (appointed under the Social Security Act, 1938); the Licensing Control Commission (appointed under the Licensing Amendment Act, 1948); the Government Service Tribunal (appointed under the Government Service Tribunal Act, 1948); the Soil Conservation and Rivers Control Council (appointed under the Soil Conservation and Rivers Control Act, 1941); the Local Government Commission (appointed under the Local Government Commission Act, 1946).

Another class of judicial tribunal is one whose constitution is already provided for by statute, but which does not come into existence until the happening of a specified event. This category includes the court required to be constituted under the Shipping and Seamen Act, 1952, to investigate shipping casualties on or near the coasts of New Zealand. It also includes Assessment Courts [14] under the Rating Act, 1925, which although constituted do not in practice assemble unless there are objections to rating valuations for their determination; boards of inquiry constituted for various purposes, as occasion may require, for example to investigate matters affecting the administration of railways; and tribunals to which State and other employees may appeal on the ground that they are aggrieved by certain decisions of their employing authorities affecting their official careers.

CONSTITUTIONAL POSITION AND DUTIES OF JUDICIARY AND MAGISTRACY

In New Zealand, as in other British constitutions, the absolute freedom and independence of its judicial officers are considered to be essential to the due administration of impartial justice. Hence all judicial appointments are made by the Governor-General on behalf of Her Majesty the Queen as the fountain of justice. There are no elective judicial offices in the Dominion, the advantages of having appointments made by the Governor-General being, first, that it is not necessary for prospective appointees to ingratiate themselves with any section of the community or political party and, secondly, that the Governor-General's advisers are enabled to maintain a high standard of efficiency and integrity in the Dominion's machinery of justice by being able to select from the best that the country has to offer without regard to, or even cognisance of, political affinities.

The independence and impartiality of the Bench are preserved in a number of different ways, some statutory and some by long standing custom, of which a few of the most important call for some attention. In the first place, appointments of judges and magistrates are for life *quamdiu se bene gesserint*, subject to retirement at the age of seventy-two in the case of judges and sixty-eight in the case of magistrates, and subject to Parliament's right to remove by way of a specially prescribed parliamentary procedure. The Crown and its Ministers can thus exert no pressure upon the judiciary through fear of dismissal. Financial independence is secured by the theoretical adequacy of remuneration and pension rights, and the protection of salaries given by statute. The salaries of judges are fixed by statute and are thus not subject to annual appropriation. They are further entrenched (so far as it is possible to bind future administrations) by a provision in the Judicature Act, 1908, virtually repeating the proviso to section 65 of the Constitution Act, 1852, that they shall not be diminished during continuance in office. Stipendiary magistrates'

---

[14] These courts exercise jurisdiction only where the system of rating is on the annual value. Where properties are rated on the unimproved or capital value of the land, the Land Valuation Court is the appropriate tribunal.

salaries are also protected by a statutory provision fixing the amount to be paid and providing for their payment without further appropriation than is authorised in the statute itself. By convention appointments to the salaried bench offer no hope of advancement to any higher office, hence nothing is to be gained in this direction from seeking the patronage of anyone. Appointees to the judiciary and magistracy are usually assigned to districts other than those in which they were in practice of the law so that they are removed as far as is reasonably practicable from all former associations both business and personal. The judiciary and magistracy exercise their functions under the protection of certain immunities, which serve to enable them to adjudicate without fear of action by persons dissatisfied with their decisions. But whatever safeguards may be prescribed or observed, the public receives its greatest assurance of justice from the personal integrity of those chosen to fill the Dominion's judicial offices.

It will be pertinent for the purposes of this sketch to mention the immunities enjoyed by those in judicial office. The judges of the Supreme Court are each exempt from all civil liability for acts done by them in the execution of their judicial functions. So long as the jurisdiction vested in them is not exceeded, their exemption is absolute, extending not merely to errors of law and fact, but to malicious, corrupt or oppressive exercise of their judicial powers. It is deemed better to risk the perpetration of an occasional injustice under the protection of immunity from suit than to risk weakening the independence of the judicature and the strength of the administration of justice by subjecting the judges and magistrates to frivolous, unfounded and vexatious charges of error, malice or incompetence brought by disappointed litigants. There are appropriate remedies by way of appeal for errors, and the criminal code lists judicial corruption as a serious indictable offence, it being however provided that no one holding judicial office may be prosecuted for that crime except with the leave of the Attorney-General, and, in the case of judges, except where the prosecution is by the Attorney-General pursuant to a resolution of Parliament.

But where the illegal act complained of is beyond the jurisdiction of the judicial officer, it is not definitely settled whether, in the case of a superior judge, he is free from liability, or whether, in the case of an inferior judicial officer, he is civilly responsible for such excess of jurisdiction. It is clear, however, that to establish exemption as regards proceedings in an inferior court, the magistrate or justices, as the case may be, must prove that he or they had jurisdiction. In the case of proceedings against a judge of a superior court, on the other hand, the plaintiff has the burden of proving want of jurisdiction. Subject to this, it seems that the liability of superior and inferior judicial officers is the same.[15]   In *Palmer* v. *Crone*,[16] Talbot J. said that if a judicial officer acts outside his jurisdiction he is not acting as a judicial officer at all, and he is in no better position than anyone else.

The maxim *nemo debet esse judex in propria sua causa* is of strict application in this Dominion, the smallest pecuniary interest in the subject-matter of proceedings serving to disqualify the interested judicial officer from adjudicating thereon.

Judicial proceedings in the Supreme Court are, as we have seen, either before the judge alone or before a judge and jury. There are no juries in the inferior courts. In all proceedings tried by a judge and jury, questions of law are decided by the judge and questions of fact by the jury. The judge, when sitting alone, or the magistrate or justices, as the case may be, combine the two functions and decide the issues both of law and fact. In all cases the judge, magistrate and justices are required to administer the laws as they find them, whether or not the benefits or obligations actually conferred or imposed by those laws accord with their private views as to what the law ought to be. Before taking office, a judicial officer is required to take a judicial oath the effect of which is that he will well and truly serve Her Majesty, her heirs and successors, according to law, in his office ; and that he will do right to all manner of people after the laws and usages of New Zealand, without fear or favour, affection or ill-will.

As to the conduct of judicial proceedings, the general rule, which is however not without exceptions, is that he who asserts must prove. Thus in criminal trials, where everyone is presumed innocent unless and until proved guilty, the onus rests with the prosecution to prove the guilt of the accused, and the onus is not discharged unless guilt is proved beyond reasonable doubt. In civil cases, it is generally accepted that a less stringent though still exacting standard of proof is required.

As in other parts of the Commonwealth, the importance of judicial precedents has always been a characteristic of the New Zealand system of administration of justice.[17] A judicial precedent speaks in New Zealand with authority, and this is so whether the precedent is a judgment of the New Zealand courts or of any other superior court in the Commonwealth. The guiding principle is that in all parts of the Empire where English law prevails, the interpretation of the law should be as nearly as possible the same. On this basis, every court in New Zealand is

---

[15] *Salmond on the Law of Tort*, 11th ed., p. 733. It would seem that, as in New Zealand the magistrates' courts in both their civil and criminal jurisdiction are inferior courts of record, the common law relating to the immunity of judges of such courts, being wider, would prevail over the statutory provision made by s. 344 of the Justices of the Peace Act, 1927, which is to the same effect as s. 19 of the Justices Protection Act, 1848 (U.K.).

[16] [1927] 1 K.B. 808.

[17] See generally *Salmond on Jurisprudence*, 10th ed., pp. 176 *et seq*.

absolutely bound by the decisions of all courts superior to itself according to the recognised table of superiority. Thus the magistrates' courts are bound by the decisions of the Supreme Court, the Supreme Court is absolutely bound by the Court of Appeal, which in turn is bound by the advices of the Privy Council. Decisions of courts of inferior jurisdiction are conditional authority in courts of equal jurisdiction. That is to say, in all ordinary cases they are binding upon one another, but it would seem that they may be overruled or dissented from when they are not merely wrong but so clearly and seriously wrong that their reversal is demanded in the interests of the sound administration of justice. Thus, in a recent case [18] the Court of Appeal considered itself free to overrule a judgment of that court which was contrary to the current New Zealand authority theretofore existing, or which, though not expressly overruled, was in principle in conflict with a decision of the House of Lords or the Privy Council or inconsistent with a judgment of the High Court of Australia. In respect of decisions of the superior courts in other British jurisdictions, the policy is to treat them as persuasive precedents, entitled to the highest respect, to the end that consistency of decision with the courts of Great Britain and of the Dominions shall be maintained.

THE LEGAL PROFESSION

In the early days of the Colony, expediency required that recognition be given to law practitioners who had qualified abroad. The Ordinance of Session No. II (1841), No. 1, by which, it will be recalled, the Supreme Court was established, directed the court to enrol to practise therein as barristers such persons only as had been admitted as barristers or advocates in Great Britain or Ireland, or who should after the date of the enactment be admitted under the authority of any law that might be passed for the purpose. The same Ordinance directed the enrolment as solicitors of such persons only as had been admitted as solicitors, attorneys or writers in one of the courts of Westminster, Dublin or Edinburgh, or Proctors in any ecclesiastical court in England, or who had served such term of clerkship with a solicitor of the court as would be required by the rules thereof, or who had established themselves in the exercise of their profession on or before December 22, 1841. It was also provided that barristers of the court could act as solicitors, and vice versa, but this privilege was to continue for only five years unless the court should in the meantime order to the contrary. In fact, however, although for a number of years the court was empowered to segregate the professions, the amalgamation which was probably instituted only as a matter of temporary expediency has subsisted to this day.

[18] *Re Rayner, Daniell* v. *Rayner* [1948] N.Z.L.R. 455.

In 1853 admission to the profession was extended to all who had been admitted as barristers, solicitors, attorneys or proctors in any court in Australia or Van Diemen's Land and had served a portion of their term of clerkships in Great Britain, Ireland or any part of Australia and had completed the term in New Zealand. In 1856 enrolment as solicitors was opened to persons who had been admitted to practice as writers or solicitors in any Sheriff Court in Scotland.

A stiffening of the qualifications is to be observed from the year 1861 onwards. The Law Practitioners Act of that year, which was a consolidating and amending measure, continued the previous provisions for the benefit of practitioners qualified abroad, except solicitors in sheriffs' courts. In the case of solicitors, however, the qualifications for future admissions were to include passing an examination on the law of New Zealand so far as it differed from the law of England. At the same time, examinations for qualification as barristers and solicitors of persons who had undertaken the requisite course of training in New Zealand were introduced, and it was expressly declared that the final of the examination for solicitors was to be consonant with that prescribed in England for attorneys and solicitors of the superior courts at Westminster. In 1865 graduates of universities in the United Kingdom or Colonies were made eligible for admission subject to passing the examination on the law of New Zealand previously referred to. In these early years the examinations were under the control of the judges of the Supreme Court, and so they remained until 1931, although the University of New Zealand had in fact for many years been the teaching and examining institution.

In the year last mentioned there was constituted a Council of Legal Education consisting of two judges, two members of the New Zealand Law Society, and two professors or lecturers of law to be appointed by the Senate of the University. The Council was given power to make recommendations to the Senate through the Academic Board with respect to legal education, particularly in reference to courses of study and examinations. The examination of candidates for admission became the statutory province of the University of New Zealand, whose certificate became one of the essential qualifications necessary for admission. A slightly less comprehensive course of study and examination is prescribed for solicitors than for barristers.

The law relating to the legal profession is now contained almost entirely in the Law Practitioners Act, 1931, which replaced the previous consolidation of 1908 and its amendments. By this statute the public and the profession are mutually protected. It provides for the admission and enrolment of practitioners, a procedure for striking practitioners from the rolls, rules as to taxation of bills of costs, the establishment and maintenance of a fidelity fund to insure the public against dishonesty, and provision for trust accounts and the audit thereof.

We have seen that the profession of barrister and solicitor are amalgamated in New Zealand, and the majority of practitioners do in fact practise both professions. Nevertheless, a barrister may practise exclusively as such, and when he is a Queen's Counsel must do so ; and a solicitor may practise solely in that capacity and, indeed, is precluded from practising as a barrister until he has fulfilled the requirements for admission to the Bar.

The Supreme Court may admit as a barrister any fit and proper person of good character and over the age of twenty-one years who :

(a) has passed the prescribed examination in general knowledge and law ; or

(b) is a solicitor and has passed such additional examination as may be prescribed in general knowledge and the law ; or

(c) is admitted as a barrister in any superior or Supreme Court in any part of the Commonwealth other than New Zealand, and who has passed the prescribed examination in the law of New Zealand in so far as it differs from the law of England (the examination being, however, dispensed with where the candidate has been in practice in England as a barrister for not less than three years) ; or

(d) is a solicitor of five years' standing who has been in active practice as a solicitor continuously for the five years immediately preceding the date of his application or has been managing clerk to a solicitor in active practice or who, if an officer employed in a Department of State, has been engaged therein for at least five years continuously in the performance of legal work of such a character as in the opinion of the court justifies him to be admitted as a barrister ; or

(e) qualifies for admission pursuant to reciprocal arrangements with other British countries.

Barristers have all the powers, privileges, duties and responsibilities that barristers have in England, and no person is entitled to act as a barrister who is not a barrister on the rolls.

A candidate for admission as a solicitor of the Supreme Court must be a fit and proper person [19] of good character and over the age of twenty-one years who :

(a) has passed the prescribed examination ; or

(b) is a barrister ; or

(c) is admitted as a solicitor elsewhere in the Commonwealth and who has passed the prescribed examination in law, including the law of New Zealand in so far as it differs from the law of England

---

[19] Applicants for admission as solicitors must take the oath of allegiance. Aliens are therefore excluded from admission, as only British subjects can subscribe to that oath : *Re Heyting* [1928] N.Z.L.R. 233.

(this being, however, unnecessary in the case of a solicitor who has practised as such in the United Kingdom for three years); or

(d) qualified for admission pursuant to reciprocal arrangements with other British countries.

By the Law Practitioners Amendment Act, 1935, at least three years' legal experience was made a necessary qualification for solicitors, subject to the court's discretion to relax this condition. Any person acting as a solicitor while not enrolled as such is subject to heavy penalties.

In 1869 the New Zealand Law Society was constituted by statute, and it retains its constitution under the Law Practitioners Act, 1931. The general functions of the Society are expressed to be, inter alia, the promotion and encouragement of proper conduct amongst all members of the legal profession ; to suppress illegal, dishonourable or improper practice ; to preserve and maintain the integrity and status of the legal profession ; to provide opportunities for the acquisition and diffusion of legal knowledge ; to consider and suggest amendments to the law ; to provide means of settling professional differences amicably ; and to protect the interests of the legal profession and of the public in relation to legal matters. There are in addition a number of district Law Societies with the same functions as those of the parent body, whose Council they elect.

In 1939 there was passed in New Zealand a Legal Aid Act, the purpose of which was to authorise the making of rules which would ensure that poor persons would have legal aid available to them. The advent of the Second World War precluded immediate implementation of the Act, and it has not yet been put into operation. However, there has not been any great public demand for a scheme to be developed, one of the reasons being that it is a tradition with the profession that lack of funds shall not deprive a person of legal assistance when he is in need of it. The Poor Prisoners' Defence Act, 1933, makes provision for the defence of accused persons without means, solicitors' and counsels' fees according to a prescribed scale being paid by the State.

THE COUNCIL OF LAW REPORTING

To conclude this chapter, a brief note may be added as to the system of law reporting in the Dominion. Cases determined by the Privy Council, Court of Appeal, Supreme Court, Compensation Court, Court of Arbitration and Land Valuation Court are reported in the New Zealand Law Reports and Gazette Law Reports. The former publication is the work of the New Zealand Council of Law Reporting, an association incorporated by statute [20] and consisting of the Attorney-General, the Solicitor-General,

[20] The New Zealand Council of Law Reporting Act, 1938.

the President of the New Zealand Law Society and eight other barristers representing the principal District Law Societies of the Dominion. The Gazette Law Reports[21] are the work of a private firm of publishers. Both series are now protected by a provision in the New Zealand Council of Law Reporting Act that it shall not be lawful for any person, firm or company other than the Council to commence the publication of or to publish a new series of reports of decisions of the Supreme Court, Court of Appeal or Land Valuation Court except with the consent of the Council of the New Zealand Law Society which may only be given on the ground that the Council of New Zealand Law Reporting has failed to arrange for publication within a reasonable time and at reasonable cost of adequate reports of the Supreme Court and Court of Appeal.

The magistrates' courts judgments and decisions are reported in two concurrent series of reports, the Magistrates' Courts Reports[21] and the Magistrates' Courts Decisions, both of which are published privately by independent firms of publishers.

---

[21] Publication of these Reports ceased with the supplement in each case for March, 1953.

CHAPTER 4

PUBLIC ADMINISTRATION AND ADMINISTRATIVE LAW

THE new functions assumed from time to time by the New Zealand State have naturally reflected the problems facing the country at each stage of its development. In Chapter 1 we have broadly indicated the nature of those problems, and have outlined the solutions found in Crown Colony days and by the successive political régimes of the past hundred years. In general, the legislative tempo set by a government has determined not only the range of State activities but also the size of the Executive. By way of illustration the legislation passed by the Liberal-Labour Government that took office in 1891 resulted in a substantial increase in the work of the Executive, and the same was true of the Labour Government that took office in 1935.

Governor Hobson brought with him from New South Wales a small group of public officials to form the nucleus of a public service. Several months later, a small military force was also sent over from New South Wales. In May, 1841, the principal offices within the Executive were :

Colonial Secretary.
Attorney-General.
Colonial Treasurer and Collector of Customs.
Clerk of Councils and Sheriff.
Surveyor-General.
Colonial Surgeon.
Harbour Master.
Chief Protector of Aborigines.
Colonial Storekeeper.
Commissioners of Land Claims.
Superintendent of Works.
Postmaster-General.
Registrar of the Supreme Court.

The main problems facing the Crown Colony were land and its development, and relations with the Maoris. The office of Surveyor-General was created by Hobson to comply with the British Government's instructions that the Governor should begin a thorough survey of the country. In view of the serious disputes with the New Zealand Company over land ownership an English attorney, William Spain, was sent out from England in 1841 with wide powers ' to investigate and determine titles and claims to land in New Zealand, with an absolutely unfettered discretion '. Lt.-Col. McCleverty was appointed by the British Government in 1845 to adjust difficulties which had arisen from awards made by Governor Fitzroy on the basis of the findings of Spain.[1]

The office of Chief Protector of Aborigines was created also in accordance with instructions from the British Government. In 1846 this office was abolished and a Native Secretary was appointed for each of New Zealand's two main islands. Native Land Purchase Commissioners were also appointed to facilitate the acquisition by the Crown from the Maoris of large tracts of land. In 1852 there was a further change in the administration of Native affairs with the formation of a Native Department in place of the Native Secretaries, but although New Zealand had secured representative and responsible government by 1856, we have already seen in the first chapter that it was not until some years later that the administration of Maori affairs was assumed by a Minister responsible to the New Zealand legislature.

The construction of roads, bridges and public buildings was, of course, essential to the development of the country. In the Colony's Estimates for the year commencing May 2, 1841, an amount of £5,354, over a tenth of the Government's proposed expenditure, was allocated to the Department of Public Works and Buildings.[2] The provincial governments which were established under the Constitution Act of 1852 embarked upon public works but eventually their lavish programmes caused financial difficulties leading to the intervention of the central government in 1867 to control the raising of loans. Finally in 1870 the function of public works was taken over by the central government from the provincial governments and the Public Works Department was constituted as a preliminary to an extensive programme for the development of the country. This Department built roads and bridges, constructed railways, and was entrusted with the administration of immigration policy until a separate Immigration Department was formed in 1872.

In 1866 the number of public servants employed by the central government had grown to 1,602. In addition, there were about 600 servants employed by the nine provincial governments whose functions included ' the conduct of immigration, the construction of public works and the preservation of life and property in settled districts '. The provincial governments also acted as the agents of the central government in some branches of administration, *e.g.*, the survey, sale and management of land.

---

[1] R. L. Jellicoe, *The New Zealand Company's Native Reserves*, pp. 40, 51.
[2] Hight and Bamford, *The Constitutional History and Law of New Zealand*, p. 166.

It was not long before the State was intervening in fields traditionally those of private enterprise. A State bank was in business between 1850 and 1856 with a monopoly of the note issue. It is characteristic of the mood of the Colony that the Royal Commission which investigated the public service in 1866 should recommend that where private enterprise failed to carry mails at reasonable rates, the Government should take over the carriage of mails until such time as the terms of the Government were met. Within the next decade the Government Life Insurance Department and the Public Trust Office, both trading concerns, were created.

When the provinces were abolished in 1876, further functions were assumed by the central government and a fresh framework was provided for local or regional participation in some aspects of public administration. Crown lands were to be administered through a system of Land Boards, subject to Ministerial control. In 1877, as part of the policy for free and compulsory education, a central Education Department was created with a system of regional boards. In the expansion of the nineties the Liberal Government was responsible for a number of new Departments, including Agriculture, the State Advances Office, Labour, Valuation, Pensions, Mines, and Industries and Commerce. Early in the present century two Departments, Health and the State Fire Office, were created, and the new function of catering for tourists was entrusted to an existing Department.

The avalanche of new legislation had come almost to a halt in the dying years of the Liberal régime and when the conservative party, known as the Reform Party, took over in 1912, its administration was marked by an absence of spectacular measures. However, in its first year of office, the Reform Government placed the public service under the control of an independent public official called the Public Service Commissioner. Other Departments formed in the less spectacular period between the Liberal and Labour Governments, were the State Forest Service [3] in 1919, the Department of Scientific and Industrial Research and the Prime Minister's Department in 1926, and the Transport Department in 1929, the last being the creation of the United Party which contained remnants of the once vigorous Liberal Party. We have already seen that the twenties were noteworthy for the formation of marketing boards to deal with different types of primary produce. In 1934 a further extra-departmental agency was introduced into the Dominion's primary industry by the establishment of the Executive Commission of Agriculture for the purpose of co-ordinating the activities of the various bodies administering the Government's agricultural policy.

When the Labour Government came to power in 1935 there was a flood of legislation which raised the number of public servants by a

[3] Hitherto forestry had been a function of the Lands and Survey Department.

greater proportion than that of the first Liberal Government, although it did not result in a comparable increase in Departments. Although new functions were assumed, much of the legislation was directed to re-shaping the institutions already in existence. For instance, broadcasting and railways which had previously been controlled by boards were brought under direct Ministerial control. The Reserve Bank and the Mortgage Corporation were reconstituted and brought closer to Minis-terial control. A Department was established to control the disposal of primary produce destined for both New Zealand and overseas markets. The Bureau of Industry was established for the purpose of licensing and fostering secondary industries. Exchange control administered by the Reserve Bank, export control administered by the Customs Depart-ment, and import control administered also by the Customs Department but with the assistance of the Industries and Commerce Department, were all introduced in 1938.

A Department of Housing Construction was created in 1936 to organise the erection of State houses for letting. In 1939 the Social Security Department (replacing the old Pensions Department) was established to administer the Government's comprehensive Social Security Scheme, and in 1943 a Department of External Affairs appeared for the first time to handle New Zealand's relations with other countries, both inside and outside the Commonwealth.

The year 1945 saw some substantial additions and alterations to the administrative structure. Public corporations, subject to directions from Ministers of the Crown, were formed to take over the Bank of New Zealand, the linen flax industry and the main civil airways ; the National Employment Service was created to administer the full employment policy of the Government (amalgamated in 1947 with the Labour Depart-ment), while the State Hydro-electric Department was established to administer the hydro-electric undertakings which hitherto had been under the control of the Works Department.

As can be seen from this briefly sketched development of just over a hundred years the evolution of our administrative system has occurred in a variety of ways. New Departments may be created to perform new functions. Old Departments may take on new functions. A branch of an existing Department may become a separate Department. Two or more Departments may be amalgamated. Because of this almost constant process of change there is little point in detailing the various Depart-ments as they exist now, but reference is made to many of them in other parts of this volume.

At the present time there are over forty Departments of the central government, a large number of administrative tribunals and a few public corporations. In addition, there is the usual system of local government.

Sir John Salmond in 1918, as Solicitor-General, defined ' Department ' in these words [4] :

' A Department, at least in its normal and typical sense, may be defined as a branch of the Government Service separately organised under the control of a Permanent Head who is not himself under any control except that of a Minister in charge.'

Except where so provided by statute, Departments of the Government have no independent legal existence which enables them to enter into legal relations with one another ; they are merely the separate agencies of the Crown. Although they are organised on an hierarchical basis the distribution of authority and responsibility within Departments can be determined by legislation and there are cases where a subordinate official has a measure of statutory autonomy in the discharge of his function, even though for the purposes of discipline he is subject to hierarchical control.

Statutes and regulations lay down what is required of Government Departments in the discharge of their functions. Procedure may be defined in this authoritative way but often there are internal instructions issued by the Department to its staff. These instructions are designed to promote the execution of policy and the efficient working of the Department and are of no interest to the public, except to the extent that efficiency in Government institutions is a matter of public concern. But where the rights or obligations of private persons are affected, the instructions must find their authority in statute or regulation.

Apart from legislation peculiar to a particular Department, there are controls which run horizontally across most Departments of State. The control of the collection and expenditure of public moneys is vested in the Treasury under the Public Revenues Act. There is also a system of audit administered by a public official responsible to Parliament. Finally the power to appoint public servants is vested in an independent statutory commission which also regulates their conditions of employment, classification, promotion and discipline ; it is also concerned with efficiency in departmental organisation and methods.

Public corporations enjoy more freedom than the ordinary Department. They are not under continuous Ministerial control in the same way as ordinary Departments, but the measure of their political independence varies. First of all, persons are appointed to the controlling boards by the Government, either for a term or at pleasure. In some cases permanent public servants are *ex officio* members of these boards and perform this work on a part-time basis in the course of their official duties. In one case, the Wheat Committee,[5] a Minister is the chairman.

[4] Not published, but known in administrative circles.
[5] This body markets wheat and flour, fixes prices for those commodities, and regulates growers, brokers, and millers : The Board of Trade (Wheat and Flour) Regulations, 1944/94.

Under the Labour Government the practice was growing of conferring on a Minister the power to issue directions on policy. A typical provision was :

> ' In the exercise of their functions and powers the directors shall have regard to any representations that may be made by the Minister in respect of any functions or business of the Corporation, and shall give effect to any decision of the Government in relation thereto conveyed to the directors in writing by the Minister.'[6]

In addition, there was the usual requirement that an annual report be submitted through a Minister to Parliament.

Some of the corporations are free from financial control, particularly those that are handling moneys from the nature of their activities, such as the Wheat Committee and the Reserve Bank. Where, however, a corporation requires financial aid from the central government there are usually provisions for close financial control including such requirements as Ministerial consent before funds are borrowed. There is no uniformity in the provisions governing audit ; the accounts of some require to be audited by the Audit Office, while others may be audited by auditors outside the Public Service. Most corporations are beyond the control exercised by the Public Service Commission over personnel.

In New Zealand the system of local government rests entirely on statute. There are special Acts of Parliament providing for various types of local authorities such as borough councils, county councils, road boards, harbour boards and hospital boards. The powers and duties of these authorities are defined by statute and they cannot exercise any power which is not expressly or impliedly conferred by statute. They are subject to judicial control to keep them within their jurisdiction. There is also a measure of administrative control by the central government, also defined by statute, which is stringent in the matter of raising loans.

ADMINISTRATIVE LAW

The wide scope of public administration in New Zealand inevitably places great emphasis on the law which governs administrative activity. This activity may be that of the orthodox Government Department, a board or public corporation, an administrative tribunal, a local authority, or any other agency which exercises public functions. We are here concerned with the legal relations between citizens and public authorities of various types. The powers which these authorities have, their status, duties and procedure are the subject matter of administrative law, likewise the extent to which their work can be controlled by the ordinary courts. ' Administrative law includes the law that is made by as well as the law that controls the administrative authorities of a government.'[7]

[6] New Zealand National Airways Act 1945, s. 18.
[7] Hart, *An Introduction to Administrative Law*, p. 3.

The scope given the subject here exceeds what was contemplated by Sir John Salmond, when he expressed the view that administrative law was concerned with the multitudinous forms and instruments in and through which the lower ranges of governmental activity were manifested.[8] But the accelerated increase in the importance of the administrative function since Salmond wrote is enough to justify the more comprehensive approach.

Administrative law is the ugly duckling of the legal family. However much realism demands that this branch of the law be clearly delineated and given greater recognition, it is for most lawyers an unpleasant reminder of the growth of State control with its encroachment on their traditional domain. The attitude of the profession and the judiciary has meant that the recognition of administrative law as a distinct branch of the law has been slow. In the traditional division of law for study purposes no separate place was given to administrative law, and there are still those who see little justification for its separate treatment. In New Zealand it is taught in the law degree as a division of constitutional law, to which it is closely allied and which in some areas it overlaps. Some attempt has been made by university teachers to have administrative law taught as a distinct subject, but the practising lawyers and judges on the Council for Legal Education have successfully checked this attempt, leaving us with the compromise that now exists. Sir Michael Myers, a former Chief Justice, who was a member of the Council when this compromise was reached, afterwards commented that so far as he knew the term ' administrative law ' was not known to or recognised by the courts. He said he did not know the precise meaning of the term and thought that for the most part it was used by academicians.[9] The term, however, is an accepted one in the judgments of the Supreme Court of the United States of America. Harlan Stone, a former Chief Justice of the Supreme Court of the United States of America, and Lord Wright, a distinguished English judge, appear to have had no difficulty in using the term.

It is true that various portions of administrative law could be studied under traditional heads. Some portions could be treated under the head of procedure. The insistence that administrative officers entrusted with judicial powers should exercise them fairly is an illustration. The provisions governing proceedings by a subject against the Crown are largely procedural. But as public administration now impinges on the citizens more closely at a variety of points it is preferable to have a classification with meaning and utility rather than one which involves excursions into various branches of the law to find the material relevant to the field of public administration. To give administrative law a coherent form means the selection of material from various well-established branches

[8] *Salmond on Jurisprudence*, 10th ed., pp. 506, 507.
[9] *Journal of Public Administration* (N.Z.), Vol. 3, No. 2, p. 41.

of law including contract, torts and procedure. It means also the study of statutes over a wide range.

In this chapter we propose to discuss first, subordinate legislation, second, administrative tribunals, and third, proceedings against the Crown. It is not possible to cover administrative law adequately in one chapter but there is relevant material in the next five chapters dealing with social, industrial and economic developments.

SUBORDINATE LEGISLATION

The legislative powers of the Executive are of two kinds : prerogative powers and powers delegated by statute. Prerogative powers subsist in a particular field only so long as that field has not been covered by statute legislation. When New Zealand's constitutional history opened, the prerogative powers that can be called legislative were already confined within the two fields of legislation for a conquered or ceded colony to which a representative legislature had not been granted, and legislation restricting enemy commerce in wartime. New Zealand was neither a conquered nor a ceded Colony. The only prerogative legislation that has been part of the law of New Zealand has been the legislation of both World Wars restricting enemy commerce. This legislation took the form of Contraband Proclamations and Orders in Council Restricting Enemy Commerce.

The convention became established between the wars, partly by changes in practice and partly by resolutions of the Imperial Conferences of 1926 and 1930, that in any matter concerning a Dominion the Crown would act only on advice from Ministers in that Dominion. The issuing of prerogative legislation comes within the scope of this convention ; but prerogative legislation was not separately considered at the Imperial Conferences of 1926 and 1930, and no procedure was laid down, for in- stance requiring the recital of the advice on which the legislation was issued. The Order in Council of November 27, 1939, which was the first Order in Council Restricting Enemy Commerce issued during the Second World War, recited that ' the Allies of His Majesty are associated with Him in the steps now to be announced '. Probably, if the Allies had been consulted and had concurred, so had the Dominions ; and, though the recital was not repeated in later Orders in Council and Proclamations, probably the advice to issue them was based on similar consultation and concurrence. Since the change in convention it has been conceivable that a divided Crown would issue prerogative legisla- tion as part of the law of part or parts only of the Commonwealth ; so the question raised by prerogative legislation now is not exactly whether it extends to New Zealand as part of the law of New Zealand but merely whether it is part of the law of New Zealand.

The Governor-General has no expressly delegated power to issue prerogative legislation, but could possibly do so under his implicit authority to exercise the prerogative.[10] The occasion, however, has never arisen.

Some United Kingdom delegated legislation has extended to New Zealand, and such of this as is unrevoked is still in force in New Zealand except to the extent that it is repugnant to any New Zealand statute enacted since New Zealand's adoption in 1947 of the Statute of Westminster, or to any regulation issued under any such statute. The most important instances are such regulations issued under the Merchant Shipping Act, 1894, as extend to New Zealand. A United Kingdom statute granting to the United Kingdom Executive the power to issue delegated legislation that extends to New Zealand would come within the provisions of the Statute of Westminster; it would be a statute extending to New Zealand, and no United Kingdom statute enacted after New Zealand's adoption of the Statute of Westminster can extend to New Zealand unless it is expressly declared in the statute that the United Kingdom Parliament has enacted it at the request and with the consent of New Zealand; and the Statute of Westminster Adoption Act, 1947, provides that such request and consent may be made and given only by the New Zealand Parliament. The Statute of Westminster does not limit the power of the United Kingdom Executive to issue delegated legislation extending to New Zealand; this power, however, is limited by the convention that in such a case the Crown would act only on the advice of New Zealand Ministers. The limitation would no doubt similarly apply where the delegate of legislative power is a public authority other than the Crown.

Legislative powers have been delegated to the New Zealand Executive both by United Kingdom statutes and by New Zealand statutes. An illustration of a delegating provision in a United Kingdom statute is section 205 of the Merchant Shipping Act, 1894, which is still in force. This section authorises the Governor-General to issue regulations concerning the supply of anti-scorbutics for the use of ships. In at least one case legislative power that had been delegated to the United Kingdom Executive was sub-delegated to the New Zealand Executive: the Western Samoa Order in Council of March 15, 1920, issued under the Foreign Jurisdiction Act, 1890, gave the Executive Government of New Zealand interim legislative power in respect of Western Samoa, to subsist until the New Zealand Parliament should otherwise provide.

The delegation of legislative power by the New Zealand legislature has been a common device since the earliest days of government in New Zealand. At the end of 1841 an Ordinance of the Legislative Council empowered the Land Registrar to make rules subject to the approval of

[10] A. B. Keith, *The Dominions as Sovereign States* (1938), p. 210.

the Chief Justice. Early in 1842 provision was made for by-laws in the Municipal Corporations Ordinance (which was disallowed) and wide legislative power was granted to the Governor-in-Council under the Regulation of Harbours Ordinance. Legislative power was quite frequently delegated to the Executive throughout the period that New Zealand was a Crown Colony. With the establishment of a representative legislature under the 1852 Constitution the case for using delegated power became stronger because parliamentary sessions were short and at first infrequent. During the first seven years of the General Assembly's existence its sessions totalled little over twelve months, and on two occasions the recess between sessions lasted almost two years. Actually, however, the delegation of legislative power was not as common during these years as it had been while New Zealand was a Crown Colony. No doubt the explanation is that Ordinances already passed gave the Executive most of the legislative power it required. Since 1852 the practice of delegating legislative power has become gradually more common, and the output of delegated legislation has grown gradually in volume.

The delegation of legislative power to the Executive is thus not merely a twentieth-century phenomenon. What has been a novel development in the twentieth century has been the enactment of emergency statutes giving powers of unprecedented scope. Prior to the First World War the delegation of legislative authority was never more than an incidental provision in a statute enacting government policy on a particular subject. Since the outbreak of war in 1914 four emergency statutes have been passed that have departed from standard practice in two important respects : the powers have been virtually unrestricted as to subject-matter, and they have extended to matters of principle. These statutes have been the War Regulations Act, 1914, the Public Safety Conservation Act, 1932, the Emergency Regulations Act, 1939, and the Supply Regulations Act, 1947.

Many important regulations were issued under the powers given by the War Regulations Act, 1914 and additional powers given by amending Acts. This legislation was originally for twelve months only, but was extended in 1915 till the end of the war with Germany, and was further extended in 1916 till twelve months after the end of the war. In 1920, within twelve months of the proclamation of the end of the war, the regulations still in force were given indefinite validity by the War Regulations Continuance Act, and the delegated legislative authority was reduced to a limited power to amend the regulations that remained in force. The War Regulations Continuance Act remained in force until 1947, when it was repealed by a statute that extended the validity of certain regulations which had been issued under the Emergency Regulations Act, 1939. Not a great deal of use was made of the War Regulations Continuance Act. For one thing, most of the permanent legal changes

initially made by war regulations had been given statutory form before
the Continuance Act was enacted. The most striking use that was made
of the Continuance Act was in a prosecution concerning political activities
in 1932 : the accused were charged under this Act and were dealt with
summarily, although substantially identical charges could have been laid
under the Crimes Act, under which they would have been entitled to
trial by jury ; and after conviction they were given sentences exceeding
in duration the maximum provided by the Continuance Act, the authority
being a blanket provision for reformative detention in the 1910 amendment to the Crimes Act. The procedure was approved by the Court
of Appeal.[11] Some observers believed that the accused should not have
been denied trial by jury and that the use of extended powers to award
reformative detention was peculiarly inappropriate in a political prosecution. The supposed abuse of power in a case based on war regulations
is often thought of as an instance of abuse by the Executive of a power
to issue delegated legislation. It is noteworthy, however, first, that the
delegated legislation was admittedly appropriate to the circumstances
in which it was originally issued ; second, that the prosecution was based
on statute law ; and, third, that the legislature had full opportunity to
appreciate the import of what it was enacting in 1920, since the text of
the regulations affected was set out in a Schedule to the Bill.

The Public Safety Conservation Act was passed in April, 1932, shortly
after unemployed citizens had rioted in Auckland and Wellington. This
Act gave the Governor-General power to proclaim a state of emergency
(for not more than one month at a time) and gave him wide powers to
issue emergency regulations which would be valid for the duration of
the state of emergency (as originally proclaimed or as later extended).
The powers given by this Act have only twice been used. A state of
emergency was proclaimed on September 1, 1939, when war was imminent,
and in the first thirteen days of September emergency regulations were
issued that occupy 191 pages in the annual volume of Statutory Regulations. Most of these regulations had been drafted in advance under the
supervision of the Organisation for National Security, which had been
set up in the Prime Minister's Department in 1937 at the suggestion of
the British Government. On September 14, 1939, the Emergency
Regulations Act, 1939, was passed, providing that the emergency regulations issued under the Public Safety Conservation Act should be deemed
to have been issued under the Emergency Regulations Act. The second
occasion was in 1951, when far-reaching regulations were issued under
the authority of the Act as a means of quelling industrial disorders on
the waterfront.[12] The Public Safety Conservation Act is still in
force.

---

[11] *Griffin* v. *Police* [1933] N.Z.L.R. 225.
[12] See Chap. 6.

The Emergency Regulations Act, 1939, gave virtually unlimited powers. These powers were sometimes abused by issuing regulations on matters of principle while Parliament was in session and by issuing regulations on subjects that had no particular relation to the war emergency. In 1947 the legislation was substantially amended. Some of the regulations still in force were continued in force as emergency regulations under the Emergency Regulations Continuance Act, 1947, and the others were continued in force as supply regulations under the Supply Regulations Act, 1947. The Continuance Act conferred a limited power of amending emergency regulations that remain in force, and also extended certain provisions of the Emergency Regulations Act and the 1940 Amendment Act that are required to govern the interpretation of the emergency regulations that are still in force. Since then the regulations in force have been steadily reduced in number and importance.

The extension of existing regulations was only a minor provision in the Supply Regulations Act, 1947. The main provision was a delegation of legislative authority almost as wide as that contained in the Emergency Regulations Act, 1939 ; in fact, the provision in the Supply Regulations Act was in substitution for the earlier provision, which was repealed at the same time as the Supply Regulations Act was enacted. The Bill as introduced invites comparison with its British counterpart, the Supplies and Services (Transitional Powers) Act, 1945. In each case a Labour Government sought power to extend existing regulations and to issue new regulations in furtherance of its social policies ; in each case the Bill was introduced in the first session of a new Parliament ; and in each case the authority was sought for a term corresponding to the maximum life of a Parliament—five years in the United Kingdom and three years in New Zealand. But the New Zealand Bill was materially amended to meet Opposition objections. Not only was the expiry date brought forward from the end of 1950 to the end of 1948, but the scope of legislative powers granted was reduced by the dropping of a sub-clause, struck out on the Minister's motion, giving eight specific powers borrowed from the 1939 Act, including powers ' authorising the taking of possession or control, on behalf of His Majesty, of any property or undertaking ' and ' authorising the entering and search of any premises '. The Act authorised the Governor-General to issue such supply regulations ' as appear to him to be necessary or expedient for maintaining, controlling and regulating supplies and services essential to the well-being of the community, and for contributing to the equitable distribution of goods in short supply throughout the world '. The regulation-making power given by the Supply Regulations Act has been used only for the purpose of revoking or mitigating the force of regulations originally issued under the Emergency Regulations Act, 1939.

Apart from the four emergency Acts, power to issue regulations is confined to amplifying the policies embodied in the empowering Act. These policies, however, are sometimes defined only in very broad terms. The Labour Government of 1935–49 on occasions obtained wide powers to issue regulations in pursuance of its economic policies. Thus the Primary Products Marketing Act, 1937, inter alia gave the Marketing Department (*i.e.*, the Minister of Marketing or his delegate) power to fix prices and conditions of sale of certain specified food-stuffs, gave the Governor-General power to add to the list of food-stuffs, and also gave him power to issue regulations authorising the Department to commandeer such food-stuffs. In a country where primary industries play so large a part, these powers could be of the greatest significance. An unusual blanket authority is contained in the Civil Aviation Act, 1948, which gave the Governor-General power to issue regulations bringing into force any future amendments that might be made to the 1944 Chicago Convention on Civil Aviation or to any Annex thereto.

The power to amend statutes is often given, though there is only one instance of a Henry VIII clause in the narrow sense in which it is defined in the Report of the Committee on (United Kingdom) Ministers' Powers : ' power . . . to modify the provisions of the Act . . . for the purpose of bringing the Act into operation.'[13]   Following the enactment of the Education Act, 1914, section 6 of the Education Amendment Act, 1915, provided : ' The Governor-General may make such regulations as he thinks necessary or expedient for avoiding any doubt or difficulty which may appear to him to arise in the administration of the principal Act by reason of any omission or inconsistency therein, and all such regulations shall have the force of law, anything to the contrary in the principal Act notwithstanding '. Instances of powers to override the empowering Act are contained in the Banking Act, 1908, and some of its amendments, the Education Amendment Act, 1919, the Factories Act, 1946, and the Civil Aviation Act, 1948. The Factories Act, to take one illustration, contains provisions regarding holiday pay and Sunday pay, and authorises the Governor-General to issue modification orders modifying the application of the appropriate sections of the Act to particular factories or classes of factories. Power to override other Acts is given in the four emergency Acts and in very few others. Instances are the Banking Amendment Act, 1914, and the Emergency Forces Act, 1950. A power similar to the one in the Factories Act (though technically not a legislative power but a suspending power), was delegated to the Minister of Labour by the Labour Legislation Emergency Regulations, 1939, enabling the Minister to suspend the operation of any Act, regulations, orders, awards or agreements restricting the working of extended hours. In a similar category is conditional legislation, such as the Legislative Council Act,

13 Cmd. 406, p. 36.

1914, which provided for the re-constitution of the Legislative Council and was to come into force on a date to be fixed by Proclamation ; it was repealed in 1950 when the Legislative Council was abolished. The rules of procedure of the Supreme Court and the Court of Appeal are a curious composition. The Code of Civil Procedure and the Court of Appeal Rules containing the rules governing the practice and procedure of those courts are enacted as integral parts of the Judicature Act, 1908, to which they respectively comprise the Second and Third Schedules. With the concurrence of the Chief Justice and any four or more of the members of the Rules Committee (constituted by the Judicature Amendment Act, 1930), of whom at least one shall be a judge, the Governor-General in Council has power to alter or revoke such rules, and to make additional rules, such additional and altered rules to be deemed part of the Code of Civil Procedure or Court of Appeal Rules as if they had been included in the Schedules. The 1930 Act further provides that the power to make rules of Supreme Court and Court of Appeal procedure conferred in any other Act should be exercised in the same way.

Some statutes authorise the making of retrospective regulations. An example is the New Zealand Army Act, 1950. The Emergency Regulations Act and the Supply Regulations Act provide indemnification in advance for such acts done in anticipation of the issue of regulations as would have been lawful if done after the issue of the regulations. So far as is known, reliance has never been placed on either of these provisions. The Leader of the Legislative Council said of the Supply Regulations Bill that the power would be used only in the most exceptional circumstances, and instanced as a proper case the seizure of drugs on a vessel about to depart from New Zealand if the drugs were needed to cope with an epidemic that had just broken out. The indemnification is in some ways undesirable, but there is no doubt that the provision would be availed of only in circumstances that furnish a clear justification.

The original delegate of legislative authority is usually the Governor-General. In the Royal Titles Act, 1947, a quasi-legislative power is given to the Crown. This Act was passed to assent to an alteration in the Royal Style and Titles and to the issue by His Majesty for that purpose of His Royal Proclamation under the Great Seal of the Realm. His Majesty issued a Proclamation accordingly on June 22, 1948. Where the delegate is the Governor-General, it is sometimes expressly provided that the powers are to be exercised in Executive Council. Occasionally the powers are to be exercised only on the recommendation of a specified authority or with the concurrence of a specified authority. An instance is the Clerks of Works Act, 1944, designed to give semi-professional status to clerks of works, which provides for the establishment of a Clerks of Works Registration Board and confers on the Governor-General authority to issue regulations on the recommendation of the Board. Much the same effect is attained in the Public Service Act, 1912, which gives regulation-making power to the Public Service Commission subject to the approval of the Governor-General in Council. The New Zealand National Airways Corporation Act, 1945, authorises the Governor-General to make regulations and also authorises the Corporation to make by-laws subject to the approval of the Governor-General in Council. Delegation to a specified Minister is exceptional. Under the Government Railways Act, 1926, the Minister was empowered to issue by-laws, but when the railway legislation was re-consolidated by the Government Railways Act, 1949, this provision was replaced by one giving the Governor-General power to issue regulations. No statute gives an unconditional delegation of legislative power to a public servant, but public servants are frequently given powers by sub-delegation. Sub-delegation is expressly authorised by many Acts, including the Emergency Regulations Act and the Supply Regulations Act. Local authorities, of course, have legislative authority. Bodies governing autonomous functional institutions, such as the University of New Zealand, lie outside the scope of this book.

Subordinate legislation is given a variety of names. The 1949 volume of Statutory Regulations contains proclamations, regulations, rules, emergency regulations, orders, notices and warrants and an exercise of statutory powers by the Minister of Marine that is headed ' Defining River, Extended-River and Extreme Limits '. The term by-laws is usually reserved for the legislation of local authorities, though two other instances of its use are cited in the preceding paragraph. Proclamations, though traditionally not used for legislative purposes, may be so used under the Civil Aviation Act, 1948, which authorises the Governor-General to make proclamations regulating or prohibiting the use of aircraft in case of war or national emergency.

The phraseology of the clauses delegating legislative authority varies from statute to statute. A common formula is : ' The Governor-General may from time to time, by Order in Council, make all such regulations as may in his opinion be necessary or expedient for giving full effect to the provisions of this Act and for the due administration thereof '. Among other formulas in current use are : ' making provision for any matters deemed necessary for the due administration of, and for giving full effect to, the provisions of this Act ' ; ' as he thinks necessary in order to give full effect to this Act ' ; and ' for any purpose for which regulations are contemplated or required by this Act '.

Regulations are all drafted in the Law Drafting Office. They are usually well drafted ; the worst-drafted sets of regulations are better examples of the draftsman's art than the worst-drafted statutes. The reason is, no doubt, that a large proportion of legislation is hurried through Parliament in the last few weeks of a session. Again, afterthoughts can be neatly dovetailed into sets of regulations, but amendments to Bills are sometimes hasty and ill-considered.

Till the coming into force of the Regulations Act, 1936, the complete text of subordinate legislation was published in *The New Zealand Gazette*. To make the text available in a form more convenient for purposes of reference, a separate publication, *Rules, Regulations and By-Laws*, was instituted privately in 1910. In 1936 this publication was superseded by an official series, *Statutory Regulations*, instituted under the Regulations Act, 1936, and since then all that has been published in the *Gazette* has been a notification that regulations have been issued. The Act provides that the annual series may include ' regulations made under any Imperial Act or under the prerogative rights of the Crown and having force in New Zealand '. Under this provision the prerogative legislation of the Second World War and the 1948 Proclamation with effect under the Royal Titles Act, 1947, have been published in the series. The inclusion of prerogative legislation in a series entitled *Statutory Regulations* is no doubt anomalous, but is convenient. A useful provision enables sets of regulations to be reprinted with amendments incorporated ; under this provision three sets of regulations were reprinted in 1950 and two sets in 1951. The Attorney-General may exempt any specified regulations or class of regulations from publication in the series. The 1950 volume contains 232 sets of regulations, and lists 179 other sets of regulations excluded as having only local or temporary importance, more than half of them price orders issued by the Price Investigation Tribunal. Since 1950 an explanatory note has been published with each set of regulations, not forming part of the regulations but indicating their general effect.

The necessity for laying regulations on the table of the House varies from statute to statute in an apparently capricious way. The War Regulations Act makes no provision ; the Public Safety Conservation Act and the Emergency Regulations Act require regulations to be tabled as soon as may be ; and the Supply Regulations Act requires regulations to be tabled within twenty-eight days if Parliament is in session, or, if Parliament is not in session, within twenty-eight days of the opening of the next ensuing session. About half the statutes conferring legislative powers require tabling. Where there is a requirement, the periods are now always of twenty-eight days ; formerly periods of fourteen days were sometimes fixed.

Three Acts provide that regulations shall expire after short specified periods unless they have in the meantime been confirmed by Parliament. The Public Safety Conservation Act, under which regulations must be laid on the table as soon as may be, provides that regulations shall expire fourteen days after being laid unless they are sooner confirmed by resolution. The regulations issued under this Act in September 1939

were confirmed within fourteen days by the Emergency Regulations
Act, and those issued in 1951 were confirmed by resolutions within the
prescribed time.   The Agriculture (Emergency Powers) Act, 1934,
under which regulations are to be laid on the table within twenty-eight
days of issue or of the opening of the next session, provides that all
regulations tabled during any session shall expire on the last day of the
session unless sooner confirmed by Act of Parliament.   Confirming Acts
have been passed at the end of each session since the principal Act was
passed.   The Primary Products Marketing Act, 1953, provides that
regulations will expire at the end of the session in which they have been
tabled unless they have in the meantime been validated or confirmed
by Act of Parliament.   Even when confirmation by Parliament is not
required by the empowering Act, it is sometimes given to remove doubts
as to validity.   Annual validation has been the practice with regulations
issued under the War Regulations Act, the Emergency Regulations Act
and the Supply Regulations Act, and sometimes other regulations have
been expressly validated.   .

During the debate on the Supply Regulations Bill at the end of the
1947 session, the Government agreed to the establishment of a Select
Committee to consider future policy regarding the regulations that were
being extended under the Supply Regulations Act and the Emergency
Regulations Continuance Act.   The Committee reported in 1948, and
its recommendations were embodied in that year's annual legislation.
The Committee has not been re-constituted in later sessions.   In any
case, its utility as a parliamentary check on Executive action was limited
by the narrowness of its terms of reference.   Consideration of the delegating clauses in current Bills lay outside its jurisdiction, and so did most
existing regulations and all new regulations then being issued.   The
Attorney-General of the National Government has stated that ever
since his Government took office in 1949 all regulations have been
referred to him before issue to enable him to question the desirability
of any regulations that appear to him to be unusual in form or undesirable
in content.

The Government cannot, of course, avoid parliamentary debate by
embodying its legislation in regulations instead of Bills.   The Opposition
seizes the first opportunity to attack regulations of which it disapproves.
Perhaps the one political rather than legal difference between Bills and
regulations is that in the case of a Bill debate precedes enactment and
in the case of regulations debate cannot ensue until after the regulations
have been issued and in most cases after they have gone into effect.
Thus, where legislation is issued in the form of regulations, interested
parties have no opportunity to use their parliamentary influence to
secure the amendment *ab initio* of provisions they consider objectionable ;
but a mitigating factor is the practice of consulting interested parties in

the drafting stage. Whether Bills or regulations are used, the Opposition may voice its criticism, and in either case the Government decides which Opposition objections, if any, to meet. The use of regulations may postpone the debate but is not likely to affect the content of the legislation.

Control by the courts has taken much the same form as in the United Kingdom. The crucial legal question is whether regulations are *intra vires* or *ultra vires*, and in decisions on this question no novel principles have been evolved. Several regulations have been declared invalid, the most important being the Import Control Regulations of 1938.[14] No regulations issued under any of the four emergency Acts have been declared invalid, and it is difficult to see how any could be. But at least one set of emergency regulations has been interpreted restrictively. In this case the Supreme Court held that the Price Stabilisation Emergency Regulations, issued in 1939 under the Public Safety Conservation Act, 1932, and validated by the Emergency Regulations Act, 1939, being necessarily of a temporary nature because originally issued under a statute that gave sub-legislative power for a period of only one month at a time, could not be read as impliedly repealing the Auckland Metropolitan Milk Act, 1933, which was a special statute dealing with a special position and providing a special code.[15] The interpretation to be placed on the regulations in question was determined by the nature of the statute under which they were originally issued, and was not affected by the nature of a subsequent validating statute.

As long ago as 1900 the Municipal Corporations Act provided: ' All regulations made by the Governor under this Act shall be of the same force and effect as if contained in this Act.' Similar provisions exist in the Public Safety Conservation Act and the Emergency Regulations Act, but not in the other two emergency Acts. Another case is the Agriculture (Emergency Powers) Act, 1934, but that is an Act under which prompt confirmation by Parliament is required. In other statutes the provision is very rare. The courts have never accepted the view that such a provision debars them from considering whether regulations are *ultra vires*[16] ; they have always taken the view that only *intra vires* regulations are to have the same force and effect as if contained in the Act, and that the provision means only that statute and regulations must be interpreted as if they constituted a single document. Another and more effective way of removing the question of validity from the purview of the courts was opened up in a 1942 case [17] where the dissenting minority of the Court of Appeal considered that, where a Minister is empowered to issue such regulations as appear to him to be necessary or expedient for a particular purpose, it is not competent for the court to inquire

14 *Jackson* v. *Collector of Customs* [1939] N.Z.L.R. 682.
15 *Thompson* v. *Auckland Metropolitan Milk Council* [1942] N.Z.L.R. 42.
16 *Campbell* v. *Frerichs* [1949] G.L.R. 275, 278.
17 *Jensen* v. *Wellington Woollen Co.* [1942] N.Z.L.R. 394.

into the Minister's state of mind. The minority were applying a very recent decision of the House of Lords,[18] to the effect that, where the criterion of validity is that a particular individual should have reasonable cause to hold a particular belief and the individual recites that he has such reasonable cause a court cannot inquire into the truth of the recital. Lord Atkin observed that if a subjective term like ' satisfied ' were used, the case would be even stronger. The term ' satisfied ' has rarely been used in New Zealand in a delegation of legislative authority. It is used in the Primary Products Marketing Act, 1953, which provides in S. 2 (3): ' The Minister shall not recommend the making of any regulations under this Act establishing a Marketing Authority unless he is satisfied, on such evidence as he considers adequate, that a majority of the persons engaged in the production of the primary product to which the proposed regulations relate are in favour of the establishment of a Marketing Authority in respect of that product.' The courts have not yet been asked to interpret such a provision.[19]

The delegation of legislative authority is a necessary device of government in New Zealand, and has proved perhaps even more useful than in the United Kingdom, first because parliamentary recesses are longer and secondly because the State's responsibilities are wider in domestic matters or, at any rate, were till 1939. On the other hand, pressure of parliamentary time is not as acute as in the Commons : sessions are shorter, standing committees are not used, much time is spent on matters of unimportant detail, and even so in 1946 Parliament had to be adjourned for a week because the Government had run out of Bills.

Powers of unjustifiable amplitude have often been granted but seldom been abused. The defect in the system has not been that the Executive has usurped the proper function of the legislature, or that the judiciary has been precluded from discharging its proper function, but that the legislature has precluded itself through faulty organisation from discharging efficiently its own functions of delegation and supervision. The legislature needs a Select Committee that will enable it to give informed consideration to every clause that delegates legislative authority and will report what use is being made of the powers previously granted to the Executive.

Controversy tends, however, to centre round the role of the Executive rather than that of the legislature. So-called ' government by Order in

[18] *Liversidge* v. *Anderson* [1942] A.C. 206.
[19] Such use of 'satisfied' is contained in s. 32 of the Shops and Offices Act, 1921–2. The word 'satisfied' is also contained in s. 35 of this Act, though not with reference to a legislative power, and in *Wilkinson* v. *Associated Chemists Ltd.* [1948] N.Z.L.R. 216, the court declined to inquire whether the Minister was satisfied in terms of this section. It may be argued that, as the power of specific direction given to the Minister by s. 35 is related to the legislative power given to him by s. 32, this case should be treated as an authority to the effect that the courts will not inquire into a state of mind when a condition of the exercise of a legislative power is that a specified individual should be 'satisfied'.

Council' is often the object of attack by whichever party happens for the time being to be in opposition. The legal profession is also persistent in its criticism, claiming that the Executive has broken the rule of law by usurping the functions of the legislature. This unrealistic approach is probably a confused expression of dismay at the growth of Executive power in general. The subject will probably continue to be discussed more on the plane of controversy than on the plane of scholarship until New Zealand has a Committee on Ministers' Powers to clear the air.

ADMINISTRATIVE TRIBUNALS

The legislation inherent in a programme of State controls has inevitably encroached upon the interests of individuals. This trend has also been accelerated by the demands of two major wars. The State is now regulating many phases of economic life. It is in this environment of control intensified by the demands of war that most of our administrative tribunals have been conceived. As the interests of some individuals are usually prejudiced by regulatory legislation a tribunal working on judicial lines is often offered as a safeguard.

The term 'administrative tribunal' does not seem to have attained a settled precise meaning but is used here to embrace those public officials who are not members of the ordinary judiciary or magistracy but who have judicial powers or follow a judicial procedure when exercising their administrative powers over persons and property. Often they have the power of moving on their own initiative and are thus to be distinguished from the ordinary civil courts, which do not move until a party sets the machinery in motion. On the other hand, they resemble the ordinary courts in that there is provision for a hearing with its corollary of reasonable notice. Although administrative tribunals must act judicially, their procedure tends to be less formal than that of the ordinary courts. The policy which each has to apply is defined in the empowering Act or regulations and it is the tribunal's duty to apply this policy to actual situations by means of a judicial procedure. There are of course the legal boundaries within which the tribunals must work ; but where, as is often the case, the tribunals have been endowed with discretionary powers they must in the exercise of these powers give substance to the shadowy form of policy.

Administrative tribunals can be classified into three broad types according to their distance from political control. First there is the professional public servant, who by virtue of some statutory office he occupies within the Executive is called upon to exercise his powers in a judicial manner. The Commissioner of Patents exercises wide judicial powers. For instance where there is opposition to the grant of a patent, he may hear the parties and make a determination including the awarding of costs. Before a title can carry a State guarantee, the District Land Registrar must adjudicate on the relevance, adequacy and operation of deeds or instruments evidencing land transactions in his district. There is a right of appeal to the Registrar-General of Land on the legal efficacy of land transactions. Judicial powers are also exercised by the District Land Registrar and the Examiner of Titles jointly when they are adjudicating on the validity of claims based on long possession or on operation of law. Claims based on long possession may only be made with respect to land held under the Deeds System or under Land Transfer certificates of limited guarantee. An illustration of a claim based on operation of law is that of a person applying for registration of his interest as the executor of a registered proprietor who is deceased. Where the District Land Registrar and the Examiner of Titles fail to agree, there is a right of appeal to the Registrar-General of Land. These officials come under the control of the Public Service Commission for the purpose of discipline, efficiency, and conditions of service. Although these officials are members of a Government Department under the normal pattern of Ministerial control and could be more easily subjected to improper pressure in the exercise of their judicial functions, there is no evidence to suggest that any such interference occurs. The legislation which conferred these functions on them is of long standing and firmly accepted. As at present conceived the duties of these officials are in harmony with the individualistic concept of property and differ from those imposed by much modern legislation which erects the community interest at the expense of individuals or groups of individuals. There are of course recent instances where professional public servants have been given judicial functions following legislation of this nature, but the general trend in recent years has been for those functions to be performed by persons appointed from outside the regular public service.

Secondly there is the intermediate type of organ, which lies outside the orthodox Government Department, and which is usually more independent of the political Executive. Its members are recruited as a rule from outside the regular public service. The last decade or so has seen many illustrations of this type, which will be discussed more fully later.

Thirdly there is the special administrative court, which is still farther removed from the political Executive than the second type and is autonomous. It is usually a court of record, and has, therefore, the power to punish for contempt. An example is the Court of Arbitration constituted in 1894 as part of the system for compulsory arbitration in industrial disputes. A further example was the Land Sales Court, which coordinated the work of Land Sales Committees and heard appeals from the decisions of those committees. The committees, however, fell within the second type as discussed above.

As will be seen from the illustrations of the first and third type of administrative tribunal, there is nothing new in the use of this administrative device. It is the frequency with which the device is used that is typical of modern administration, particularly during time of war. For most of the tribunals created during the last war the curtain did not fall with the cessation of hostilities and they now form an integral part of the administrative structure in the post-war period. Even those tribunals which disappeared when hostilities ceased are significant for the reason that they may form the basis for future tribunals. It is now proposed to examine most of the tribunals created within the last fifteen years, which of course includes the war period.

Functions

Three of the tribunals, the Price Tribunal, the Goods Services Charges Tribunal, and the Land Sales Tribunals performed important functions in connection with the stabilisation policy of the country. The Price Tribunal fixed prices for goods and services. It maintained a survey of the prices charged, investigated complaints made about charges, and initiated legal proceedings where appropriate. It had a general duty to prevent profiteering or the exploitation of the public. In 1947 its position was redefined in legislation but without any great change in its character and it is now operating in a peacetime economy. The Goods Services Charges Tribunal prescribed and reviewed charges to be made for the conveyance of goods and mails in goods services. It was abolished in 1948 when the Transport Charges Appeal Authority was created.

The Land Sales Court had two principal functions :

(*a*) to hear and determine objections to the compulsory taking of farm lands for settling ex-servicemen and to fix the compensation payable for land so taken ;

(*b*) to control the prices for sale or lease of rural and urban land.

For the most part, the court acted as an appellate tribunal from the decisions of Land Sales Committees to whom applications to the court were normally referred in the first instance. These tribunals were abolished in 1948 and their functions taken over by new tribunals known as the Land Valuation Court and the Land Valuation Committees. The new tribunals were given the additional functions of disposing of claims for compensation for land taken over by the Crown for public works and of hearing objections to valuations made for rating and revenue purposes. As a result of legislation in 1950 the control of the sale or lease of urban land was removed, and the control in respect of rural land was substantially modified with provision for its expiry on June 30, 1952.[20]

The Government Railways Industrial Tribunal determines the remuneration and conditions of service of railway employees in certain categories. In its deliberations the tribunal is obliged to have regard to the promotion of efficiency in the railways service. An Emergency Disputes Committee is set up to settle a particular industrial dispute which is referred to it by the Minister of Labour and which in his opinion is likely to result in a strike or lockout. The Transport Appeal Authority was created in 1941 to determine appeals from the decisions of Transport Licensing Authorities. Originally this function was performed by the Minister of Transport, but when the portfolios of transport and railways were later held by the same Minister, it became desirable to set up another appeal authority because the railways service was an interested party in the transport field. In 1949 the Transport Appeal Authority became the Transport Licensing Appeal Authority. The authority is a judge of Supreme Court status who at the present time is also the Transport Charges Appeal Authority. The Industrial Efficiency Appeal Authority [21] was created by statute in 1942 to hear appeals from decisions of the Bureau of Industry on the granting, transferring and cancelling of licences in industry. In determining appeals the authority has regard to the general purposes of the Industrial Efficiency Act, 1936, in particular to the economic necessity of securing efficiency and co-ordination in industry. The Sea-Fisheries Licensing Appeal Authority, which was created in 1945, hears appeals from decisions of licensing authorities either refusing licences to fishermen or cancelling existing licences.

The Armed Forces Appeal Boards were responsible for hearing appeals for exemption from military service on the grounds of hardship, conscience, the public interest or ineligibility for service. At a later stage in the war they dealt with applications for release from the armed forces. Where an appeal was allowed on grounds of conscience the appellant became subject to the jurisdiction of the Special Tribunal, which could make orders ensuring that for the duration of the war the appellant's financial position was no better than it would have been if he had served in the armed forces. This tribunal could also determine the type of civilian work in which the appellant should engage. In 1945 Revision Authorities were set up to deal with the applications of military

[20] The Land Settlement Promotion Act, 1952, has since been enacted. It is designed to prevent the undue aggregation of farm land. The Act also adopts the general principle that purchasers of farm land should reside on the land personally and farm it personally. The Land Valuation tribunals have functions under the new legislation.

[21] Previously the appeal authority had been the Minister who referred the appeals to Sir Francis Frazer and acted on the latter's recommendations. To meet criticism that politics entered into the Minister's decisions, the Act was passed and Sir Francis Frazer was formally appointed as the appeal authority.

defaulters for release on parole from defaulters' detention. The primary function of the Aliens Authority was to report to the Minister on every alien registered in its district and to classify aliens within categories specified in the regulations. An alien who had been refused a licence to work in a particular occupation or locality could appeal to the Aliens Authority. An alien had the right of appeal to the Aliens Appeal Tribunal against any classification of him which had been made by the Aliens Authority in its report to the Minister. There was also power in the Minister to refer questions to the Aliens Appeal Tribunal for its advice. The principal function of Industrial Manpower Committees was the determination of appeals from the decisions of District Manpower Officers on questions affecting the movement of workers within the employment field. The War Pensions Board decides whether a claimant is entitled to a pension or allowance under the War Pensions Act, 1943. It can review a decision made by the Secretary of the Board in terms of powers delegated to him. There is a restricted right of appeal to a higher tribunal designated the War Pensions Appeal Board.[22] The question whether death or disablement is attributable to or aggravated by service in the forces can be the subject of appeal, as well as any assessment of pension based on medical grounds. The appellant's position is specially strengthened by legal presumptions relating to medical grading and evidence.

Some of these administrative tribunals have or had both legislative and adjudicative powers. Not only did the Goods Services Charges Tribunal have power to vary charges payable under an individual contract, but still using judicial procedure it could vary the schedules of charges applicable to a group of operators within a given area. Apart from the judicial form of the procedure, a decision of the latter type has the generality of a legislative act, although within a narrow field. The Price Tribunal has an interesting collection of powers. First it can legislate in the sense of making a price order which will be generally applicable to one class of goods. Secondly it can adjudicate in respect of applications submitted to it by individual traders. Thirdly it is acting administratively when it initiates proceedings in the ordinary courts for breaches ; similarly when its staff makes the investigations preliminary to a price order or price approval. Adherents of Dicey will shudder at the grouping of three such powers within the one organ. The Land Sales Court apart from dealing with appeals in individual cases could issue general directions to Land Sales Committees and could move without its aid being invoked by a party. An order of the Railway Industrial Tribunal can have general application within a particular category. Moreover, when a tribunal such as the Railways Industrial Tribunal must have regard to the promotion of efficiency, its approach must

[22] Similar tribunals had been functioning since the 1914–18 war.

necessarily be wider than that of the ordinary courts, and this brings it nearer to the administrative process.

Numerical Strength of Tribunals

Tribunal	Number
Aliens Authority	1
Aliens Appeal Tribunal	3
Armed Forces Appeal Board	3
Emergency Disputes Committee	7
Goods Services Charges Tribunal	5
Industrial Efficiency Appeal Authority	1
Industrial Manpower Committee	3
Land Sales Committee	3
Land Sales Court	3
Price Tribunal	2
Railways Industrial Tribunal	3
Revision Authority	1
Sea-Fisheries Licensing Appeal Authority ..	1
Special Tribunal	1
Transport Appeal Authority	1
War Pensions Board	3
War Pensions Appeal Board	3

It will be seen that in most cases a tribunal does not exceed three members, but there may be many tribunals of a particular type distributed throughout the country. The latest legislation governing the Price Tribunal provides for a president, one or more ordinary members and one or more associate members. In the case of the Railways Industrial Tribunal assessors may be appointed to take part in the hearing of an application as though they were members of the tribunal, but they do not have any voting power.

Tenure of Office

The general rule is that members of these tribunals hold office during the pleasure of the Governor-General (acting alone or in Council), or of the Minister. Although members of the War Pensions Board and the War Pensions Appeal Board hold office during pleasure, no member can serve for a continuous period of more than three years without re-appointment. Members of the Railways Industrial Tribunal are appointed for a term of three years. The Industrial Efficiency Appeal Authority, the Sea-Fisheries Licensing Appeal Authority and the two Transport Appeal Authorities are appointed for terms not exceeding three years, but there is power to re-appoint them. Where the Act provides for appointment for a term, it is usual to provide for removal on the grounds of neglect of duty, misconduct, or disability.

Qualifications for Appointment

Representation of interests and the need for specialised knowledge have been factors in the recruiting of persons for some of the tribunals. The legislation may expressly provide for the recognition of these factors or it may be the policy of the appointing authority. The War Pensions Appeal Board is an illustration. Two members of the board are medical practitioners, one of whom is appointed as a representative of ex-servicemen on the nomination of the New Zealand Returned Services' Association.[23] The chairman of the board is usually a lawyer with judicial experience. The lower bodies, the War Pensions Boards, consist of at least one medical practitioner and one member appointed as a representative of ex-servicemen on the nomination of the New Zealand Returned Services' Association. Lawyers preside over these bodies.

Land Sales Tribunals [24] were recruited in the main to obtain a blend of legal experience and knowledge of building and land values. For instance, the chairman of the Wellington Urban Committee was a practising lawyer, the second member was a former Government architect well versed in building values, and the third was a land agent. The first president of the Price Tribunal was a lawyer with judicial experience, the second member was an economist, and two associate members represented the interests of consumers.

The chairmen of the Armed Forces Appeal Boards were usually practising lawyers or stipendiary magistrates and the other members were recruited in the main to give representation to employer and employee interests. Lawyers were selected for the Special Tribunal, the Revision Authority, and except for one appointee for the Aliens' Tribunal and the Aliens' Appeal Tribunal. The Industrial Manpower Committees were representative in character to the extent that one member represented the employees and one the employers. For an Emergency Disputes Committee three are selected to represent the employees and three the employers. The chairman of the Railways Industrial Tribunal is a deputy judge of the Court of Arbitration, the second member is the Government representative, and the third a representative of the staff organisations of the railway service. A judge of Supreme Court status holds office as the Industrial Efficiency Appeal Authority.

In some cases the legislation imposes disqualifications. No person can act as the Transport Licensing Appeal Authority or as the Transport

---

[23] The tribunal travels and the two medical members are drawn from the centre where the sitting is held.

[24] Land Valuation Committees, which took the place of Land Sales Committees, have a magistrate as chairman and one other member who has experience in the valuation of real property.

Charges Appeal Authority if he is financially interested in or associated with the transport industry. A person who is financially interested in the industry to which an appeal relates cannot act as the Industrial Efficiency Appeal Authority. No one can be a member of the Railways Industrial Tribunal if he is a serving member of the department or of a staff organisation.

Procedure

A common provision is that these tribunals may admit such evidence as they think fit. Such a provision, however, is probably subject to the restriction that the evidence must be of such a nature as to lead the tribunal to believe that it is in all probability true.[25] Moreover, the provision would not enable the admission of evidence which offended against decency, morality or public policy. These tribunals regulate their procedure as they think fit, subject to any requirements that may be set out in the enabling Act or regulations. With most tribunals a formal hearing is necessary together with adequate notice to the parties concerned of the date for the hearing. A formal hearing, however, is not necessary where a tribunal reaches a decision without adversely affecting the interests of the subject. A Land Sales Committee could consent to a sale at a figure acceptable to the vendor and the Crown without holding a formal hearing, but where agreement was not reached the vendor was entitled to a formal hearing. The volume of work that fell to the Price Tribunal during the war obliged it to deal with the great bulk without formal hearings, although an aggrieved party could insist on a formal hearing. The Transport Licensing Appeal Authority deals with appeals without a formal hearing unless Government Departments are directly concerned or an oral hearing is sought by an interested party or considered desirable by the Appeal Authority. Most of the cases are actually disposed of without a formal hearing. When this procedure is followed the documents submitted to the Appeal Authority comprise the official transcripts of proceedings before the subordinate licensing authority, the written submissions of the parties, the comments of each party on the other's submissions, the comments of the subordinate licensing authority, together with a précis made by the Transport Department and references to the licences involved. Before the Goods Services Charges Tribunal dealt with an application for general increases in a town or country area, the accounts of a selected number of operators within the area were checked by the Transport Department's investigating staff. The revenue accounts and balance sheets, along with certain other statistical data, were then placed before a committee of accountants (one representative each of the transport industry, users,

[25] *Seed* v. *Somerville* (1904) 7 G.L.R. 199.

and the Department) which adjusted the accounts in accordance with conventions laid down by the tribunal. The adjusted accounts were then summarised and copies forwarded to the parties interested in the application.

Formal hearings are usually in public, except in the case of the Price Tribunal during wartime and the War Pensions Tribunals. A hearing before a Land Sales Tribunal could be held in private, if the tribunal considered this to be in the interests of all the persons concerned. A similar provision applied to the Armed Forces Appeal Board. An Industrial Manpower Committee could hear a case in private, if it thought that this was in the public interest. The Special Tribunal and the Revision Authority were exceptions to the general rule in that no person other than the party directly affected could attend a hearing except with permission, nor could a report of proceedings be published except with the consent of the tribunal.

Before almost all the tribunals, parties can be or could be represented by counsel or by a lay person with the tribunal's consent. With the Railways Industrial Tribunal no person may be an advocate unless he is a member of the department or is the general secretary or assistant general secretary of a service organisation. In the case of the Industrial Manpower Committee it was competent for a worker or employer to be represented by his organisation. The trend with some English administrative tribunals of discouraging legal representation is not so obvious here, although it would be an advantage in the case of some of the tribunals. Those who have observed tribunals at work in this country cannot help noticing that the friendly informal atmosphere which often prevails vanishes on the appearance of the lawyer-advocate. The chairman of the tribunal, if he is a lawyer, adopts a more formal procedure, but if he is not a lawyer he and the other lay members tend to assume a defensive attitude.

Most of these tribunals are deemed to be commissions under the Commissions of Inquiry Act, 1908, which is discussed in the preceding chapter. The only point that need be mentioned here is that the procedure under that Act for stating a case on a point of law for consideration by the ordinary courts is seldom used by administrative tribunals.

Quorum and Decision Making

Where a tribunal comprises three persons, the quorum is usually two, although in the cases of the Land Valuation Court and the Railways Industrial Tribunal the judge or chairman must be one of the members present. All three members of the War Pensions Appeal Board must attend to make a quorum as was the case with the Armed Forces Appeal Boards and the Industrial Manpower Committees. The members of an

Emergency Disputes Committee, three representing employers and three the employees, are all obliged to attend. Any member who, without reasonable excuse, fails to attend a meeting commits an offence. This is necessary as conflicting parties in a dispute may be reluctant to meet.

Not fewer than two members (other than associate members) must be present at any sitting of the Price Tribunal, and where there are only two present both must concur in a decision. If more than two are present, the decision is that of the majority and if the voting is equal the chairman has a casting as well as a deliberative vote. A majority decision of the Land Sales Court was not possible unless the judge was one of the majority, and where only two members were present the decision of the judge prevailed. Where there is an equal division of opinion in the Railways Industrial Tribunal, the decision is that of the chairman. The chairman of the War Pensions Board has a deliberative as well as a casting vote, but two members must concur in a decision. In the Goods Services Charges Tribunal the chairman had a deliberative as well as a casting vote. The decision of the majority (excluding the chairman) is the decision of an Emergency Disputes Committee but if the members are unable to reach a decision, the chairman's decision becomes that of the committee.

Extent of Independence

The degree to which these bodies are autonomous varies. They could be abolished, of course, by an Act of Parliament and in some cases by Order in Council. Control by the Executive exists when persons are being selected for administrative tribunals. Where members hold office during pleasure there is also the unrestricted power to remove them at any time, although it is a step seldom taken. Members of the Emergency Disputes Committees, the War Pensions Board, and the War Pensions Appeal Board, are appointed by Ministers as were those of the Goods Services Charges Tribunal, the Armed Forces Appeal Board, the Industrial Manpower Committees, the Alien Authorities and the Aliens Appeal Tribunal. The Minister of Justice was the appointing authority for the two tribunals last mentioned. The Governor-General in Council is the appointing authority for the Land Valuation Tribunals and the Railways Industrial Tribunal, but in the latter case the Act provides that the appointments are made on the recommendation of the Minister. The Governor-General without sitting in Council is the appointing authority for the Price Tribunal, the two Transport Appeal Authorities, the Industrial Efficiency Appeal Authority and the Sea-Fisheries Licensing Appeal Authority, but in the first-mentioned instance it is expressly provided that he acts on the recommendation of a Minister. Where a tribunal comprises more than one person, the person to preside is normally chosen by the authority empowered to constitute the tribunal. It is not the practice to have chairmen in rotation.

The power to appoint and to dismiss is an effective instrument in the hands of the Executive, but it is necessary to probe further to see whether there are other provisions enabling the Executive to influence the policy of these tribunals. The regulations creating the Aliens Authority and the Aliens Appeal Tribunal contemplated close relations between these tribunals and the Minister. An Aliens Authority in its main task could do no more than make recommendations to the Minister. The regulations also provided that it was to have regard to the Minister's directions whether general or particular. The Aliens Appeal Tribunal heard appeals from the recommendations of an Aliens Authority and also advised the Minister on matters he referred to it. The Goods Services Charges Tribunal could not complete one aspect of its work without reference to a Minister. If it decided that an increase in rates was justified the incidence of that increase whether to be borne by the consumer or by subsidy had to be stated by the Minister and his direction embodied in the order.

The Acts or wartime regulations which created most of the tribunals are generally silent on the subject of Ministerial control of policy. The Minister can usually initiate regulations which will affect the policy to be applied by the tribunals. For instance, regulations promulgated in 1946 for Land Sales Tribunals went beyond the realm of procedure and laid down policy in one important aspect, but the substance of these regulations was later embodied in an Act of Parliament.

Apart from the power to initiate regulations there is sometimes a means of contact established for the Minister. For instance, it is laid down that the Minister may refer complaints to the Price Tribunal. The Minister in the Labour Government once made it clear in Parliament that he expected the Price Tribunal to conform with his policy, but it should be remembered that under the regulations important powers given to the Tribunal could not then be exercised except with the consent of the Minister.

To some extent the degree of independence is governed in practice by the nature of the tasks to be performed, by the extent to which the status and duties of tribunals have been defined in the empowering instruments, and by the quality and prestige of the personnel comprising the tribunals. Control of manpower was vital in wartime and policy had to react quickly to changing situations. Ministerial statement of policy is of value and desirable if announced in proper form, and this course was followed when the Goods Services Charges Tribunal was created. It seemed, however, that in a few cases Industrial Manpower Committees responded to views emanating from sources other than those contemplated by the enabling regulations. This does not seem to have arisen in the case of the other tribunals.

The Lewis Case

In what circumstances a member of an administrative tribunal should be removed from office was hotly debated in Parliament in 1946.[26] A practising lawyer, Lewis, had been appointed chairman of the Hamilton Land Sales Committee by the Governor-General in Council and held office during pleasure. Later the Minister of Lands wrote to him :

> ' On several occasions my attention has been drawn to press reports of the meetings and decisions of the Hamilton Land Sales Committee. I have asked for official reports and after considering them very carefully have reluctantly come to the conclusion that you are not rightly disposed to, nor have a true appreciation of, the principles which the Act seeks to apply. Moreover, on several occasions it would appear that your dealings with Crown officers and witnesses have been biased and unduly harsh.
>
> ' In view of these facts neither I nor the administration can have the confidence in your chairmanship that is necessary for the effective operation of the Act. As I do not want to create a situation that may cause you the slightest public embarrassment, I respectfully suggest that you tender your resignation from the Office of Chairman of the Hamilton Land Sales Committee.'

The Minister's action became the basis of a vote of no confidence in the Labour Government.

The Opposition contended that there had been political interference with a judicial officer, and that Lewis was being removed because the judgments of his committee did not suit the Government. They stressed that although the committee had handled about 4,800 cases, there had been no more than thirty-one appeals to the Land Sales Court. Although the committee was charged with consenting to transactions at excessive figures, yet in ten of the appeal cases the Land Sales Court had seen fit to increase the figures fixed by the committee. Of the appeals eleven had been lodged by the Crown, but in only one case did the Crown succeed in having the figure fixed by the committee reduced. These points were used to urge that the committee had functioned efficiently but that in any event the Crown if dissatisfied with a committee's decision could appeal. As Lewis, according to the Minister, had a bias against the Crown, and this was said to be common talk within the legal profession, the District Law Society had written to the solicitors practising in the district, most of whom replied. These replies declared that there was no foundation for the assertion that the chairman had shown any bias against Crown valuers. The Opposition in stressing the judicial character of the tribunal contended that a member should not be removed on

[26] N.Z. Parliamentary Debates, 3rd session, 1946, Nos. 6, 7, 8.

flimsy evidence and that it was essential that there be an impartial inquiry during which the member should be given full opportunity to answer the charges.

Speakers for the Government stressed that the Minister had a clear duty to see that the spirit of the legislation was applied and that there was no maladministration. Land Sales Committees were not judicial bodies in the ordinary sense but were quasi-judicial bodies exercising regulatory powers. The Prime Minister emphasised that the issue was simply whether the administrative action of the Minister was justified or not. According to another speaker, Lewis was asked to resign not because of one act but because of a series of acts which showed that he was no longer fit to hold office. Cases were discussed in detail, and charges emerged. In one case an application had been made to the committee for its consent to the transfer of one of the sections of a subdivision. When the case came before the committee the chairman decided to fix the basic price for all the sections. The Crown representative protested that the application concerned only one section, but after a heated discussion he was ordered to sit down. Other cases were quoted to show that Lewis had been unduly harsh with the Crown representative and with Crown witnesses. He had lightly treated the evidence submitted by the Crown and on occasion had denied the right of the Crown representative to call witnesses, address the committee, and cross-examine the witnesses for other parties. In one case at least he was alleged to have given a decision without consulting his colleagues on the committee. In another case Lewis in his capacity as solicitor for the applicant asked that the application should be dealt with by the other members without the need for a formal hearing. As the Crown representative objected to this procedure there was a formal hearing when the basic rent of the property was fixed at a figure substantially below that agreed upon by the parties. Under the legislation there was discretionary power to increase the basic value, but it was asserted that the committee had made excessive use of this provision. The fact that few appeals had been lodged was explained in part by the fact that the court had not been sitting for some months pending the appointment of a new judge. That so many lawyers came forward to defend Lewis, was merely a tribute to their professional solidarity.

In rejoinder the Opposition reminded the Government that it was the function of the tribunal to administer the law as it was written and that the tribunal was not concerned with the spirit of the legislation apart from its expression in the words of the statute. Lewis could give a satisfactory answer to each of the charges. He should have the same traditional immunity from political control as those who formed the ordinary judiciary. His action in proceeding to fix the basic value of all sections within a subdivision instead of confining himself to the one section was a common-sense procedure. Friction had been caused by the inexperience of the Crown representative. The evidence submitted by the Crown had not been disregarded but had been weighed in the judicial manner required by the Act. It was inconceivable that any decision would be made by the chairman alone, because the Act required that two members of a committee should concur and any failure here could easily be remedied. In the case where he was the applicant's solicitor, he had not sat as a member of the tribunal but had merely asked that the application should be dealt with by the other members without a formal hearing as was the procedure for most of the applications dealt with by Land Sales Committees. Lewis had already filed evidence by a valuer, but as this valuer had since died a formal hearing would have involved a fresh valuation with added expense. Furthermore this case was not decided until weeks after the Minister had taken action against Lewis.

If the facts were as stated by speakers for the Government, the Executive was clearly justified in proceeding with the removal of Lewis, but in the welter of charge and counter-charge and the conflicting versions of the various cases thrown into the debate it was impossible to elicit the facts. The Government when introducing the legislation in 1943 emphasised the judicial character of the machinery but in the Lewis debate the emphasis was changed. It was clear, however, that the Minister had been scrupulously careful not to interfere in individual cases. The Opposition maintained that Lewis as a judicial officer was entitled to the same traditional immunity as a stipendiary magistrate. Although Land Sales Committees performed their tasks by means of a judicial procedure, it is important to remember that there were several administrative features which distinguished them from the ordinary courts. A committee might before the hearing or during any adjournment exercise its powers of inquiry and investigation. The exercise of powers in this manner is not a normal judicial function, but it appears that for the most part committees with the encouragement of the court confined themselves to a consideration of the details given in a formal application before deciding whether to consent or to insist on a formal hearing. The Land Sales Court had power first to review of its own volition any decision of a Land Sales Committee and second to issue general directions to Land Sales Committees. Viewed from the angle of the ordinary courts these initiatory and administrative powers were unusual. Ordinarily to invoke the aid of a higher court, a party must appeal ; nor do we find an ordinary court giving general directions to be followed in future by inferior courts or tribunals. The justification for vesting these powers in the Land Sales Court was to give it adequate control over Land Sales Committees and so secure harmony and uniformity in their decisions throughout the Dominion. It is true that the Land Sales Court did not see fit to exercise these powers in the manner apparently intended by the legislature, but the fact that the provisions existed does make it clear that the analogy with the ordinary judiciary should not be pushed too far.

There was no doubt that the Executive had unrestricted legal power to remove Lewis. A similar power when vested in the President of the United States of America has been stated thus :

> ' The President need not have any reasons for such a removal ; if he has reasons they need not be good ones ; and he need not give the officer any opportunity to be heard or to answer charges. Neither explanation nor courtesy is required.'[27]

Lewis was given more courtesy than Governor Fitzroy gave Spain, a commissioner who was appointed to investigate and determine claims to land : in 1845 Fitzroy abruptly put an end to Spain's work by threatening to have him forcibly ejected from his office by the Commissioner of Public Works.[28] The political question however was whether the administrative steps taken in respect of Lewis were fair and justified, but as the surrounding facts were not satisfactorily proved there is little point in carrying the discussion much further.

The standard of behaviour demanded of a member of a tribunal and the extent to which a government could determine the policy of a tribunal were two issues which became intertwined and confused in the debate. If the policy of a tribunal is to be determined from time to time by a government in the manner contemplated by some of the speakers, then it is necessary that Parliament should so provide and such determinations should be publicly declared in formal communications to a tribunal.

Contribution to Legal Development

The law which controls administrative tribunals is not as significant as the law which they make. Operating as they do in a variety of fields and sometimes at different points in the same field, the sum total of their contribution to legal development is apt to be underestimated. Mere enumeration of the quantum of their decisions would be impressive enough, but the radiations of these decisions are often no less significant. Standards are evolved which are more difficult to apply than rules because of the greater discretionary element inherent in a standard.

The influence of the Land Sales Court on valuation methods was an interesting illustration of the evolution of standards. The court had to determine from the expert evidence of valuers the basic value of a particular property. The primary step was to settle the market value of the property as at December, 1942. Valuers varied considerably in the methods they used in arriving at their valuation of improvements

---

[27] Cushman, *The Independent Regulatory Commissions*, p. 466.
[28] R. L. Jellicoe, *The New Zealand Company's Native Reserves*, p. 46.

and while this continued, the work of the tribunals was protracted and made more difficult.

Standards were ultimately formulated for the valuation of both farm and urban property. They were elastic enough to meet features which might be peculiar to a particular case. The rigidity of a legal rule was avoided, yet there was some restraint on the adoption of too empirical an approach.

For a detailed illustration it will suffice to discuss the standard that was evolved for the valuation of urban property. It was considered desirable that there be a common basis for assessing value. Normally the cost of building a house bears a close relation to its value. The object, therefore, was to ascertain what an average house would have cost to build in December, 1942. Evidence as to contract prices of dwellings erected at this date was given by some valuers and an average cost ascertained in terms of area of floor space. However, this method was not entirely reliable owing to the wide variations in design, size and quality of the houses under consideration, and, to ensure greater accuracy, there was evolved a formula for a standard house. This house was deemed to be one of good design, built of particular materials and containing the number of rooms and amenities of the average modern home.

Plans and specifications of the standard house were prepared and an accurate estimate of its cost in labour and materials as at December, 1942, was made. When an actual house had to be valued for the purpose of the Act, valuers would compare it with the standard house and make adjustments for any variations in design, size and quality. This method had the approval of the Land Sales Court and was generally adopted by valuers with the result that for the purposes of the Act a common standard for the valuation of houses was achieved.

Judicial Control

In the words of Sir Michael Myers, the ordinary courts are the guardians of the rights and liberties of the subject, and it is their duty to see that justice is done between man and man and between King and subject.[29] The control exercised by the Supreme Court over all inferior courts and over all persons or tribunals exercising judicial or quasi-judicial functions which affect the rights of subjects is, to use the words of Sir John Salmond, an essential point of civil freedom and public policy.[30] Another judge in approving this statement has stressed that the controlling authority is for the purpose of keeping all such tribunals within the scope of their appointed jurisdiction : it is vital to the liberties

[29] *Journal of Public Administration* (N.Z.), Vol. 3, No. 2, p. 45.
[30] *N.Z. Waterside Workers' Federation* v. *Frazer* [1924] N.Z.L.R. 689, 703.

and rights of the subject that the power of control should be jealously guarded and freely used.[31]

The citizen may do as he pleases providing he does not infringe the law. The public official, however, may do only what is authorised by legislation or by some rule of common law. Tactically he is in a worse position than the citizen. The general rule is that a decision of an administrative tribunal can be upset if it has exceeded its jurisdiction or if it has acted contrary to the principles of natural justice. ' Natural justice ' is used here in a technical sense and refers to procedural aspects such as the insistence on a fair hearing and the giving of reasonable notice.

The control exercised by the Supreme Court is administrative in essence, and the remedies take the form of orders. A writ of prohibition may issue to prevent an administrative tribunal from dealing with a matter beyond its jurisdiction. Where, however, the administrative tribunal has already exceeded its jurisdiction, the appropriate remedy is a writ of certiorari. ' Prohibition goes to prevent the doing of a judicial act which would be beyond the jurisdiction of the inferior court ; certiorari goes to quash and declare invalid a judicial act already done in excess of that jurisdiction.'[32] A writ of mandamus may issue to compel an administrative tribunal to perform a duty which is cast upon it by the law. An injunction can be granted to restrain a public official or tribunal from proceeding on a particular course. The cases in which these remedies have been granted range over a wide field of administrative activity.

The jurisdiction of Land Sales Committees and of the Land Sales Court was examined by the Supreme Court in a case [33] that came before it in 1946. The defendant had agreed to purchase a property subject to the consent of the Land Sales Court. His application for the consent of the Land Sales Court was made by letter, which omitted some of the particulars required, and which was not verified by the prescribed statutory declaration. The Supreme Court held that the jurisdiction of the Land Sales Court and Land Sales Committees was founded on an application for consent which had to be in substantial compliance with the provisions of the Act. The omission from the application of the verifying statutory declaration was fatal to the jurisdiction of the tribunal, and it was not within the power of the tribunal to cure such a defect. The court held that the tribunal could be restrained. The appropriate remedy was a writ of prohibition, as the application had not been formally heard by the committee. The same case also illustrated one possible application of the remedy of mandamus. The plaintiff no longer wished to treat with the defendant but as he feared that the Land Sales

[31] *Boyes* v. *Carlyon* [1939] N.Z.L.R. 504, 516, 517.
[32] *N.Z. Waterside Workers' Federation* v. *Frazer* [1924] N.Z.L.R. 689, 709.
[33] *Ryan* v. *Evans* [1946] N.Z.L.R. 75.

Committee might refuse to hear an application arising from a transaction with a fresh party, he sought a writ of mandamus to compel the committee to deal with a new application. The Chief Justice, however, thought it unnecessary to consider this question as the committee, in view of the decision already reached by the court, would doubtless hear such an application provided it was regular in form. If the committee, however, later failed in this respect, a writ of mandamus could doubtless issue to compel the committee to take the preliminary step of hearing an application, but such a writ could not fetter, for instance, the discretion of the committee in settling the basic value of the property for the purposes of the sale.

The use of certiorari was well illustrated in the interesting case of *Boyes* v. *Carlyon*, decided in 1939.[34] Carlyon as Chief Police Officer in the Cook Islands entered under a search warrant the office of Smith, the Resident Commissioner of the Cook Islands Administration, and seized papers relating to pending litigation. The Resident Commissioner was then the Acting Chief Judge. Carlyon's reason for this extreme step was his view that there might be a miscarriage of justice owing to the manner in which the Acting Chief Judge was conducting criminal trials. Next day Smith in his capacity as Resident Commissioner suspended Carlyon and gave him notice that he would be charged with insubordination. Boyes, one of the joint Public Service Commissioners, travelled from New Zealand, a distance of 1,600 miles, and on the morning of his arrival at Rarotonga, held a formal inquiry under the provisions of the Public Service amendment Act, 1927, which makes provision for the investigation of complaints and charges against officers. Witnesses may be summoned and examined upon oath. As the result of an investigation penalties ranging up to dismissal may be imposed by the Commissioner. There is the important provision that at any inquiry or investigation the officer shall be entitled to be represented by counsel or agent.

There were differing versions as to what happened at the opening of the inquiry, but when the case was dealt with in the Supreme Court Mr. Justice Reed held on the evidence that Carlyon claimed the right to get legal advice and representation but Boyes proceeded with the inquiry despite the protest. There were no legal practitioners at Rarotonga, and it would have been necessary for Carlyon to bring counsel from New Zealand. Carlyon had received notice of the charges and of the probable date and place of hearing more than eighteen days prior to the actual day of the hearing. As a result of the hearing the Commissioner found Carlyon guilty of the charges and ordered the deduction of a week's salary and his transfer to New Zealand.

[34] *Boyes* v. *Carlyon* [1939] N.Z.L.R. 504.

The Court of Appeal decided in favour of Carlyon on the ground that he had been denied the right to be represented by counsel or agent. The Chief Justice, Sir Michael Myers, in delivering one of the judgments said :

> ' I cannot help thinking that, where Parliament propounds a scheme such as is contained in section 11 of the Public Service Amendment Act, 1927, and as part of that scheme expressly confers upon the person whose conduct is being inquired into the right of being represented by counsel or agent, such a right is conferred for the express purpose not only of having justice done but of enabling the members of that large body of persons comprised in the public service and affected by the Act to see for themselves that everything that is done bears the appearance of justice. Where such a right is expressly conferred and an inquiry is so conducted as that the right cannot be exercised, then I cannot help thinking that there has been a denial of justice. And if there has been a denial of justice and the court is not embarrassed by any statutory enactment taking away certiorari then in my opinion certiorari should go. . . .
>
> ' I cannot see that a person whose conduct is being inquired into under section 11 of the Public Service Amendment Act, 1927, can be said to have had " a full, free, fair and ample hearing " where he has been denied in connection with the inquiry a right which Parliament has expressly conferred upon him. The provision in the statute is a special one enacted by Parliament for the protection of the person affected and to ensure that he may have the assistance of counsel or agent if he desires. If then he is prevented by the tribunal from exercising his statutory right it seems to me that there is a denial of that justice which Parliament itself has prescribed.'

The Crown asserted that certiorari was not appropriate because the commissioner was acting administratively and not judicially. The Court of Appeal, however, had no difficulty in saying that the commissioner, although for the most part an administrative officer was acting judicially when conducting an inquiry of this nature.

The case illustrated yet another rule applicable to remedies of this type. Even when it was established that the commissioner had failed to follow the proper procedure, it was still within the discretion of the court not to issue a writ of certiorari. In exercising its discretion, the court was entitled to examine all the facts of the case, including the conduct of Carlyon. For instance, he might have been slow in bringing proceedings or he might have acquiesced in the irregularity. Neither point was proved against Carlyon nor was there anything else of such a character as to disentitle Carlyon to the writ.

Even though an administrative tribunal has acted judicially there may be circumstances where a writ of certiorari is not available. In 1910 a case came before the court where a public servant, Reynolds, sought relief.[35]   A Board of Inquiry had been set up by the Governor in Council to inquire into a charge of misconduct. The Board was held to be a quasi-judicial body and its report to the Governor was in the nature of a judgment because it was a condition precedent to the power of the Governor in Council to dismiss a civil servant. If the Board exceeded its jurisdiction in conducting the inquiry, it could be controlled by certiorari. This remedy, however, was refused on the ground that the application was too late. The Board had discharged its functions and the report had gone on its way. The Governor, whether acting alone or in Council, could not be reached by judicial process.

The writ of certiorari has been used by the Supreme Court for the purpose of examining whether an industrial award of the Court of Arbitration has been made in excess of authority. Although the writ applies to judicial acts and not to the exercise of administrative or legislative authority, the court has held that the writ applies where administrative or legislative powers have to be exercised through a procedure judicial in form. Sir John Salmond's reasoning on this point is :

> ' An industrial award is in form a judicial decree, but in substance it is an act of legislative authority. It is the establishment of a set of authoritative rules regulating an industry and determining not the present rights and obligations of litigants, but the future relations and mutual rights and obligations of all persons who thereafter during the currency of the award choose to enter into contractual relations with each other as employers and employed in that industry. This is the substance but in point of form and in respect of procedure by which this legislative authority is exercised the process is judicial, and the authority is vested in a Court of Judicature. . . .
> ' How is this distinction to be applied to an act which is judicial in form and procedure but legislative in substance and effect ? For the purpose of certiorari an industrial award must be taken to be what it professes to be, namely the exercise of judicial authority by a Court of Judicature.'[36]

The general rule is that mandamus will not lie against the Crown, but it will lie against a Minister or other servant where a statute imposes on him a duty to the public or to a member of the public. Whether there is in fact such a duty is a question of interpretation. In the *Jorgensen Case* decided in 1931 the Minister of Customs had declined to grant plaintiff's application for a brewer's licence, and contended that he had an absolute and unfettered discretion. The court, however, rejected the Minister's contention and held that he must grant an application which complied with the statutory provisions and regulations.[37] In the same year the Minister of Customs was involved in another case, but here the plaintiff failed to show that there had been a breach by the Minister of a legal

---

[35] *Reynolds* v. *Att.-Gen.* (1909) 29 N.Z.L.R. 24.
[36] *N.Z. Waterside Workers' Federation* v. *Frazer* [1924] N.Z.L.R. 689, 709, 710.
[37] *Jorgensen* v. *Minister of Customs* [1931] N.Z.L.R. 127.

duty. The plaintiff had applied for a licence to distil but he did not forward plans of a building already completed and equipped. It was held that the Distillation Act, 1908, contemplated that there would be such a building available for inspection and that a licence would issue when an inspection showed that the Act had been fully complied with. Until the premises were completed, there was nothing that the court could by mandamus compel the Minister to do in relation to the issue of a licence.[38]

Mandamus has gone to compel a Land Board to fulfil its original decision to grant leases of Crown lands to certain applicants. Once the Board and the Minister had reached a decision in terms of the governing legislation, the decision was binding and the Board was obliged to execute the leases in terms of the decision. The Board and the Minister up to the point of decision had an absolute discretion but once this discretion had been exercised the Board had no other course but to execute leases in accordance with the decision. Discretion no longer existed and mandamus was thus the appropriate remedy to ensure that the Board completed its part of the bargain. An exception to this would arise if the court took the view that what purported to be a decision was so extravagant as not to be an honest exercise of the Board's authority.[39] In another case mandamus has issued to compel the Transport Appeal Authority to exercise his jurisdiction and hear an appeal, which he had declined to do because of a misconception as to the law.[40] Again, mandamus has issued to compel an official to grant an exhibitor's licence under the Cinematograph Films Act, 1928, where the applicant had complied with the provisions of that Act and the regulations made under it.[41]

Mandamus is issued to ensure that some positive step required by law is taken but injunction is used to restrain a person from taking a particular step which is contrary to law. In one case decided in 1922 the Minister of Education proposed to hold an inquiry into charges of disloyalty and insubordination made against a teacher. At the hearing it was contended that the Education Act was merely a skeleton form of legislation which had been left to be filled up by regulations. On this view the Minister had the executive power under the regulations to hold the inquiry and cancel or suspend the teacher's certificate. The court held, however, that the regulation was *ultra vires* and granted an injunction.[42]

Modern legislation contains many illustrations of attempts to limit the power of the Supreme Court to control administrative tribunals.

[38] *Smerle* v. *Minister of Customs* [1931] N.Z.L.R. 938.
[39] *McKellar* v. *Otago Land Board* (1908) 27 N.Z.L.R. 811, 829.
[40] *King* v. *Frazer* [1945] N.Z.L.R. 175.
[41] *Kerridge* v. *Girling-Butcher* [1933] N.Z.L.R. 646.
[42] *Park* v. *Minister of Education* [1922] N.Z.L.R. 1208.

For instance, there is the following provision for the Court of Arbitration :

> ' Proceedings in the court shall not be impeached or held bad for want of form, nor shall the same be removable to any court by certiorari or otherwise ; and no award, order, or proceeding of the court shall be liable to be challenged, appealed from, reviewed, quashed, or called in question by any Court of Judicature on any account whatsoever.'[43]

As to the Land Sales Court, the Act provided :

> ' Proceedings before the court shall not be held bad for want of form. No appeal shall lie from any order of the court, and no proceeding or order as aforesaid shall be liable to be challenged, removed, quashed, or called in question in any court.'[44]

A somewhat similar provision existed for a Land Sales Committee which, however, was made subject to the controlling jurisdiction of the Land Sales Court. Statute provided that the decisions of the Transport Appeal Authority were not subject to proceedings in other courts except upon the ground of lack of jurisdiction.[45] It was provided in the case of the Special Tribunal, a wartime tribunal controlling conscientious objectors, that there could be no appeal from its decisions and no other method of attack except for want of jurisdiction.[46] A similar provision covered the Revision Authorities which dealt with the applications of military defaulters for release on parole.[47]

Provisions of this type are not construed as widely as the words might suggest. Obviously the Supreme Court must give some meaning to statutory provisions of this type, but it will tend to give a meaning which least impairs its controlling power. To oust the controlling power of the Supreme Court, Parliament, in the strong words of Salmond, would have to use language so clear and coercive as to be incapable of any other meaning. The very wide provision covering the Court of Arbitration came up for interpretation by the Full Court in 1924. It was contended that this provision gave the Court of Arbitration unrestricted power to fix the limits of its own jurisdiction, and that its determination of such a question, even if wrong in law, could not be examined by the Supreme Court. This contention was rejected. Sir John Salmond in his judgment held that the provision did not confer on the Court of Arbitration an uncontrolled authority to do as it thought fit : an award, order, or proceeding was protected from examination *only if it were within the jurisdiction of the Court of Arbitration.* In Sir John Salmond's view, to admit the truth of the contention would produce an extraordinary result.

[43] Industrial Conciliation and Arbitration Act 1925, s. 97.
[44] Servicemen's Settlement and Land Sales Act 1943, s. 15.
[45] Statutes Amendment Act 1941, s. 86 (4).
[46] National Service Emergency Regulations 1940, Amendment No. 5, 4A, (8).
[47] National Service Emergency Regulations 1940, Amendment No. 17, 43 (9).

The Arbitration Court would possess uncontrolled authority to make in any matter whatever, such orders and awards as it thought fit. It could disregard the limits of its jurisdiction, infringe the jurisdiction of other courts, and violate the law of the land ; yet all orders and awards so illegally made would have to be acted upon as valid by the ordinary courts. It was settled law that the taking-away of certiorari did not extend to cases where there was want or excess of jurisdiction. The orders, convictions or judgments protected were only those which were within the jurisdiction of the court which made them. Were it not for this protection, the proceedings of the inferior court or tribunal could be examined in respect of errors appearing on the face of them or for the purpose of removing those proceedings for trial and adjudication in the superior court. The section meant merely that so long as the Court of Arbitration kept within the limits of its jurisdiction, its proceedings and judicial acts within those limits were not subject to examination, question, or control by any other court, whether on the ground of error of law or fact, irregularity of procedure, defect of form or substance, or any other ground whatever.[48] If the Court of Arbitration exceeds its powers either through a misconception as to the law or as to a question of fact which is basic to its jurisdiction, then it can be checked by the Supreme Court. For instance, in 1937 the Court of Appeal decided that an award embracing clerical workers was made *without jurisdiction*, and certiorari was granted.[49]

The same principle was discussed in the case of *Boyes* v. *Carlyon*, *supra*. If the Public Service Act had provided that the decision of the commissioner was final and that no writ of mandamus, prohibition or certiorari could lie to any court, the commissioner would have been in a stronger position. In that event Carlyon, according to the Chief Justice, would not have succeeded in his proceedings for certiorari unless he had shown that the commissioner had acted ' altogether without jurisdiction '.[50] The Land Sales Court itself recognised the controlling jurisdiction of the Supreme Court. A Land Sales Committee had attempted to compel a vendor to accept a purchaser selected by the Committee. It was held by the Land Sales Court that a power of such novelty and far-reaching effect would be a serious invasion of private rights and would need to be clearly conferred by legislation ; until it was so conferred the Supreme Court could doubtless interfere by certiorari.[51] As has been seen earlier in another case, the Supreme Court held that the jurisdiction of a Land Sales Committee was founded on an application for consent, which must at least be in substantial compliance

[48] *N.Z. Waterside Workers' Federation* v. *Frazer* [1924] N.Z.L.R. 689, 701, 702, 703.
[49] *Re Otago Clerical Workers' Award* [1937] N.Z.L.R. 578.
[50] *Boyes* v. *Carlyon* [1939] N.Z.L.R. 504, 510.
[51] *Re a proposed sale : Giles to Burns* [1946] N.Z.L.R. 260.

with the Act. The omission from such an application of the prescribed verifying declaration was fatal to the jurisdiction of a committee, notwithstanding the protective section.[52]

General Observations

On the whole administrative tribunals have proved equal to the tasks which were imposed on them during and since the war. Although the black market in urban property reached a scale which even the dogs in the street noticed, this was not a reflection on the work of Land Sales Committees. Lord Byron once said in irony that the Luddites could be repressed with the aid of a Judge Jeffreys and a jury of twelve butchers. Failing such measures, there is little left but to reflect on how far legislation should go in advance of the socio-ethical standard of the community.

Most of these administrative tribunals in their framework, powers, and procedure are fashioned on a broad pattern evolved from experience. History gives many illustrations of new agencies which thrived for a time and were later absorbed into the orthodox judicial system, but there is nothing to suggest that a similar fate awaits the New Zealand administrative tribunal of today. On the other hand we do not see administrative tribunals merging into the administrative organisation of the ordinary Government Department. Their existence is possibly a reflection on both the judiciary and the ordinary Government Department. In contrast with the ordinary courts the administrative tribunal can be recruited from specialists who are fully acquainted with the particular sphere which is the subject of the legislation and who can maintain greater continuity in policy. A simplified procedure makes for speed and cheapness. On the other hand, although there are outstanding exceptions arising from the standing and quality of the personnel, administrative tribunals tend in practice to be less independent than the ordinary courts and display a lower standard of objectivity and impartiaᴋty.

According to one English writer [53] the trend away from the ordinary courts and from the use of lawyers on administrative tribunals will depend mainly on two related factors :

(1) On the extent to which public opinion continues to regard impartiality based on independence and absence of any prior knowledge of the facts as preferable to a specialist's familiarity with the problem and its implications ; and

(2) on the extent to which the outlook of the judiciary lags behind public opinion.

Although the recruitment of lawyers has obvious advantages in the case of some tribunals, for instance the Land Sales Tribunals, it is doubtful

[52] *Ryan* v. *Evans* [1946] N.Z.L.R. 75.
[53] L. C. B. Gower, *Modern Law Review* (England), Vol. 9, No. 3, p. 214.

whether they are best suited for the handling of complex economic issues. The lawyer who has an intimate understanding of the working of economic forces is a *rara avis*, but in such a class was the late Sir Francis Frazer, who brought to his task an honours degree in economics in addition to his legal qualifications and who had both administrative and judicial experience. He acted as the Transport Appeal Authority, the Industrial Efficiency Appeal Authority and the Sea-Fisheries Appeal Authority. He was also chairman of the Goods Services Charges Tribunal and the War Pensions Appeal Board.

The Tariff Commission of 1933 dealt with the question whether there should be an appeal to the ordinary courts on technical matters.[54] Section 20 of the Customs Amendment Act, 1921, provided:

> ' Where any dispute arises as to the true meaning and application of any terms used in the Tariff and therein printed in italics, the Minister may determine such dispute in such manner as appears to him just, and his decision thereon shall be final.'

This section was criticised by some importers who suggested that it be amended to provide a right of appeal from the Minister to the court. The commission said: ' The evidence did not convince us that the complaints in this connection were of a serious nature. Very few specific grievances were referred to by witnesses, and they appeared to be unimportant. The main grievance appears to arise in connection with the classification of goods under the tariff headings, and with the fact that appeals do not lie from these classifications.

' In our opinion the present law and practice are in the public interest, and should stand unaltered. It will be appreciated that, with the multiplicity of tariff items, and the infinitely greater multiplicity of commodities imported, the tasks of classification are difficult and complex, demand a highly technical knowledge of various commodities which can be acquired only by considerable experience, and are not matters upon which Supreme Court judges are specially qualified by experience and training to adjudicate, and upon which we are inclined to think they would be unwilling to be asked to adjudicate. Most of the questions over which real difficulty arises involve rather fine distinctions, and for the purpose of satisfactory administration require to be settled expeditiously. The Supreme Court, if this class of case were forced upon it, would have no precedents arising out of its own experience for its guidance, and would presumably have to decide the issue on the basis of hearing a number of witnesses on both sides. This would cause very considerable delay, and possibly considerable trouble through conflicting decisions by different judges, because the questions at issue are in the main matters of fact and not of law. It might congest the work of the Supreme Court, cause considerable uncertainty in Customs administration, and make the tariff difficult of consistent

[54] Appendices to Journals of H. of R. 1934, H.-28, (f) (4).

and expeditious administration. Incidentally, especially if appeals on points of classification went beyond the Supreme Court, the situation thus created might in some instances be ridiculous. The present procedure is likely to give a much more expeditious and satisfactory decision on matters of Customs classification than the Law Courts of the land. The suggestion that the Minister, in exercising his discretion under the Act, is acting as judge in his own case is a travesty of the situation. The Minister is not judging his own case, but acting as arbiter between the community as a whole and the importer, and, after taking the advice of his responsible officers, is a much more competent arbiter for this class of problem than any lay tribunal possibly could be.'

It is doubtful whether the ordinary courts are the best fitted to pass upon the determinations of modern administrative tribunals. The experience of recent years indicates that very few of the decisions of these tribunals are attacked in the ordinary courts. This does not necessarily prove a high standard of performance on the part of the tribunals. In some instances the justice was rough, and there were disquieting features present on occasion, which could have been removed had there been an inexpensive and speedy means of appeal to a higher body on the merits of a decision. One of the great weaknesses has been the empirical manner in which these tribunals have been created. Perhaps this is not so serious if a high standard is set in the appointment of persons to these tribunals or if, as with a few of the tribunals, such as the War Pensions Boards, there is a right of appeal to a higher administrative tribunal.

In the long run a final administrative court to hear appeals from all or most administrative tribunals would possibly provide a desirable apex for the administrative tribunal system. A prerequisite would be a good deal of reorganisation of administrative tribunals designed to produce more uniformity in their structure, powers, and procedures. The attainment of the prerequisite would be a major hurdle in itself. However, in recent years there have been some desirable trends. First, we have noted that for a few of the tribunals there is already a right of appeal to a higher administrative tribunal. Second, the same person may be the appellate authority for a number of administrative tribunals of various types. Third, the creation of the Land Valuation Court is of interest for it represents an attempt to give to one appeal authority a number of appellate functions connected with the one subject-matter, namely the valuation of land. These and other similar trends should be allowed to run freely for a further period because they would help to provide a more positive answer to the question whether or not a final administrative court should be constituted. They would also help in determining how such a court should be organised and the type of person that should be chosen for the court. For these reasons there is little to be gained by the creation of a final administrative court at this particular stage of our development.

There is something to be said for a wider adoption of the principle that administrative tribunals should give reasoned grounds for their decisions, enunciate the principles they are following, and facilitate the publication of their decisions. A few of the tribunals maintain a good standard in these respects. The advantages are obvious. The public tend to have greater confidence in the tribunals, which in turn are encouraged to attain consistency in their work. At the same time a fund of data is provided for use by other tribunals when faced with analogous situations.

Although the administrative tribunal is usually less independent than the ordinary court, it has more independence than the Government Department. Public confidence in the administration of controversial legislation is fostered if the work is entrusted to an administrative tribunal rather than to a Government Department. Furthermore, where the State adds to its regulatory functions it may be desirable for the interests affected to have a voice in the administration of the new policy, or it may be necessary to recruit these tribunals from outside the public service because the service lacks specialists of the type required. If the latter is true it may be an indictment of training policy in the public service, particularly when the trend could have been foreseen. In so far as this recruitment depends on the need to obtain impartiality it may also contain a reflection on the quality of personnel in the public service. A judicial attitude but without the impediment of legalism is required at many points in administration, and can be developed within Departments even though in the ultimate they are subject to political control. It is better that this quality should be developed from within than that it should be imposed from without by the ordinary courts or by legislation. The virtue of the *droit administratif* is that it evolved as a mode of self-discipline within the French administration itself. For this country something of the spirit of the Conseil D'État is required. By meeting these demands the public service can reduce the need for the creation of administrative tribunals, but it is apparent that tribunals of this type will continue to be appointed on other grounds. In times of crisis such as war it may be the essence of wisdom to enlist the aid of citizens in the country's administration. It eases the burden on the civil service when the call on manpower is acute and at the same time gives an outlet for public energy and thus promotes a more healthy spirit in a democracy.

PROCEEDINGS AGAINST THE CROWN

Early in the history of New Zealand there was a swing against the historic rules of the common law that the Crown could not be sued in its own courts, and that the Crown could do no wrong. These rules were limited in their operation so long as the State confined itself to such functions as the defence of the realm and the maintenance of law and order, but they imposed hardship as soon as the modern State appeared with its armoury of social and economic powers. For practical purposes they ceased to be of importance in New Zealand when the Crown Proceedings Act, 1950, came into force on January 1, 1952.

Apart from statute the position at common law was that a servant of the Crown who committed a civil wrong could be sued personally even though the Crown itself could not be sued, but that a servant of the Crown did not become personally liable under a contract, unless he expressly made himself liable. In the course of its evolution the common law gave the subject a method of proceeding by petition of right against the Crown for the recovery of property and money, where he would have had a remedy except for the fact that the defendant was the Crown. This remedy applied to cases of breach of contract, but the common law gave no effective remedy against the Crown in tort.

The legislative approach in New Zealand was to adopt from the common law the remedy of petition of right and gradually to widen its scope. By the Crown Redress Act, 1871, the subject could proceed against the Crown under a contract made with the authority of the Colonial Government. There was, however, an express restriction : the subject could not proceed against the Crown either for the performance of a contract for the sale of any lands of the Crown or for damages for breach of any such contract. By later legislation in the seventies, the subject was conceded a remedy for a limited class of civil wrongs. The Crown Suits Act, 1881, which was largely a consolidation of the earlier legislation, provided that a subject could proceed against the Crown in cases where he would have had a remedy if the defendant had been a fellow subject, and the cause of action fell within one of these categories :

(*a*) breach of contract ;
(*b*) wrong or damage, which was independent of contract, and which arose from a public work.

'Public work' was defined as meaning any railway, tramway, road, bridge, electric telegraph, or other work of a like nature which was used by the Government or constructed by the Government out of moneys voted by Parliament, and whose revenues formed part of the general revenue of the Colony.

The decade prior to the introduction of the 1881 Bill had seen a rapid increase in the range and intensity of State activity including the construction of railways, roads and other public works and the creation of trading departments. The Bill when first introduced contained a proviso protecting the Crown from proceedings under a contract respecting land held by the Crown. Despite the strong efforts of the Attorney-General, Parliament was in no mood to conserve the position of the Crown and the proviso was dropped.

The Crown Suits Amendment Act, 1910, expanded the limited class of civil wrongs and enacted that a petition of right could be filed for :

(*a*) breach of contract ;

(*b*) any cause of action for which a petition would lie at common law ; and

(*c*) any other injury which would give rise to an action between private persons.

During the passage of this legislation the Attorney-General stressed that the State had extended its operations widely and that in these circumstances it was reasonable that the Crown should accept the same risks as private enterprise. The Act, however, imposed some important restrictions. The Crown could not be made liable under the head of employer's liability for the acts or defaults of the Governor-General, a judge, magistrate, justice of the peace, or other judicial officer. The category of wrongs or injuries was limited : under the Act the Crown could not be sued for assault, false imprisonment, malicious prosecution or erroneous judicial process. Libel and slander were excluded, as was any action where malicious motive was an essential element. The Crown, however, was bound by the Deaths by Accidents Compensation Act, which gave the deceased's relatives a remedy where negligence was the cause of death. The 1910 Act placed a limit of £2,000 on any amount which could be recovered in this way, but this limit was removed in 1943.

A person who had a claim or demand against the Crown within the legislation could set forth details in a petition to be filed in the court. No petition could be filed in the court unless one month's prior notice in writing had been given to a Law Officer. The notice had to state explicitly the claim or demand, the nature of the relief sought and the office of the court in which it was intended to file the petition. The proceedings on a petition were conducted in the same manner and with almost the same rules of practice as applied to an ordinary action between subject and subject. The court gave such decision as it would give in any action between subject and subject and similarly there was a right of appeal. If the decision was against the Crown, the registrar gave the petitioner a certificate in the prescribed form. On receipt of the certificate the Governor-General might cause to be paid, out of any money specially appropriated by Parliament to that purpose, such damages as were awarded to the petitioner, together with any costs allowed him by the court, and might also perform any decree or order pronounced or made by the court.

Despite this legislation the subject in New Zealand was still at a disadvantage in some respects. In an action by the Crown the defendant could not launch a counterclaim as he could where the plaintiff was not the Crown. A subject proceeding by way of petition could not obtain an order against the Crown for the production of documents, nor could he have another defendant joined with the Crown. The Law Officer had the right to select the place of trial. If the subject was successful in his petition, interest did not run on the amount of the judgment, with ensuing hardship to the subject if there was delay in meeting the judgment : in one case because the Crown saw fit to contest a judgment right up to the Privy Council, it was almost three years before the judgment was met.[55] There was no procedure for the enforcement of a judgment. A judgment on a petition of right had no coercive operation.[56] It was not capable of execution. It was merely a declaration by the court as to the liabilities of the Crown. It rested with Parliament to say whether or not any sum found by the court to be payable should be paid.

A party may be estopped by his conduct from denying the truth of some evidence, but this rule did not apply to the Crown. Nor could the Crown be prejudiced by the ineptness of its servants. This was illustrated in litigation between the Crown and the City of Wellington in 1896.[57] It was provided that the Governor could grant a certain piece of land to the Corporation for use as a public street subject to conditions. It was held that if it were proved that the Corporation had erected unlawful structures on the land, the rights of the Crown would not be prejudiced merely because its servants stood by and allowed the structures to be erected without question. Moreover, the Crown's claim in one capacity could not be offset by any sum which it might owe in another capacity. Nor could the Crown be compelled, as a subject can be, to give security for costs before proceeding with an appeal : such a requirement was held to be inconsistent with the principle that even when judgment was given against the Crown, payment was still within the discretion of the Crown.[58]

The Crown Proceedings Act, 1950, goes a long way towards bringing the procedure in actions by or against the Crown into line with the procedure in actions between subjects. We have seen that New Zealand early gave the subject a remedy for a limited class of civil wrongs, but the similarly named English Act of 1947 was a stimulus for the assumption by the Crown in New Zealand of a much wider liability in tort. The English Act served as a basis for many of the provisions of the New Zealand Act. The petition of right as a form of procedure for the aggrieved subject is abolished as is a variety of writs which were available only to the Crown. The Crown cannot now proceed by way of informations in civil suits unless such proceedings are expressly authorised by any Act. A number of important enactments which hitherto did not bind the Crown are made binding on the Crown.

---

[55] Broad v. The King [1916] N.Z.L.R. 609.
[56] Rayner v. The King [1930] N.Z.L.R. 441, 457, 458.
[57] The Queen v. The Mayor, Councillors and Citizens of City of Wellington (1896), 15 N.Z.L.R. 72.
[58] Broad v. The King [1916] N.Z.L.R. 609.

The general principle is that any person as of right may take civil proceedings against the Crown to enforce any claim against the Crown in respect of any of the following causes of action :

(*a*) the breach of any contract or trust ;

(*b*) any wrong or injury in the nature of a tort ;

(*c*) any cause of action founded on any Act ;

(*d*) any cause of action for which an action lies for damages or to recover property ; and

(*e*) any other cause of action in respect of which a petition of right would lie against the Crown at common law or in respect of which relief would be granted against the Crown in equity.

The Act thus covers practically the whole field of civil proceedings. It treats the Crown as a private person of full age and capacity for the purpose of liability in respect of certain defined torts. First of all, the Crown assumes liability for torts committed by its servants or agents including independent contractors. Second, the Crown assumes the liability of an ordinary employer for any breach of those duties which an employer at common law owes to his servants or agents. Third, it assumes liability for any breach of duties attaching at common law to the ownership, occupation, possession, or control of property. The Crown also assumes liability in tort for failure to comply with a statutory duty where the relative statute that binds it to perform that duty similarly binds persons other than the Crown and its officers. It will be seen that the Crown's liability in tort has been considerably extended and that remedies for such torts as assault, libel, and slander are not excluded. There are, however, provisions in other Acts which still confer immunity on the Crown and its officers. The Act itself makes it clear that proceedings cannot be taken against the Crown in respect of '. . . anything done or omitted to be done by any person while discharging or purporting to discharge any responsibilities of a judicial nature vested in him, or any responsibilities which he has in connection with the execution of judicial process '.

Where any servant or agent of the Crown with its authority infringes a patent, a registered trade-mark or any copyright in a design, civil proceedings may be taken against the Crown.

Where a subject is bringing an action against the Crown in respect of a statutory or other public duty, it is still necessary for him to give prior notice of the proposed action and of the circumstances upon which it is based.

It is not possible to obtain an injunction against the Crown or an order for specific performance, but the court may make orders declaratory of the rights of the parties.

The Crown may be required to answer interrogatories or make disclosure of documents to the same extent as a subject except where to answer any question or to disclose any document would be injurious to the public interest. A person sued by the Crown now has the same rights in regard to counterclaim or set-off as he would have if the proceedings were taken by another person, but rules may be made to exclude any question of a set-off or counterclaim in respect of taxes, duties, or penalties.

The ordinary rules as to interest on judgment debts and as to costs are made to apply to the Crown. The Crown, however, is still not required to give security for costs, this being regarded as unnecessary. A special procedure is defined for the satisfaction of judgments against the Crown. Judgments may be satisfied by the Governor-General without further appropriation than the section in the Act and an annual statement is to be laid before Parliament showing all amounts paid in this manner.

CHAPTER 5

SOCIAL LEGISLATION

FOR its era the old-age pension scheme of 1898 was an important piece of legislation attracting widespread interest beyond New Zealand. Less spectacular but no less important has been legislation designed to promote the welfare of children and to improve standards of health. The impetus for much of the legislation dealing with education and health has come from the failure or inability of voluntary bodies to provide a universal service of a satisfactory standard.

In 1872 the first comprehensive measure dealing with public health was passed and considering the period it was noteworthy for the extensive powers taken to interfere with the liberty and property of the subject in the interests of public health. Fear of disease was the driving force here. In 1877 the principle of free, secular and compulsory education was introduced. Although there was coercion in this measure, it was more significant for its emphasis on the creation of an educational service through a combination of central, regional and local effort. Administratively the care, custody and education of neglected and delinquent children has been linked with the Education Department since 1880 but the first comprehensive legislation on the subject was passed as early as 1867. The old-age pension scheme of 1898 was the beginning of an era conferring monetary benefits on different groups within the population and reaching a climax in the Social Security Act, 1938. The latter Act also provided a system of health benefits.

In the last chapter we mentioned that a Government Department had been established in 1936 to organise the erection of houses for letting. Since the nineties the State had concentrated for the most part on advancing moneys to people to enable them to erect their own houses. The programme inaugurated by the Labour Government in 1936 of building houses for letting was pursued vigorously until it was substantially reduced in the middle of the war years. However, it was not long before the programme was resumed, and it reached high peaks in the years 1948–49 and 1949–50. After the National Government came to power in 1949 the tenants of State houses were given the opportunity to purchase their houses on favourable terms. Houses are still being built by the State, and in addition finance on easy terms is made available to local authorities to enable them to inaugurate housing schemes.

We have selected for treatment here the legislation dealing with health, education, child welfare, social security and the welfare of the Maoris.

This is not exhaustive but elsewhere in the volume are discussed such matters as factory employment and the fixing of fair rentals. We shall see from the next chapter that allowance is made for the family responsibilities of workers in determining what their award wages should be. In Chapter 8 we discuss the allowance made for a producer's family responsibilities in calculating the guaranteed price to be paid to him under the scheme for the marketing of dairy produce.

HEALTH

The Public Health Act, 1872, was based substantially on English legislation. The Act dealt with the control of disease and the provision of hospitals. There were elaborate provisions governing quarantine and vaccination. Local Boards of Health and a central Board of Health for each province were established. In 1876 the central Boards of Health for the provinces were replaced by one central Board of Health for the whole Colony.

The Colonial Secretary when introducing the Bill of 1872 had stressed that public health was becoming a pressing question. Although the legislation that was passed then seemed sound enough in content, the Colony did not escape serious outbreaks of infectious disease. The incidence of typhoid fever was high. It is significant that in the seventies the number dying from typhoid averaged over 160 a year, whereas sixty years later the comparable figure was seven a year. As was the case in so many other fields, much of the weakness lay in the administrative machinery. Local Boards of Health too often proved unequal to their responsibilities because of ignorance and local pressure. The central Board of Health could achieve little in the face of this situation. Chadwick, in his efforts to lift the standard of health administration in England, had been faced with the indifference, ignorance and opposition of local authorities. The problem was similar in New Zealand, at least until the turn of the century.

The Public Health Act, 1900, was the response to this challenge. When introducing that measure the Colonial Secretary said that Parliament should remove from local authorities the duties then devolving upon them, which were never or hardly ever carried out. As a result of this legislation the central Board of Health was abolished, and a Government Department with a staff of medical officers and inspectors was created to take the initiative in the drive for an improvement in the public health. Local Boards of Health were abolished and the ordinary local authority was substituted. This change in itself was more nominal than real as the local Board of Health under the earlier legislation was usually the ordinary local authority for the district. The significant change was that through a redistribution of powers and duties the central government was placed in a stronger position to enforce compliance with minimum health standards.

In 1920 a further Act was passed which created a Board of Health. In some respects the powers of the Department were strengthened Some powers of lesser importance were delegated to local authorities and their existing powers and duties were defined with greater clarity. The Act is still in force.

It will be seen that the administration of legislation dealing with health is both a national and a local effort. Drastic powers affecting liberty and property are vested in the various agencies which administer the health legislation. The Department of Health works in close association with local authorities and with the Board of Health. The chairman of the Board is the Minister of Health, and there are representatives of the Department, the medical profession, the Faculty of Medicine in the University of Otago, the Municipal Association, the Counties Association, hospital boards, and civil engineers. There is also a woman to represent the interests of women and children. The role of the Board is to hold inquiries into and make recommendations concerning special health problems and to see that local authorities perform their statutory duties, but it has the power to exempt a local authority from its statutory functions, which are then taken over by the Department of Health. However, there are signs that the Board has receded in administrative significance.

The Department of Health is organised into these ten Divisions :

(*a*) public hygiene ;

(*b*) hospitals ;

(*c*) child hygiene ;

(*d*) nursing ;

(*e*) clinical services ;

(*f*) tuberculosis ;

(*g*) maternal welfare ;

(*h*) dental hygiene ;

(*i*) occupational health ; and

(*j*) mental hygiene.

The Dominion is divided into fourteen health districts, each the charge of a Medical Officer of Health, who is a medical practitioner specially qualified in sanitary science and employed by the Department of Health. It is his duty to see that the legislation is observed and to advise local authorities on their responsibilities for health administration. Local authorities fall into two groups. One group consists of local authorities of which city councils, borough councils and county councils are illustrations, and health administration is simply one of their many activities. The other group is represented by boards, which are specially created to administer public hospitals and associated activities.

General Local Authorities

The detailed duties and powers of authorities of this type are set out in the legislation. They may be compelled by the Board of Health to provide sanitary works and services, but there is a right of appeal to a stipendiary magistrate and two assessors against a requisition of the Board. A local authority must also comply with regulations made under the Health Act and applicable to its district. It is empowered to make by-laws for the protection of the public health in its district, and it must arrange for the regular inspection of its district to ascertain if there are nuisances or conditions which are offensive or likely to be dangerous to health. Periodical reports on diseases and sanitary conditions within its district must be made by the local authority to the Medical Officer of Health.

The machinery of the magistrates' court is used to enforce compliance with the provisions of the Act. A person who is responsible for a nuisance is liable to a fine. An order may also be made for the effective abatement of a nuisance and prohibiting its recurrence. A magistrate may specify the works to be done in order to abate the nuisance or prevent its recurrence, and the time within which they shall be done. If a magistrate is of opinion that by reason of the nuisance any dwelling or other building is unfit for human occupation, he may prohibit its use for that purpose until the nuisance has been effectively abated to his satisfaction, or until provision has been made to his satisfaction to prevent its recurrence.

Where premises or dwelling-houses fail to meet the requirements of the Act, the local authority may issue closing-orders and must do so if required by the Board of Health. A closing-order is served on the owner or occupier of premises prohibiting the use of the premises for human habitation or occupation until such repairs, alterations, or works as may be specified in the order have been carried out to the satisfaction of the local authority. Except on the direction of the Director-General of Health, a local authority cannot issue a closing-order unless the owner or occupier has failed to comply with a prior notice served on him calling on him to attend to the matters specified in the notice within a given time. An owner or occupier may appeal from a closing-order to a stipendiary magistrate, who may cancel the order or confirm it subject to such conditions as he deems just.

The procedure for the more serious step of demolition begins with a certificate by the Medical Officer of Health or by a surveyor or engineer of a local authority that a building or part of it should be demolished. On receipt of the certificate a local authority may by requisition in writing require the owner to take down and remove the building, or the part which is the subject of the requisition, within the time specified in the requisition. The Board of Health can require the local authority to take this course. If the owner fails to comply with the requisition, a stipendiary magistrate, on the application of the local authority, may make an order that the building or part of it be taken down and removed at the expense of the owner and within a specified time.

The Housing Improvement Act of 1945 represents a more comprehensive approach to the problem of unsatisfactory housing conditions. Under that Act the Governor-General, on the recommendation of the Minister of Works and the Minister of Health, may make regulations, by Order in Council, prescribing standards of fitness for houses. Regulations may also be made to prevent overcrowding in houses. The Act too provides a procedure for the reclamation of overcrowded areas.

If a local authority is of opinion that any house does not comply with the regulations applicable to it, the local authority may cause to be served on the owner a notice giving him not less than one month to carry out specified repairs, alterations, or works including partial demolition. Alternatively, if the local authority is of opinion that it is impracticable to make the house comply with the regulations, the notice may require the owner to pull down the house. There is no provision for closing orders as is found in the Health Act.

The proviso to the more drastic step of complete demolition reflects the current housing shortage. A local authority cannot require any house, in which a person resides at the time of the notice, to be pulled down so long as that person continues to make the house his residence, unless the local authority is satisfied that suitable alternative accommodation will be available for that person when he leaves the house. The owner or any other person having an estate or interest in the land may appeal to a stipendiary magistrate against a notice given by a local authority under this legislation. Where a local authority fails or neglects to take such steps as, in the opinion of the Minister of Works, are necessary or desirable for the improvement of housing conditions in its district, the Minister may exercise the powers that could have been exercised by the local authority.

This procedure is alternative to that provided in the Health Act. In choosing which procedure to use, local authorities will doubtless be influenced by the fact that the regulations made under the Housing Improvement Act lay down standards which are more precise than the general provisions of the Health Act. There is of course no provision in the Health Act requiring a local authority to be satisfied that there is suitable alternative accommodation available, but in these days it is most unlikely that any local authority would flout public opinion to the extent of pressing for demolition of a house when there was no suitable alternative accommodation available for a family residing in that house.

Hospital Boards

Early in the life of the Colony it was found impracticable to follow the former English method of leaving to voluntary effort the erection of hospitals and their control, and the provincial governments undertook some responsibility for the care of the sick. The first central measure was taken in 1885 when Parliament provided a scheme for the creation of hospital boards to administer public hospitals. The boards, in addition, were to assume the function of granting charitable aid, a step which, it was contended, would make old-age and sickness pensions unnecessary. Most of the governing legislation is now in the Hospitals Act, 1926.

New Zealand is divided into thirty-seven hospital districts, each with its board of elected representatives. The functions of a board are to maintain public hospitals and to provide a certain measure of outdoor medical and nursing service. Charitable aid is also one of its functions but the volume of work done under this head has fallen substantially since the introduction of the Social Security scheme. In addition to hospitals the boards may establish, with the approval of the Minister of Health, institutions for children including nurseries and institutions for old people, maternity homes, inebriates' homes, and reformatories for women or girls. Health services of a preventive nature may also be established.

The extent to which institutions of various types, apart from hospitals, are now in operation is of interest. There appears to be only one children's home established by a hospital board, although another one is subsidised by a hospital board. Presumably this is because of the institutions that have been established by the Child Welfare Division of the Education Department and by voluntary or religious bodies. No nurseries have been established, although this may be due to the fact that the power to establish them was not conferred until 1948. There are a few old people's homes. The power to establish maternity homes is widely used, but where there is no maternity home it is the practice for the board concerned to provide for maternity patients within the public hospital. There are no inebriates' homes provided by hospital boards, although an inebriate may be admitted to a psychiatric ward in a public hospital. Several homes for inebriates are maintained by a religious organisation which is aided by a grant of State funds. Reformatories for females are not now provided by hospital boards as the main responsibility for institutions of this type has been directly assumed by the State.

Mental hospitals are not controlled through boards and are State institutions under the direct control of the Health Department, as are a few hospitals of special types. Private hospitals operate under a central system of licensing and supervision to ensure that they reach a satisfactory standard in accommodation, equipment and staff.

On the one hand important powers cannot be exercised by a board except with the approval of the Minister or of his Departmental delegate. On the other hand the Minister or the Director-General can compel a board to do certain things. It has been seen that institutions of various types mentioned cannot be provided except with the Minister's approval. Although a board has power to recruit staff, it must meet such minimum requirements for medical and nursing staff as may be fixed by the Director-General. It is the duty of a board to maintain the institutions which are established. The Director-General has power to inspect the administration of the institutions including the care and treatment of patients. A board must comply with his directions. A board may make grants or pay subsidies to medical or nursing associations, benevolent institutions, private philanthropic associations, or private hospitals, provided that the Minister approves. A board has power to make by-laws for the administration of the various institutions under its control. These by-laws, however, cannot come into force without the approval of the Minister. Moreover, the Governor-General has the power to disallow by-laws at any time.

The Social Security Act, 1938, affected the revenue of hospital boards in one important respect. Where a patient is entitled to benefits under the Act, a hospital board must now accept fees from the Social Security Fund in full satisfaction of its claim against the patient for his care and treatment. Revenue from this source is approximately equal to 30 per cent. of the maintenance expenditure of a board. The balance is recovered partly by a levy on the contributing local authorities and partly by a Government subsidy granted on the levy. At the beginning of each financial year a board submits for the Minister's approval estimates of its proposed expenditure for capital and maintenance. These estimates form the basis for computing the subsidy to be paid by the central government, and at the same time enable the programme of a board to be controlled. The levies made on local authorities within a hospital board's district are shared by them according to the capital values of rateable property within their areas. There is now statutory provision for a gradual reduction in the rate of the levy until 1957 when the levy will cease to be made. This arrangement involves increased grants from the State.

The Department of Health

One of the most important duties of the Department is to take steps to prevent, limit and suppress infectious and other diseases, including industrial ones. For any disease which falls within the ' notifiable infectious ' class the responsibility for notifying the Department lies primarily on the medical practitioner attending the case. The Medical Officer of Health may enter premises where he suspects that there is a person suffering from such a disease and may order that person's removal to a hospital. In the event of the outbreak of any infectious disease the Medical Officer of Health, with the authority in writing of the Minister, may exercise certain drastic powers. He may take possession of lands and buildings, whether public or private, for the accommodation and treatment of patients. He may requisition vehicles, drugs, food and drink. A person who suffers any loss or damage through the exercise of these powers is entitled to compensation, which is determined in case of dispute by a stipendiary magistrate, whose decision is final.

For the purpose of attempting to prevent the outbreak or spread of any infectious disease a wide variety of special powers may be exercised by the Medical Officer of Health upon the authority of the Minister. These powers directly affect the property and liberty of the citizen. For instance, the use of any land, building, or thing which the Medical Officer of Health has declared to be insanitary may be prohibited. The Medical Officer of Health may cause any insanitary building to be pulled down and the materials destroyed. Insanitary things and infected animals may be destroyed. A person injuriously affected by the destruction of any building, animal, or thing under these particular powers, may claim compensation providing the destruction did not become necessary by reason of his breach or neglect of duty or of the ordinary rules of sanitary carefulness or cleanliness. Disputes are determined by a magistrate whose decision is final.

The movement of persons may be severely restricted and they may be required to report themselves or submit themselves for medical examination. Places of assembly may be closed. Powers of quarantining incoming vessels, aircraft and persons are also given. This does not exhaust the category of special powers but indicates their variety and scope.

Venereal diseases are covered by the Health Act and the Social Hygiene Act, 1917. Regulations establish a system of control and impose duties on persons suffering from such diseases to obtain treatment. Medical practitioners and medical officers of hospitals are required to notify the Medical Officer of Health of such cases.

Tuberculosis

The Tuberculosis Act, 1948, provides for the treatment, care and assistance of persons suffering or having suffered from tuberculosis and for preventing the spread of the disease. The Act sets up a system of control which begins from the time a medical practitioner has reason to believe that a patient of his is or may be suffering from tuberculosis. Where persuasion fails, a person suspected of suffering from tuberculosis can be compelled to undergo an examination to determine whether he is suffering from that disease. The Medical Officer of Health has statutory power to enter premises where persons suffering or suspected of suffering from tuberculosis are residing or working.

On the application of the Medical Officer of Health, a magistrate may order a person, who is suffering from tuberculosis and is in an infectious condition, to be removed to an institution for treatment. Before this drastic action can be taken three conditions have to be fulfilled :

(*a*) that it is in the patient's interest that he should be properly attended and treated ;

(*b*) that the patient's circumstances are such that proper precautions to prevent the spread of the infection cannot be taken, or that such precautions are not being taken ;

(*c*) that there is a substantial risk of other persons being infected.

The period of detention covered by a particular order cannot exceed three months, but further orders can be made from time to time. An appeal against a magistrate's decision lies to a judge of the Supreme Court in chambers.

The Act gives the Minister of Health power to establish a vocational guidance service for patients. There is also power to establish and maintain vocational training or industrial rehabilitation courses. Specially constructed shelters or huts and furniture can also be supplied for the use of tuberculous persons.

An interesting provision confers legal immunity on a person who does any act in pursuance or intended pursuance of any of the provisions of the Act. It matters not that there has been want of jurisdiction or a mistake of law or fact. There is, however, no immunity where a person has acted in bad faith or without reasonable care, but no proceedings can be brought except by leave of a judge of the Supreme Court.

Infirm and Neglected Persons

Where any aged, infirm, incurable, or destitute person is living in insanitary conditions or is not receiving proper care or attention, the Medical Officer of Health may apply to a stipendiary magistrate for an order committing the person to a suitable public institution.

Professional, Vocational and Technical Standards

A series of statutes control those groups which work in the field of health. Medical practitioners, dentists, nurses, midwives, masseurs, and opticians are all subject to a control which follows a common pattern. The same is true of those plumbers who engage in sanitary plumbing. The administration of each Act is vested in a special body on which interested parties, including, as a rule, the Department of Health, are represented. The Acts establish the principle of registration, which ensures that persons who enter those occupations have reached a proper standard of education and training and are of good character. The provision for the cancellation of registration is an important sanction in the maintenance of ethical standards.

There is a right of appeal against the decisions of the controlling body. For instance, if the Medical Council has declined to direct registration the applicant may apply to the Supreme Court for an order that he be registered, and it is within the discretion of the court to make such order as it thinks fit. The name of a medical practitioner cannot be removed from the register for misconduct except upon an order of the Supreme Court. Where the Medical Council in the exercise of its disciplinary powers inflicts a fine, or with the written consent of the Attorney-General suspends a practitioner, there is a right of appeal to the Supreme Court. The provisions for dentists are similar.

The appeal provisions for the other groups do not use the machinery of the Supreme Court in the same way as those for medical practitioners and dentists. Appeals from the decisions of boards controlling masseurs, opticians, and nurses and midwives go to a Board of Appeal consisting of a stipendiary magistrate and two assessors whose decision is expressed as being final and conclusive. Where, however, the Nurses and Midwives Board refuses to approve a private hospital or private charitable institution as a training school or revokes a prior approval, there is a right of appeal to the Supreme Court.

The legislation controlling pharmaceutical chemists differs in a minor respect from that controlling other groups. There is no representative of the Department of Health on the Pharmacy Board, but one member of the Board is a barrister appointed by the Minister of Health and he acts as chairman of the Board's Disciplinary Committee. The Pharmacy Board cannot cause a name to be removed from the register for grave impropriety or infamous conduct unless the Disciplinary Committee so recommends. There is a right of appeal to a Board of Appeal consisting of a magistrate and two assessors.

Registration places members of these various groups in a privileged position. As a rule they may sue for fees. In addition the unqualified person is liable to heavy penalties for describing himself as being registered or for practising or professing to practise as a member of one of the professions or occupations controlled by the legislation.

Medical Advertisements

Under legislation passed in 1942 the Medical Advertisements Board has wide powers to deal with quackery in medical advertisements. The chairman of the Board is the Director-General of Health and amongst the members are an analyst and a medical practitioner. A medical advertisement is defined as an advertisement relating to any drug, cosmetic, or dentifrice, and includes one relating to ' any article, substance, preparation, instrument, apparatus, or method of treatment, manufactured, prepared, or advertised for diagnosing, preventing, alleviating, treating, or curing any ailment, disorder, deformity, or defect of the human body, or for altering the nutrition or structure or any function of the human body '. A medical advertisement must contain the true name and address of the person for whom or on whose behalf it is published. The Act does not apply to any advertisement or scientific matter which is distributed or published amongst members of professions concerned with the health of the human body.

An important and interesting feature of the legislation is the power of the Board to call upon an advertiser to prove to the Board's satisfaction any claim or statement made or implied in an advertisement. An advertiser who fails to prove his claim or statement is prohibited from repeating it unless he has the prior consent of the Board. Where an advertiser proves his claim or statement he cannot make any reference to that fact in subsequent advertising. In protecting the public the Board can take the initiative and publish statements relating to matter contained or implied in medical advertisements. Statements of this kind are privileged.

There are detailed provisions dealing with the use of testimonials in advertising. Persons are forbidden from offering, giving, or receiving consideration for testimonials which are published as medical advertisements. It is within the power of the Board to require a person to cease publishing copies of a testimonial in any medical advertisement. The Board may call upon an advertiser to produce the original of a testimonial used for advertising. A person commits an offence who knowingly uses fictitious testimonials or who publishes a copy of a testimonial which is not a true copy in every material particular. Similarly it is an offence to use for advertising a testimonial given by a person who has died more than three months before the publication of the advertisement.

In the early years following the passing of the Act there was evidence that the Medical Advertisements Board was actively performing its functions. However, there is nothing to suggest that the Board is still active. This may be a mere matter of administrative reticence, but in any event the Act has deterrent value.

Other Regulatory Functions

One of the most important functions of the Department is the regulation of the sale of food and drugs to maintain standards of purity and to guard against adulteration. Food premises are liable to inspection and must conform to standards laid down by the Department. Offensive trades are controlled. The sale of poisons of certain classes is controlled. The establishment and administration of cemeteries and crematoria are controlled by the Department under the provisions of the Cemeteries Act, 1908.

Health Education and Other Services

Although we have outlined the regulatory functions of the Department of Health, it is important to bear in mind that the emphasis in recent years has changed to health education and to the provision of special facilities. An intensive campaign is conducted to make the public aware of the factors leading to good health and to encourage the public to comply with the basic rules. Tuberculosis has been attacked in this way. Various forms of publicity are used for this purpose. Schoolchildren are also given periodical medical examinations and their parents are notified where medical care is required. There is, however, no compulsion on parents to respond unless the case is one for criminal proceedings on the ground of neglect. The Department provides facilities for inoculation of children against typhoid. There are clinics provided for immunization against diphtheria. Vaccination against whooping-cough is available for infants. The Department administers the Milk-in-Schools Scheme, which provides for the issue of pasteurised milk to schoolchildren free of cost. Health camps are also established for delicate and undernourished children. Clinics providing free dental care for children are established throughout the country. Medical research is fostered.

Health Benefits

The Department administers that portion of the Social Security Act, 1938, which provides for a wide range of health benefits to all persons ordinarily resident in New Zealand. The object of the scheme is to relieve the patient in whole or part of the cost of medical, hospital and other related services.

The policy which the Act enunciated was that every person should receive free of charge most of the services normally given by a medical practitioner in the course of a general practice. This, however, could not operate unless a medical practitioner was willing to enter into a special contract with the Minister which specified the nature of the services to be provided, the obligations of the practitioner, and his rate of remuneration. A prospective patient would fill up the prescribed form, which he would then present to a medical practitioner of his own choice. The medical practitioner, if willing to accept the patient, would add his signature to the form which would then become an agreement between himself and the patient. For each of these patients the medical practitioner would receive an annual capitation fee plus mileage fees where appropriate.

Only a minority of medical practitioners entered into this scheme, and in 1941 an alternative scheme had to be prepared which provided that a medical practitioner who rendered any of the prescribed services was entitled to receive from the Social Security Fund a fixed fee for every occasion on which he rendered one of the prescribed services. Mileage fees could also be claimed. As some of the profession were still antagonistic to the legislation, it was necessary to provide that the patient was to receive a refund up to a specified rate on production of the medical practitioner's receipt. The charge to the patient is usually in excess of this rate.

As has been seen already, a public hospital is obliged to accept a standard contribution from the Social Security Fund in full satisfaction of its claim against a patient for treatment. For other hospital institutions, including private ones, the contribution from the Social Security Fund is accepted in partial satisfaction of their claims against patients. A hospital board is also entitled to a grant from the Social Security Fund to meet a portion of the expenditure it incurs in providing out-patient treatment. Separate schemes confer benefits to meet the cost of maternity, X-ray and laboratory diagnostic services, massage, pharmaceutical supplies, home-nursing, domestic assistance, dental services and artificial aids and appliances.

EDUCATION

The Education Act, 1877, which was passed shortly after the abolition of the provinces adopted the principle that primary education should be free, secular and compulsory. It provided for the establishment of a Department of Education, and also for regional and local administration by *ad hoc* bodies : Education Boards and School Committees. The Act envisaged that the school committees would take the leading part in administration, but their powers of independent action soon began to decrease in scope, and after a few years the Education Boards became the dominant authorities. Till the turn of the century the Department did little more than pay out to the Education Boards the funds appropriated by Parliament. Since early in the present century the Department's powers have steadily increased.

School Committees

A meeting of the householders in each school district is held once every two years to elect a school committee. A committee is subject to the general supervision and control of the Education Board, and is responsible for the care of school buildings, grounds and equipment and for sanitation. It receives financial grants from the Education Board on a basis defined by regulations. From these grants a committee meets the cost of cleaning and heating of the school and the purchase of school requisites. A committee can, of course, and does, go beyond this outline of functions to raise money by voluntary effort for school purposes, much of which is subsidised by Government grants. Each committee is required to submit to its Board an annual report on its activities and a statement of its accounts. A committee has the power to make a recommendation to its Education Board for the appointment, transfer, suspension or dismissal of a teacher, but under the present system, rarely recommends the appointment of a teacher. It may suspend a teacher for immoral conduct or gross misbehaviour. The position of the committee in relation to the Board is strengthened by the provision that no appointment, suspension or dismissal can take place until the committee has been first consulted by the Board.[1] An exception arises where a teacher is guilty of immoral conduct or gross misbehaviour, when the Board can suspend or dismiss the teacher without consulting the committee. The teacher has a right of appeal to a special tribunal which will be discussed later.

Education Boards

There are ten Education Boards in the Dominion. Members of an Education Board are elected by the members of School Committees within the education district. A Board is deemed to be an agent of the Crown in respect of its property and the exercise of its functions. It is entitled to all the privileges which the Crown enjoys in respect of exemption from taxation and the payment of fees or charges and from other obligations. The land and buildings of all public primary schools in an education district are legally vested in the name of the Education Board for that district.

The Board appoints and transfers teachers in accordance with a procedure carefully defined in legislation and regulations. It has disciplinary powers as already mentioned. It pays teachers in accordance with national scales laid down by regulation. It is responsible for establishing, consolidating, maintaining and controlling schools, but Ministerial approval or consent is needed in some circumstances, for example, in the case of school transport systems or proposals for consolidation or for new school buildings. For all these purposes it receives from the Department funds which have been appropriated by Parliament. The Board is bound to apply the funds in a specified manner and to follow a prescribed accounting system. An annual report and an audited balance sheet must be forwarded to the Minister. The Board may make such by-laws in accordance with the Act and regulations as in its opinion are necessary or desirable to enable it to exercise the duties and functions

---

[1] It is not necessary for an Education Board to consult a School Committee in respect of any appointment, transfer, or dismissal of a teacher of a "normal" school.

imposed by the Act, and to direct and control its officers and the schools in the district.

Post-Primary Schools[1a]

An Education Board may apply to the Minister for the establishment of a secondary school, a technical high school or a district high school. The Minister himself may take the initiative and after consultation with the Board may establish a school of any of these types. A secondary school is controlled by a board of governors whose powers and duties are defined in a scheme of management approved by the Minister. The relationship of the principal to the board of governors is also defined in the scheme. A secondary school does not come under the control of an Education Board, but is subject to a measure of central control because financial grants made by Government must be spent for the most part on specified purposes. Since 1945 regulations have laid down the courses of study to be taught. Regular inspections are made by officials from the Department. Each governing body must forward to the Minister an annual report and balance sheet. A somewhat similar procedure is adopted for technical high schools. Most of these schools have their own boards of managers but a few of them come under the control of an Education Board. A scheme of management is not drawn up, as there are regulations which govern the situation. District high schools are controlled in the same way as primary schools, and thus come under the general system of control. They are schools providing facilities for a post-primary as well as a primary education.

The Department of Education

Under the control of the Minister of Education, the Department of Education has the function of administering the education legislation. Apart from what may be done by persuasion and leadership, the Minister and the Department are in a strong position because the funds required by Education Boards and boards controlling post-primary schools are almost wholly supplied by the Department. The ultimate application of the funds is also subject to a measure of central control.

An Education Board can be compelled to carry out certain directions of the Minister who, for instance, can direct a board to arrange for the transport of children to and from an existing school, instead of establishing a new school. The consent of the Minister is required before a board can close a school. The Minister, himself, can initiate action for the closing of a school. Every public school must be organised and conducted in accordance with the regulations, and the Act itself mentions the subjects to be covered in the programme of primary instruction. The Department has a system for the inspection of all State schools

[1a] Post-primary schools in a district may now be grouped under the broad control of a post-primary Schools Council: Education Amendment Act, 1953.

and registered private schools, and in this way is able to maintain satisfactory standards throughout the country. The services of specialists in particular fields of education are provided by the Department for the benefit of schools.

The Department is responsible for the formulation of regulations which establish a uniform salary scale and a system of certifying and grading teachers. It conducts examinations for schoolchildren and awards bursaries. Other functions of the Department include the control of Maori schools and the correspondence schools, which provide courses for those who cannot attend school usually because their home is too far from the nearest school. The Department administers the child welfare legislation, which is separately discussed. Vocational guidance centres are directly controlled by the Department. The Music-Teachers Registration Board is associated with the Department. The Director of Education is a member of the National Council of Adult Education which is a statutory body promoting adult education and which receives a grant from the State. A large number of publications are issued by the Department.

Appeal Tribunals for Teachers

The position of teachers is protected in a number of ways. First, a primary or post-primary teacher has a right of appeal against the cancellation of his certificate and the removal of his name from the Teachers' Register. Second, he has a right of appeal against his dismissal, suspension or transfer. Third, a primary teacher in certain circumstances has a right of appeal if he has not been appointed to a position for which he has applied. Fourth, a primary teacher may also appeal against the position allotted to him on the numerical grading list, and a post-primary teacher against his personal classification.

Separate tribunals are set up to deal with each of the four different types of appeal. Administrative tribunals have already been fully discussed in Chapter 4, but it is worthy of mention that no solicitor or counsel may appear before the Teachers' Court of Appeal which deals with appeals against dismissal, suspension or transfer. In the case of the Primary Teachers' Appeal Board which hears appeals from unsuccessful candidates for appointment as primary teachers, the rule is that witnesses are not heard unless the circumstances are exceptional. The appellant, however, may appear in person or be represented by a teacher or by any officer of an approved teachers' organisation. An appellant may conduct his own appeal before the tribunal dealing with appeals against classification or grading or he may be represented by another person who is not a solicitor.

Judicial Control

On occasion the Supreme Court has had the task of defining the respective roles of school committees, Education Boards, and the Department of Education. Most of the litigation that has resulted in the delineation of the powers and duties of the three bodies has been initiated by teachers. An early attempt by an Education Board to ignore a school committee was restrained by the court in these words : ' The committee have by law a right to be asked and to give their advice on the question of whether a master is to be dismissed. If a duty is placed upon the Board to ask the advice of the committee, it is plainly part of that duty to furnish them with all the materials in its possession which are not in the possession of the committee, so as to enable the advice to be given. A man who asks his lawyer or his doctor what he thinks of his case, and omits to state the facts or symptoms, is either completely fatuous or has no real intention of seeking advice'.[1b] An attempt by an Education Board to appoint teachers from year to year was declared illegal by the Supreme Court in 1909.[2] The Board introduced this system to avoid that part of the Education Act which gave a teacher a right of appeal. In the opinion of the judge the legislature intended to vest in a teacher a certain kind of limited security of tenure of office, and the system adopted by the Board was not contemplated by the Act. Furthermore such an appointment not only purported to deprive the teacher of his right of appeal but also purported to deprive school committees of their right of consultation upon its termination.

An indirect attempt by the Minister to take a power which properly belonged to an Education Board was checked by the court in 1922.[3] In an address given by Sir Michael Myers in 1940, this case was discussed in these words :

' Section 161 of the Education Act, 1914, empowered the Governor-General to make regulations " for any purpose for which regulations are by this Act authorised or required to be made and generally for any purpose which he thinks necessary in order to secure the due administration of this Act ". The Education Act also enacted that all such regulations shall fix a day on which the same shall come into force *after which they shall have the force of law.* Regulations were made which purported to give the Minister of Education the power of cancellation or suspension of a teacher's certificate, or licence to teach. Certain charges of disloyalty and insubordination were made against a teacher and the Education Board held an inquiry with a view to the suspension or dismissal of the teacher in the event of the charges being substantiated. The result of the inquiry was in the teacher's favour and no further action was taken by the Board. But the Minister (which may have

[1b] *Wilkinson* v. *The Education Board of Otago* (1888) 6 N.Z.L.R. 307, 310, 311.
[2] *The New Zealand Educational Institute* v. *The Marlborough Education Board* (1909) 28 N.Z.L.R. 1091.
[3] *Park* v. *Minister of Education* [1922] N.Z.L.R. 1208.

been the Minister of his own motion or being moved by the departmental head) being dissatisfied with the methods and results of the
Board's investigation, proposed to institute a further inquiry into
the same or similar charges with a view to the cancellation or suspension of the teacher's certificate in pursuance of the regulations.
If that procedure was in order then the teacher's certificate could
have been cancelled or suspended by the Minister, and the teacher's
career ruined, without appeal or other legal remedy or redress. The
Minister insisted that he had the right to act as he proposed and
an action was commenced for an injunction to restrain him from
taking his threatened proceedings. It was argued on his behalf that
the Education Act was merely a skeleton form of legislation which
had been left to be filled up by regulation, that the Minister had
the executive power under the Regulations to hold the inquiry and
cancel or suspend the teacher's certificate and that the court had no
jurisdiction over him. That argument fortunately did not succeed.
Mr. Justice Salmond, who heard the case, held that the regulation
was *ultra vires* and void and granted an injunction.'[4]

In his decision, Sir John Salmond stressed that teachers of public schools
under the Education Act were not servants of the Crown but of the
Education Boards.[5] In a case two years earlier, mandamus went to
compel the Director of Education to take steps to put into effect the
decision of a Teachers' Appeal Board on a question of grading. The
court then said, ' He [the teacher] has a right to take the necessary
steps to ensure that whenever his " record leaps to light, he never shall
be shamed " by the appearance thereon of a less number of marks than
those which have been awarded him by the proper authorities '.[6]

CHILD WELFARE

In 1867 an Act was passed to deal with the problem of ' neglected and
criminal children '. The superintendent of any province was authorised
to establish industrial schools for neglected children and reformatory
schools for those children who, having been convicted of an offence,
were directed to be sent there. There were also private institutions
which were recognised for the purpose of the Act and which received
grants from public funds. Children under the age of fifteen came
within the scope of the Act. The next significant piece of legislation
was the Industrial Schools Act, 1882, which moved away from the
conception behind the earlier legislation of relying primarily upon institutions as the best method of coping with the problem. The administrative policy was now to board as many younger children as possible in
approved private homes, and the new Act was framed to meet this policy.
Provision was made for the appointment of inspectors of industrial

---

[4] *Journal of Public Administration (N.Z.)*, Vol. 3, No. 2, p. 52.
[5] *Park* v. *Minister of Education* [1922] N.Z.L.R. 1208, 1213, 1214.
[6] *Jaffrey* v. *Mulgan* [1920] N.Z.L.R. 251, 254.

schools and for the supervision of those children who had been licensed out to private homes. In 1900 the age limit was raised and children under sixteen came within the scope of the Act.

During the First World War an experiment was conducted in Auckland in the handling of young delinquents. Many delinquent boys who would otherwise have been sent to institutions were allowed to remain in the community but under the supervision of a Juvenile Probation Officer. The experiment was successful and in 1917 the system was given statutory recognition to the extent of a provision authorising the appointment of Juvenile Probation Officers throughout the country. The whole child welfare system was re-cast in 1925 when legislation was passed embodying some of the recommendations of the Superintendent of Child Welfare who had visited the United States of America and Canada to study the methods in operation there. The early emphasis on punishment had given way to greater emphasis on a more humane and constructive approach.

The Child Welfare Act, 1925, provides for the maintenance, care and control of children who are specially under the protection of the State and generally for the protection and training of indigent, neglected or delinquent children. The Act is administered by a superintendent, under the control of the Minister and Director of Education. The superintendent exercises rights of guardianship, to the exclusion of all other persons, over all children committed to his care by the courts. He is assisted by a group of public servants styled as the Child Welfare Division of the Department of Education and also by a large number of honorary child welfare officers.

There are various State institutions for the reception of minors and in addition there are private institutions which are recognised for the purposes of the legislation. Under statutory authority there is a system for the registration and inspection of all private institutions for children. A statutory duty is cast on such officers of the Child Welfare Division as are chosen for the purpose to inspect these institutions and to interview the inmates. Officers of the Division are responsible for the supervision of all children under the age of six years who are living apart from their parents. State institutions for deaf and for mentally backward children are controlled by the Division.

A child committed to the care of the superintendent may be placed in one of the institutions established by the Division, or in a private institution, or in a foster-home, or may remain in his own home under the oversight of a field officer but still under the formal, legal guardianship of the superintendent. Preventive work is an important duty of the superintendent and of those assisting him. The policy is not to remove a child from his own home unless the home is unsatisfactory and remedial measures fail. If it is desirable that a child be removed from his own home, then an endeavour is made to place him in a foster-home, with specified provisions for his maintenance, education, training, and employment. It is only as a last resort or as a temporary measure that a child is committed to an institution. The Act says specifically that where children are placed in the care of the superintendent they are not to be permanently maintained in an institution, save in exceptional cases to be determined by the superintendent.

The superintendent may assume control of a child if a parent, guardian or other person having for the time being the custody or control so applies. The agreement entered into by the superintendent and the parent, guardian or other person does not confer legal guardianship on the superintendent.

Control, and with it guardianship, is normally conferred on the superintendent by court action. A complaint may be filed by any constable or any Child Welfare Officer that a child is neglected, indigent, or delinquent, or is not under proper control, or is living in an environment detrimental to its physical or moral wellbeing. A justice may then issue a summons to any person having the custody of the child requiring him to appear before a Children's Court. Where a justice considers that a child should be forthwith removed from his surroundings he may issue a warrant for the removal of the child to an institution until the complaint has been disposed of. If it is not convenient or advisable to place a child in an institution meanwhile, the warrant may authorise other satisfactory provisions for the temporary maintenance and care of the child. If, on the hearing of a complaint a Children's Court is satisfied as to the truth of the complaint, or if where a child is charged by the police with an offence the court decides that the charge is proved then it may make an order for the committal of the child to the care of the superintendent or may place the child under the supervision of a Child Welfare Officer. An order must specify the religious denomination in whose faith and doctrines the child is to be educated.

An inmate is deemed to be a destitute person within the meaning of the Destitute Persons Act, 1910. The word 'inmate' is defined in the Child Welfare Act to include not only a child maintained in an institution but any child for the time being under the care of the superintendent, whether or not the child is for the time being in an institution. It is the duty of the superintendent in the appropriate case to apply for a maintenance order against any person liable under the Destitute Persons Act for the maintenance of the child, unless the superintendent is satisfied that there is no such person of sufficient ability to contribute towards the cost of the maintenance of the child. The superintendent may agree with any person who is responsible for the maintenance of a child that that person will pay the cost or a portion of the cost of the child's maintenance.

Out of the wages earned by a State ward in employment, the ward may receive for his personal use such amount as the superintendent may approve, and the balance is paid into the Post Office Savings-Bank, to an account in the name of the superintendent but in trust for the ward. Any public moneys expended for the benefit of the ward, for example, equipping him for employment, may be recouped from this account, but it is the present practice of the Department to supply the initial outfit free of charge. The amount at credit of the account may be paid over to the ward on his discharge, or with the approval of the Minister, it may continue to be held in trust for him after his discharge and paid to him as the superintendent thinks fit.

With the approval of the Minister a person may be discharged from control before he attains twenty-one if the superintendent is satisfied that this is in the best interests of the person. There is statutory provision that a person is discharged on attaining the age of twenty-one. Where, however, in the superintendent's opinion, any person is morally degenerate, or is otherwise not a fit person, for his own sake or in the public interest, to be free from control, the superintendent may apply to a magistrate exercising jurisdiction in a Children's Court for an order extending the period of control. Any such order may extend the period by four years, and there is provision for further extensions. A magistrate, when he receives an application for extension of the period of control, must assign counsel to the person and the Act provides that counsel is to be given all reasonable means of ascertaining the full facts of the case. If a magistrate orders an extension of the period of control, the person is treated for legal purposes as a minor.

Private or Public Institutions

A measure of control is imposed on local authorities, private organisations or individuals who desire to establish children's homes. Institutions of this type must be registered. There is provision for inspection prior to a decision being made on the question of registration and also during the currency of registration.

Not only must the premises be suitable for a children's home, but there must be suitable provision for the staffing and equipment of the premises and for the welfare of the children. Proper records must be kept. Plans of the proposed new buildings or for substantial structural alterations of existing buildings must be submitted to the Minister for his prior approval.

Registration may be cancelled, if the controlling authority of a children's home fails to comply with a requisition to effect repairs, alterations, improvements or additions within a specified time. A similar step may be taken by the Minister, with the concurrence of the Governor-General in Council, if it appears to the Minister that satisfactory provision is not being made for the welfare of the children or that the conduct of the home is unsatisfactory in any way.

Infants' Homes

Under the Infants Act, 1908, it is unlawful for any unlicensed person to receive or retain in his care or charge a child under the age of six years for the purpose of nursing or maintaining it apart from its parents or guardians for a period longer than seven consecutive days. The Minister may exempt the following from this legislative prohibition :

(*a*) an institution that is supported wholly or in part by moneys of the Crown or by public subscription ; or

(*b*) any person who, being a near relative of an infant, desires to take charge of the infant ; or

(*c*) any person as to whom the Minister is satisfied that such provisions should not apply.

The licensing system is administered by the Superintendent of Child Welfare. The granting of a licence depends on the character and fitness of the applicant and on the suitability of the house proposed to be used by the applicant as a foster-home. The maximum number of infants that can be received and maintained at any one time is specified in the licence. A record-book in the prescribed form must be kept by the foster-parent. There is provision for inspection of foster-homes. The Minister may revoke a licence at any time during its currency. A foster-parent is not permitted to receive any consideration for the maintenance of an infant except under an agreement which has been approved by the Department. In any prosecution for an offence against this provision, the burden of proving that no payment or reward has been received by the defendant lies upon the defendant.

If there is default in the payments due under the agreement, the superintendent has power in some circumstances to pay the amount due to the foster-parent, and to recover the amount from the defaulting party. Where the agreement is for the payment of a lump sum, the moneys must be deposited with the Department, and the foster-parent is entitled to receive out of these moneys a weekly payment of such amount as may be agreed between the superintendent and the foster-parent. The foster-parent has no further claim against the moneys after the infant leaves the foster-home, and the residue must be applied from time to time, as the superintendent thinks fit, in the further mainten-ance of the infant and in the payment of any medical expenses incurred. If the infant dies, the funeral and medical expenses are deductible from the moneys held by the superintendent. Any moneys still remaining must be repaid to the person by whom the lump sum was deposited.

A duly appointed officer may at any time in cases of emergency (of which he is the sole judge), remove an infant from any foster-home. It is unlawful for any other person to remove a child (whether under or over the age of six years) from a foster-home or for the foster-parent to permit such removal, except with the written consent of the superintendent or other authorised officer. The procedure to be followed in the case of an infant who dies in a foster-home is set out in the Act. The coroner, after receiving a report from a registered medical practitioner as to the cause of death, may decide that an inquest is necessary. It is the duty of the coroner at such an inquest to inquire not only into the immediate cause of death, but also into all the circumstances relating to the treatment and condition of the infant during life which in his opinion should be inquired into in the public interest.

Illegitimate Births

The Registrar of Births has a statutory duty to notify the Superintendent of Child Welfare of all illegitimate births. It is then necessary for a Child Welfare Officer to ascertain the condition of the child and its mother. The welfare of the mother and her child thus becomes the concern of the Child Welfare Officer. He may assist to place the child in a suitable home, and where necessary, advise the mother on legal procedure to establish the paternity of the child and obtain maintenance from the father. On the written request of the mother the superintendent himself may initiate proceedings for the making of an affiliation order against any person alleged to be the father. The superintendent, if he thinks fit, may take steps to have the child committed to his care. An obligation to maintain secrecy is expressly imposed on Child Welfare Officers dealing with illegitimate children.

Children's Courts

An important feature of the Child Welfare Act of 1925 is the provision for a system of Children's Courts. Specially appointed magistrates and justices of the peace exercise jurisdiction within these courts. Honorary associates of either sex are appointed to advise the court on the cases that come before it. They are appointed on the ground of special knowledge or experience deemed to be of advantage to the court in the exercise of its discretionary powers, but the decision of the court does not depend on their concurrence. No judicial proceedings can be heard or determined in any Children's Court unless and until a Child Welfare Officer has had an opportunity to investigate the circumstances of the case and to report thereon to the court. Most judicial proceedings normally within the jurisdiction of a stipendiary magistrate or a justice but relating primarily to any child or children and involving the attendance of children at any court, must be heard and determined by a stipendiary magistrate or a justice sitting in a Children's Court for the district. For the purpose of the court's jurisdiction a child is defined as a person under the age of seventeen, but the ordinary courts may refer to Children's Courts cases of minors who though over the age of seventeen are not more than eighteen years. The proceedings may relate to offences committed by children or to complaints that children are neglected, indigent, not under proper control, living in a detrimental environment, delinquent or have failed to comply with the conditions of a supervision order. Children appearing on complaints may be committed, placed under supervision or admonished and discharged. Those charged with offences may be similarly dealt with or the court may impose upon them any penalty or make any order that could have been made in other courts. On occasions an offender has been obliged to write an essay or to memorise a psalm.

In the case of an indictable offence which is not triable summarily, the normal procedure outside of a Children's Court is for the stipendiary magistrate or a justice to commit the accused to the Supreme Court for trial or sentence, or to dismiss the information. The Children's Court, however, has jurisdiction to dispose finally of cases which come before it, except that proceedings relating to a charge of murder or manslaughter cannot be heard in a Children's Court.

There are special provisions designed to remove the Children's Court from the formal atmosphere of an ordinary court hearing and to give it a wide discretion in the way it handles the cases that come before it. In practice the method of handling cases varies : the atmosphere of one court may resemble that of a clinic, whereas that of another may be more formal. For many years it had been the practice for a magistrate to deal with children in the privacy of his room. The principle behind this practice was embodied in the Child Welfare Amendment Act, 1927, which provided :

> So far as practicable persons attending any sittings of a Children's Court shall not be brought into contact with persons in attendance at any other court ; and for this purpose the sittings of the Children's Court shall not, except in cases where no other suitable room is available, be held in any room in which any other court ordinarily exercises jurisdiction ; nor shall a sitting of the Children's Court, if held in the same premises as any other court, be held at a time when such other court is sitting, if other arrangements can reasonably be made.

No child is required to give evidence on oath. The court may dispense with the normal procedure of requiring an offender to plead. It is not necessary for the court to record a conviction against a child even though the charge may be proved. A stipendiary magistrate competent to exercise jurisdiction in a Children's Court may discharge an information without a hearing if, after considering the report of a Child Welfare Officer, he is of the opinion that the matter is trivial.

The court is not open to members of the public. It is unlawful for any person to publish a report of any proceedings taken before a Children's

Court. The only exception is when the special consent of the presiding magistrate or justice is given, and even then there can be no publication of the name of the child, or of its parents or guardian, or any other name or particulars likely to lead to the identification of the child.

If a child is jointly charged with another person who is not a child within the meaning of the Act, a magistrate competent to exercise jurisdiction in a Children's Court has a discretion whether or not the proceedings should be heard in the Children's Court. Where the proceedings are being heard in the Children's Court, it is competent for that court, at any stage, to order that the proceedings be removed out of the Children's Court, and the case is then dealt with as though no Children's Court had been established. Where a person is charged before a stipendiary magistrate or a justice with the commission of an offence against a child, the proceedings may be heard in a Children's Court, but the ordinary court may in its discretion deal with the case, even though the proceedings may involve the attendance at court of children. Where a child charged with an offence has been committed to the Supreme Court for trial or sentence, a judge of the Supreme Court may, in his discretion, refer the case to a Children's Court for determination. He also has a discretion at any stage of the proceedings to make any order in relation to the child that could have been made by the Children's Court.

SOCIAL SECURITY

One phase of the social security legislation has already been discussed in the shape of the medical, hospital and other similar benefits which are administered through the Department of Health. We now turn to another group of benefits, which are monetary ones administered by the Social Security Commission. The commission in the exercise of its powers is under the general direction and control of the Minister of Social Security.

Prior to the Social Security Act, 1938, the legislative approach had been piecemeal. The old-age pension introduced in 1898 had been the first step, and this was followed by the widow's pension in 1911. Miners unable to work because of phthisis became eligible for pensions in 1915. Pensions for the blind came in 1924. Two years later the Family Allowances Act gave some relief to the poor by authorising a small weekly allowance for the maintenance of each child in excess of two, providing the total family income did not exceed a prescribed minimum. In 1936, invalids were given pensions.

As the old-age pension scheme of Seddon's Government appealed to the electorate, so did the social security scheme of Savage's Labour Government appeal to the electorate in 1938. Although the Social Security Act, 1938, was built on schemes which had been evolved over a period of forty years, it went considerably further in increasing those benefits, in making the conditions less restrictive, and in creating new types of benefits.

There are now ten different types of benefits as follows:

(1) *Superannuation Benefit* for those who have attained the age of sixty-five. This benefit is not the subject of a means test but a person already in receipt of a social security benefit of another type is ineligible for a superannuation benefit.

(2) *Age Benefit* for those who have attained the age of sixty. This benefit is the subject of a means test.

(3) *Widow's Benefit.* A widow, who is the mother of one or more children under the age of sixteen, is entitled to a benefit. Where, however, a widow has no child or children under the age of sixteen she may still qualify for a benefit providing the duration of her marriage was not less than fifteen years, and providing she has had a child of the marriage. Where the duration of the marriage has been less than fifteen years the widow can still qualify if she can show that the duration of the marriage, plus any subsequent period during which she has had the care of a child under sixteen is not less than fifteen years. Where a widow does not have the ' child ' qualification, she can receive a benefit if the duration of the marriage was not less than five years and if at the date of her husband's death she had attained the age of fifty. In addition a widow who is not less than fifty years of age, but who lost her husband after she had attained the age of forty, is eligible providing the duration of her marriage was not less than ten years and providing not less than fifteen years have expired since the date of her marriage. Under these provisions no widow whose age is less than fifty can qualify unless she has had one or more children.

A married woman who satisfies the Social Security Commission that she has been deserted by her husband can be treated as a widow for the purpose of receiving a benefit, but she is required to take proceedings against her husband for a maintenance order under the Destitute Persons Act, 1910. Once a benefit is granted any maintenance collected under an order of the court is paid to the Social Security Fund but where the maintenance exceeds the benefit the excess is paid to the wife. Should the wife receive any money direct from her husband the benefit may be reduced by the amount so received. A married woman, whose husband is the subject of a reception order under the Mental Defectives Act, 1911, or is an inmate of a mental institution is entitled to apply for a widow's benefit.

(4) *Orphan's Benefit.* This benefit is payable for an orphan child under the age of sixteen.

(5) *Family Benefit.* The father or mother of any child under sixteen may apply for a family benefit. Where a child is continuing its

education as a full-time day pupil at a school or college, the commission may continue the benefit until the end of the year in which the child attains eighteen. An applicant is not entitled to this benefit unless the child is in fact maintained as a member of the applicant's family, nor is the benefit payable if another type of social security benefit is payable in respect of the child. A significant provision is that the benefit is paid to the mother, unless in special circumstances the Social Security Commission considers that it should be paid to the father or to some other person for the benefit of the child.

(6) *Invalid's Benefit*. A person of the age of sixteen and upwards is entitled to an invalid's benefit if he or she is totally blind or is permanently incapacitated for work as the result of an accident or by reason of illness or of any congenital defect. An applicant must show that his incapacity for work was not self-induced or in any way brought about to qualify for a benefit.

(7) *Miner's Benefit*. A miner's benefit is payable to any person who, while engaged as a miner in New Zealand contracted miners' phthisis and is thereby permanently and seriously incapacitated for work; similarly where a miner has contracted any other occupational or heart disease and is permanently and totally incapacitated. To qualify for a benefit a person must have been employed as a miner in New Zealand for not less than two and a half years. If a person receiving a miner's benefit dies, leaving a widow, the widow becomes entitled to a benefit during widowhood.

(8) *Unemployment Benefit*. A person over the age of sixteen who is not qualified to receive an age benefit is entitled to an unemployment benefit if he satisfies the Social Security Commission on each of these three points:

(a) that he is unemployed;

(b) that he is capable of undertaking and is willing to undertake suitable work;

(c) that he has taken reasonable steps to obtain employment.

Unless there are special circumstances, no benefit is payable for the first seven days of any period of unemployment. The commission has the power to defer for a period not exceeding six weeks the commencement of the benefit or to terminate the benefit, in any of the following circumstances:

(a) if the applicant has voluntarily become unemployed without good and sufficient reason;

(b) if the applicant has lost his employment by reason of any misconduct as a worker;

(c) if the applicant or beneficiary has refused or failed, without a good and sufficient reason, to accept any offer of suitable employment;

(*d*) in the case of a seasonal worker, if his earnings for the season are sufficient for the maintenance of himself and his family notwithstanding a period of temporary unemployment.

(9) *Sickness Benefit.* A person over the age of sixteen who is temporarily incapacitated for work through sickness or accident, and who as a result has suffered a loss of earnings, is entitled to a sickness benefit. Unless there are special circumstances, no benefit is payable for the first seven days of incapacity.

(10) *Emergency Benefit.* Where a person for any reason is unable to earn sufficient for the support of himself and his dependants and is not eligible for any of the preceding benefits, the Social Security Commission may grant him an emergency benefit on the grounds of hardship. If the commission considers that an applicant should undergo training, medical examination or treatment or undertake work, the benefit may be made subject to compliance with the commission's requirements. The commission has a discretion as to the amount of a benefit but usually fixes the amount to equal the amount of the benefit for which the applicant most nearly qualifies.

Residential Qualifications

No one is eligible for any of these benefits unless he complies with the appropriate residential qualification. A person is not entitled to a superannuation benefit unless he was a resident in New Zealand on March 15, 1938, and has resided continuously in New Zealand for not less than ten years immediately preceding the date of his application for a benefit. Continuous residence is not deemed to have been interrupted by absence from New Zealand if :

(i) the total period of absence does not exceed one year ; or

(ii) the total period of absence from New Zealand exceeds one year but does not exceed that period by more than six months for every year of residence in New Zealand in excess of a period of ten years, and the applicant has been actually resident in New Zealand for the twelve months immediately preceding the date of his application.

There are special provisions designed to protect seamen serving on any ship registered or owned in New Zealand, also persons serving in Her Majesty's Forces or absent on Government service. Where an applicant was not resident in New Zealand on March 15, 1938, he can still qualify for a benefit providing he can show that he has resided continuously in New Zealand for not less than twenty years immediately preceding the date of his application. In his case also, continuous residence in New Zealand is not affected by absences which do not exceed specified periods.

The residential qualifications for age benefits are similar to those laid down for superannuation benefits. A widow's benefit is not payable unless the woman and her husband resided in New Zealand for not less than three years immediately preceding the death of the husband, but there is no such condition if the widow has one or more dependent children under sixteen. An orphan's benefit is not payable unless the orphan was born in New Zealand or the last surviving parent resided in New Zealand for the three years immediately preceding his or her death. For a family benefit, the child, in respect of whom it is payable, must have been born in New Zealand or must have resided there permanently for twelve months.

An applicant for an invalidity benefit must have resided in New Zealand for not less than ten years immediately preceding the date of his application but there is the usual provision that allows absences from New Zealand up to a certain total period. In addition an applicant in respect of blindness must show that he was born in New Zealand or that he became blind while permanently resident in New Zealand. Every other applicant must show that he was born in New Zealand with the condition to which his incapacity for work is attributable, or that he became incapacitated for work by reason of an accident happening in New Zealand or by reason of illness contracted in New Zealand. These provisions covering birth and incapacity do not apply to an applicant who was actually resident in New Zealand on September 4, 1936, or who became resident in New Zealand after that date and has resided continuously in New Zealand for not less than twenty years immediately preceding the date of his application.

For a miner's benefit the minimum period of continuous residence is five years, and for both the unemployment and sickness benefits it is one year.

Character Provisions

Age, widow's, invalid's and miner's benefits are not payable unless the applicant is of good character and of sober habits, and can be cancelled if there is any lapse in this way. Furthermore an age or miner's benefit can be declined if a married applicant has failed to meet his or her domestic obligations. Superannuation, orphan's, family, unemployment and sickness benefits have no character qualification.

Rates of Benefits

For most of the benefits the maximum payable is £3.7.6 per week, but this, in effect, is doubled in the case of age, invalid's, miner's, unemployment and sickness benefits, where the beneficiary has a dependent wife not on benefit in her own right. With some of the other benefits the maximum can be increased. A widow who has dependent children may receive a mother's allowance as well as the ordinary widow's benefit. Any of the benefits may be increased where the beneficiary is the parent of a person who died as a result of service either with the armed forces, or with the New Zealand mercantile marine during the Second World War.

The earnings of a blind person who receives an invalid's benefit are subsidised up to a maximum and in addition there is some relaxation of the means test.

The general rule is that a person in receipt of one type of benefit is not eligible for another. But this does not mean that a person can necessarily elect the type of benefit to take. For instance a person entitled to an age benefit is not eligible for an unemployment benefit or invalid's benefit. An exception to the general rule is the family benefit, which may be paid in addition to any other benefit.

Means Test

There is a means test for all the benefits except the superannuation, family and miner's benefits. The formula applied for age benefits, invalid's benefits, widow's benefits (where applicant is over sixty and has no dependent children), orphan's and unemployment benefits takes account of both capital assets and income, whereas that applied for widow's (where applicant is under sixty or has dependent children) and sickness benefits takes account of income only.

Reciprocity With Other Countries

For age benefits and invalid's benefits there has been reciprocity between New Zealand and the Commonwealth of Australia since 1943. For the purpose of age benefits and invalid's benefits in New Zealand, residence in Australia counts as the equivalent of residence in New Zealand. Residence in New Zealand counts for the purpose of the comparable Australian benefits. Total blindness or permanent incapacity contracted in either country is treated in the same way for invalid's benefits. The danger of unilateral action is avoided by the provision that the rate of benefit must not exceed the maximum of the country which has the lower maximum rate. Moreover, where the conditions for the grant of a benefit in one country are more restrictive than those in the other country, an applicant has to qualify under the more restrictive conditions.

Reciprocity with Australia was widened in scope from July 1, 1949, when an agreement came into operation covering age, invalid's, widow's, family, unemployment and sickness benefits. Residence or birth in one country is regarded as residence or birth in the other and applicants for age, invalid's or widow's benefit must satisfy the residential qualifications of both countries. Generally the qualifications for reciprocal benefits in each country are the same as for the corresponding benefits in that country but male applicants for age benefit must be sixty-five years of age.

There is also reciprocity with Great Britain and with Northern Ireland for family benefits, and residence in either of these two countries of a child who is a British subject is treated as residence in New Zealand. Similarly a child who is a British subject and who was born in the United Kingdom is treated as having been born in New Zealand.

Financing of Scheme

The various benefits are paid out of the Social Security Fund which has been established within the Public Account. The Fund derives most of its revenue from taxation on salaries, wages, and other income, including the income of companies, and this is supplemented by an annual appropriation made by Parliament. The Social Security scheme is not contributory in the sense that the potential beneficiaries contribute to the fund on the basis of a computation of risk. The effect of the scheme is to redistribute income on a large scale.

MAORI WELFARE

The economic forces unleashed by colonisation drove the Maoris off most of their best land. It is true that from the earliest days of the Colony there was official solicitude for the interests of the Maoris, and, although this was enlightened for a *laissez-faire* age, it did little more than regulate the disposal of land. It is also true that Maoris were often willing participants in the sale of their land and indeed clamoured for this right. There was, however, little thought whether the alienation of land was in the true interests of the Maoris, and constructive measures for enabling them to adjust themselves to the presence of the European came very late. The Maoris, even if they did obtain fair value, and this was not always so, did not necessarily understand that by sale they were extinguishing all interest in their land. The safeguards imposed did not go far enough to protect the interests of the Maori race as a whole.

Defeated in a war which the Maoris felt had been provoked by the white man's aggression, and which led to confiscation of land, the Maoris became more helpless and suspicious of the white man's policy. Measures to lift their health and educational standards were not favourably received in many Maori districts. For a long period Maoris were cynical of those of their race who co-operated with the white man. Special representation in Parliament merely scratched the surface of the psychological, social and material issues that were involved, although the Maori race today is far more conscious of its political strength.

The Maori social system with its emphasis on tribal authority had been impaired because the individual Maori knew that he had an interest in land which he could sell to the European settler. To allow the Maoris to become separated from their land was rudely to shake the closely knit organisation of a primitive community. The partial disintegration, which has resulted, has exposed the Maori race to the less desirable features of the white man's way of life. The excessive consumption of intoxicating liquor is a social problem among the Maoris. There is also a high incidence of crime. The Maori population is increasing naturally at a more rapid rate than the white population, and this gives point to the problem of assimilation, which must eventually be faced. Maori lands cannot provide an adequate living for them all, with the inevitable result that Maoris are steadily moving into European centres of population.

The aim of recent policy has been to restore communal strength and pride, but on the basis of progressive development towards an ultimate position where the Maoris will stand on real equality with the white man without the need for protective legislation. The general advance in social legislation in New Zealand would only serve to widen the gap if special attention were not given to Maori problems.

The Maori Social and Economic Advancement Act, 1945, is a comprehensive attempt to provide for the general welfare of the Maori race. In the words of the title the Act makes provision for the social and economic advancement and the promotion and maintenance of the health and general well-being of the Maori community. The aim is to encourage the Maoris to control their own domestic affairs but with ample encouragement, guidance and assistance from the Maori Affairs Department. The Controller of Maori Social and Economic Advancement is a high official in the Maori Affairs Department and he is assisted by a staff of Welfare Officers who are distributed through districts populated by Maoris.

For each tribal district there is a committee called the Tribal Executive and the district itself is divided into a number of areas, for each of which there is a Tribal Committee. All the members of the Tribal Committee except the Welfare Officer are elected every two years at a general meeting of the Maori residents within the area. The Welfare Officer for the district is a member of both the Tribal Committees and the Tribal Executive, on the appointment of the Minister of Maori Affairs. Apart from the Welfare Officer every Tribal Executive consists of two representatives of each Tribal Committee within the tribal district, and they are appointed by the Minister upon the recommendation of the Tribal Committees of which they are members. The Tribal Executive and the Tribal Committee took the place of the Maori Councils and Village Committees which functioned under the Maori Councils Act, 1900.

A Tribal Executive has these functions in relation to Maoris within its district :

(*a*) to promote, encourage, guide and assist members of the Maori race—

(i) to conserve, improve, advance and maintain their physical, economic, industrial, educational, social, moral, and spiritual well-being ;

(ii) to assume and maintain self-dependence, thrift, pride of race, and such conduct as will be conducive to their general health and economic well-being ;

(iii) to accept and maintain the full rights, privileges, and responsibilities of citizenship ;

(iv) to apply and maintain the maximum possible efficiency and responsibility in their local self-government and undertakings; and

(v) to preserve, revive, and maintain the teaching of Maori arts, crafts, language, genealogy, and history in order to perpetuate Maori culture ;

(*b*) to collaborate with and assist various Government agencies in the rehabilitation of Maori discharged servicemen and the placement of Maoris in industry and others forms of employment ;

(*c*) to collaborate with and assist the Education Department and any educational institutions in the vocational guidance and training of Maori children ;

(*d*) to co-operate with and assist all State Departments, local bodies, associations, institutions, clubs, trustees of Maori reservations, incorporated and unincorporated bodies, or any person or persons in connection with any matter or question arising out of or pertaining to the well-being of the Maori race or any member thereof ;

(*e*) to inquire into, recommend, and report to the Minister on any matter or question referred to it by the Minister which may affect or be likely to affect the well-being of the Maori race or any member thereof ;

(*f*) to undertake the administration of any works or duties which may be delegated to it by the Minister ;

(*g*) to make such recommendations to the Minister on any matters affecting the well-being of the Maori race as it shall deem fit ;

(*h*) subject to the powers of the Minister, to control, advise, and direct the activities and functions of the Tribal Committees within its district, to receive reports and recommendations from the Tribal Committees within its district, and to make such recommendations to the Minister in connection therewith as it shall deem fit.

The control of fishing-grounds, reserved for the exclusive use of Maoris or of any tribe or section of a tribe may be vested in a Tribal Executive or Tribal Committee. In general a Tribal Committee has the same functions as a Tribal Executive, but it is subject to the control and direction of the Tribal Executive. No member of a Tribal Committee is personally liable for any act done or omitted by the committee, or by any member of the committee, in good faith in the exercise of the powers and authority of the committee.

A Tribal Executive may make by-laws for its district and for a variety of purposes. The powers here given are similar to those conferred on the ordinary local authority although there are differences, one of which is the power to make by-laws for the prevention of gambling in any Maori village. A by-law is not invalid merely because it deals with a subject dealt with by the general law, but it is invalid if it conflicts with the provisions of any Act or regulations dealing with the same subject matter or if it conflicts with any rule of law. By-laws made by Tribal Executives cannot come into force until they have been approved by the Governor-General and published in the Gazette.

Unless the Tribal Executive directs otherwise, it is the duty of each Tribal Committee to investigate all breaches of by-laws committed in Maori villages within the area. The Tribal Committee may authorise proceedings to be taken within the ordinary courts or it may, in its discretion, exercise its jurisdiction to impose a fine up to a limited amount. A committee, however, cannot impose any penalty on an offender without giving him a reasonable opportunity of being heard in his own defence. Where a person fails to pay any penalty imposed by a committee in this way, the amount may be recovered in the magistrates' court as a debt due to the Tribal Committee. If a person who has been fined in this manner defends the proceedings, the matter must be reheard by the magistrates' court, which may give judgment as it thinks fit.

There is provision for the appointment of members of the Maori race as wardens. A Maori warden may at any reasonable time enter any licensed premises situated in or within two miles of any Maori village and warn the licensee or any servant of the licensee to abstain from selling or supplying liquor to any Maori who in the opinion of the warden is intoxicated, or is violent, quarrelsome, or disorderly, or is likely to become so, whether intoxicated or not. A warden may order a Maori to leave the premises, and if the Maori refuses or fails to leave the premises, a constable with the assistance of the warden may expel the Maori from the premises. In this respect a Maori welfare officer has the same powers as a Maori warden.

The much higher death rate among Maoris for intestinal disease can be traced to the lower standard of sanitation and water-supplies generally to be found in Maori settlements. Active measures are taken by the Health Department to deal with this problem. A Tribal Executive has power to establish within its district and administer any scheme of works, which is aimed at providing a water-supply or sanitation. By-laws may prescribe the charges to be made for such a service.

The revenue of a Tribal Executive or of a Tribal Committee may, with the approval of the Minister, be subsidised at a rate not exceeding one pound for one pound out of the moneys appropriated by Parliament for the purpose. The funds may also be augmented by gifts of money made by local authorities or by other organisations such as, for instance, the Maori Land Board. Each Tribal Executive and Tribal Committee must have prepared annually a balance-sheet and statement of account, which, after being audited, must be submitted to the Minister with a report on operations.

Although the committee system here described does allow for a progressive devolution of the administration of Maori affairs, many important measures affecting the Maori race continue to be administered by the Maori Affairs Department. Maoris have shared in the benefits of advanced social legislation which apply to the country as a whole, but instead of dealing direct with some of the Departments which administer this legislation they deal with the Maori Affairs Department, which handles these functions directly or as an agent for the particular Department. At the same time the Maori Affairs Department adapts the measures to meet the interests of the Maori race and their special problems. The development of Maori farming lands and the settlement of Maoris on these lands is one of the important functions of the Department. Land is also purchased for this purpose. In an effort to raise living conditions the Department lends moneys to Maoris for the erection of dwellings and the Department itself erects dwellings for Maori borrowers. The Horticultural Division of the Department encourages Maoris to make the best use of small areas of land. Another division of the Department provides Maoris with facilities similar to those provided for Europeans by the Public Trust Office in the administration of estates. A good deal of the work connected with the rehabilitation of Maori ex-servicemen has been done by the Department as agent of the Rehabilitation Department, while the Maori Land Court continues to exercise jurisdiction over the ownership of, and dealings with, Maori land and many related matters. The present policy is to assist Maoris to become good citizens with the emphasis on the development of self-reliance.

REFORM IN SOCIAL LEGISLATION

The legislation on human welfare is comprehensive and it is difficult to see what scope there is for major developments of a novel character. There is, however, a need for the examination of existing legislation to see whether it is achieving its objects. It is true that the various Acts have been amended from time to time in an endeavour to keep pace with developing requirements, but there has been no comprehensive examination of what is now a very wide expanse of State activity.

In our survey of the legislation we have noted the amount of administrative discretion vested in the public authorities working in the social field. The extent to which this discretion is controlled varies. Where liberty or property is involved as with some of the health legislation the normal safeguard is that important powers cannot be exercised except through the machinery of the ordinary courts or through specially constituted tribunals. Where, however, benefits are conferred as distinct from the imposition of duties, administrative discretion is not controlled to the same extent and this is illustrated by that portion of the social security scheme which confers monetary benefits. The social security scheme is financed from taxation, and lacks the correlative link that would be present in a contributory scheme. An applicant has no formal right of appeal against an adverse decision of the Social Security Commission except on an invalid's or miner's benefit and then only on medical grounds. The Social Security Commission, which comprises three members who are permanent officers of the Social Security Department, is under little restraint in the exercise of its powers, and it does seem that there is need for machinery which confers a right of appeal on claimants for benefits of the various types. It is only fair to say, however, that there is nothing to suggest that the legislation has not been fairly and properly administered to date.

There are other questions that arise in regard to existing legislation. What can be done to induce the community to play a greater part in the administration of the hospital, educational and social security systems ? Is it wise that the central government should assume the role of providing the funds ? Are the existing central agencies suitably organised for their various tasks ? To what extent does current policy and practice reflect recent advances in knowledge and techniques of social work ? Is the judicial approach as expressed in the system of Children's Courts the best for meeting the problem of the delinquent child ? Is the provision of monetary benefits under the social security scheme necessarily the best method of meeting the needs of certain types of beneficiaries ? How far should the principle of means tests be applied to social security benefits ? What proportion of the national income should be spent on social measures ?

To answer these various questions would require excursions into politics, economics, social work and administration, and would take us beyond the scope of this chapter. However, there is one dominating feature that ought to be mentioned. Over the last three generations we have seen clear evidence of the growth of centralism. This is true of public health and education, but the best illustration is the social security scheme which is administered by the central government without citizen participation. Few would question that the central government had to take the initiative at some stages to develop proper health and educational standards, and even now there may be a strong case for the central government still taking the initiative in matters of Maori welfare. But the broad trend has been at the expense of local interest and participation. There is little local interest in the work done by hospital boards or education boards. The school committee system is kept alive by a few valiant souls in the community. Few people seem to be interested in the financial and administrative soundness of the social security scheme, although there is no unwillingness to accept its benefits. The lethargy that pervades the community in these matters is one of the serious problems facing New Zealand. Efforts have been made to reverse the trend towards centralism and to encourage local communities to take more interest in and more responsibility for social work in their areas. These efforts, however, have not been notable for their success and it is difficult to see how the result can be otherwise when education boards and hospital boards, for example, depend on the central government for funds. The trend towards centralism cannot be reversed until the structure of local body administration has been altered and strengthened; but progress on this question is slow.

CHAPTER 6

INDUSTRIAL RELATIONS[1]

THE history of trade unionism in New Zealand is for the great part interwoven with that of the statutory system of conciliation and arbitration, which was established in 1894. In 1878 the Trade Union Act, which was modelled on British legislation, and which was fathered by Sir Robert Stout as Attorney-General, gave limited recognition to trade unions. Unions of employers were catered for as well as unions of workers. The purposes of any trade union were not to be deemed unlawful merely because they were in restraint of trade, and to this extent there was protection from a criminal prosecution for conspiracy and also from an attack on any agreement made by a union. The Act, however, provided that a court could not entertain any legal proceeding to enforce or to recover damages for the breach of certain types of agreements, although it did not make agreements of those types unlawful. Whilst the legislature declared that agreements of this kind could not be upset, it did not vary the rule of law that the courts would not enforce contracts in restraint of trade. These agreements were mostly those governing relations amongst members of a union and their attitude to employers, and an illustration was an agreement between members of a union as to the conditions on which they would accept employment in an industry. In one New Zealand case[2] an injunction was sought to restrain the executive of a trade union from paying sustenance to members on strike, when the strike had not been carried out in accordance with the rules of the union, but it was held that the court had no jurisdiction.

There were penal provisions designed to deal with members or officers who fraudulently failed to deliver up to their union its assets or records. A system of registration was established and a union which chose to be registered obtained some advantages but incurred some obligations. A registered union through its trustees could purchase or take on lease land not exceeding one acre : such land could be sold, exchanged, mortgaged, or let by the trustees. All real and personal estate belonging to a registered trade union was to be vested in the trustees, who could bring or defend proceedings in respect to that property. Before a union could gain registration, its rules had to cover certain points specified in the Act. For instance, the whole of the objects

[1] The writer acknowledges the valuable help he has been given by Mr. G. F. Grieve, LL.B., Office Solicitor, Labour and Employment Department. Mr. Grieve, however, is not responsible for any views expressed herein.
[2] *Riddell* v. *Dodds* (1890) 9 N.Z.L.R. 210.

for which a trade union was established had to be stated in the rules. A union was also obliged to furnish annually to the registrar statements of its assets and liabilities and income and expenditure. Few unions took advantage of registration immediately following the passing of the Act.

Indeed, at the time relatively few of the workers were organised in unions. During the eighties—a period of depression—the workers became widely aware of the need to organise in order to protect and advance their interests. This period saw a good deal of activity stimulated by developments in other more industrialised countries. The first major strike, however, failed in 1890 leaving the workers more receptive to the idea of seeking amelioration through the political machine. Later in the same year the Liberal Party won the election with the support of the working class. Factories were small and were scattered throughout the country. To organise the workers into cohesive powerful groups when they were scattered over the country and were migratory in habit was a most difficult task. Politically they were a growing force, but industrially they were under a severe handicap in negotiating with employers. In this scene the Liberal Government saw the need for State measures to foster unionism and to protect the worker in other respects.

Legislation was passed to deal with conditions in factories, shops, and coal-mines, and on ships. In the seventies legislation had been passed regulating the conditions, including hours of work, for the employment of females and children. A commission was set up in 1889 to investigate allegations of ' sweating ' and the Factories Act, 1891, was one result of its recommendations. In the eyes of the commission the purpose of the earlier legislation had been defeated through the lack of the means of enforcement. The new Act provided for the appointment of inspectors, who were civil servants. There was little of novelty in the substance of the legislation, when compared with similar provisions to be found in a more highly developed industrialised country such as England, but there was emphasis on the responsibility of the central administrative machine to safeguard the interests of the workers.

CONCILIATION AND ARBITRATION

An Act of 1894 had this significant title, ' An Act to encourage the formation of industrial unions and associations and to facilitate the settlement of Industrial Disputes by Conciliation and Arbitration '. The trade union system was to be strengthened, collective bargaining fostered, and in the last resort a dispute settled by compulsory arbitration. The employer was to gain from the outlawing of strikes. Although unions could choose to stay outside the system, employers could not escape the net if they were cited to appear at a Conciliation Council. Employers, however, could cite a union registered under the system. Once conciliation proceedings commenced, a case had to go to the Court of Arbitration for an award unless agreement was reached. The legislation was last consolidated in 1925, and although there have been amendments since then, the system of conciliation and arbitration is still in operation.

To be recognised for the purposes of the Act, a union had to be registered. To be registered a union had to reach a minimum standard in numbers. On registration a union achieved the status of a corporate body and became subject to the jurisdiction of the Court of Arbitration. Its rules, provided that they complied with statutory requirements as to substance and form, became binding on members of the union. A registered union could hold real and personal property : it could sue and be sued.

It will be seen that an industrial union under this Act occupied a different position from a trade union registered under the legislation of 1878. It was a corporation and, unlike the registered trade union, it did not require trustees for its property. Registration conferred some protection against the formation of rival unions. Under an amendment passed in 1936 the concurrence of the Minister of Labour was necessary before a new union of workers or of employers could be registered where there was already in the same industrial district an existing union registered in respect of the same industry. Since 1951, the concurrence of the Minister has also been required before the rules of a union are altered to extend its membership to include workers in any industry if there is in the same industrial district an existing union registered in respect of that industry. The amendment in 1936 also encouraged the formation and registration of what were termed New Zealand unions, providing they had branches in at least four of New Zealand's eight industrial districts. Another amendment of 1951 provides that an industrial union may be a member of, or be affiliated to, any organisation formed for the purpose of protecting or furthering the interests of workers in connection with conditions of employment throughout New Zealand.

The entrance fees and subscriptions payable by members of a union, together with the levies that may be made by a union, are controlled by the Act. The current provision is that no person can be required to pay an entrance fee exceeding five shillings. Further, it is not competent for a union to provide in its rules for the payment of subscriptions exceeding one shilling a week unless the rules on this point have been adopted by a majority of the valid votes cast at a secret ballot ; the secret ballot must be either a postal ballot or a ballot conducted in such other manner as may be approved by the Registrar of Industrial Unions. Proposals for levies must be carried by secret ballot conducted on similar lines.

Industrial unions and industrial associations [3] are required to keep in proper form a correct account of their receipts and payments. As a result of an amendment made in 1951 any financial member of a union may demand, without charge, a copy of the annual accounts and of the auditor's report. Where the registrar has reason to believe that any accounts have not been properly kept or that any moneys have been misappropriated, he may insist on the accounts being audited by a public auditor : there is no provision for the regular submission of accounts to the registrar, as was the case in the Trade Union Act, 1878.

Conciliation Procedure

No industrial dispute may be referred to the Court of Arbitration until it has been first referred to a Council of Conciliation. Either the workers' union or the employer may take the initiative in starting the machinery. It is more common for the workers' union to do so, and the following description of the usual procedure will accordingly assume that it is the workers' union which is taking the initiative. The formal procedure is for the workers' union to make a demand upon a union of employers or an industrial association of unions of employers or upon representative employers within the industrial district. If this demand is not satisfied or there is no reply, the union may then apply to the Conciliation Commissioner in the industrial district for the setting up of a Council of Conciliation to hear its claims. No such application may be made unless it has been approved by resolution by the committee of management of the union, nor may any application be made in respect of matters covered by an existing award or agreement unless within two months of its expiry. Where, however, more than one industrial district is involved an application may be made within four months of the expiry of an award or agreement. In its application the union states the names of employers' unions or representative employers whom it desires to be made parties to the proceedings.

The union supplies the Conciliation Commissioner with a list of the persons whom it recommends for appointment as its assessors to hear the dispute. The general rule is that no one is eligible to become an assessor unless he is or has been actually engaged or employed in the industry in which the dispute has arisen. The commissioner, however, may relax this rule to the extent of appointing one assessor who is not so qualified, providing he is of the opinion that it is impracticable or inexpedient for the general rule to be applied in its entirety. The number of assessors who may be appointed on behalf of one side is up to and

---

[3] Any council or other body however designated representing no fewer than two industrial unions connected with one industry or related industries of either employers or workers may be registered as an industrial association of employers or workers.

including four but this figure may be increased to seven where more than one industrial district is involved.

The Conciliation Commissioner makes a fixture for the hearing of the dispute by a Council of Conciliation and cites the respondents. He also calls upon the respondents to make a recommendation for the appointment of assessors (equal in number to those appointed for the applicants) to act on their behalf, and appoints in accord with this recommendation if he is satisfied with their qualifications. If the respondents fail to nominate qualified persons as assessors, the commissioner himself may appoint qualified persons to act as assessors. Not later than three days before the hearing the respondents must lodge with the commissioner a statement in detail admitting such of the claims of the applicants as they desire to admit or making counter-proposals, and a copy of the statement must be sent to the applicants by the commissioner. Immediately an application for the setting up of a Council of Conciliation has been filed, the commissioner himself may take special measures to settle a dispute : for instance he may call a conference of the interested parties without awaiting the formal steps leading up to a hearing before a Council of Conciliation, but this particular procedure is not often followed. However, one of the special functions assumed by a Conciliation Commissioner is to take the initiative in bringing to the conference table the representatives of parties to a dispute that may result in a stoppage of work.

The commissioner and the assessors constitute a Council of Conciliation and the commissioner presides. It is the duty of the council to endeavour to bring about a settlement of the dispute by such means as it thinks fit. Considerable elasticity is permitted in the conduct of a hearing, which may be a public or private one, but the hearing must take place within the industrial district in which the dispute has arisen. A council can determine its own procedure. No barrister or solicitor, whether acting under a power of attorney or otherwise, may appear or be heard before the council. A council can make inquiries on its own initiative. The commissioner may adjourn a hearing and confer with one side privately if he thinks that such a step is desirable.

A person may be summoned to a hearing to give evidence on oath, but he is not obliged to divulge trade secrets or details of the financial position of his business. However, if he so desires and the commissioner thinks fit, a witness may give evidence of this type or produce his books to the commissioner sitting alone. The commissioner may later inform the assessors that in his opinion, a claim or allegation is, or is not, substantiated by the evidence or the books.

Where a dispute is settled before the council, the terms are embodied in an industrial agreement which is signed by the assessors on behalf of the parties and by the commissioner. The agreement when filed with the

Clerk of Awards becomes binding on the parties. The signatures of the assessors are conclusive proof that the parties to the dispute have agreed to the terms, but a party bound by any such agreement may apply within one month to the Court of Arbitration for total or partial exemption from its terms. If the assessors so decide, they may apply to the Court of Arbitration for an award embodying the terms of a settlement and the court may make an award without hearing the dispute. If an award is made then all unions and employers in the industry within the district become bound, even those who were not parties to the original proceedings in the Council of Conciliation.

Where an agreement is not reached it is competent for the council to make a recommendation for the settlement of the dispute, providing the assessors are unanimous. Such a recommendation is published as being the council's view of the merits of the dispute but the parties are not legally bound to accept the recommendation. A recommendation, however, can develop into a binding agreement: under the amending Act of 1936 the Clerk of Awards publishes a notice embodying the recommendation and giving the parties one month to signify their dissent from the recommendation. Failing dissent and subject to further notice, the recommendation is deemed to operate as an industrial agreement executed and filed by the parties.

Access to the court was severely restricted by legislation passed in a time of depression, 1932, but this restriction was removed in 1936. During that period, if the parties refused to agree to a settlement in conciliation proceedings there could be no reference to the court unless all assessors so agreed, but in some circumstances it sufficed if all except one assessor on each side agreed. To the extent that this alteration threw emphasis on conciliation, it was desirable, but politically it was doomed because it was too closely associated with the economic policy of the Government to reduce wages.

Court of Arbitration

The court consists of three members appointed by the Governor-General, one of whom is styled as the judge of the court. No one may be appointed as the judge unless he is eligible to be a judge of the Supreme Court. It is declared that a person appointed to be judge of the Court of Arbitration is subject to the same provisions as a judge of the Supreme Court and has the same rights in matters of tenure of office, salary, and privileges. One of the two other members is appointed on the recommendation of employers' unions and the other on the recommendation of workers' unions. There is provision for the appointment of assessors where technical questions come before the court. The decision of a majority of the members present at a sitting of the court, or if the members present are equally divided in opinion, then the decision of the judge is the decision of the court. There are special provisions in the legislation enabling the council or the court to deal with contempt or obstruction. So long as the court keeps within its jurisdiction, its decisions cannot be questioned in the ordinary courts. The Court of Arbitration has jurisdiction to settle and determine any dispute that has arisen between employers and workers' unions in relation to industrial matters. Industrial matters are now specially defined as meaning:

> ' all matters affecting or relating to work done or to be done by workers, or the privileges, rights, and duties of employers or workers in any industry, not involving questions which are or may be the subject of proceedings for an indictable offence, and include all matters affecting the privileges, rights, and duties of industrial unions or industrial associations or the officers of any such union or association.'

The judge of the Court of Arbitration may in any matter before the court state a case for the opinion of the Court of Appeal on any question of law arising in the matter. The Court of Arbitration may delegate to a stipendiary magistrate any of its powers and functions, but a person may appeal to the court against a decision of such a delegate. There is also provision for the appointment of deputy judges who may exercise such powers or functions as may be delegated to them by the court, subject to a right of appeal to the court. In the case of the illness or absence of the judge of the court a deputy judge may be appointed to act in his place.

An Award

The court has jurisdiction to make an award where the conciliation procedure has not resulted in complete agreement between the parties to a dispute or where the assessors, although reaching agreement, seek an award to include those who were not parties to the dispute. An award regulates the mode, terms and conditions of the employment of workers and the wages to be received by them. In the words of Sir John Salmond, an award is, in effect, a code of rules for the regulation of the industry concerned during the currency of the award by which certain rights and obligations are conferred and imposed upon the employers and workers engaged in that industry during that period : it is in form a judicial decree, but in substance it is an act of legislative authority.[4]

The most important feature of an award is that it extends to and binds every trade union, industrial union, industrial association, or employer who is connected with or engaged in the industry to which the award applies within the industrial district to which the award relates.

---

[4] *New Zealand Waterside Workers' Federation Industrial Association of Workers* v. *Frazer* [1924] N.Z.L.R. 689, 709.

This is so even if a party has not been cited in the proceedings leading up to the making of an award, but the court may in its discretion exempt a party who although not specifically cited in the prior proceedings is caught by the award, providing the party applies for exemption within one month of the court's order. An award may be made for any period up to three years. It may allow for the issue of a permit to any worker to accept a wage below that prescribed for the ordinary worker in the trade to which the award relates. An award normally binds all persons engaged in an industry within an industrial district, but if the award is to be satisfactory in operation the citation of the interested parties becomes important. The court may at or before the hearing of any dispute take steps to ascertain whether all persons who ought to be bound by its award have been cited to attend the proceedings and it may direct that further parties be cited. In certain limited circumstances citation may be given by advertisement. An industrial agreement may be declared to be an award of the court providing it is binding on the majority of the workers in the industry to which it relates and in the industrial district in which it was made.

Of interest is the provision which exhorts the court when making an award to avoid all technicality, where possible. Another provision is that the award should state in clear terms what is or is not to be done by each party on whom the award is binding. A copy of the award or industrial agreement must be kept affixed in some conspicuous place at or near the entrance of the factory or shop. Among the things which an award must specify is its currency, which must not exceed three years. It is provided, however, that an award, even though the period has expired, continues in force until the making of a new award or industrial agreement. There is provision for the extension by the court of an award beyond the industrial district for which it was first made, even to the extent of making it operative for a particular industry throughout the whole country.

Apart from the increased coverage an award has certain advantages over an agreement, and the parties having embarked on the formal procedure almost invariably seek an award. For instance, an award is not vitiated as an agreement may be through failure of consideration. At one time when a complete agreement was reached it was usual to leave one clause as if in dispute in order to give the court jurisdiction. Now even this fiction is dropped and if the complete agreement is sent on to the court with the request that an award be issued the court will issue the award in terms of the agreement provided it is not contrary to law.

It has been customary to provide in awards and industrial agreements for the setting up of committees to deal with disputes that arise during the operation of an award or industrial agreement. This has been recognised in the legislation over a long period. The provisions were recently revised and are now contained in the Industrial Conciliation and Arbitration Amendment Act, 1951. An award or agreement may provide for the setting up of a Local Disputes Committee to deal with a dispute or difference arising out of or connected with an award or agreement but not specifically dealt with therein. Each side nominates an equal number of representatives for the committee, and in addition there is a chairman who is agreed upon or is appointed by the Conciliation Commissioner in the absence of agreement. There is provision also for the appointment of a National Disputes Committee where the dispute concerns more than one industrial district.

The decisions of these committees are final and binding on all persons directly affected by the dispute or difference. However, they have no power to make a decision which is inconsistent with the provisions of an award or agreement. There is also a right of appeal from their decisions to the Court of Arbitration.

For each type of committee the decision of the majority of the members (excluding the chairman) is the decision of the committee. Where a committee does not reach a decision the chairman may decide the matter and his decision is treated as being that of the committee. However, the chairman of a Local Disputes Committee may instead pass the matter to a Conciliation Commissioner for reference by him in his discretion either to a National Disputes Committee or to the Court of Arbitration. Where a National Disputes Committee does not reach a decision, the chairman may refer the matter to the Court of Arbitration.

Evidence and Procedure

The ordinary rules of evidence are relaxed. For instance, the court may accept, admit, and call for such evidence as in equity and good conscience it thinks fit, whether strictly legal evidence or not. This provision, however, has been restrictively interpreted to the extent that it has been held that evidence should be admitted only where full effect may safely be given to it.[5] All books, papers and other documents produced before the court, whether produced voluntarily or pursuant to summons, may be inspected by the court, and also by such of the parties as the court allows, but the information obtained therefrom cannot be made public. The proceedings of the court must be conducted in public except that at any stage the court, of its own motion or on the application of any of the parties, may direct that the proceedings be conducted in private. Lawyers are discouraged from appearing before the court by the provision that no barrister or solicitor may appear for a party unless with the consent of the other party. There is also the

[5] *Seed* v. *Somerville* (1904) 7 G.L.R. 199.

significant provision which forbids the court to allow costs on account of counsel. Barristers and solicitors, however, may appear on interpretation or penalty proceedings, and their costs may be allowed in such actions. Parties may be represented by counsel where the court is conducting an inquiry into a disputed election within a union.

Penal Provisions

Where an industrial dispute has been referred to a Council of Conciliation, the relationship of employer and employed must continue uninterrupted until the dispute has been finally disposed of by the council or the court, and those who interrupt this relationship whether they be unions, individual workers or employers are liable to fines. The dismissal or suspension of any worker, or the discontinuance of work by any worker, pending the final disposition of an industrial dispute is deemed to be a default, unless the party charged with such a default satisfies the court that such a course was not taken on account of the dispute. Workers are given statutory protection against victimisation. The employer is liable to a penalty where he dismisses any worker or alters any worker's position in the employment to his prejudice, if at any time within twelve months before his dismissal or alteration of position the worker :

(a) was an officer of any industrial union or branch of a union or was a member of the committee of management of any union or branch, or was otherwise an official or a representative of any union or branch ; or

(b) had acted as an assessor on a council of conciliation ; or

(c) had represented a union or branch of a union in any negotiations or conferences between employers and workers ; or

(d) was entitled to some benefit of an award, order, or agreement, or had made or caused to be made a claim for any such benefit for himself or any other worker, or had supported any such claim, whether by giving evidence or otherwise ; or

(e) had given evidence in any proceedings under the principal Act.

It is a defence to the employer if he proves that the worker was not dismissed or his position altered because he had acted in any of the above capacities or was entitled to or involved in a claim for a benefit. A worker is deemed to be dismissed if he is suspended for a longer period than ten days. Where there is already an award current a breach is committed if a party either alone or in combination with others takes proceedings with the intention to defeat any of the provisions of the award. Whether a contract is a device to defeat the terms of an award depends on whether it expresses the real agreement of the parties or is merely a device for concealing an agreement which is an infringement of an award.[6]

6   *Re Manawatu Flaxmillers' Award* (1903) 12 G.L.R. 102.

Inspectors of Factories are also Inspectors of Awards and it is their duty to see that the provisions of any industrial agreement, or award, or order of the court, are observed. A wages and overtime book must be kept by every employer bound by an award or industrial agreement and an Inspector of Awards may require this book to be produced for his examination. Penalties for offences committed by any of the parties are recoverable at the suit of an Inspector of Awards or of another party to an award or industrial agreement. Not only is a defaulting employer liable to fines for offences defined in the Act, but he is also liable to proceedings that may be taken to recover to the use of the worker the difference where his employer has paid wages at a rate less than that fixed by an award or industrial agreement. Proceedings to recover wages in this manner must be brought in the magistrates' court except that the inspector may commence his action in the Court of Arbitration. Proceedings for offences or breaches must likewise be taken in the magistrates' court but if the proceedings are being brought by an inspector he may bring them either in the Court of Arbitration or in the magistrates' court. If they are taken in the magistrates' court there is a right of appeal to the Court of Arbitration in the following cases :

(*a*) on any matter of fact in any case where the amount of the claim exceeds five pounds ;

(*b*) on a point of law, with the leave of the magistrate in any case where the amount of the claim does not exceed five pounds, and without such leave in any other case.

On any such appeal, the determination of the Court of Arbitration is final. A magistrate may, if he thinks fit, before giving judgment, state a case for the opinion of the Court of Arbitration.

The individual worker who despite an award or industrial agreement takes part in a strike is liable to a penalty not exceeding £50, and the individual employer who despite an award or industrial agreement is a party to a lockout is liable to a penalty not exceeding £500. Those who foment industrial trouble face these provisions :

(1) Every person who incites, instigates, aids or abets an unlawful strike or lockout or the continuance of any such strike or lockout, or who incites, instigates, or assists any person to become a party to any such strike or lockout, is liable to a penalty as follows :

(*a*) if a worker, a penalty not exceeding £50 ;

(*b*) if an officer, or a member of the committee or executive, of any industrial union, industrial association or trade union, or of the branch concerned, a penalty not exceeding £250 ;

(*c*) if an industrial union, industrial association, trade union, or employer, a penalty not exceeding £500.

A person who is guilty but is not caught by provisions (*a*), (*b*), or (*c*) above is liable to a penalty not exceeding £50.

(2) Every person who makes any gift of money or other valuable thing to or for the benefit of any person who is a party to any unlawful strike or lockout, or to or for the benefit of any industrial union, industrial association, trade union, or other society or association of which any such person is a member, shall be deemed to have aided or abetted the strike or lockout within the meaning of this section, unless he proves that he so acted without the intent of aiding or abetting the strike or lockout.

(3) When a strike or lockout takes place, and a majority of the members of any industrial union or industrial association are at any time parties to the strike or lockout, the said union or association shall be deemed to have instigated the strike or lockout.

The Minister may by notice in the Gazette cancel the registration of any industrial union or association, or may cancel any award or industrial agreement in so far as it relates to the union if he is satisfied that any discontinuance of employment has caused, or is likely to cause, serious loss or inconvenience, and that it has been brought about wholly or partly by any industrial union of workers or employers or any member thereof. This power was given to the Minister in 1939. Since 1947 it has been deemed to be a rule of every industrial union of workers registered under the Industrial Conciliation and Arbitration Act that no strike shall take place until the question has been submitted to a secret ballot of those members of the union who would become parties to such a strike. A similar provision applies to employers in respect of lockouts. In 1949 it was provided that a Conciliation Commissioner might at any time call a compulsory conference of the parties in an endeavour to settle a dispute in relation to any matter which, in his opinion, is not specifically provided for in any award or industrial agreement. He must have reasonable grounds for believing that a strike or lockout exists or is threatened in his district in respect of such a matter.

For the purpose of penal liability, a union is deemed to have instigated a strike or lockout unless it proves that, before the strike or lockout took place, a secret ballot in accordance with the statutory rule was held on the question whether the strike or lockout should take place. A union may escape liability by showing that no officer of the union had the means of knowing of the imminence of the strike or lockout, or that each officer took every step possible to ensure compliance with the secret ballot requirements and to prevent the strike or lockout.

Where a proposal for a strike has not been carried by secret ballot before the event, every member of the union who is a party to the strike is liable to a fine not exceeding £100. An officer or member of the committee of the union is liable to a fine not exceeding £500 unless he proves that he had no means of knowing of the imminence of the strike or that he took every step possible to ensure compliance with the statutory requirements for a ballot and to prevent the strike. There are corresponding provisions for lockouts, except that members of an employers' union who are parties to a lockout are liable to a fine not exceeding £1,000.

If in any action judgment is given, whether by a magistrates' court or by the Court of Arbitration, against any industrial union or industrial association, and is not fully satisfied within one month thereafter, all persons who were members of the industrial union or industrial association at the time when the offence was committed in respect of which the judgment was given, are jointly and severally liable on the judgment in the same manner as if it had been obtained against them personally. All proceedings in execution or otherwise in pursuance of the judgment may be taken against them or any of them accordingly, except that no person is liable under this provision for a larger sum than five pounds. The statutory protection given to wages against attachment is removed by the provision that wages beyond a certain amount may be attached to recover penalties imposed on workers. In addition the registration of a union convicted of a breach can be suspended for such period as the court thinks fit, not exceeding two years. During any period of suspension, the union or association is incapable of instituting, or continuing, or of being a party to any conciliation or arbitration proceedings under the Act, or of entering into any industrial agreement, or of taking or continuing any proceedings for the enforcement of an award or industrial agreement, or of making any application for the cancellation of its registration.

It should be noted that there are penal provisions which apply to certain industries irrespective of whether or not unions in those industries are registered under the Industrial Conciliation and Arbitration Act. The industries concerned were selected for special treatment in view of their social and economic importance, and are listed below :

(*a*) the manufacture or supply of coal-gas ;

(*b*) the production or supply of electricity for light or power ;

(*c*) the supply of water to the inhabitants of any borough or other place ;

(*d*) the supply of milk for domestic consumption ;

(*e*) the slaughtering or supply of meat for domestic consumption ;

(*f*) the sale or delivery of coal, whether for domestic or industrial purposes ;

(*g*) the working of any ferry, tramway, or railway used for the public carriage of goods or passengers.

if any person employed in any of these industries strikes without having given to his employer, within one month before so striking, not less than fourteen days' notice in writing, signed by him, of his intention to strike, or strikes before the expiry of any notice so given by him, the striker is liable to a fine not exceeding £75. If any employer engaged in any of these industries locks out without having given to his employees, within one month before so locking out, not less than fourteen days' notice in writing of his intention to lock out, or locks out before the expiry of any notice so given by him, such employer is liable to a fine not exceeding £750. Every person who incites, instigates, aids, or assists any person who has struck or locked out in breach of these provisions to continue to be a party to the strike or lockout, is liable to a penalty as follows :

(a) if a worker, a penalty not exceeding £75 ;
(b) if an officer, or a member of the committee or executive, of any industrial union, industrial association, or trade union, or of the branch concerned, a penalty not exceeding £350 ;
(c) if an industrial union, industrial association, trade union, or employer, a penalty not exceeding £750.

A person who is not caught by provisions (a), (b), or (c) above, is liable to a penalty not exceeding £75.

LABOUR DISPUTES INVESTIGATION ACT, 1913

Apart from the provisions discussed in the preceding paragraph, there is a code that governs those few unions which have chosen to stay outside the jurisdiction of the Court of Arbitration. The Labour Disputes Investigation Act, 1913, which is modelled on Canadian legislation, applies to ' societies of workers (whether incorporated or not, and whether registered under any Act or not), and to the members of any such society who are not, for the time being, bound by any award or industrial agreement under the Industrial Conciliation and Arbitration Act, 1908, and to the employer or employers of any such workers '. It is unlawful for a society of workers in this category to use the strike weapon unless requirements as to prior notice have been met and a secret ballot has been held. Furthermore, if a society has chosen to be a party to an agreement which has been filed with the Clerk of Awards, as provided in the Act, then its members cannot legally take part in a strike before the expiration of the currency of the agreement and may be punished for this or other breaches of the agreement. There are a few instances of unions which, although registered under the Industrial Conciliation and Arbitration Act, have made agreements under the Labour Disputes Investigation Act, 1913.

The notice referred to in the preceding paragraph is a written one given to the Minister of Labour. It specifies the parties to the dispute and sets out the claims which are made by the society and which must arise from a dispute relating to conditions of employment. On receipt of such a notice the Minister must refer the matter either to a Conciliation Commissioner, appointed under the Industrial Conciliation and

Arbitration Act, to take action in an endeavour to settle the dispute, or to a Labour Dispute Committee which is specially set up for each dispute and which consists of an equal number of the workers and the employers. The committee thus appointed proceeds to elect some other person as chairman. Each committee consists of not less than three nor more than seven members as determined by the Minister. The Minister may appoint where the parties fail to appoint members of a committee or where the members of a committee fail to elect a chairman.

It is the duty of the chairman to appoint a time and place for the investigation of the dispute, and to give public notice of investigation by newspaper advertisement. Any person or society of workers or employers affected by the dispute, whether a party to it or not, is entitled to appear before the committee in such manner as the chairman determines. The committee investigates the matter of the dispute, endeavours to effect a settlement, and as soon as practicable makes a report to the Minister. If a settlement of the dispute is not arrived at, the committee includes in its report such recommendations for the settlement of the dispute as it thinks fit. If the members of the committee are equally divided in opinion, the committee may, in lieu of making recommendations, submit to the Minister not more than two proposals for the settlement of the dispute. Each proposal is included in the report of the committee, and is signed by the members concurring in it. On receipt of the report the Minister causes the recommendations or proposals contained in it to be published in such newspaper or newspapers circulating in the district as he thinks fit.

If a dispute is not settled within fourteen days after notice has been given to the Minister, then the Registrar of Industrial Unions must forthwith conduct or cause to be conducted a secret ballot of those members of the society of workers who are directly concerned in the dispute. Where recommendations for the settlement of the dispute have been made by a Labour Dispute Committee, the question is whether the recommendations shall be adopted but where recommendations have not been made the question is whether a strike shall take place. The result of the ballot must be published in such newspaper or newspapers circulating in a district as the registrar thinks fit. At any time during the continuance of a strike which is not an unlawful strike the registrar may, on the requisition of not less than 5 per cent. of those workers who are directly concerned in the strike being members of a society or societies, proceed to conduct or cause to be conducted in the prescribed manner a secret ballot of all such members directly concerned in the strike on any question relating to the strike that may be proposed by the requisition. There are corresponding provisions for lockouts.

A Conciliation Commissioner may at any time, if he thinks fit, whenever he has reasonable grounds for believing that a labour dispute, to which the Labour Disputes Investigation Act, 1913, would apply, exists or is threatened in any district within which he exercises jurisdiction, take such steps as he deems necessary, whether by way of recommending a conference of the parties or otherwise, with intent to procure a voluntary settlement of the dispute.

Penalties are provided for those persons or societies who incite, instigate, aid or abet an unlawful strike or lockout. When a strike or lockout takes place and a majority of the members of any society of workers or employers are at any time parties to the strike or lockout, the society is deemed to have instigated the strike or lockout. Certain disciplinary provisions of the Industrial Conciliation and Arbitration Act forbidding the interruption of the relationship of employer and employed are made applicable as are the provisions dealing with contempt of or obstruction to a tribunal.

The Labour Disputes Investigation Act is exceptional for this wide power which is conferred on the Minister of Labour :

> Notwithstanding anything in the foregoing provisions of this Act, the Minister may in any particular case, having regard to the special circumstances and to the interests of all the parties concerned, reduce any period of notice to be given under this Act or the time within which anything may be done thereunder, and may also, if he thinks fit, in any such case dispense with the publication of the recommendations of a Labour Dispute Committee or of the result of any ballot.

THE COURT OF ARBITRATION

Now that we have outlined the provisions that govern unions in New Zealand we return to the Court of Arbitration to discuss the role it has played in the industrial and economic life of the country. The court has seen a change of emphasis in its functions. Originally conceived as a body to settle the occasional industrial dispute, it quickly became flooded with work because the conciliation system did not function as intended. It also increasingly exercised a legislative function in the granting of industrial awards which covered large sectors of the country's economy. It was the major force in the formulation of industrial codes which went far beyond the fixation of wages to embrace conditions such as hours, factory hygiene and amenities. At stages in its history the court has been the instrument for the execution of economic policy as expressed in legislation. In a time of trade recession it has reduced wages : at another time it has increased wages and improved conditions in accordance with the legislative policy of a Government, for instance that of the Labour Government on the question of a forty-hour week. During wartime it has had the job of stabilising wage rates. In its evolution the court has risen to a commanding position in the economic life of the country. The task of the court in establishing uniform wage standards has been greatly assisted by the fact that the dominating characteristic of New Zealand's economy is its reliance on the export of agricultural produce.

Theoretically many of the tasks entrusted to the Court of Arbitration could have been executed by an ordinary Government Department working under Acts of Parliament with the usual power to initiate regulations. However, there are great advantages in giving a judicial form to the expression of economic policy where fairness and the appearance of fairness are so important. Parliament could have legislated from time to time and in greater detail, but it is unlikely that this process would have been fast or adaptable enough to cope with relations in the industrial field.

The legislative character of the court's work was emphasised by the task given to it in 1936. Under legislation passed in that year, the court was obliged, of its own motion, to make a general order fixing a basic rate of wages for adult male workers employed in any industry and also for adult female workers to which any award or industrial agreement related. The court could from time to time at intervals of not less than six months amend any general order by a subsequent general order either on its own motion or on application by any industrial union or industrial association. In fixing a basic rate of wages the court had to have regard to the general economic and financial conditions affecting trade and industry in New Zealand, the cost of living, and any fluctuations in the cost of living since the last order. The basic rate of wages for adult male workers was to be such a rate as would, in the opinion of the court, be sufficient to enable a man in receipt thereof to maintain himself and a wife and three children in a fair and reasonable standard of comfort. Any general order made could provide for the issue to any worker of a permit to accept a wage lower than the basic rate.

The idea of fixing basic rates of wages by a general order was doubtless borrowed from legislation of this type in several of the Australian states. The particular standard adopted, namely, what is sufficient to enable a man to maintain himself and a wife and three children in a fair and reasonable standard of comfort, had been adopted by the Australian Federal Arbitration Court as early as 1907.[7] It is significant that in fixing a basic rate of wages the court is required to look at the general economic and financial conditions, and there is no reference to the position of individual industries. In recent years there has been increasing pressure from women's organisations for the acceptance of and application of the principle of ' equal work, equal wages ', but although there has been some weakening in the opposition to this pressure the economic

[7] Mazengarb, *Industrial Laws of New Zealand* (1947), p. 133.

implications of the principle stand as a substantial barrier to its fulfilment. Mazengarb in his work[8] has this comment to make :

> 'The principle of "equal work, equal wages" is both in New Zealand and Australia taken to be over-ridden by the paramount principle of enabling a male worker to support his family. It would seem, however, in New Zealand that since the rate is fixed for a family of three children the young single man is given a great economic advantage, to the detriment of public interest, over the large family unit, and today this is by no means compensated by the system of family allowances or by taxation exemptions.'

In its early years the court was working in a period of rising prosperity and its decisions were almost invariably in favour of the workers although the employers lost little time in passing on the increases to the consumer. It was generally recognised that the interests of the workers had suffered severely in the depression of the eighties and that as a result there was considerable leeway to be made up. The first judge of the court, Sir Joshua Williams, reflected this outlook in his sympathetic attitude towards the claims of workers. But in the years from 1908 to 1913 the trend of the court's judgments was more in favour of employers because of altered economic conditions : whereas the employers had previously been critical of the court, they began to support the institution at a time when workers had become critical of it. The court is never likely to be applauded by both parties at a given time. The writer well remembers a remark of the late Sir Francis Frazer, who sat as a judge of the court over a long period, that he felt that justice had been done if one side howled for no more than a short period, but if it continued to howl over a long period, he then began to doubt the soundness of the court's decision.

The court is a stabilising influence ; it tends to be slow in increasing wage rates but it also tends to be slow in reducing wage rates. Parliament has intervened on occasions to accelerate a trend, downward in 1931 and upward in 1936. Apart from the occasional though significant legislation which indicates the path to be trodden by the court, there is a wide area of discretion vested in the court. The court is empowered to determine all matters ' in such manner in all respects as in equity and good conscience it thinks fit '. It is in the power of the court to refuse to make an award in an industrial dispute, if it considers that for any reason an award ought not to be made.

Apart from occasional legislation to meet special economic conditions, no attempt has been made by Parliament to express in law the social and economic policy to be followed by the court. The judgments of the court while refraining from enunciating a policy in precise terms, have endeavoured to see that fairness is achieved, even if the approach has been

[8] Mazengarb, *Industrial Laws of New Zealand* (1947), p. 134.

empirical. It was in this way that minimum wage standards were first evolved although the court has since had statutory power to include in awards a minimum rate of wages. Profit-sharing schemes, however, have not been sanctioned except in a few cases such as awards for shearers and shed hands and for some fishermen. The court gave early recognition to the principle of preference for unionists as is discussed in this extract from a judgment [9] of Mr. Justice Ostler in 1937 :

> ' There was nothing in the Act giving the Court of Arbitration express power in its awards to grant preference to unionists, but in one of the earlier awards Williams J. allowed such a provision to be inserted upon the condition that the industrial union of workers concerned provided in its rules that membership should be open to all workers in the industry of good character and sober habits upon payment of the prescribed dues. From that time preference to unionists upon that condition was provided for in nearly every award or agreement.'

Compulsory Unionism

The Full Court, however, held that an award made by the Court of Arbitration embodying compulsory unionism with the consent of the parties was beyond the jurisdiction of the Court of Arbitration.[10] One judge, Mr. Justice Herdman, went so far as to say that compulsory unionism would be a ' flagrant piece of despotism '.[11] It was left to the Labour Government to introduce compulsory unionism by legislation in 1936. The policy of the legislation was to ensure that those benefiting by a union's efforts should assume the obligations of membership of that union. An employer bound by an award or industrial agreement was not permitted to employ adult persons in any jobs within the scope of that award or industrial agreement unless such persons were for the time being members of a workers' union bound by the same award or industrial agreement. Where a person was obliged by this provision to become a member of a particular union, he was of course entitled to apply for membership of that union, but a union was not obliged to admit him if this would mean that the maximum membership as fixed in any award or order of the Court of Arbitration would be exceeded. Since 1951 a person may apply for exemption from membership of a union on religious grounds but if his application is successful he is required to pay to the Social Security Fund an amount equal to the subscription otherwise payable to the union. Applications for exemption are heard by the Conscientious Objection Committee appointed under the Military Training Act, 1949.

[9] *Re Otago Clerical Workers' Award* [1937] N.Z.L.R. 578, 610, 611.
[10] *Butt* v. *Frazer* [1929] N.Z.L.R. 636.
[11] *Ibid.*, 646.

Problems Facing the Court of Arbitration

The court in the exercise of its power has met with difficult problems caused by the nature of industrial organisation. There is the predominance of small industrial units, the variation in the deployment of workers within a unit, and the fact that units tend to be extensive rather than intensive in their industrial activity and thus a business may embrace a number of trades. It is not practicable for awards to run in parallel lanes without encroaching on one another, and even within an award there may be organic difficulties in its application. It is inevitable that sometimes a worker whilst in one employment would seem to be covered by different awards by reason of his differing tasks.

The Attitude of the Ordinary Courts

In the main the attitude of the ordinary courts has been favourable to the development of the Court of Arbitration, and doubtless this was assisted by the fact that in the period from 1894 to 1921 presidents of the Court of Arbitration were drawn from the Supreme Court bench. There was also an understanding of the complexity and difficulty of the court's task and a reluctance to embarrass the court in the discharge of its functions. The question of preference for unionists was considered by the Court of Appeal in 1900.[12] An order of the Court of Arbitration contained a provision that the employers should be bound to employ members of the union in preference to non-members, provided that there were members of the union equally qualified with non-members to perform the particular work required to be done, and ready and willing to undertake it. The court decided that the Court of Arbitration had jurisdiction to direct in its award that preference of employment be given to unionists over non-unionists. The Chief Justice remarked that many of the industrial disputes that had arisen were disputes between workmen and employers as to whether non-unionists should be employed along with unionists, and that it would have been strange that this fertile source of strikes and disputes should have been excluded from the jurisdiction of the court.

In 1908 the Court of Appeal had occasion to examine the penal powers of the Court of Arbitration.[13] The Court of Arbitration had fined a miners' union but as the fine had not been met, the court later made an order for the payment of the fine by the individual members of the union. A majority of the judges in the Court of Appeal held that the individual members of the union could be made liable in this way. In the view of the Chief Justice, the Court of Arbitration could proceed contrary to law or to fact in dealing with matters under its jurisdiction and from these

[12] *Taylor and Oakley* v. *Edwards* (1900) 18 N.Z.L.R. 876.
[13] *Blackball Miners* v. *Judge of Court of Arbitration* (1908) 27 N.Z.L.R. 905.

decisions, however erroneous, there was no right of appeal. The position, of course, is different where the court acts without jurisdiction. The case is also interesting for two legal principles which were competing for application. On the one hand there is the statement of Mr. Justice Williams, who delivered one of the majority judgments, that :

> ' If the Act contemplates, as it undoubtedly does, that in certain events the individual members of a union shall be liable, there is no reason to suppose that the legislature would intend the enforcement of such liability to be hedged in with difficulties unless such intention were made perfectly plain from the language of the act.'

On the other hand, there is the statement of Mr. Justice Edwards, who delivered a dissenting judgment, that :

> '. . . the doubt should be resolved in favour of the members of the union. The liability sought to be enforced is of a penal character . . . If the legislature had intended that such a liability should be imposed, it appears to me that it would have been imposed in clear words.'

The judgments of the majority in this case show a clear disposition to give a broad interpretation to the powers of the court.

In 1916 the attempt was made to introduce compulsory unionism into the provisions of an award, but the Court of Appeal held that a provision in an award requiring every non-unionist employed in any establishment covered by the award to become and remain a member and declaring that his failure to do so was a breach, was *ultra vires*.[14] Although the Chief Justice in his previous judgments concerning the court had been liberal in his approach, he was opposed to the conception of compulsory unionism. He considered that compulsion was the antithesis to unionism, that unionism imported voluntary action and that if all became unionists, unionism would cease to be a differentiation of workers. This case marks the beginning of a slightly less beneficent attitude towards the court. In 1923 the Full Court, with the Court of Arbitration in contemplation, is seen stressing the power of the Supreme Court to keep all other courts within the scope of their appointed jurisdiction.[15] It may be significant that since 1921 the president of the court has not generally been appointed from the Supreme Court bench, but in any event the trend towards a stricter delineation of the court's powers had already begun. Another factor in this trend may have been that the aid of the Supreme Court was sought more than formerly and that employers and workers were more jealous of their rights.

There is always the danger of conflicting decisions because of the separate paths laid down for the recovery of wages and for breaches of

---

[14] *Magner v. Gohns* [1916] N.Z.L.R. 529.
[15] *New Zealand Waterside Workers' Federation Industrial Association of Workers v. Frazer* [1924] N.Z.L.R. 689, 695, 703.

awards. Claims for wages may be brought in the ordinary courts and if they are dealt with in the magistrates' court there is a right of appeal to the Supreme Court. Where, however, a magistrate is dealing with a claim for a penalty arising from a breach of an award, the appeal is to the Court of Arbitration. In either case it may be necessary to construe an award, and in his civil capacity a magistrate may say and in fact has said that he is not bound by the decisions of the Court of Arbitration even though those decisions bind him in another capacity.[16] However, there has been no sustained difference of treatment. In a life of nearly sixty years the Court of Arbitration has produced a mass of case law but the court has endeavoured to be consistent with its own previous decisions. The Supreme Court for its part has not departed greatly from the course of decision in the Court of Arbitration. Since 1941 there has been provision for the Inspector of Awards to be heard in any civil action for wages, salary or damages under a contract which involves an award or industrial agreement. The provision that allows the Court of Arbitration to state a case for the Court of Appeal tends towards the building up of a common approach, but if the ordinary citizen is to be saved the inconvenience of facing two conflicting bodies of law dealing with the same subject matter, then it is desirable that the Court of Arbitration should follow the current of decisions of the Supreme Court, and vice versa.

The Health of Unions

For good or for ill the court has largely determined the course of unionism in New Zealand. It has encouraged the formation and growth of unions. The legislation was deliberately framed to ensure that in general individual workers had no status before the Court of Arbitration. Many unions were formed primarily to take advantage of the arbitration system and the system has also served to buttress the small union. Although amending legislation in 1936 and 1937 gave further encouragement to unionism, there still remain a few groups which because of smallness or dispersal, or both, are too weak to be formed into unions, and which have to rely on such minimum standards as are embodied in the general law. Several powerful unions, relying on their own bargaining strength, have remained outside the system, but most unions turn naturally to the court for the redress of their grievances, and this has been an important factor in the promotion of industrial peace. It is sometimes urged, however, that the paternalism shown by the legislation for unions does not make for their healthy democratic development, and that many of them exist purely to advance or to protect the interests of workers before the court with little attempt to develop other activities. It is also argued that compulsory unionism assures the union of a steady

[16] *Scott* v. *Empire Printing and Box Manufacturing Co. Ltd.* (1942) 2 M.C.D. 307.

income from fees, leaving the secretary with less incentive to promote a good corporate spirit within the union. Thus the union tends to be dominated by its secretary and by a few active members. Although there is a good deal of truth in this criticism, the fact remains that the control of a group by a few is not a phenomenon peculiar to the trade union movement. A further point is that within the trade union movement there is some misgiving on the question of compulsory unionism because it adversely affects the conception of a ' closed shop '. In 1950 employers and unions successfully opposed a Government proposal that there should be provision for a secret ballot within a union on whether membership of that union should be compulsory, and their paradoxical reason was that the removal of compulsory unionism would tend to result in the control of a union falling to a militant few.

The court does provide a constitutional method for the settling of grievances, and for the most part the trade union movement has relied on this machinery, although it has not hesitated to use its political power in an endeavour to promote its interests where the court has been unable to accede to its claims. In 1936 the Labour Government was responsible for legislation which permitted the use of trade union funds for political purposes such as contributions to the funds of a political party. This provision has been criticised as being undemocratic : workers, irrespective of their political beliefs, are compelled to join a union and it is argued that it is unfair that the union should use its funds to make contributions to a political party when there are bound to be varying political views amongst its membership. It is true that the liberty of the individual is infringed but a union would be seriously handicapped if it were prevented from taking political action simply because this was opposed by a minority. At worst, even if the wishes of a minority are disregarded by a union, the members of that minority have the other opportunities available to citizens for expressing their beliefs and engaging in political activity.

At times the court has been almost submerged by the volume and complexity of its work. During the last war power was conferred on the Minister of Labour to set up *ad hoc* tribunals to settle disputes and there was no right of appeal from the decisions of such bodies. They could reach decisions which varied the provisions of existing awards. The justification for their use was the need for speed in dealing with disputes, which were usually local although sometimes potentially serious. Most awards provided for the setting up of a special committee to deal with disputes of this character, but there remained the right of appeal to the court. In practice, there was a tendency for parties to make no sustained effort to settle a dispute at the committee stage, but to await the airing of the dispute before the court. The court in its procedure was slow because its approach was necessarily more comprehensive. It was also faced with a steady stream of work in the interpretation of existing awards and agreements and in their revision as they expired. The *ad hoc* tribunals served a useful purpose in easing the burden of the court but in their operation they could not be expected to have the perspective and consistency of the court in dealing with disputes and in carrying out the stabilisation regulations. Their frequent use would ultimately have led to the undermining of the authority, prestige, and effectiveness of the court.

STRIKES

We have already outlined the penal provisions for dealing with unlawful strikes. The occasions, however, are few when proceedings have been instituted to recover penalties, and this has been true of periods when governments, less sympathetic to the worker than Labour, have been in power. The main aim in a time of strike has been to get the workers back to work, and when this has been achieved there has been a disinclination to prosecute for breaches and thus run the risk of further discord. Under wartime regulations the monetary penalties were increased and a penalty of another type, namely, imprisonment up to three months, was introduced, but the reluctance to enforce penalties remained. As mentioned earlier, a sanction of still another kind had been introduced in 1939 when the Minister was given power to cancel the registration of a union or to cancel an award or industrial agreement. Cancellation of an award or industrial agreement would enable employers to engage workers who were not unionists. The more serious step of cancelling a union's registration would pave the way for the formation of a new union.

Vigorous steps were taken by the Government to deal with the watersiders' strike of 1951. The Public Safety Conservation Act, 1932, which gives the Governor-General power to proclaim a state of emergency and to issue emergency regulations, was invoked : exceptionally wide and diverse powers were taken by regulation. Funds of the union were vested in a receiver. The registration of the union was cancelled. These measures were eventually successful in bringing about a resumption of work but were assisted by a division within the trade union movement. Later in the same year the Industrial Conciliation and Arbitration Amendment Act was passed.[17] We have already embodied under other heads some of the changes made by this Act. It brought under closer control the internal affairs of unions. The Registrar of Industrial Unions was given wider powers to ensure that the rules of a union provided where practicable for the election of officers by such democratic methods

[17] Although some provisions of the Industrial Conciliation and Arbitration Act, 1925, as amended, still apply to the waterfront industry, there is now a special tribunal which regulates pay and conditions of work and decides disputes within that industry: see Waterfront Industry Act, 1953.

as a secret postal ballot of the financial members of a union. The registrar may refuse to record rules, which in his opinion are unreasonable or oppressive, but there is a right of appeal to the Court of Arbitration. Inquiries into disputed elections in unions may be conducted by the Court of Arbitration which has the power to make remedial orders.

A twin measure was the Police Offences Amendment Act, 1951, which deals in the main with sedition and intimidation. The waterfront strike, it was urged, had been fomented by communists who had engaged in the clandestine distribution of leaflets vilifying and defaming persons in authority, and leaders of workers' unions which were not in sympathy with the strike. It was also asserted that some of the propaganda was calculated to incite or encourage violence, lawlessness or disorder.

There was already provision in the Crimes Act for sedition in its more serious form, with a right of trial by jury in the Supreme Court. This provision was not altered but there was created a separate offence triable before a magistrate and carrying a penalty of imprisonment for a term not exceeding three months or a fine not exceeding £100 or both. The provisions dealing with intimidation are comprehensive and the offence is wide enough to embrace intimidation of a worker's wife, child, or parent. Picketing is made illegal and the police are given special powers to deal with it. The Bill when first introduced had drastic provisions shifting the burden of proof to the defendant. These were modified as a result of strong criticism inside and out of Parliament, and apart from other safeguards the sections provide as a minimum that a defendant is entitled to be acquitted if the evidence is such as to raise a reasonable doubt of his guilt.

Under modern conditions it seems inevitable that the State should be given a wide range of coercive powers for dealing with emergencies created by recalcitrant unions and their members, but there is still room for an administrative policy which fosters a more healthy atmosphere in industrial relations and which places greater emphasis on the principle that prevention is better than cure. The Industrial Relations Act, 1949, is a step in this direction. It provides for the setting up of an Industrial Advisory Council including representatives of employers and workers. The functions of this Council are to inquire into and make reports and recommendations to the Minister on such ways and means of improving industrial relations and industrial welfare as from time to time appear to be practicable. Included are such matters as incentive-payment, profit-sharing, and similar schemes, the safety and health of workers, the provision of amenities, and the establishment of works committees and other employer-worker organisations. Advisory councils for specified industries or localities may be set up and they make their reports and recommendations to the Industrial Advisory Council.

CHAPTER 7

MONOPOLY AND PRICE CONTROL

MONOPOLIES

LEGISLATION dealing with combinations of capitalists came at a later stage than that dealing with combinations of workmen, and the approach was different in character. The complaints of New Zealand manufacturers of agricultural implements that they were suffering from unfair competition from importers of implements from foreign countries led to legislation first in 1905. Flour and other products were the subject of legislation in 1907. All this legislation was consolidated in the Monopoly Prevention Act, 1908. More stringent legislation was introduced in 1910 to repress monopolies. Parliament was not content to leave the problem to the evolution of the common law and its choice was justified by the turn of events even if the Crown has had an unhappy run in the judicial interpretation of at least one important provision.

The method chosen by Parliament to deal with the question of agricultural implements was to set up a board to investigate any complaint by two or more New Zealand manufacturers that the price of any implement on importation into New Zealand had been materially reduced, and that unfair competition was being carried on by importers of implements from foreign countries. The board would report in writing to the Minister of Customs the result of its inquiry and state whether or not in its opinion the price of any implement had been materially reduced. If the board recommended that relief be granted, it was lawful for the Minister to grant to the manufacturers of implements in New Zealand such bonus, not exceeding 33 per cent., as he deemed necessary to enable manufacturers to compete with importers of such implements. For the purposes of these provisions implements manufactured in the United Kingdom were deemed to be manufactured in New Zealand.

Another part of the Monopoly Prevention Act, 1908, deals with wheat, flour, and potatoes. Where it is found that the wholesale market price in New Zealand of any of these commodities is unreasonably high, the problem can be tackled by exempting the commodity from customs duties and thus facilitating imports to force down the price. The formula provides that the price of any of these commodities is deemed to be unreasonably high if the average price in New Zealand has, by reason of any combination among the holders of stocks, or by reason of any complete or partial monopoly established by any such holder, been raised above the price which would have been determined by unrestricted competition. It was provided that the machinery of the Court of Arbitration would be used in the administration of this portion of the Act. If the court on an inquiry found that the price was unreasonably high, it would recommend the Governor-General to declare, by Order in Council, that the commodity in question should be admitted to New Zealand free of all customs duties.

It will be seen that the policy behind the preceding legislation was to use such economic weapons as the payment of a bonus or the variation of the customs tariff, but in actual practice these weapons do not seem to have been used to any appreciable extent. The Commercial Trusts Act, 1910, however, is a more direct attack on monopolies, and its title is ' An Act for the Repression of Monopolies in Trade or Commerce '. The Act in its approach resembled the Sherman Act in U.S.A., but was more stringent than comparable Australian legislation. The policy behind the Act is that free and unrestricted competition is necessary if prices are to be kept fair or reasonable. Distrust of foreign oil and meat interests was the force behind the passing of the Act. The goods to which the Act now applies are :

(*a*) agricultural implements ;

(*b*) coal ;

(*c*) any article of food for human consumption, and ingredients used in the manufacture of any such article ; and

(*d*) petroleum or other mineral oil.

Offences are created to cope with the practice of exclusive dealing and with the refusal of one party to deal with another. One section makes it illegal for concessions to be given in consideration of exclusive or principal dealing, or restrictive dealing, or because a purchaser is a member of a commercial trust, or acts or intends or undertakes to act in accordance with the policy of any commercial trust with respect to the sale, purchase, or supply of any goods. In a judgment delivered in 1927 the Privy Council held that this section had no application to the case of an advantage given or promised by or on behalf of one of the parties to the dealing to his own agent.[1] Another section catches a person who refuses, or agrees only upon relatively disadvantageous conditions, to sell goods to or buy goods from another person because such other person deals with a person or class of persons or because he will not undertake to deal with a person or class of persons. It is also an offence if the refusal is because a person has not undertaken to deal exclusively with or will not become a member of a commercial trust, or does not act in accordance with the policy of a commercial trust. The commercial conduct caught by these sections is regarded as evil in itself and it is not necessary to show that it is contrary to the public interest.

[1] *Crown Milling Company Limited* v. *The King* [1927] A.C. 394.

It is also an offence for any person to conspire with another to monopolise wholly or partially the demand for or the supply of any goods : similarly to control wholly or partially the demand for or supply or price of any goods. Such monopoly or control, however, must be of such a nature as to be contrary to the public interest, but it is enough if it is obtained through breaches of the law of the type discussed in the preceding paragraph.

Other offences are created to embrace any person who sells goods at a price which is unreasonably high, if that price has been determined, controlled, or influenced by any commercial trust. The provisions are wide enough to include a person who is not a member of a commercial trust but who follows its price policy. If a commercial trust itself sells at a price which is unreasonably high, every member of that trust is guilty of an offence, and in addition the trust, if a corporation, is guilty. The price of any goods is deemed to be unreasonably high if it produces or is calculated to produce more than a fair and reasonable rate of commercial profit to the person selling or supplying, or offering to sell or supply, those goods, or to his principal or to any commercial trust of which that person or his principal is a member, or to any members of any such commercial trust. Those who aid and abet the commission of offences are also liable. The strict rules of evidence are relaxed to enable evidence to be admitted in proof of any fact in issue, even if such evidence is not admissible in other proceedings. A person is not excused from answering any question or from producing or making discovery of any document on the ground that this would tend to criminate him in respect of any offence against the Act.

Under the Board of Trade Act, 1919, and its Amendment of 1923, the Minister of Industries and Commerce was given power to investigate industrial matters and to hold judicial inquiries to obtain information for these purposes :

(*a*) the due control, regulation and maintenance of the industries of New Zealand ;

(*b*) the due observance, enforcement or amendment of laws relating to the industries of New Zealand ;

(*c*) the discovery and prevention of breaches of those laws ;

(*d*) the prevention or suppression of :
  (i) monopolies ;
  (ii) unfair competition and other practices detrimental to public welfare ; and

(*e*) the proper regulation in the public interest of prices of goods and rates of services.

Although these inquiries must be held in private, the Minister may authorise publication of certain matters and such publication is made under the shelter of absolute privilege. The Minister may institute an inquiry of his own motion or on a reference of the Governor-General, or on the complaint of any person. Under the legislation regulations may be made by the Governor-General in Council for a variety of purposes including the prevention or suppression of monopolies and of unfair competition : the same authority may fix prices of commodities. Regulations have been made under the Board of Trade Act regulating specific trades and products including such things as the sale of wheat, flour, bread, sugar, raw tobacco, wool and the production of wool-packs.

The Act itself makes it an offence for goods to be offered for sale or sold at an unreasonably high price. An offence is also committed by any person who is in possession of goods for trading purposes but who destroys or hoards and refuses to sell such goods or to make them available for sale, if this action raises or tends to raise the retail price of similar goods. A prosecution for either of these offences cannot be launched without the consent of the Minister of Industries and Commerce. In practice it was difficult to secure convictions against traders for profiteering, because the words ' unnecessarily high ' were too wide.

The Commercial Trusts Act, 1910, was first tested in proceedings before the Chief Justice, Sir Robert Stout, in 1912.[2] A sugar company, by arrangement with an association of merchants and some individual firms, members of the association, issued a scale of discounts to be allowed on the purchase of sugar. The scale was framed so as to prevent merchants not belonging to the association from earning the maximum discount. It had the effect of giving the association the control of the distribution of sugar within the Dominion, and also had for one of its results the protection of the company from foreign competition. The company allowed a nominee of a group of merchants to purchase sugar on their behalf so as to earn the maximum discount, and paid the discount to the nominee. It refused to give the same discount to an outside firm which was in competition with the group.

It was held that the company, the merchants' association, and the individual firms were guilty of the conspiracy offence. Secondly, the company, in giving discounts to a nominee of the merchants, was guilty of an offence under the section that makes it illegal for a person to give to another person a discount ' for the reason or upon the express or implied condition that the latter person is, or becomes, or has been, or has undertaken, or will undertake to become, a member of a commercial trust '. Thirdly, the company, in refusing to deal with the outside firm on the same basis as with the nominee of the group, was guilty of an offence. Fourthly, the merchants' association and the individual firms who arranged the transaction were guilty of an offence under the

[2] *R. v. Merchants' Association of New Zealand* (1912) 32 N.Z.L.R. 1233.

aiding and abetting section. Heavy fines were imposed. The judgment was sustained by the Court of Appeal.[3]

It was argued that, as the Act was a penal one, it should be strictly construed against the Crown. The Chief Justice thought, however, that the statute was clear and precise.

'It is said this is a new law and a very stringent one, and thus necessitates a stringent construction. The law is new in a sense, but it must not be forgotten that before English industry was developed as it is now there were many laws that infringed individual liberty in the buying and selling of goods more than this statute does.'[4]

The Chief Justice discussed the context in which the legislation had arisen:

'There have been many laws in recent years passed to supervise and control monopolies, the aim being not to limit liberty but to promote true freedom. I apprehend such is the aim of our many labour laws. That there are vast and difficult industrial problems before all civilised communities is admitted by all who have studied our present-day industrial conditions. The industrial condition has been considered in the United States, in Australia, in the Continent of Europe, and in New Zealand ; and the question really is, Is the State to be dominant and to see that such liberty is granted as makes for the liberty of all, or must the State be placed under the control of large industrial organisations ? There have been struggles in the past between the State and various organisations. At one time they dominated the State ; and there have sprung up in the development of industries, in the concentration of industries, and especially in the growth of capital and the easy mode of transportation, huge combinations, recently termed "trusts", and the question really is, Ought the State to interfere with those trusts ? This is really for the legislature to answer and not for the courts. It may be that this present law may fail, or it may be that this present law only touches the fringe of the question. It is not the province of this court to criticise the method the legislature has adopted in dealing with industrial questions. The duty of the court, as well as of all good citizens, is faithfully to obey the provisions of our statutes. If the statute is ineffective or wrong in principle the appeal must be to the legislative power to alter it, not to the courts to construe it so as to set it aside.'[5]

In discussing the conspiracy section the Court of Appeal said :

'All that the court has to consider is the nature of the monopoly or control, and whether such nature is contrary to the public interest. The effect of the monopoly and control sought to be obtained by the merchants was to keep up the price of sugar to sub-purchasers, which, had it not been for the monopoly, would have been reduced, and to make it impossible for the public to get the benefit of such reduction.

---

[3] *Merchants' Association of New Zealand v. R.* (1913) 32 N.Z.L.R. 1259.
[4] *R. v. Merchants' Association of New Zealand* (1912) 32 N.Z.L.R. 1233, 1251.
[5] *Ibid.*, 1251, 1252.

Prima facie such a monopoly would, in our opinion, be of a nature contrary to the public interest. There may, however, be other considerations which negative this conclusion. Thus, if the monopoly is reasonably necessary in order to prevent the destruction or crippling of an important local industry, or if it is reasonably necessary in order to secure the efficient and economical distribution of the product of the industry, the monopoly might not be contrary to the public interest although it tended to keep up prices. In the present case, however, it appears to us that there is no justification for the contention that a monopoly of distribution by the merchants is necessary to protect the Sugar Company from foreign competition. Nor is there any reason to believe that the monopoly is necessary in order to secure efficient and economical distribution of the manufactured article.' [6]

The Crown Milling Case

The question whether or not a monopoly or control is of such a nature as to be contrary to the public interest was thoroughly thrashed out by the New Zealand courts[7] in a case which reached the Privy Council in 1926. The defendant company was formed for the purpose of acting as sole selling agent, on a commission basis, for flour, bran, and pollard for all such flour-millers as should enter into agreements with it to that effect. The agreements were all in the same form, and provided (inter alia) that the millowners who were parties thereto should not make any sales direct to the public or sell otherwise than through the agency of the company. The company undertook to sell each month a proportionate quantity of each millowner's output of flour, the quantity in each case being determined according to a certain fixed scheme. Provision was made for ascertaining from time to time the current price at which flour was to be sold through the agency of the company. The effect of the combination created by the agreements with the company was admittedly to create a commercial trust having a partial monopoly of the supply of flour and controlling the supply and price of flour in part of New Zealand. By the time the case reached the Privy Council, it had been considered by six judges. The judge of first instance had decided against the Crown, but the Court of Appeal had allowed the Crown's appeal by a majority of three to two. Thus, on a counting of heads, the New Zealand judges were equally divided on the answer to be given. The case provides an interesting illustration of judges wrestling with a difficult economic issue and justifies more than passing treatment.

In the Supreme Court, Mr. Justice Sim thought that to determine whether or not a monopoly was contrary to the public interest, the court had to consider the potentialities of the monopoly in the future, as well as its actual effects in the past. A monopoly could be so inherently vicious

---

[6]　*Merchants' Association of New Zealand* v. *R.* (1913) 32 N.Z.L.R. 1267, 1268.
[7]　*The King* v. *Crown Milling Co. Ltd.* [1925] N.Z.L.R. 258, 753.

or so full of potentialities for evil as to be embraced by the section, but where its vice was not gross and palpable the court had to examine the whole subject to say whether the evils outweighed the virtues. After reviewing the circumstances in which the company had been formed, the judge did not think that it had been established with any sinister design or that its main purpose had not been to stabilise the flour-milling industry by eliminating unrestrained competition with its attendant evils. The operations of the company had been conducted in substantially the same manner with substantially the same scope and object as the operations which the Government for some years previously had conducted continuously through the agency of the Board of Trade and the Wheat Controller. The price secured by means of a monopoly might be higher than would have been obtained under free competition, but this did not make the monopoly contrary to the public interest unless the price were unreasonably high. The consumer might derive benefit for a time from cut-throat competition but in the long run it was not in the public interest to have such competition. The judge also thought that other provisions in the same Act and in the Board of Trade Act, 1919, were sufficient to deal with any attempt to charge excessive prices. He rejected the assertion that the inevitable tendency of the scheme was to remove from each miller the natural inducement that previously existed to produce the best flour he could.

In the Court of Appeal the Chief Justice, Sir Robert Stout, was strongly of the view that the contract was of such a nature as to be contrary to the public interest because it gave the company these powers :

(*a*) fixing prices ;

(*b*) fixing the amount of production ;

(*c*) fixing where the production was to take place ; and

(*d*) declaring that flour produced in New Zealand must be exported.

He thought that the mere fact that the monopoly controlled food and its price was enough to justify the court in saying that it was contrary to the public interest. Decisions in England dating back from the middle of the eighteenth century had shown that any restraint of trade, especially dealing with people's food, was contrary to the public interest. He surveyed the history of the wheat industry in New Zealand and showed that the price in New Zealand was appreciably above that in Australia.

Mr. Justice Reed concluded that the association was a combination which had these potentialities for evil to the public :

(i) the fixing of an unreasonable price for flour ;

(ii) the preventing of active competition between millowners ;

(*a*) lowering the standard of the quality of the flour ;

(*b*) removing all inducement to improve the machinery of mills and the methods of manufacture ;

(c) removing all inducement to render the organisation in milling
companies more efficient.

He thought that it was better for the public that there should be
unrestricted competition.

> ' We know that there is three times as much milling capacity in
> the mills in New Zealand as is required to supply the demands of
> the people for flour. Which is better for the public—that by paying
> an unreasonable price for flour the shareholders should receive
> interest on this dead capital, or that through unrestricted competi-
> tion there should be a survival of the fittest, and the well-organised,
> well-equipped mills should survive, whilst those which are not
> efficiently managed and kept up to date should go to the wall ? ' [8]

In his judgment the test to be applied was whether the restraint was
such only as to afford a fair protection to the interests of the party in
favour of whom it is given, and not so large as to interfere with the
interests of the public.

> ' Let that test be applied to the present case, and we find, first,
> that the combine affects a commodity—flour—of which the public
> must have a constant supply ; a commodity which the poorest
> member of the community must buy ; a commodity which it is
> essential, in the interests of the whole of the public, should be kept
> at as cheap a price and be of as good a quality as is possible. We
> find that the price of flour in New Zealand is above the parity of
> other wheat-producing countries ; that the formation of the com-
> bine largely removes the incentive to improve either the methods
> of manufacture or the quality of the flour, or to reduce prices. The
> interests of the general public are thus seriously affected by the
> combine. Does it afford only a fair protection to its members ?
> Upon this point evidence was called. I need not examine it. What-
> ever the interested parties may say, there is the incontrovertible fact
> that for over eighty years flour-milling had been carried on in New
> Zealand without any restraint on competition until the extraordinary
> circumstances created by the war necessitated Government control.
> The circumstances that then arose no longer exist ; and, however
> satisfactory it may have proved to flour-millers to be able to rely
> on a fixed price for their flour, it is not in the interests of the public
> on the withdrawal of Government control, to substitute that of the
> flour-millers themselves. As for eighty years, with open and un-
> restricted competition, flour-millers were able to carry on without
> the suggested dire results following, it would require the most
> cogent evidence that circumstances had so changed that at the
> present day it would be ruinous to private parties engaged in the
> industry if a return to such unrestricted competition were made
> before the court should assist in imposing upon the public such
> an extremely detrimental monopoly. The evidence called entirely
> failed in that respect.' [9]

[8] *Ibid.*, 810.
[9] *Ibid.*, 814, 815.

Mr. Justice McGregor thought that the primary and paramount ' public interest' was the need for an uncontrolled supply of cheap and good flour in the Dominion.

> ' Any monopoly that on the whole tends in that direction is of such a nature as to be " in the public interest ". Any monopoly that on the whole tends in the opposite direction is prima facie of such a nature as to be " contrary to the public interest " however beneficial it may be to the private interest of the flour-millers and others engaged (as in this case) in the production and distribution of wheat and flour.'[10]

It was not necessary to prove an intent to control the supply or price to the detriment of the public, or to show that any detriment had happened to the public. All that the court had to consider was the nature of the monopoly or control, and whether such nature was contrary to the public interest. In his view the main features of the monopoly were :

(i) to eliminate competition between flour millers ;
(ii) to restrict the saleable output from each mill ;
(iii) to establish a fixed price for all flour, irrespective of quality ;
(iv) to ensure that this fixed price should be determined from time to time by the ' commercial trust ' itself ;
(v) that the public should be compelled to accept whatever brand of flour that the trust should select—purchasers being carefully excluded from dealing direct with any individual flour-miller.

It was difficult to see how a monopoly in the staple food of the people, created in the private interests and for private profit, could fail in the result to be of such a nature as to be contrary to the public interest. The nature of a private monopoly appeared to be inherent and immutable, and its pernicious results tended to be inevitable. He reviewed the steps in the creation of the monopoly and concluded that the flour-millers had deliberately conspired together to perpetuate under their own control the State monopoly which the Government itself was about to abandon as undesirable in the public interest. It had been proved that in 1923, shortly after the monopoly had commenced to operate, the broad tendency was for the price of flour to become higher and for its quality to become lower. These results were the essential traits of the nature of a monopoly and were contrary to the public interest.

Mr. Justice Herdman, who was one of the minority judges, stressed that the question for decision was not whether all monopolies were inherently vicious but whether this particular one was of a nature to be contrary to the public interest. It was therefore necessary to understand something of the history of flour-milling in New Zealand during recent years, and to have some knowledge of the circumstances which gave rise to the combination. He examined the measures of control taken by

[10] *Ibid.*, 817.

the Government from 1917 until the formation of the combination and concluded that the twin aim of the Government was to ensure that the people could buy bread at a reasonable price and that the local wheat-grower was protected. He thought that the public as a whole was interested in having large industries maintained, and in avoiding a campaign of price-cutting, which might bring about the paralysis of large business undertakings and widespread unemployment. If a combination raised prices to an unreasonable height, or if it effected its purpose by any illegal means, or if profits which were unreasonable were exacted from the public, then there would be justification for the complaint that there existed something which was of a nature to be contrary to the public interest, but he found that none of these things existed in this case. Moreover, he could not ignore the fact that the Crown could invoke other legislative powers even within the same Act to deal with abuses, of which excessive prices were an illustration.

The other dissenting judge, Mr. Justice Alpers, thought that a judge who is called upon to decide whether a course of conduct is or is not consonant with public interest, whatever other test he might apply, should at least not adopt the standard of an economic theory at variance with the settled policy of the country. In a country professedly democratic and reasonably educated the public themselves might fairly be deemed the best judges of what is in their interest. He pointed out that it had been the settled policy of the Government to make the country self-contained for wheat production. A protective tariff on flour had been in force since 1888 and an embargo on importation existed from the beginning of 1917 to the beginning of 1925. It could be assumed, therefore, that the public, in so far as they understood their own interest, did not believe it to consist of cheap bread to the exclusion of all other considerations. A court would be chary of convicting a body of men of an offence when they have acted upon a view of the meaning of ' public interest ' which has found support for a number of years in legislative enactments imposing tariffs, in Orders in Council regulating prices, and in official utterances of Cabinet Ministers responsible to Parliament in which the same view of the meaning of ' public interest ' is expressed in unambiguous terms. He refused to accept the argument of the Crown that competition in such an article as flour—' the one staple of public diet '—was imperatively necessary. He said, ' In this country of eaters of meat and drinkers of tea, with luxurious standards of living, I much doubt if bread bears any higher proportion to the total expenses of an average household than did Falstaff's " Halfpenny-worth of bread to this intolerable deal of sack ".'[11] The Government had complete facilities for controlling the combination and checking possible abuses, both under the other provisions of the Commercial Trusts Act and under the Board

[11] *Ibid.*, 831.

of Trade Act, 1919. By removing the embargo or lowering the duty the Government could at any time give full play to foreign competition; nor was domestic competition excluded, because one-fourth of the domestic output of flour was produced by mills outside the combination. There was some evidence from which it could be said that the monopoly had been beneficent in operation. Three important industries—wheat-growing, flour-milling and baking—had been saved from the price-cutting that was threatened when State control was withdrawn.

On appeal the Privy Council[12] reversed the decision of the Court of Appeal and restored the judgment of Mr. Justice Sim given in the Supreme Court. The Privy Council considerably restricted the scope of the question by saying: ' It is not for this tribunal, nor for any tribunal, to adjudicate as between conflicting theories of political economy.'[13] They thought that the legislature had in view that there might be cases of monopoly or control which would not be contrary to the public interest. That a monopoly was contrary to the public interest had to be established in each particular case of prosecution. The burden of proof was upon the Crown, and this applied with special force when the commission of crime was in question. The issue in the circumstances of the case was really one of fact and could not be decided merely as a matter of law. The Privy Council did not think that the Crown had discharged the burden of proof which lay upon it in this case. They reached this conclusion after reviewing and weighing the evidence, but in the judgment there is no detailed analysis of the evidence leading up to this conclusion.

The judgments of the various courts reveal an interesting divergence of opinion amongst the judges in the approach to be adopted in determining whether a monopoly is of such a nature as to be contrary to public interest. So framed the question is a difficult one opening up wide territory for examination. The judgments reveal how the political and economic ideas of judges affect their approach to a case of this kind.

The Chief Justice, Sir Robert Stout, had been prominent as a Liberal politician before his elevation to the Bench. He favoured State action to protect the poor and the weak. The case reflects his humanitarianism, his intense solicitude for the consumer and his distrust of combinations which sought to restrain trade, particularly in food. He had taken a strong line in the sugar case already discussed. The need for cheap and good flour was postulated by Mr. Justice McGregor. He was merciless in his examination of the motives and conduct of the combination. Mr. Justice Reed came out in favour of free and open competition as the best corrective for an over-capitalised industry, and he did not think that the consumer should bear the burden of increased prices arising

[12] *Crown Milling Co. Ltd.* v. *The King* [1927] A.C. 394.
[13] *Ibid.*, 402.

from this condition.   He was concerned at the potentialities for evil in such a combination.

> ' Evidence that its past behaviour has been in no way detrimental to the public interest is not a factor in considering the possibilities of the situation.   It is inconceivable that a combine that purposes to prey upon the public would be sufficiently wanting in common sense as to show its hand at once.'[14]

This view may be contrasted with that expressed by one of the dissenting judges, Mr. Justice Herdman, that ' one must assume that those who control a monopoly which is lawful will continue to obey the law '.[15] A similar sentiment was echoed by the other dissenting judge, Mr. Justice Alpers, when he said that ' opulent corporations, like humbler persons accused of offences against the law, are entitled to " the benefit of the doubt ".'[16]

The judgment in the Supreme Court and the minority judgments in the Court of Appeal show a less unfriendly attitude to big business and an appreciation that combinations may promote industrial efficiency. Free and unrestricted competition should not be pushed to the point of causing economic dislocation in important industries even if this meant some increase of price providing the increase were not excessive. It was stressed that this was consistent with the protectionist outlook of the country.   Both the sugar and the flour industry had grown in the shelter of the customs tariff.   Mr. Justice Alpers, before his elevation to the Bench, had practised in the city of the most important wheat-growing province and was doubtless aware of the economic consequences flowing from a declaration that the monopoly was contrary to public interest. Mr. Justice Herdman had been Attorney-General in the ' Reform ' Government which had been more kindly disposed towards big business than the Liberal Government in its heyday.

It would be wrong to suggest that the New Zealand judges divided in a manner reminiscent of the Supreme Court of the United States when it was passing upon ' New Deal ' legislation.   A glimpse at the political character of the successive Governments which appointed the various judges who adjudicated does not yield any decisive conclusion, nor does an investigation of the social background of the judges.   It is true that the dicta of such judges as Sir Robert Stout and Mr. Justice Herdman reveal a consistency with their earlier political affiliations.   A strong factor, however, was the emerging economic view that big units were not inherently vicious.   This trend, of course, had to cope with the majestic sweeps of the Chief Justice in defence of little units, be they small traders or consumers.

[14] *The King* v. *Crown Milling Co. Ltd.* [1925] N.Z.L.R. 753, 808.
[15] *Ibid.*, 800.
[16] *Ibid.*, 833.

The community was becoming more accustomed to big enterprises. The early twenties had seen the creation by the legislature of a number of marketing boards, and it is not unlikely that their existence did something to reduce the suspicion attaching to a combination, even if it did not have the backing of legislation as did the marketing boards. As has been said by Lord Wright :

> ' We live in days of conferences, marketing schemes, voluntary and compulsory combinations, international cartels ; to say that such organisations, which necessarily involve restraint of trade, are, unless effected by statutory authority, invalid and unlawful, is a mischievous figment. The legal rules of public policy must march with the times in actuality as they are supposed to do in theory.'[17]

The law as expressed by the Privy Council did not accept the challenge to resolve the economic issues, despite the efforts made by the New Zealand judges. The dictum of the Privy Council that it was not its function to adjudicate as between conflicting theories of political economy has been criticised for its positivism, and, in a way, it is a disguised defence of a *laissez-faire* philosophy. The decision, however, was more in harmony with the emerging view that the growth of large economic units in the modern State was ' both inevitable and desirable '. But it is obvious from the experience of this case that the statutory formula is too wide. If the ordinary courts are to be entrusted with the control of monopolies, the formula needs to be more precise. It seems, however, that the task could be better handled by a special tribunal equipped to analyse and weigh economic data.

Export Control and Internal Prices

Export control is another method that has been used to control internal prices and this type of control was applied to butter during the First World War. Prior to that war, there was power to prohibit exports which fell within particular categories, but this power was not conferred as part of an economic plan. The Governor-General in Council had the power to prohibit the exportation of any goods which, in his opinion :

(*a*) could be used for any purpose of war ; or

(*b*) should be kept in New Zealand for the preservation of the flora or fauna.

A similar power could be invoked to protect the revenue or to prevent fraud or deception. The Governor-General in Council could also prohibit the exportation of goods which were not free from disease or which might endanger life or property at sea.

Shortly after the outbreak of war, the Regulation of Trade and Commerce Act, 1914, was passed to provide that at any time when the

[17] *Legal Essays and Addresses,* p. 380.

country was at war, the Governor-General by Order in Council could fix the maximum price in New Zealand of any class of goods. The Governor-General by Order in Council could also prohibit the exportation of any goods where this, in his opinion, was necessary in the public interest. Under the Customs Act, 1913, the export of certain classes of goods could be prohibited either absolutely or subject to conditions.

The internal price of butter rose because of its higher export value and numerous complaints were made to the Board of Trade that the consumer in New Zealand was paying an unreasonably high price for butter. After an investigation by the Board of Trade, an Order in Council was made in 1916 prohibiting the export of butter or cheese unless it had been manufactured at a factory in respect of which an export licence had been issued and was in force at the time of shipment. Another Order in Council fixed a maximum price for butter sold for consumption within New Zealand.

Every factory was entitled to have and retain an export licence provided it was willing to submit to and observe the conditions as laid down in the relevant Order in Council. There was no administrative discretion comparable to that under the Import Control Regulations of 1938; an exporter in New Zealand was free to export if he accepted the conditions and every exporter was to be treated alike.

One of the conditions for the grant of an export licence was the payment to the Crown of a charge on all butterfat consumed by the licence-holder in the manufacture of butter or cheese. The charge was at a uniform rate, but the rate could be varied from time to time by the licensing authority with the approval of the Board of Trade. All manufacturers of butter in New Zealand who elected to join the scheme, whether they were selling for home consumption or for export, received the same net return from each pound of their produce and made the same rateable contribution towards the cost of administering the scheme. Moneys paid by way of charge were held in a deposit account and applied first in payment of the expenses of administration and secondly in payment to the licensees of fair compensation for any loss incurred in disposing of butter for home consumption instead of for export. Any residue remaining was refunded to the licensees.

The scheme was attacked in the courts[18] on the ground that the Order in Council was *ultra vires*. It was contended that the wartime legislation which amended the Customs Act, 1913, should be read in the context of that Act and given a narrower interpretation. Other grounds were:
(*a*) that the payment enacted from the licensees was a tax or charge within the meaning of the Petition of Right and was therefore invalid because not assented to by Parliament;

[18] *Taratahi Dairy Co. and Mangorei Dairy Co.* v. *Attorney-General* [1917] N.Z.L.R. 1.

(b) that the fund created was money of the Crown, and as such could only be disposed of by Parliament under the Constitution Act;

(c) that none of the powers conferred by the legislation could be delegated by the Governor in Council to the licensing authority created by the Order in Council; and

(d) that the Governor in Council had no power to make the Order retrospective.

The judgments of the Full Court illustrate two distinct approaches. Those of the two judges forming the majority show a liberal attitude to the Order in Council, while the dissenting judgment of the Chief Justice, Sir Robert Stout, shows a restrictive attitude. The Chief Justice made the fine point that the charge was not fixed on the butter and cheese exported but was fixed on butterfat, which was not exported. He also took the view that all that the 1914 Act did was to enact that the power of prohibition was not confined to any class of goods but was during the war applicable to all. It did not mean that conditions could be imposed which were not authorised by the 1913 Act. To his mind, it could not be assumed that the Parliament of New Zealand by inserting the word ' conditions ' in the Customs Act of 1913, and by re-enacting it in the Act of 1914, meant to say that the word authorised the abrogation of the constitutional practice of England which had existed since the time of the Stuarts; Parliament did not intend to hand over to the Governor and his Executive powers of taxation without its being consulted. He held that the charge came within the words of the Petition of Right: ' That no man hereafter be compelled to make or yield any gift, loan, benevolence, tax or suchlike charge, without common consent by Act of Parliament.' In his view the charge that was made in the Order in Council had not received the assent of Parliament. The Solicitor-General, Sir John Salmond, contended that as it was wartime, Parliament meant to confer upon the Executive extraordinary powers. The Chief Justice, however, rejected this view on the ground that there was no clear and emphatic statement that Parliament had abrogated its function of legislating or levying taxes or charges. He twitted the Solicitor-General with the similarity his argument bore to that of the Crown in Stuart times when it urged the greatness of the kingly power, particularly in time of war. He considered that the Governor in Council even if he had power to impose the charge could not delegate this authority to a public official designated as a licensing authority; the Order in Council had given the licensing authority power to fix the charge at any rate he pleased but with the approval of the Board of Trade. The money in his view, was Crown money, which could not be spent without the sanction of Parliament. The Order in Council, therefore, in purporting to deal with Crown money was invalid.

A contrary view was taken by Mr. Justice Edwards. He declined to regard the 1914 legislation as an amendment to the 1913 legislation and held that it was a substantive enactment, passed for a widely different purpose of the most transitory character. In his view the reference in the Act of 1914 to the Act of 1913 merely embodied those of the powers given by the Act of 1913 which were applicable to the purpose of the later enactment. The words in which those powers were couched had to be read and construed as though the same powers had been reproduced in full in the Act of 1914. He then proceeded to say that the Governor in Council had the absolute power to prohibit all exports in his discretion. It followed that if the Governor chose to relax the prohibition to allow the exportation of goods subject to conditions or restrictions, the exercise of his discretion in this way was beyond control, provided the power had been exercised for the regulation of trade and commerce in time of war. Because there was statutory authority to prohibit exportation, the enaction of a charge was not contrary to the Petition of Right. The money collected in this way did not form part of the revenue of the Crown, as it was held on trust. Because the Governor in Council had the absolute power to prohibit exportation, he could impose upon those who came under the system the obligation to enter into an agreement which gave delegated power to the licensing authority. For the same reason, there was no objection to the retrospective provision in the Order in Council. The foundation for the validity of the Order in Council was the absolute and uncontrollable power of the Governor to prohibit the exportation of goods.

Mr. Justice Chapman followed in somewhat similar vein. He pointed out that there were two leading features of the 1914 Act, first its title, ' An Act to make provision for the Regulation of Trade and Commerce in Time of War ', and second the provision that any Order in Council made under the Act remained in force only until His Majesty was at peace with all foreign States and Princes. In his view these features showed it to be an emergency Act of an exceptional character. The key to the whole question was to be found in the provision empowering the Governor absolutely to prohibit the exportation of any class of goods. When a functionary was expressly empowered to do a certain act in itself of a stringent nature, and he was at the same time empowered to do this subject to conditions as to relaxation to be laid down by himself, there was a strong presumption that he was thereby empowered to exercise his authority in a less stringent way if he thought fit. The 1914 Act was not to be construed as an amendment to the 1913 Act; the 1914 Act had to be regarded as the dominant enactment. The charge raised by the Order in Council was not a tax in any sense ; it was not levied for the enrichment of the Treasury. He regarded the fund as an ordinary trust fund which could be disbursed without the need for parliamentary authority. He did not accept the argument that the delegation of powers to a licensing authority was invalid. He returned to the point that there was the overriding power to prohibit exports and that there was power to relax this prohibition on conditions which in this instance applied in favour of parties who were willing to enter into an agreement settling the terms and conditions on which they might export butter and cheese. The conditions were valid because it was open to an exporter to apply in the terms of the Order in Council for a licence, and to subject himself for his own benefit to the conditions set out. Similarly there could be no objection to the retrospective provision.

Subsequent Trends

We have already pointed out the weaknesses of the statutory formula for the control of monopolies, but in any event the central administrative issue has been the wider one of how best to control prices, whatever be the factors operating in the economy. It is significant that, since the *Crown Milling Case*, the Executive has turned to a greater use of the regulatory powers conferred under the Board of Trade legislation. For instance, in 1936 the Labour Government introduced (by regulation) a detailed scheme for fixing the prices of wheat, flour, and bread. Another development was legislation designed to make the law more precise on the question of profiteering, and three years later a comprehensive and detailed system of price control was introduced.

Profiteering

The Prevention of Profiteering Act, 1936, created an offence called ' profiteering '. The significant provision was that proceedings were to be taken before a stipendiary magistrate, whose decision was to be final and conclusive. No prosecution could be commenced except by an officer of the Department of Industries and Commerce acting by direction of the Minister. The penalty was a fine not exceeding £200, or imprisonment up to three months in the case of an individual, or a fine not exceeding £1,000 in the case of a company or corporation. The principle adopted by this Act was to fix a basic price, which was to be the lower of the following prices :

(*a*) the current price at which on June 1, 1936, goods of the same nature and quality were saleable in the same locality if sold in the same quantity and on the same terms as to payment, delivery, and otherwise ; or

(*b*) the actual price at which on June 1, 1936, goods of the same nature and quality were being sold by the defendant, in the same locality, in the same quantity, and on the same terms as to payment, delivery, or otherwise.

The performance of services other than those involved in the relationship of master and servant was embraced by the same formula.

The offence of profiteering was committed where the price or rate exceeded the basic figure by an unreasonable amount. In determining whether any increase above the basic figure was unreasonable, the magistrate had to take into consideration the following matters :

(*a*) the extent by which the expenses of the defendant had since June 1, 1936, been increased by the operation of any amendment of the law relating to the rates of remuneration of any workers, or to the working hours of any workers ;

(*b*) the extent by which the business of the defendant had been or was likely to be increased by reason of an increased demand for goods of the kind sold or for services of the kind performed by him, due to the increased purchasing-power of persons requiring such goods or services.

This Act provided a more precise formula for determining what was profiteering and it was much easier to prove an offence under this Act than under the Board of Trade legislation where the test was the wider and more difficult one of whether the price were unreasonably high. The Labour Government had embarked on a deliberate policy of raising wages and the new Act was designed to restrain the resulting tendency for prices to rise.

These provisions were criticised in a public address in 1940 by the then Chief Justice, Sir Michael Myers, in these words :

'. . . in the case of an ordinary trivial offence against the law under the Justices of the Peace Act a fine of £5/1/- gives a general right of appeal, whereas under this particular Act of 1936 a man may be fined £200 or sentenced to three months' imprisonment—the decision may be palpably wrong, but he has no right of appeal. And this—although the charge may involve difficult and intricate questions of both fact and law which may be of general importance to the whole mercantile public. But see how unfairly the 1936 Act can work. The question of prosecution is one for the Minister. He may prosecute a person before one magistrate and fail and then lay other informations against other defendants in different districts before other magistrates until perhaps in some case a conviction is obtained, and there is no opportunity of correcting the magistrate's mistake if he has gone wrong. And, be it observed in passing, that the Act provides that a stipendiary magistrate upon whom is conferred the special jurisdiction under the Act shall be entitled, in addition to his salary as fixed by the Magistrates' Courts Act, to such extra salary or allowances (if any) as may be approved by the Governor-General in Council. Can you agree that all this is right ? '[19]

No prosecutions appear to have been launched under this legislation, which was repealed in 1947. The Act seems to have been more of a

[19] *Journal of Public Administration* (N.Z.), Vol. 3, No. 2, p. 50–51.

gesture by the Labour Government to its followers, although it may have had some moral effect on traders.

PRICE CONTROL[20]

As preparation for a wartime economy the Price Investigation Tribunal was set up in June, 1939, under the Board of Trade Act with advisory and investigational powers delegated to it by the Minister of Industries and Commerce. Later in the same year, the Price Stabilisation Emergency Regulations, 1939, were made which provided that the prices of goods and the rates for services ruling as at September 1, 1939, could not be raised without the prior consent of the Minister of Industries and Commerce who, in practice, delegated the work to the Price Investigation Tribunal, now called the Price Tribunal. The regulations embraced goods of the same nature and quality, and were later amplified by the addition of the word ' substantially '. The defendant in a prosecution had to show that the goods were not of substantially the same nature and quality.

Under this procedure the onus was on the trader to submit a proposed increase in price or rate to the Price Tribunal for its approval. The Price Tribunal, in fixing a price, was not obliged to say how it had arrived at that price. Some goods, for example textiles—the subject of fashion changes—were outside the ' same nature and quality ' rule, and the powers of the Price Tribunal were extended to embrace the power to declare that particular commodities or classes of commodities were subject to control. The effect of such a declaration was that it became an offence to sell a commodity except at a price fixed on application. To fix a price the Price Tribunal had of course to make an investigation of costs. The Price Tribunal was also empowered to make price orders which had legislative character in the sense that the price of a commodity could be fixed for part or for the whole of the Dominion.

The general rule was that the price of goods or services could not be raised except to the extent of the actual increase in the cost of those goods or services, and then only to the extent that the Price Tribunal was satisfied that the merchant or person providing the service was unable to absorb the increase. This meant that, in general, no extra profit could be claimed, thus running counter to accepted commercial practice, which had been recognised by the Supreme Court in the ' *Big Ben* ' *Case* of 1920.[21] Under the Board of Trade Act, 1919, the price of any goods was deemed to be unreasonably high if it produced, or was calculated to produce, more than a fair and reasonable rate of commercial profit to the person selling or supplying those goods, or to his principal. In the ' *Big Ben* ' *Case* the question was the meaning of the words ' commercial

[20] Control of rents is dealt with in Chap. 11.
[21] *Christie* v. *Hastie, Bull & Pickering Ltd.* [1921] N.Z.L.R. 1.

profit' as used in the Act. An American manufacturer of 'Big Ben' alarm clocks had raised the prices at which they would sell to traders and also the prices at which traders were to sell to the public. After the prices had been raised the New Zealand traders involved in the case held in their stock clocks which had been purchased by them when the prices were lower. The established usage of the trade was that in such a case the trader selling to the public would sell at the increased price ruling at the time of the retail sale. The Solicitor-General, however, contended that the trader should sell at the lower price ruling at the time when he purchased the goods from the manufacturer.

It was held that the intention of the Act was to prevent the abnormal conditions following the war from being used by traders for their own aggrandisement. ' In a word, it intended to prevent what is now known as " profiteering ".' It was not intended to disturb established customs or usages of trade. 'Commercial profit' meant with respect to each article such profit as was considered fair and reasonable by reputable traders before the abnormal conditions resulting from the war arose, or such further profit as might be found by reputable traders to be fairly necessary in a free market. The court thought that commercial business could never be successfully carried on if traders were precluded from selling their goods at the prices current in a free market. Unless traders were allowed to pursue their invariable course of business with reference to replacements, as it existed prior to the war, the strong probability was that many would be driven out of business, and the result would be most detrimental to the public interest. It was also held that the custom for merchants who were both wholesalers and retailers to charge retail prices to retail customers was both necessary and beneficial to the public. The customs and usages of trade had been reached by experience which showed them to be most to the advantage of the public, otherwise competition would have brought them to an end.

Hardship would be caused if the Act were given an interpretation inconsistent with the conception of free competition and with the trade usages which flowed from it. Traders faced the certainty that prices would rise and fall and in effect they must be enabled to make gains on some items in order to compensate for losses on others. Overseas manufacturers would refuse to supply New Zealand traders if the latter were unable to comply with the provisions relating to the price at which retail sales were to be made from time to time. To insist that the selling price of an article had to be based on its actual cost would mean an inquiry in every case to determine first, what had actually been paid and second, what was a 'fair and reasonable rate of commercial profit'. At the one time traders could be selling articles of the same description at different prices depending on what those articles had actually cost them.

The difficulties portrayed in this judgment of twenty years before did not deter the Price Tribunal from adopting a formula of price control which excluded the factor of replacement cost. This was possible because price control was closely tied to a policy of stabilisation which embraced wages, rents, income, as well as prices of commodities and of land. The Price Tribunal was empowered to increase prices to the extent of actual additional costs, but only in respect of those goods which had cost more, and only to the extent of any increase which it considered could not be absorbed by the vendor.

Where the Price Tribunal was satisfied that there was a case for an increase in price, and the commodity was one of those ' stabilised ' by the Government, the tribunal had to consider whether the position should not be met by a grant of a subsidy from the Government. During the Second World War, and in the years following, considerable use has been made of the subsidy system for a wide range of commodities. The grant of subsidies eases the pressure for prices to rise. Subsidies are in the unfettered discretion of the Executive. Rationing has also been used to ensure an equitable distribution of goods.

Mere control of prices would not have been enough if nothing had been done on the question of value. It is the statutory function of the Standards Institute to encourage the evolution and maintenance of standard specifications, but progress in this field has been necessarily slow. Standards of this origin were embodied in a few of the Price Tribunal's orders. Where there was no officially recognised standard, it was the practice of the tribunal to specify in its decisions, not only the price, but such matters as quality, quantity, and size.

No proceedings could be taken for a breach of the regulations unless the Price Tribunal first issued a certificate that it considered that there was a prima facie case of a breach. Hundreds of prosecutions were successful. With this method of control it is easier to establish breaches than where the test is the wider one of whether a price is excessive—a question that has to be settled empirically by the court on the facts of each case.

In essence the powers vested in the Price Tribunal were not different in character from those already vested in the Executive. For instance, in the years of the First World War the maximum prices of wheat, flour, bread, bran, and pollard had been fixed by Order in Council, but the control exercised by the Price Tribunal in the Second World War was far more intensive and extensive in its operation throughout the economy of the country. The profiteer, whether a monopoly or a small trader, was caught in the meshes of a wider policy which sought stability through a controlled economy. There were provisions designed to eliminate profiteering, black-marketing, hoarding, and other evasions of price control. Although price control was more successful than in the period of the First World War, it was buffeted by the rising cost of imports and by the fact that although a wide range of controls was introduced the economy of the country was never completely controlled. Even where controls ran there remained the physical difficulties of enforcement, and this was the weakest aspect of the system. The dilemma is that when the case for controls is strong as in a time of war there is usually an acute shortage of manpower.

The price control structure had been built on the foundation of Emergency Regulations but in 1947 the Control of Prices Act was passed to give the Price Tribunal statutory form, as part of a peacetime policy of price control. Although the Act introduced some changes, it did not result in any substantial change in the character and powers of the Price Tribunal. The Act, however, provided that the tribunal with the written consent of the Minister of Industries and Commerce, could delegate to the Director of Price Control its powers excepting that of making Price Orders. There was a right of appeal to the tribunal against any decisions made by the director under powers delegated to him by the tribunal. The stated object of this provision for delegation was to free the tribunal of administrative and enforcement duties. Another change made was that the sittings of the tribunal were to be open to the public unless the tribunal made an order for any case or any class of cases to be heard in private. This should be contrasted with the Control of Prices Emergency Regulations, 1939, which provided that sittings of the tribunal were to be held in private unless in any case the tribunal otherwise decided. The court has since held that this emphasis on public hearings ' points to a more judicial approach to questions before the tribunal under the Act than under the previous regulations '. This and other provisions enabled the court to say that the tribunal in its procedure is required to act judicially.[22]

The Act recognises three different types of price control. First there is the Price Order which may be made by the Price Tribunal with the authority of the Minister of Industries and Commerce, and which fixes the actual or the maximum or the minimum prices that may be charged for particular goods. Secondly the tribunal may by ' special approvals ' authorise a selling-price in respect of the sale of particular goods. Thirdly, there is a statutory formula governing those goods which are not the subject of Price Orders or Special Approvals. Under this formula maximum prices cannot exceed those ruling for goods and services of the same kind on a prescribed date. There is provision for exempting goods or services from this type of control. Since the National Government took office in 1949 the scope of price control generally has been considerably narrowed by the exemption from control of a wide range of items and this has been greatly facilitated by the Control of Prices Amendment Act, 1953.

[22] *F. E. Jackson & Co. Ltd.* v. *Price Tribunal* (No. 2) [1950] N.Z.L.R. 433.

Industrial Efficiency

Questions of monopoly and price control inevitably raise those concerned with industrial efficiency. The more intensive the control the more it becomes involved with the efficiency of the units which are the subject of the control. Furthermore, it will be noted later that the Industrial Efficiency Act of 1936 had the effect of granting monopolies to those industries which were licensed under its provisions.

Although primary production was, and still is the main feature of the country's economy, the growth of secondary industry has had some encouragement from the State. Bounties were used as an instrument of protection from the early eighties. The awards of the Court of Arbitration have relied in part for their efficacy upon a tariff system. When awards provided for an increase of wages, it was inevitable that the prices of New Zealand goods would tend to rise, and had there been no tariffs it would have been easier for foreign goods to compete on the New Zealand market. By the turn of the century there were a number of instances where protective duties had been imposed, and they are now an established part of government policy. The Labour Government came to power in 1935 determined to provide better employment opportunities for the labour force, and it saw the promotion of secondary industry as an important step towards this goal. A more balanced economy was sought, and there was also a desire to ensure that inefficient and uneconomic units were not fostered. Thus the Industrial Efficiency Act, 1936, was passed with this title :

' An Act to promote the Economic Welfare of New Zealand by providing for the Promotion of New Industries in the most Economic Form and by so regulating the General Organisation, Development and Operation of Industries that a Greater Measure of Industrial Efficiency will be secured.'

Scheme of the Act

The Act establishes a registration and licensing system. It also makes provision for the preparation and execution of a plan for the organisation of any industry or related industries, and an Industrial Committee may be appointed to carry out or to assist in the carrying out of a plan. The main organ created by the Act is a Bureau of Industry to administer the Act. There is a right of appeal against any decisions of the bureau on applications for licences.

The bureau consists first, of ordinary members who are public servants with special knowledge or qualifications for the work of the bureau and second, of special members who represent respectively manufacturing industries and agricultural and pastoral industries. Special members may also be appointed at any time to represent any particular industry or group of related industries, and the workers in any such industry or group of related industries may also be represented by special members. Members of the bureau are appointed by the Minister of Industries and Commerce and hold office during his pleasure.

The principal function of the bureau is to make recommendations to the Minister on matters concerned with the promotion of industry, and its healthy development. In addition to its functions as an advisory body, the bureau has functions in respect of industrial plans and licensing. It is expected to facilitate collaboration between Departments of State on matters affecting the administration of the Act. It has the function of maintaining a continuous survey of industries, their finance and methods, and of disseminating industrial information. Another function is that of collaborating with research and other organisations and arranging for the publication and distribution of information amongst persons or organisations concerned with increasing the general standard of industrial efficiency. It also has the function of collaborating with the New Zealand Standards Institute in the work of evolving official standards and of simplifying materials, processes, or products. The bureau is clothed with all the powers of a commission under the Commissions of Inquiry Act, 1908.

The Minister may at any time direct the bureau to prepare an industrial plan for the organisation of any industry or related industries. A provisional plan is then prepared by the bureau, which has the power to require any person or persons to furnish written or oral statements on matters relevant to the plan. When the provisional plan is submitted to the Minister by the bureau, he must give public notice of the material proposals and special notice to all such persons or organisations as in his opinion will be directly affected if and when the plan is brought into operation. Recommendations or objections to the provisional plan are referred to the bureau, which may modify or extend or alter the plan as it thinks fit. After this process the plan is submitted to the Minister with the bureau's recommendations. The plan if approved by the Minister is brought into force by regulations made by the Governor-General by Order in Council, but the Governor-General in Council must be satisfied that the material proposals have been approved by a majority of the persons engaged as principals in the industry or have been approved by persons employing a majority of the workers engaged in the industry. Levies may be imposed to provide funds to meet the cost of preparing or of carrying out plans, including the payment of compensation.

Registration and Licensing

To enable registers to be compiled, the Minister has the power to specify the matters in respect of which particulars are required to be furnished, the forms in which such particulars shall be supplied, and the persons by whom they shall be supplied. The provisions have been described in these words :

> ' The Minister is empowered by notice published in the Gazette to declare that a specified industry shall be carried on only pursuant to a licence issued by the Bureau of Industry. Such a declaration may be made in respect of an industry then being carried on in New Zealand, or in respect of an industry that is not at the time engaged in within New Zealand. No appeal lies against the Minister's decision to declare an industry to be a licensed industry. The general effect of the declaration is to require any person already carrying on the industry to apply for and obtain a licence authorising him to continue to carry on the industry, and to prohibit any other person from being engaged in the industry unless and until he is granted a licence. The legal effect of the declaration may be described as negative ; that is, a person may *not* continue to carry on an existing industry without a licence, and a person may *not*, without a licence, become engaged in an existing industry or commence a new industry.'[23]

The Bureau of Industry is the controlling authority for the issue, suspension, revocation, and control of licences. In considering an application for a licence, the bureau must give to the applicant, and to all other persons who in its opinion will, whether directly or indirectly, be materially affected by its decision, a sufficient opportunity to produce evidence or to make representations to the bureau with respect to the subject-matter of the application.

Where an application is made for a new licence or for a renewal of a licence, the bureau must have regard to a wide variety of matters, all of which come under the general heading of promoting the economic welfare of New Zealand by ensuring the most efficient conduct of its industries.

The bureau may, in its discretion, refuse to grant a licence or may grant a licence subject to such conditions as, having regard to the intent and purposes of the Act, it thinks fit to impose. If in any case the bureau refuses to grant a licence it must, in notifying its decision to the applicant, state the grounds of its decision. The bureau, on giving to the licensee not less than six months' notice of its intention so to do, may revoke any licence granted in any of these cases :

   (a) if the licensee fails to comply with any of the provisions of the Act or of any regulation or industrial plan made under the Act ; or

   (b) if the licensee commits a breach of any of the conditions of his licence ; or

   (c) if, in the opinion of the bureau, the licensee is not achieving economic production in the industry in respect of which he is licensed or is not able to produce goods of suitable quality ; or

[23] Decision of 3/12/45 of Industrial Appeal Authority in Appeals by *M. Michelin & Co. Ltd. and Others*. Not reported.

(*d*) if, in the opinion of the bureau, the licensee is not meeting, or is unable to meet changing needs of markets due to inventions, advances in science, technology, or custom.

No licence granted under the Act may be transferred by the licensee except with the authority of the bureau.

Any person who is aggrieved by a decision of the bureau in respect of his application or licence may appeal to the Industrial Efficiency Appeal Authority. Any other person who, in the opinion of the Appeal Authority, is materially affected by the decision of the bureau may, with the leave of the Appeal Authority, appeal from such decision. In determining an appeal, the Industrial Efficiency Appeal Authority must have regard to the general purposes of the Act and, in particular, to the economic necessity of securing efficiency and co-ordination in industry.

The Governor-General may from time to time, by Order in Council, make all such regulations as in his opinion are necessary or desirable for enforcing the provisions of any industrial plan, or for effectively carrying out any such plan, or generally for the purpose of giving full effect to the intent and purposes of the Act. Without limiting this general authority, the Act states that regulations may be made for a number of specific matters, some of which are :

(i) the fixing of prices or rates, or of maximum or minimum prices or rates, for any classes of goods or services, or the fixing of fixed or maximum or minimum rates of royalties, fees, discounts, rebates, concessions, or considerations, of any kind whatsoever in respect of any goods or services, or in respect of any patent or other proprietary rights ;

(ii) the control of production by the fixing of quotas or otherwise, and the control of the marketing and distribution of products ; and

(iii) the standardisation and simplification of materials, processes, and products.

Regulations must be laid before Parliament within fourteen days after the making thereof if Parliament is then in session and, if not, then within fourteen days after the commencement of the next ensuing session.

The Policy of the Appeal Authority

The decisions of the Appeal Authority are interesting for their treatment of economic issues. The Appeal Authority has ruled that the Act requires the bureau, after

' carefully weighing all the pros and cons, to determine whether the establishment of a new industry for which a licence is sought will be to the advantage of New Zealand ; and, until it has reached an affirmative decision on that issue and has also satisfied itself that the new industry will be economic in itself and will be carried on in the most economic form (in respect of which the Bureau is empowered to lay down conditions), to withhold a licence.'[24]

Apart from the matters specifically mentioned in the Act, the Appeal Authority took the view in a 1945 decision[25] dealing with the grant of licences for the manufacture of rubber tyres and tubes that other matters that may be deemed relevant are the strategical value of a new industry; the effect of its establishment on Commonwealth relations, particularly those with the United Kingdom; the necessity for conserving dollar exchange; the reasonable claims of overseas manufacturers who have in the past supplied the New Zealand market; and the maintenance of a balanced economy in New Zealand.

' It is axiomatic that New Zealand should purchase as great a part as possible of her requirements for manufactured goods from the United Kingdom, which is the principal purchaser of her primary products. It is accepted that extreme economic nationalism is detrimental to real welfare; and that, in general, a country should concentrate on the commodities that it is best able to produce and should export the surplus in exchange for commodities that other countries are better able to produce, and should not embark on the production of commodities that cannot be produced economically. This statement of general principles does not, however, negative entirely the desirability of a primary-producing country establishing and maintaining suitable secondary industries, provided they are economic.'[26]

In another case[27] decided in 1945, a company held a licence to assemble radio receiving sets, and its application was for an extension of this licence to include the complete manufacture of receiving sets. This application was declined on the ground that the New Zealand manufacturers already in the field were capable of meeting the probable post-war demand for high quality radio receiving sets.

In an application for a licence to manufacture women's footwear, which was decided in 1946, the Appeal Authority, after reviewing the economic condition of the industry, concluded that the division of the materials and labour then available among a larger number of manufacturing units could not materially increase the total volume of production and might even reduce it. The potential manufacturing capacity of existing licensed units was, under normal conditions, substantially in excess of the probable demand. To grant additional licences would result, sooner or later, in destructive competition, which was bad.[28]

---

[24] *Ibid.*
[25] *Ibid.*
[26] *Ibid.*
[27] Decision 16/4/45 of Industrial Appeal Authority in appeal by *Amalgamated Wireless (Australasia) Ltd.* Not reported.
[28] Decision 28/1/46 of Industrial Appeal Authority in appeal by *Footgluve Shoe Manufacturing Co. Ltd.* Not reported.

In a case decided in the preceding year, an application for a licence to manufacture electric ranges and stovettes was declined on similar grounds. The case is of interest for these remarks on the objects of the Act:

> ' The Industrial Efficiency Act is designed, not to foster mono-polies or quasi-monopolies without regard to efficiency or economy, but to ensure that there shall be an adequate (but not excessive) number of efficient and economic units in a gazetted industry, and that their operations shall be supervised. If a unit proves to be uneconomic or inefficient, its licence can be revoked, and, if there is scope, a licence in replacement can be granted to a new unit. If the efficient and economic licensed units reach an optimum output, beyond which further economies cannot reasonably be expected, the grant of an additional licence to a new unit may properly be considered. I think that this fairly summarises the underlying objects of the Act. In so far as the facts of the present appeal are concerned, there is uncontradicted evidence that the eight existing licensed units are efficient and economic, and there is ample incon-trovertible evidence that their number is adequate, if not more than adequate to meet all probable post-war demands for some years. They have not yet reached the optimum in production. In these circumstances, if my interpretation of the Act is right, I cannot allow the present appeal. If I were to do so, I would run the risk of substituting destructive and uneconomic competition for the healthy competition that at present exists. In my view, it is neces-sary, under the legislation, to draw a line between the two types of competition, provided of course that the licensed units continue to be efficient, progressive, and economic.'[29]

In the course of its life the Act has not been applied to industry on a wide scale. Only a few industrial plans have been brought into operation. It is in the licensing sphere that more use has been made of the Act, but even here there has been a substantial decline in the number of licensed industries. In 1948 the number of industries licensed was twenty-seven, but in 1952 the figure had fallen to thirteen. The administration of the Act has been criticised for its tendency to protect those industries already in the field without subjecting them to keener tests of their efficiency. Some of the new industries which have grown up under the shelter of import control are marginal ones needing periodical review. The Act itself is expansive in conception, but its administration has not developed in the fullness envisaged by Parliament. The current trend in dealing with inefficient units is away from State intervention of this character and towards other less direct remedies such as the modification of import control.

[29] Decision 29/6/45 of Industrial Appeal Authority in appeal by *Bradley's Electrical Co. Ltd.* Not reported.

CHAPTER 8

MARKETING AND THE PRIMARY PRODUCER

IN the First World War the main primary products were ' commandeered ' on behalf of the British Government as a war measure and this involved submission to a measure of export control. When the commandeer arrangement ended with the return of peace, it was not long before there were demands from producers for organised marketing controlled along limited guild lines. The main aim of the producers was to market to the best advantage and to avoid price fluctuations as far as possible. The twenties saw the creation of a number of statutory marketing bodies vested with extensive coercive powers over the export of primary products. Meat, dairy produce, fruit, honey and kauri gum were each the subject of special legislation ; the only important exception was wool. The pattern of control was similar in each case and may be illustrated by reference to meat and dairy produce.

THE MEAT PRODUCERS' BOARD

A preamble has the legal significance of being the key to the intention of the legislature and, in the case of the Meat Export Control Act, 1921–22, ran thus :

> ' Whereas the economic welfare of New Zealand has lately been adversely affected by reason of a reduction in the net returns receivable by persons engaged in the business of the production of meat for export, such reduction being due in part to falling prices and in part to the charges payable in respect of freight and other services: And whereas conferences have lately been held of representatives of the Government and of persons whose business is the production of meat for export, and it has been resolved that the public economic welfare will be promoted by the establishment of a Board of Control, with power to act as the agent of the producers in respect of the preparation, storage, and shipment of meat, and in respect of the disposal of such meat beyond New Zealand : And whereas it is desired to give effect to the resolutions aforesaid, and to provide by law accordingly : And whereas it is further deemed necessary and desirable that the expenditure of the Board of Control should be subject to audit as if it were public expenditure, and that the expenditure of the Board should be guaranteed by the Government of New Zealand.'

A board was created with extensive powers to control the export of meat. It is proposed to discuss the Board as it exists at the time of writing. The Board is a body corporate with perpetual succession, and is capable of holding real and personal property. It is deemed to be the agent of the owners of all meat of which it assumes control under the Act. The law governing principals and agents applies to this statutory relation-ship, except that the Board may exercise its powers without the authority of the owner of meat. Members of the Board are not personally liable for any act or default which in good faith is done or omitted by the Board in the course of its operations.

The Board now consists of *nine* members as follows :

(*a*) two persons appointed as representatives of the New Zealand Government ;

(*b*) five persons appointed as representatives of the producers of meat for export, on election by the producers ;

(*c*) one person as a representative of stock and station agents [1];

(*d*) one person as a representative of the dairy producers.

A representative of the Government holds office during the pleasure of the Governor-General. A representative of the producers holds office for two years, is eligible for re-appointment following re-election, but may at any time be removed from office by the Governor-General on the recommendation of the Board. The representative of stock and station agents is appointed for two years, is eligible for re-appointment, but may at any time be removed from office by the Governor-General on the recommendation of the Board. The person representing the dairy producers is appointed for two years by the Governor-General on the recommendation of the New Zealand Dairy Board and is eligible for re-appointment. He may be removed from office by the Governor-General for inefficiency, disability, insolvency, neglect of duty, or misconduct. The Board appoints one of its members as chairman.

For the purpose of enabling the Board effectively to control the export, sale, and distribution of New Zealand meat, the Governor-General may use the machinery of the Customs Act to prohibit the export of any meat except as determined by the Board. Licences issued under earlier legislation may be made subject to such conditions and restrictions as may be imposed by the Board.

The Board has full authority to make such arrangements and give such decisions as it thinks proper for the following matters :

(*a*) for the grading, handling, pooling, and storage of meat ;

(*b*) for the shipment of such meat on such terms and in such quantities as it thinks fit ;

(*c*) for the sale and disposal of meat on such terms as it thinks advisable ;

(*d*) for the insurance against loss of any such meat either in New Zealand or in transit from New Zealand, and until disposed of ;

---

[1] These are concerns which trade with and finance farmers.

(e) for the exhibiting and advertising of New Zealand meat and the doing of anything else, for example, experimentation to improve quality and to promote sales ;

(f) generally for all such matters as are necessary for the due discharge of its functions in handling, distributing, and disposing of New Zealand meat.

For the purpose of enabling the Board to carry out its functions, the Governor-General may make such regulations as he thinks necessary for the purpose of enabling the Act to be carried into effect.

The Board may determine from time to time the extent to which it is necessary that it should exercise control over the export of meat from New Zealand. The control may range through any degree of limited control up to absolute control, but irrespective of the nature of the control, no contract for the carriage by sea of meat for export shall be made except by the Board or in accordance with conditions to be approved by the Board. There are provisions which govern the mode in which notice of intention to assume control is to be given but where limited control is assumed, the extent of the control can be defined in agreements between the Board and the owners of the meat. The Board can take steps to protect the interests of producers in the slaughtering of stock for export. Meat under absolute control would be graded, shipped, and sold by the Board or under its direction. There was provision for a levy on all meat exported from New Zealand : the rate to be fixed by the Board within a maximum limit prescribed by regulations made by the Governor-General. The operation of this provision has been suspended and payments to the Board are now appropriated by Parliament.

The application of all moneys received by the Board is defined by the Act. The balance remaining after provision has been made for the Board's expenditure and for a payment into a reserve fund to enable the Board to carry on its operations, is payable to the owners of the meat subject to control. The proportions are fixed by the Board by reference to the quantity and grade of the meat handled.

The Board has power to purchase land and to erect stores thereon for the purpose of carrying on its operations. Its powers of borrowing are confined to the provision that the Minister of Finance may from time to time borrow on the security of Treasury Bills, or otherwise on the security of the public revenues of New Zealand, any moneys that may be required by the Board to enable it to carry on its operations. The Government may guarantee the repayment of moneys raised either by the Board or at its request to enable advances to be made to owners of meat controlled by the Board.

The Board has never purported to assume either absolute or limited control over the export of meat. It has concentrated on making collective bargains on behalf of the producers with ship-owners and others engaged in the business of handling, storing, and selling meat. Substantial reductions have been achieved in some of the charges for these services. Although the Board has never exercised its legal powers of control, it has regulated the flow of meat through the medium of freight contracts and shipping allotments.

THE DAIRY-PRODUCE CONTROL BOARD

The Dairy-Produce Export Control Act, 1923, was the first measure to provide for the organised marketing of dairy produce. The Act did not come into force until its provisions had been approved in a poll taken of all suppliers of milk or cream to factories manufacturing dairy-produce for export. When the provisions had been approved in this way, the Act was brought into operation by Proclamation and the Dairy-Produce Control Board was formed. The Board consisted of twelve persons : nine were elected by the producers, one represented the proprietary interests in the dairy industry, and two represented the Government. No one who had been rejected in an election for the producers' representatives could be appointed as one of the Government representatives. The Board appointed a chairman from one of its members. The Board was a body corporate with perpetual succession, and was capable of holding real and personal property.

To enable the Board to control the export, sale, and distribution of New Zealand dairy-produce, the Governor-General was empowered to use the machinery of the Customs Act to prohibit the export from New Zealand of any dairy-produce except in accordance with a licence. This licence was to be issued by the Minister of Agriculture subject to such conditions and restrictions as might be approved by the Board.

The Board could determine from time to time the extent to which control was necessary for the effective operation of the Act and for the fulfilment of its purposes. Before assuming control, the Board had to give notice as set out in the Act. The Board, if it so wished, could intervene to make contracts for the shipping and carriage by sea of all dairy-produce. It could make a levy within specified limits, on all dairy-produce exported from New Zealand. It could insure dairy-produce against loss.

The various provisions in the Act were, for the most part, identical with those for the Meat-Producers Board, with one important difference : there was no provision for a Government guarantee of repayment of advances that might be made by the Dairy-Produce Control Board in the event of it assuming absolute control.

Only in one season, 1926–27, did the Board assume absolute control, including the fixing of sale prices, but this move to reduce costs between producer and consumer excited organized opposition from London

trading interests and came at a time when other adverse factors led
to a fall in prices. After this unhappy experience, the Board turned
to a policy of arranging freight contracts and regulating the flow of
dairy-produce from New Zealand.

MARKETING BOARDS AND THE COURTS

In the few cases that have arisen, the attitude of the court has been
generally sympathetic to these boards in its interpretation of their powers.
In 1927, the Full Court[2] reviewed the legislation governing the operations
of the Meat-Producers' Board. As the Act had been passed to safeguard
the economic welfare of the Dominion, the court thought that the
principle of strict construction, which was applied to ascertain the powers
of an ordinary company operating for private gain, was not appropriate
here. It commented that the production of meat was one of the leading
industries in the country. In its view the Act should receive such a fair,
large, and liberal construction as would best attain its object. On this
principle, the court held that it was lawful for the Board to expend its
funds in the acquisition of land in London and in the erection of
meat-stores thereon.

The powers of the Dairy-Produce Control Board were considered
by the court[3] in 1926. The question was whether the Board could agree
to pay a newspaper for the publication of material dealing with the
activities and transactions of the Board, and also of information calculated
to promote the interests of the dairy industry. There was no express
power to enter into such an agreement, but the court held that the
Board had the right and the authority to tell the producers what it was
doing, and that there was implied power to enter into such an agreement.
The court took into account the importance of the activities of the
Board and its responsibility to the producers.

We have seen that the Board in 1926 assumed absolute control of
the export of dairy-produce, but there was a special statutory provision
which exempted from complete control any dairy produce which was
the subject of a contract of agency entered into in writing on or before
a stated date. Produce which came within this exemption could be
marketed in England free of control, but the agent could not make shipping contracts, for that was the exclusive function of the Control Board.
It was in the interests of those who wished to escape the control that an
expanded meaning should be given to any contracts of agency that came
within the statutory exemption. In a case[4] that reached the Court of
Appeal in 1927, a contract of agency had been made in 1921 for the

[2] *New Zealand Meat-producers Board* v. *Attorney-General* [1927] N.Z.L.R. 851.
[3] *New Zealand Dairy Control Board* v. *Attorney-General* [1926] G.L.R. 11.
[4] *Southland Dairy Co. Ltd.* v. *New Zealand Dairy-Produce Control Board* [1927]
N.Z.L.R. 305.

disposal of a company's output. In 1926, after the Board had assumed absolute control, the company entered into subsidiary agreements with several other dairy companies whereby the latter were to cease to carry on business on their own account, but were in future to manufacture butter as agents of the first-mentioned company. The company then asserted that the whole of its output, including that manufactured by the agent companies, was exempt from control by the Board. It is not necessary to examine here all the legal issues that were involved, but the general view taken by the court was that, to hold that the company was entitled to establish factories from one end of New Zealand to the other for the purpose of increasing its production of butter, and that the agent was bound to handle that output, was placing a construction on the document which the parties never intended when they made their bargain in 1921.

In another case,[5] a strong attempt was made to restrict the operation of the Act to a particular class of dairy company. ' There are in New Zealand two different classes of dairy companies engaged in the manufacture of dairy-produce, *i.e.*, butter, cheese, and dried milk. There is first the class known as the co-operative company, in which the suppliers are the shareholders, and the whole of the profits are divided among the shareholders ; and secondly, the class known as the proprietary company, in which the suppliers hold no shares, but sell their milk or cream to the company for either a fixed price or a price based on the market price in London from time to time of butter and cheese. It was strenuously contended that the Act should be construed to apply only to the produce of co-operative companies, and that the produce of proprietary companies was not within its provisions ; but the Court decided against this contention and held that the Act applied to all dairy-produce in New Zealand intended for export. The effect of this decision was that the power to control the export and sale of their dairy-produce was taken from those proprietary companies and vested in the Board. This was an extreme instance of the taking away of private rights by the legislature, but the words were too clear for any doubt as to the intention of the Act."[6]

In one case,[7] however, the operations of a marketing board were checked. It was not a case where its substantive powers were restrictively interpreted, but one where, in the exercise of its powers, it had failed to comply fully with procedural requirements. The New Zealand Fruit-export Control Board wished to assume control of the export of

---

[5] *Waitaki Dairy Co.* v. *New Zealand Dairy-Produce Control Board* [1927] N.Z.L.R. 543.
[6] *Southland Dairy Co. Ltd.* v. *New Zealand Dairy-Produce Control Board* [1927] N.Z.L.R. 305, 323, 324.
[7] *J. A. Redpah and Sons Ltd.* v. *New Zealand Fruit-export Control Board* [1929] N.Z.L.R. 369.

fruit from certain districts and notice of its intention to assume control was published in newspapers circulating in those districts. However, the Board failed to publish the notice in the New Zealand Gazette as was prescribed by regulations and the court held that, as a result, the control was not in operation. In the view of the court the general powers of control conferred on the Board by legislation involved a substantial interference with the right of the individual to carry on his own business in his own way, and it was therefore obvious that the provisions governing publicity should be fully applied.

FURTHER MARKETING LEGISLATION

In 1934 Parliament established the Executive Commission of Agriculture to co-ordinate the work of most of the boards controlling primary products. The Governor-General might, from time to time, by Order in Council, transfer to the commission any of the powers vested in the boards dealing with meat, dairy-produce, fruit, honey and poultry. No such transfer, however, could take place except after consultation with the board concerned. The legislation creating the Executive Commission of Agriculture was drastic in character, and it is particularly significant that it was introduced by a Conservative Government. It reflected the general anxiety felt for the welfare of the dairy industry, which was then passing through an intense economic crisis. In the same legislation the Dairy-Produce Export Control Board was reconstituted to become the New Zealand Dairy Board with seven members, three of whom were elected by dairy companies, and three appointed by the Governor-General in Council, and one appointed by a large dairy company. Two significant powers were conferred. First, the Board could regulate production, and second, it could control dairy produce intended for local consumption.

The Executive Commission of Agriculture was not destined to play for long its full role. As a result of legislation introduced by the Labour Government in 1936, the Minister of Marketing stood in the shoes of the commission for the purpose of the transfer to him of the powers vested in the various boards. Power was taken to abolish the commission by Order in Council. Pending abolition the commission exercised such powers as were delegated to it by the Minister of Marketing. In particular its activities were directed to effecting economies in the manufacture of dairy-produce by minimizing overlapping in the collection of milk or cream. It allocated areas or cream collection routes to particular dairy companies. It also arranged for and effected the amalgamation of dairy companies and the closing of uneconomic factories ; the aim being to eliminate proprietary dairy companies and extend the co-operative movement within the industry.

Although the course subsequently followed for dairy-products does not run parallel with that for any of the other products, it is profitable to trace developments in the dairy industry because that is the field where experimentation in forms of control has gone furthest. Under the 1936 legislation, the Dairy Board, shorn of much of its power, was reconstituted once again and prevented from exercising its powers, functions, or discretions except with the approval of the Minister of Marketing. The central principle was the guarantee by the State of prices for dairy-produce. The Crown was empowered to purchase dairy-produce and then to arrange for its sale in New Zealand, or for its shipment and sale overseas. Marketing functions were entrusted to a Department under the control of the Minister of Marketing. The prices to be paid by the Crown to producers were to be fixed by Order in Council in accordance with a formula laid down by Parliament. The supply and distribution of butter and cheese to the internal market was controlled and prices were so fixed that those who supplied the internal market did not suffer in relation to those who supplied the export market. The formula had to have regard to the prices paid over the immediately preceding period of eight to ten years for dairy-produce manufactured for export. Additional factors in the formula were :

(a) the necessity in the public interest of maintaining the stability and efficiency of the dairy industry ;

(b) the costs involved in the efficient production of dairy-produce ;

(c) the general standard of living of persons engaged in the dairy industry in comparison with the general standard of living throughout New Zealand ;

(d) the estimated cost to the Marketing Department of the dairy-produce concerned, and also the cost of the general administration of the Act ; and

(e) any other matters deemed to be relevant.

The prices were to be such that any efficient producer engaged in the dairy industry under usual conditions, and in normal circumstances, would be assured of a sufficient net income from his business to enable him to maintain himself and his family in a reasonable state of comfort. However, there were to be gradations in price according to the quality of the produce. This method of leaving the price fixation to the Crown remained in force for over a decade, but the pressure of the industry for fixation by a more independent body was met to some extent by the creation of special committees, which, although no more than advisory bodies, foreshadowed the next change in legislation.

In 1947 a corporate body, the Dairy-Products Marketing Commission, was established to acquire and market butter and cheese manufactured for export, and to determine the price to be paid upon acquisition.

By an amendment made in 1948 'Dairy-Produce' is defined as
including :

(*a*) milk and cream[8] ; and

(*b*) butter, cheese, and all other products of milk or cream, whether
derived therefrom by manufacturing processes or otherwise.

The commission already had power to control butter and cheese, but
the amendment gave the commission power first, to acquire and market
other types of dairy-produce and second, to prohibit, restrict, and control
their export by other persons. The commission has authority to make
and carry out such arrangements and give such directions as it thinks
proper for any of the following purposes :

(*a*) for the handling, pooling, transport, and storage of dairy-produce ;

(*b*) for the shipment of dairy-produce that is intended for export,
on such terms and in such quantities as it thinks fit ;

(*c*) for the insurance against loss of dairy-produce ;

(*d*) for the further treatment, processing, or packing of dairy-produce ;

(*e*) for furthering the sale of dairy-produce overseas, whether by
advertising, experimental shipments, or otherwise howsoever ; or

(*f*) generally for such matters as are necessary for the exercise of
the functions and powers of the commission.

The commission consists of seven members, three representing the dairy
industry, and three the Government and a chairman appointed by the
Government. Those recommended by the Minister to represent the
dairy industry must be selected from a panel of names submitted by
the Dairy Board.[9] Each member of the commission is appointed for
five years. The Minister of Marketing must consult the Dairy Board
and obtain its views before he makes any recommendation to the Governor-
General for the appointment of any member of the commission, whether
as chairman or otherwise.

Members of the legislature or of the Dairy Board are not eligible
for appointment to the commission. There is also a special provision
disqualifying a person from holding office as chairman if he is in the
employ of the Crown, or if he falls into some other similar relationship
as more particularly defined in the Act. He cannot engage in any business
except farming. Any member of the commission may at any time be
removed from office by the Governor-General for disability, bankruptcy,
neglect of duty, or misconduct.

Whereas the guaranteed prices had previously been fixed by the

---

[8] Note, however, that the supply and distribution of milk and cream for consumption within New Zealand is controlled by the Milk Act 1944. Under
s. 36 (1) of the Milk Amendment Act 1951, milk is so defined as to exclude
milk intended for manufacture into butter, cheese, casein, dried milk, condensed
milk, or condensed cream.

[9] The latest legislation governing the Dairy Board is the Dairy Board Act, 1953.
Its main function is a developmental one.

Governor-General by Order in Council, the commission can now fix the prices but in accordance with a formula stated in its empowering Act. If the accounts of the commission, however, disclose a debit, or a debit is likely to occur within a period of twelve months, the commission must consult the Minister before it fixes any prices. The only substantial variation from the previous formula was the addition that the commission had to have regard to the promotion of the general economic stability of New Zealand. The price so fixed still carried the Government guarantee. Although the commission was given power to control supplies to the domestic market, it was not conceded the power to fix prices on that market. Whatever the figure at which butter or cheese is sold on the local market, the Act provides for an adjustment to ensure that the dairy company obtains no more or no less than it would have obtained if the produce had been acquired for export.

The moneys of the commission are held in the Dairy Industry Account at the Reserve Bank which is authorised to grant the commission accommodation by way of overdraft within a specified limit. The Minister of Finance is authorised to advance to the commission out of the Public Account such sums as may be necessary, without further appropriation by Parliament. There are several safeguards. Cheques on the account must be countersigned by the Audit Office. The prior consent in writing of the Minister of Finance is required before an overdraft with the Reserve Bank can be increased beyond a defined limit and before the commission can borrow moneys in any other manner or mortgage or charge any of its property. His authority is also required for the making of investments beyond the narrow field authorised by the Act. The payments to be made out of the Account are defined in the Act and there is provision for the commission, the Dairy Board, and the Minister of Marketing to agree upon the payment out of the account of moneys for any purpose they deem to be of benefit to the dairy industry. The accounts of the commission must be audited by the Audit Office.

The commission is under a statutory obligation to report to the Minister of Marketing from time to time on trends and prospects in overseas markets in respect of dairy produce and on movements in costs or prices, or on other factors likely to prejudice the economic stability of the dairy industry. The commission is also required to furnish annually to the Minister of Marketing a report of its proceedings and operations, together with a copy of its accounts for the year. The report and accounts must also be laid before Parliament. There is a significant provision that the commission must comply with the general trade policy of the Government and with any general or special directions given by the Minister to the commission in pursuance of the policy of the Government. No such direction, however, can be given in relation to the fixing of prices.

An interesting provision is the one dealing with the making of regulations. The Governor-General may, from time to time, by Order in Council, make regulations, but he cannot do so except in accordance with recommendations made by the commission to the Minister. Included in the purposes for which regulations may be made are these :

(a) regulating the kinds, grades, or qualities of butter or cheese which may be manufactured for consumption in New Zealand ;

(b) regulating the distribution and sale of butter or cheese in New Zealand, and authorising the commission to acquire for resale in New Zealand, and to sell, any butter or cheese ;

(c) licensing persons engaged in the business of distributing or selling (otherwise than retail) butter or cheese intended for consumption in New Zealand ;

(d) obtaining any information or particulars that may be required for the purposes of the Act.

The regulations must be laid before Parliament.

The history of experiments in the dairy industry over the last twenty-five years is a most fruitful lesson in the interaction of economics and politics and its expression in the law. First, there was the period of board control with State assistance on the assumption that the interests of the industry at least for the most part coincided with those of the country as a whole. Towards the end of this period, the fall in returns owing to the economic conditions of the early thirties led to a heart-searching. A policy of export control could not avoid looking back to production and could also be adversely affected by uncontrolled sales on the domestic market. Furthermore, if Great Britain imposed quotas on her imports of New Zealand produce, production within New Zealand would have to be controlled in the light of those quotas. There was a demand for the co-ordination of the activities of all marketing boards. This culminated in the Executive Commission of Agriculture of 1934. Co-ordination, however, could do little to cope with the problem of insecurity caused by severe falls in prices overseas. It was in this context that the notion of a guaranteed price, based largely on an average of prices over a long period of years, was introduced by the Labour Government in 1936. The social flavour of the legislation is seen in the insistence that the efficient producer should be assured of sufficient net income to maintain himself and his family in a reasonable state of comfort. Parallel legislation was passed to protect the interests of workers in the employ of producers. Reliance was placed upon standards which, although vague in many respects, show the spirit behind the legislation.

With the State giving a guaranteed price, it was almost inevitable that a Government Department should be established to bring the industry under closer and continuous control. A Department was established but, although it performed its duties efficiently, it could not compete against the demand of a powerful group of producers to be allowed greater participation in the control and disposal of their produce. The notion of a guaranteed price appeals to producers in a time of recession, but it has not quite the same appeal in prosperous times when the free market shows a higher return. However, the producers, although on occasion dissatisfied with the actual price fixed, were not seeking the abolition of the principle of the guaranteed price. They wanted the price to be fixed by a body more independent of the Executive, and a Government that had become the target for some criticism acquiesced. So, the upshot was the Dairy Products Marketing Commission, which is a step away from direct Executive control and yet which is subject to some Government control.

To obtain the financial backing of the State and yet be free of Government control was the aim of the industry. The State, however, could not abdicate where it was assuming heavy financial responsibilities, nor could it overlook the economic importance of the industry to the country as a whole. The legislation setting up the Dairy Products Marketing Commission is full of compromise with emphasis on mutual consultation and on the interlocking of powers. To meet distrust of the Executive, there are interesting attempts to control the Executive in the exercise of such powers as it has. For instance, we have seen that the Minister must consult the Dairy Board before he recommends the Governor-General to appoint a person to be a member of the commission. Regulations cannot be made unless they are in accordance with the recommendations of the commission. In its turn, the commission, in some respects, cannot move without consultation with the Executive, and there are some powers which it cannot exercise without the approval of the Executive. The danger of partisanship from either side is met by the special disqualifying provisions governing membership of the commission. The provision that the commission should carry out the trade policy of the Government is almost too vague to interpret, and in any event, it is unlikely that the courts will have much opportunity to elucidate it before the next turn of the legislative wheel. Other provisions depend for their force on the efficacy of constitutional conventions, and several in the last resort require good faith on the part of the Executive, leaving the ultimate sanction to be a political one.

INTERNAL MARKETING

Under legislation passed in 1937, the Marketing Department was given the power to fix the wholesale or retail prices at which dairy produce, fruit, honey, and eggs could be bought or sold within any part of New Zealand. Price margins could be fixed within which these foodstuffs might be bought or sold. The Department could also fix the general conditions under which these foodstuffs were to be sold. The range of foodstuffs could be extended by Order in Council from time to time and, in 1939, this provision was expanded to cover such goods or classes of goods as might be specified by Order in Council.

To secure economic and orderly marketing in New Zealand, the legislation of 1937 gave the Department power to take the foodstuffs enumerated above. This power, however, could not be exercised without authority conferred by regulations made by Order in Council. Regulations could be made :

(a) authorising the Department to take, at prices to be fixed by the same or any subsequent Order in Council, any such foodstuffs, and to export so much thereof as, in the opinion of the Minister, would not be required for consumption in New Zealand ; or

(b) authorising the Department to control the export of any such foodstuffs by any person or authority other than the Department.

Where foodstuffs became subject to the above measures of price control, or were acquired by the Department, there was provision for the Minister to pay to those persons equitably entitled sums for the purpose of equalising, as far as practicable, the net returns received or payable in respect of such foodstuffs.

An important feature of the scheme was the purchase by the State of a private concern trading in foodstuffs of the kinds specified in the Act. The Marketing Department was empowered to trade, and it did so for the purpose of setting a comparative standard not only in prices but in quality.

The Department assumed control of citrus fruits in 1937, partly to protect the New Zealand consumer against exploitation when imported supplies were scarce, and partly to ensure that oranges from the Cook Islands were marketed for the benefit of that Dependency. During the Second World War, the Department took over the export of apples and pears as overseas markets had become disrupted and it was necessary to ease the pressure on the internal market.

We have seen in our discussion of the various marketing boards that they sprang from the pressure of producers and that little attention was paid to the interests of the consumer. It is true that a substantial factor behind the Internal Marketing legislation of 1937 was the desire to advance the interests of those who were producing foodstuffs for the internal market. The Labour Government however had to meet the consumer interest, and it is significant that, in the course of time, the Department placed greater stress on seeing that consumers were fairly treated in the way of supplies, quality, and prices. It was inevitable that

this policy would run counter to the interests of producers, and it was
not long before internal marketing became a lively political issue. From
1947 the Department began to decline as an economic force. Its activities
substantially shrank when the marketing of butter and cheese passed to
the Dairy-Products Marketing Commission in 1947. Another step in
the decline was the setting up of a special board to handle apples and
pears, although the Department operated as agent for that board. In
1953 the Department was abolished and its small residue of functions
transferred to the Department of Agriculture.

FURTHER RECENT LEGISLATION

The Primary Products Act, 1953, reflects the policy of the Government
to give the producer more say in the marketing of his own produce.
Machinery is provided for the establishment of a marketing authority
for the purpose of regulating the marketing of any primary product
within the scope of the Act. ' Primary product ' for the purpose of the
Act means any product of agriculture, horticulture, grazing, poultry
farming, or beekeeping, but does not include dairy-products, wheat,
potatoes, apples, pears, tobacco, wool, livestock, or meat. The excluded
items are, of course, the subject of special schemes.

Under the Act, regulations may be made establishing marketing
authorities and defining their constitution, powers, and functions. The
Act provides, however, that regulations cannot be made unless the
Minister of Agriculture is satisfied, on such evidence as he considers
adequate, that the majority of the persons engaged in the production of a
product are in favour of the establishment of a marketing authority
for that product. The purposes for which regulations may be made
cover a wide range relating to marketing. These purposes, as well as the
other provisions of the Act, embody the long experience that the country
has now had of marketing schemes. The only point that need be noted
here is that marketing beyond New Zealand is contemplated as well as
marketing within New Zealand.

In conferring the power to make regulations, the Act recites that
one of the purposes is to enable producers to control the marketing of
their own products. The interests of the consumer, however, are protected to some extent by the provision that at least one member of each
marketing authority must be appointed as Government representative,
and he, as the Act says, represents the interests of consumers of the
primary product concerned, in addition to his other functions as a member
of the authority. A further safeguard is that regulations made under
the Act must ultimately have the sanction of Parliament. The regulations
require to be laid before Parliament within twenty-eight days after the
date they are made, if Parliament is then in session or, if it is not in

session, then within twenty-eight days after the commencement of the next session. The regulations expire on the last day of that session except so far.as they are expressly validated or confirmed by an Act passed during the session. Finally, a marketing authority must comply with the general trade policy of the Government and with any general or special directions given by the Minister of Agriculture in pursuance of that policy.

CHAPTER 9

EXCHANGE CONTROL AND BANKING

THE year 1938 was a crucial one in the economic history of New Zealand and the measures taken in that year set a pattern that has, in many respects, endured to the present. Overseas funds began to decline during the 1936–37 season and this movement continued until late in 1938 when a dangerously low level was reached. It was at this point that control was introduced to conserve overseas funds for the purpose of meeting overseas debt services and essential imports. Three inter-related steps were taken ; first, there were the Export Licences Regulations ; secondly, the Import Control Regulations ; and thirdly, the suspension of the obligation of the Reserve Bank to give sterling in exchange for its banknotes. These profound changes were not made by specific Acts of Parliament.

EXPORT CONTROL AND OVERSEAS FUNDS

The objective of the Export Licences Regulations was to provide a system for following and conserving overseas funds and providing for their application. Provisions of this type were not new as a measure of export control, for a somewhat similar purpose had existed in the slump period of the early thirties. The regulations, which are still in force, establish a licensing system for the export of goods from New Zealand. Goods include New Zealand products (whether raw or manufactured). Animals are included, as is any other movable personal property which the Minister of Customs, by notice in the Gazette, declares to be goods for the purposes of the regulations. The general rule is that goods cannot be exported from New Zealand except in accordance with the terms of a licence. A licence is granted on condition that the overseas credits earned by the goods are sold to a New Zealand bank in return for New Zealand currency.

The regulations do not apply to :

(a) any goods exported or proposed to be exported through the Post Office, unless in any case the Minister determines that the export of any such goods through the Post Office shall be subject to the regulations ;

(b) any goods exported as ships' stores ; or

(c) any other goods in respect of which the Minister, by direction in writing, determines that the regulations are not to apply. Such a direction may be at any time varied or revoked by the Minister.

There are three types of licence. The first is a particular licence for the export of specified goods in a specified ship. This licence is for the occasional shipment. The second type is a general licence to export goods from specified ports over a specified period. This caters for those who make periodical or frequent shipments. Such a licence may apply to goods of all kinds, or be limited to specified kinds of goods. A general licence may be revoked at any time by the Comptroller of Customs. The third type is a purchaser's licence to export goods that have been purchased in New Zealand with credits from overseas. From every decision of the Comptroller of Customs or Collector of Customs there is a right of appeal to the Minister, whose decision is final.

Particular licences and general licences are issued subject to special conditions. The licensee is required to deliver the relevant shipping documents or drafts to the trading bank named in his application. Where goods are exported for sale, the licensee must arrange for the net proceeds of the sale to be paid to a branch or agent of the local bank in London, or in the place where the goods are sold. At the same time, the branch or agent of the local bank must be supplied with a statement giving particulars of the sale and proceeds. In the case of a general licence, there is the further requirement that within six days after a certificate of clearance has been granted to the ship in which the goods have been exported, the licensee must deliver to the Collector of Customs a statement giving various particulars of the goods and showing whether the goods have been exported for sale or for any other purpose.

The local trading bank is obliged to arrange for the net proceeds of the sale to be paid by its overseas branch or agent to the Reserve Bank or its authorised agent. It must also notify the Reserve Bank in Wellington of the receipt and disposal of the moneys by its overseas branch or agent, with particulars of the sale. The Reserve Bank, in its discretion, may in any case permit the local bank to dispose of the moneys in some other manner.

Where a foreign credit is paid to the Reserve Bank, or its agent, the Reserve Bank must pay to the local bank an amount equal to the value of the foreign credit, converted into New Zealand currency at a rate not less than the then current rate of exchange. This amount is then held to the credit of the licensee, subject to any agreed or customary charges and to any contractual rights and liabilities as between the bank and the licensee. The licensee is deemed to have irrevocably appointed the local bank as his agent to receive and dispose of the proceeds in the manner prescribed by the regulations.

Where credit or currency has been made available in New Zealand in exchange for an overseas credit or currency, so that goods may be purchased in New Zealand for export, special provisions apply. As foreign credit is made available and is used in New Zealand in the purchase of goods for export, there must be paid to the Reserve Bank, or its agents, such amount of foreign credit as equals in value, at the current rate of exchange, the New Zealand credit or currency used in the purchase of the goods. It is in the discretion of the Reserve Bank, however, to vary this provision.

As with particular and general licenses so in the case of a purchaser's licence, the Reserve Bank on receipt of a foreign credit must pay over an amount equal to the value of the foreign credit, converted into New Zealand currency, at a rate not less than the current rate of exchange.

A purchaser's licence cannot be granted unless the Collector of Customs is satisfied that foreign credit has been paid to the Reserve Bank, or its agent, or that arrangements, satisfactory to the Reserve Bank, have been made for this payment or that the Reserve Bank has authorised the foreign credit to be disposed of in some other manner.

Before any licence is issued, the applicant can be required to give security for compliance with the conditions of the licence and with the regulations. Those who commit offences against the regulations are liable to heavy penalties.

IMPORT CONTROL

In 1934 the minority report of the New Zealand Monetary Committee made this comment:

> 'We recognise that it is possible but not easy to maintain a stable internal price-level and at the same time maintain parity of exchange with a country which has a fluctuating price-level. We definitely prefer stability of internal price-level; and, so far as exchange variation may become a problem beyond the dimensions of a reasonable stabilization fund, we would recommend that it be dealt with by rationing the exchange. In such rationing preference should be given to essential commodities not available from our own resources.'[1]

The comment was made by a group, most of whom were members of the Labour Party which was then the Opposition but which became the Government in 1935. Although the minority was thinking primarily of the trade recession of the early thirties and of the instability produced internally by restriction of credit and by depreciation of the currency, the report did portend the method that was to be adopted by the Government in the crisis of 1938.

Under the Import Control Regulations, goods cannot be imported unless a licence has been obtained or an exemption granted. It is in the discretion of the Minister of Customs to grant a licence in respect of all goods included in any application, or in respect of part only of such

[1] N.Z. Appendix to Journals H. of R., 1934–1935, Vol. I, B.-3, 87.

goods, or to decline to grant any application. He may impose such conditions as he thinks fit and, in particular, any licence may specify a period within which goods comprised in the licence may be imported. He may revoke or modify the terms and conditions of a licence, providing the licensee is notified in writing prior to the actual shipment of the goods from the country of export to New Zealand.

The Minister may at his discretion from time to time by notice in the Gazette exempt from the requirements of a licence any particular goods or classes of goods or goods imported from particular countries. By a similar procedure an exemption may be withdrawn but goods which have been shipped from the country of export to New Zealand at the time of the withdrawal are protected.

The Minister may from time to time delegate to officers of Customs the powers of granting, revoking, and modifying licences. Where an applicant or licensee is dissatisfied with a decision given under delegated power, he may by notice in writing apply to the Minister for reconsideration of the act complained of, and may submit in writing such considerations as he thinks fit in support of his application. The decision of the Minister upon reconsideration is final.

It was not long before these regulations were challenged in the Supreme Court.[2] Leaving aside for the moment whether the regulations were within the powers conferred on the Executive by Parliament, the court examined the regulations for their meaning and concluded that they surrendered the whole field of importation to the uncontrolled discretion of the Minister of Customs unguided by any settled principles. In the view of the judge they conferred upon the Minister of Customs these powers :

(*a*) Except in so far as he has for the time being created general exemptions of named goods from the licensing system by the exercise of the discretion given to him under the regulations, nothing can be imported into New Zealand without his consent, or the consent of one of his delegates. If consent be refused, no reason need be given for refusal, and from the Minister's final refusal there is no appeal.

(*b*) In exercise of his powers, the Minister may from time to time at his discretion, (i) permit all importation not otherwise prohibited in which New Zealanders desire to engage ; or (ii) prevent any importation at all ; or (iii) sanction parts, but only parts, of the importation in which New Zealanders desire to engage.

(*c*) The Minister is not bound to proceed upon any defined or definable principle or principles or according to any settled practice or practices in the exercise of his powers.

[2] *F. E. Jackson & Co. Ltd.* v. *Collector of Customs* [1939] N.Z.L.R. 682.

(*d*) If he should choose to proceed from time to time upon any defined principle or according to any settled practice, he is not bound to make any announcement as to what that principle or practice is or will be. If, however, he should choose to make any such announcement, it is at least difficult to see how, in view of the terms of the regulations, he could be compelled by any legal process to adhere to such announcement.

(*e*) He is not compellable to consider merely classes of goods as such. He is free to consider classes of goods ; the countries from which they are exported ; the purposes for which they will probably be used if and when imported ; the persons who wish to import them ; the extent to which an importer has, as a matter of business, imported such goods in the past ; the circumstance that an importer has, by expenditure of time and money, prepared himself to engage in a particular branch of importing business ; whether particular prohibitions would tend to create unemployment, and if so, to what extent, and whether such unemployment would be readily absorbed by other activities the growth of which the particular prohibitions might encourage ; for how long particular prohibitions, if imposed, might be expected to last, and whether their imposition might encourage the growth within New Zealand of other methods of meeting the demands of consumers which might be left in a difficult position by the removal of the restrictions. But the terms of the regulations entitle the Minister to give to any considerations that he may think relevant, from time to time, and in individual cases as much or as little weight as he from time to time thinks fit. And, if he thinks fit to ignore any or all of the considerations mentioned above, it is difficult to see how that could be made the subject of any successful legal proceedings by any one.

(*f*) In the result, he is not compellable, and may well consider it not to be his duty to treat all importers in the same way with regard to the same classes of goods, even when they are imported from the same country and are intended to be used for the same purposes. Nor is he obliged to treat the same importer in the same way as to the same quantity of the same goods on different occasions. In fact, he has express power to revoke a licence at any time prior to actual shipment from the country of export. This power appears to be exercisable notwithstanding that the importer, on the faith of the licence, had entered into a contractual obligation to pay for the goods or had actually paid for them.

(*g*) Licences may be refused for importations even though such importations can be accomplished without any immediate demand for the exchange of New Zealand currency into sterling, and no matter for how long such demand may be shown to have been postponed by contract between exporter and importer. Indeed, it appears to be within the power of the Minister to refuse a licence for importations although it is demonstrated to him that the goods sought to be imported are the subject-matter of a bequest or gift from a person abroad to a person in New Zealand.

(*h*) In granting a licence the Minister may impose such conditions as he thinks fit.

Having found the meaning of the regulations the judge then turned to the question whether there were statutory provisions which gave power to make regulations so wide and far-reaching in their content. The preamble to the regulations ran thus :

> ' Pursuant to the Customs Act, 1913, and the Reserve Bank of New Zealand Amendment Act, 1936, and to all other powers enabling him in this behalf, and being of opinion that the prohibition of the importation of goods hereinafter referred to is necessary in the public interest and to the end that the economic and social welfare may be promoted and maintained and to enable the Reserve Bank of New Zealand to fulfil its functions of regulating and controlling the transfer of moneys from New Zealand and the disposal of moneys that are derived from the sale of any New Zealand products and for the time being are held overseas, His Excellency the Governor-General, acting by and with the advice and consent of the Executive Council, doth hereby make the following regulations : '

In his examination of the Customs Act, 1913, the judge found that the provisions relied upon by the Crown did no more than to empower the Governor-General in Council to prohibit the importation of *classes* of goods specified in the Order in Council : there was no power to prohibit the importation of all goods collectively.

> ' The actual language used in section 46, the history of the legislation, and the purpose of the Act are all against such a large interpretation as that the Governor-General is empowered to prohibit totally importation as such. I am disposed to concede that the Customs Act is more than an Act for collecting a certain kind of revenue, and that it is also an Act for regulating and controlling departments of trade or commerce, including importation. But, if so, it regulates and controls importation on the basis and assumption that importation will continue, and will not be extinguished. . . .
>
> ' To decide that importation as such is permanently or temporarily not in the public interest is, in my view, to decide a question different, not merely in degree but in kind, from deciding that the importation of specified classes of goods is not in the public interest. . . .
>
> ' I do not believe that the language relied upon should be interpreted so as to attribute to Parliament that it has empowered the Governor-General in Council to introduce, even temporarily, so remarkable a change in our national life.'

The judge thought it was significant that, although the Act made mention of a power to prohibit the importation of goods from any specified person, there was no mention of a power to prohibit importation by any person. Furthermore, the Governor-General in Council had no authority to delegate his powers and responsibilities to the Minister of Customs.

Turning to the Reserve Bank legislation, the judge found that a decision to exclude imports was not a decision as to a ' monetary policy ' which could be communicated to the Bank by the Minister of Finance in terms of the legislation.   This was so even if the decision to exclude imports was in consequence of a monetary policy of exchange control. On the same day as the Import Control Regulations were made there were made the Export Licences Regulations, which placed the proceeds of the sale of exported goods under the control of the Reserve Bank. On the day following, the duty of the Reserve Bank to give in exchange for its own notes sterling for immediate delivery in London was suspended.   From this material the Crown invited the court to perceive that it was, for the time being, the monetary policy of the Government to control and limit the free transfer of New Zealand currency into sterling and that the forcible control of the importation of goods into New Zealand followed as a logical step.   The judge held, however, that decisions to limit imports were not decisions of a monetary character, although he was disposed to accept that the limitation of imports was an indirect method of effecting exchange control and he quoted economic authority for this view.   He also quoted from an official publication of the League of Nations to show the importance of the functions committed to the Minister of Customs : the successful operation of the system required an extremely high degree of State interference with, and control of, all branches of economic life.   Even if the Governor-General in Council had power to legislate by regulation in this field, there was no express power enabling him to hand the field over to be regulated or controlled by someone else.   To assume power to deal with all cases in a certain field by a series of particular exercises of discretion is not a valid exercise of a power to make regulations concerning that field.   .

In the result, the regulations could not be sustained under the Customs or Reserve Bank legislation, or by the combined effect of both statutes, and were invalid.   The judge accepted the view that he should give the Acts such fair, large, and liberal interpretation as would best attain their object, but decided that the powers conferred upon the Minister of Customs by the Import Control Regulations were so great that much clearer language than Parliament had employed was required to justify the attempt to confer them.   He agreed that there was force in the argument of the Solicitor-General :

> ' that those cases cited during the argument which illustrate the jealous care with which the Courts foster and protect trade and commerce are of little assistance in construing an enactment which

authorises exchange control, and incidentally authorises its consequences. But this consideration does not warrant an assumption that Parliament intended to permit that a person, or the holder for the time being of an office not mentioned by it, should have power to distribute the inevitable dislocation, still less that he should have power to distribute it from time to time according to his uncontrolled discretion and without any enunciation of rules or principles which might assist those who were likely to be affected to regulate their own affairs accordingly.'

Later in the same year, Parliament met the position by an amendment declaring that the Import Control Regulations were and had always been valid. The amendment, however, did not affect judgments given prior to its date. Although this amendment has been made, the judgment that has been discussed is valuable for its exhaustive examination of the effect of the regulations.

BANKING

We have already seen the role of the Reserve Bank in relation to the conservation of overseas funds. Its role in other fields is of growing significance and demands examination in the context of the New Zealand banking scene.

The attitude of the State towards commercial banking has passed through a number of phases. First of all, apart from a brief interlude between 1850 and 1856 when there was a State bank with a monopoly of note issue, the State contented itself with granting banks authority to begin business and to issue bank-notes. Banking was regarded by the public as the field of private enterprise and the State confined itself to the provision of safeguards to protect depositors and the general public. The first stage may be said to have ended in 1914 on the outbreak of the First World War. From then to the early thirties is the second stage. In that period there was close co-operation between the Government and the banks in financing war expenditure. There was also a growing awareness that banking affected the economic condition of the country as a whole and that what served the interests of a bank did not necessarily serve those of the public. Towards the end of this period there was pressure for the creation of a central bank. The third phase quickly followed with the creation of the Reserve Bank with the exclusive right of note-issue. The Reserve Bank, although initiated by the State, was given a measure of independence and its share capital was subscribed by the public. The fourth and present phase is one where the Reserve Bank is owned completely by the State but the method of control has varied with the Government in power.

Over a long period the legislation dealing with currency and banking did not fit the economic situation. The assumptions behind the legislation were not real, but at least the legislation was not a strait-jacket impeding economic development; its faults were more those of formulae which were unreal or too wide. The legislation had assumed that New Zealand was on the gold standard, but at no time in its history was this true. The cash and credit resources of the country were not regulated by the quantity of gold held within the country for monetary purposes, nor did gold ' ebb and flow freely into and out of the country ' in harmony with transactions on foreign exchanges. The London balances arising from trading operations were, however, convertible into gold. The traditional policy of the banks was to link sterling and New Zealand currency by an exchange rate which moved within certain narrow limits. Most of our external trade was with the United Kingdom and moneys for the development of the country were borrowed on the London market. It was inevitable that the London balances should ultimately regulate the credit policy of banks. New Zealand became sensitive to sterling movements and changes in the British price level inevitably affected the New Zealand price level. The Reserve Bank Act, 1933, clearly recognised that New Zealand was on the sterling exchange standard, although sterling by then had ceased to be convertible into gold.

Treasury, in a survey prepared for the New Zealand Monetary Committee of 1934, explained the system in these simple terms :

> ' The banks maintain offices in London, and these offices receive the proceeds of the sale of our exports. The exporters receive credit for the amounts due to them, plus or minus exchange at the ruling rate, in the books of their respective bankers in New Zealand. These credits go to swell deposits. The importers, on the other hand, pay to their bankers by cheque in New Zealand the amount of their debt due abroad, plus or minus exchange on London at the ruling rate, and the British or other overseas' merchant receives payment directly or indirectly out of the London funds of the banks.'

Treasury emphasised that, in the last resort, it was the pressure on the London balances of the banks which limited the amount of credit that could be issued in New Zealand. Currency was necessarily subordinate to credit. It was clear then that the state of the London funds was a restraint which could not be avoided without obvious consequences. In its summing-up, Treasury reached these conclusions :

(1) that the *de facto* system is and always has been a sterling-exchange standard ;

(2) that it has centred round an approximate fixed par of exchange between the British and the New Zealand pound ;

(3) that our external trade is cleared through London and the London balances of the banks are the chief factor in regulating the volume of credit in New Zealand ;

(4) that the banking habit is strongly developed in New Zealand and notes and coin are very subsidiary, being used for little beyond payment of wages, petty disbursements and till-money ;

(5) that the legislative restrictions on the note-issue have been quite inoperative, as the demand has always been considerably less than the maximum amount the banks were in a position to issue ; and

(6) that the volume of credit has regulated the note-issue and not vice versa.

The banks pursued a monetary policy of endeavouring to keep New Zealand ' on an even keel ' in regard to London funds. By long experience they had found that an increase in their advances which was disproportionate to the increase in their deposits led inevitably to a drain on the London balances. They therefore watched closely the ratio of their advances to deposits. In the absence of controls imposed by Government, the banks used the traditional methods of bringing the overseas balance of payments position into equilibrium, namely raising interest rates on advances and deposits, altering the exchange rate on London, and simultaneously exercising stricter qualitative selection of advances, discouraging and declining advances that were sought for consumption purposes rather than for essential production, particularly primary production.

There are now five trading banks which cover the country with a network of branches. Two are British banks, two are Australian banks, and one is a New Zealand bank. Each of these banks had the legal power to issue notes until this function was taken over by the Reserve Bank. The main regulatory provisions of long standing were uniform. First, the note-issue was not to exceed the amount of the coin bullion and public securities held by the bank in New Zealand, and coin was to be not less than one-third of the total. Second, the debts engagements and liabilities of a bank were not to exceed three times the coin, bullion and public securities held by it within New Zealand. As mentioned earlier, too much significance should not be attached to these legal limits because it was the London balances which limited the credit policy of the banks.

Banks doing business in New Zealand have been incorporated under special Acts or under general Companies Acts supplemented by special Acts on such matters as the issue of notes. There has also been incorporation by Royal Charter.

All banks are subject to the Banking Act, 1908, which prescribes such things as the minimum and maximum number of directors and the procedure for an increase of capital and for the transfer of shares. The Banking Act also provides that Royal Charters and Letters Patent granted to banks are as effectual within New Zealand as Acts of the New Zealand General Assembly.

Banking is done by the Post Office Savings Bank under special legislation. There are a few trustee savings banks which are regulated by special statutory provisions. The amount on which interest may be paid is fixed and interest rates may be fixed or varied by Order in Council. Stock and station agents, building and investment societies, and some trading companies accept deposits either on a time or call basis, but there is authority to fix by Order in Council the maximum rates of interest that may be paid by them on deposits ; some of these institutions, for instance stock and station agents, grant their clients cheque facilities.

RESERVE BANK

In the depression years of the early thirties, the banking system was the subject of much criticism. The tendency of the banks to treat New Zealand and Australia as one economic unit for exchange purposes had the possibility of unfairness for New Zealand. It was argued that, as Australia was a much larger economic unit, whose climatic conditions led to greater fluctuations in production, it was inequitable that purely Australian factors should adversely affect New Zealand. It was contended that the trading banks had not co-operated with the Government in its desire to alter the exchange rate and that the banks had imposed disadvantageous terms for the discounting of Treasury Bills intended to provide the Government with the funds with which to buy sterling. It was also asserted that it was a fundamental weakness in New Zealand banking organisation that the control should be in the hands of a number of independent boards of directors, only one of which possessed a head office in New Zealand. However, perhaps the strongest argument was that in a time of crisis a central bank, particularly where it had Government backing, could take a dispassionate view of the monetary steps required and could initiate steps considered desirable, regardless of the necessity to make profits. The Reserve Bank was finally established by an Act of 1933.

The temper of the times can be gauged from these passages in the majority report of the New Zealand Monetary Committee of 1934 :

> ' There can be no argument against the right of the State to control currency and credit within its borders. The paramount authority of the State must not be merely permissive and negative ; it must be active and positive. . . . In so far as legislation limited the activities of the banks, they have been controlled by the State but this control was merely a legal framework—it may have given form but it certainly did not give direction to the banking system.'

Central banking was a developing fashion and the pressure for the establishment of a central bank in New Zealand followed the trend of other British countries to set up central banks.

The primary duty of the Reserve Bank under the legislation is to exercise control over monetary circulation and credit in New Zealand so that the economic welfare of the Dominion may be promoted and maintained. Power to control the exchange rate is vested in the Bank. The Bank is required at all times to make public the minimum rate at which it is prepared to discount or re-discount Bills. Only an Act of Parliament can dissolve the Bank.

The Bank is managed by a Board of Directors consisting of the Governor and the Deputy-Governor and seven ordinary members. The Secretary to the Treasury is an *ex officio* member with voting powers. The Governor and Deputy-Governor must be persons who have had actual banking experience. While they are in office they cannot engage in any business on their own account or act as directors of any business or hold any interest in any other bank. They are appointed by the Governor-General in Council for a term of seven years and are eligible for re-appointment. Ordinary members hold office during the pleasure of the Governor-General in Council but cannot hold office continuously for a longer period than five years, although they are eligible for re-appointment. The following are ineligible for appointment as Governor, Deputy-Governor, or as ordinary members :

(*a*) members of the legislature ;

(*b*) employees of any other bank, but the Act provides that not more than one member of the Board may be a director of any other bank ;

(*c*) public servants of any Department. This provision, however, does not apply to the Secretary to the Treasury ;

(*d*) Undischarged bankrupts ; and

(*e*) those who are not British subjects by birth. In the case of one person the legislature relaxed this provision.

In 1936 the Labour Government made the Reserve Bank an instrument of its policy. The financial structure of the Bank was changed : the State provided the whole of the capital, including the General Reserve Fund. The private shareholders were repaid but the corporate identity of the Bank was preserved.

As we have seen, the sterling exchange standard had been recognised by the 1933 legislation but the amending legislation of 1936 is significant for the power given to the Minister of Finance to suspend by notice in the Gazette the obligation of the Bank to give sterling on demand in exchange for its notes.

Under section 10 of the amending legislation, the Bank was obliged to give effect to the monetary policy of the Government as communicated to it from time to time by the Minister of Finance and the Governor-General was empowered to make regulations by Order in Council enabling the Bank to fulfil its functions. The meaning of this section has never been judicially settled, although Mr. Justice Callan in the *Jackson Case*[3] had these comments to make on the difficulties raised by the amendment :

[3] *F. E. Jackson & Co. Ltd.* v. *Collector of Customs* [1939] N.Z.L.R. 682, 726, 727.

'Section 10 of the Amendment Act of 1936 is in an unusual form. It expressly refers to " the monetary policy of the Government as communicated from time to time by the Minister of Finance ". Ostler J. observed, in the passage already quoted from his judgment in *Carroll's Case*, that the courts have no concern with the policy of the Government responsible for the promulgation of a regulation. That is the ordinary rule and it is very well settled. But, in this case, arising from the way the subsection is expressed, the arguments of counsel discussed at great length the monetary policy of the Government of the day and the court was invited to concern itself with that topic. Nor is it clear that this discussion can in this case be disposed of by the method adopted by McMillan J. in *Re Sooka Nand Verma* where that learned judge said : " We have heard, in the course of the argument, something about the policy of the Ministry but, sitting in this court, we are not in any way concerned with the policy of this or any other Ministry. If the policy of the Ministry commends itself to the legislature and we find that policy crystallised in an Act of Parliament, then, and then for the first time is it brought to our notice." But upon this occasion Parliament appears to have reversed the normal process and, within some limits not easy to define, to have enabled any Government to crystallise any monetary policy into measures which have legal effect upon the lives and activities of citizens. What from time to time it is lawful for the Reserve Bank to do in certain spheres, appears to have been made dependent on what is from time to time the monetary policy of the Government. Further, a great deal of the argument appears to me to have proceeded upon the assumption that the section makes the existence, nature, and extent of the regulating power thereby conferred upon the Governor-General in Council dependent upon what is for the time being the monetary policy of the Government of the day. Since the argument, a doubt has occurred to me as to whether this is the true construction. It may be that what Parliament intended was that the Governor-General in Council should make, once and for all, such regulations as would enable the Reserve Bank to fulfil its allotted function whatever might be, from time to time, the monetary policy of any Government. But, if it be the position that the extent of the regulating power conferred by Parliament is made dependent upon what is for the time being the monetary policy of the Government of the day, the subsection may raise problems of special importance and difficulty to which it may become the duty of the courts to give careful attention in order to determine whether the subsection really is an instrument by means of which Governments, in pursuance of their policies, may subject citizens to controls of kinds never before experienced, in spheres as to which Parliament has said no express word and by such a route that the courts cannot effectively check whether in reality the regulating power exists.

'During the course of his argument, the Solicitor-General contended that, even if the court were unable to know from the available material, what, if any, was the monetary policy of the Government, it was nevertheless bound to assume, from the mere making of the regulations, that the Government had a monetary policy and to accept the opinion of the Governor-General in Council that these regulations were necessary to enable the Reserve Bank to fulfil its function of giving effect to that policy. This appears to illustrate the serious nature of the problems that may arise from the enactment.'

In 1939 the Labour Government put through an amendment expressing in clearer terms the Bank's obligation to give effect to a decision of the Government. The Government sought more direct control over monetary policy including the power to compel the Bank to carry out the Government's policy in relation to such matters as interest and discount rates. Although the change was opposed by the Governor and the Board of Directors of the Bank, the following provision was embodied in the law :

' In the exercise of their functions and powers under the principal Act, the Governor and Board of Directors shall have regard to any representations that may be made by the Minister of Finance in respect of any functions or business of the Reserve Bank, and shall give effect to any decision of the Government in relation thereto conveyed to the Governor in writing by the Minister of Finance.'

This provision was repealed in 1950 and the position now is that the Bank is required to give effect to any resolution of the House of Representatives in respect of any functions or business of the Bank.

In promoting and maintaining the social and economic welfare of New Zealand, the Bank must now regulate and control these things :

(a) credit and currency in New Zealand ;

(b) the transfer of moneys to or from New Zealand ;

(c) the disposal of moneys that are derived from the sale of New Zealand products and for the time being are held overseas.

By the 1950 amendment, the Bank is also required to do all such things within the limits of its powers as it deems necessary or desirable to promote and safeguard a stable internal price level and the highest degree of production, trade, and employment that can be achieved by monetary action.

To carry out its functions, the Bank has a variety of powers. It may accept money on deposit or on current account. It has the power to make and issue bank-notes. It may buy and sell gold and silver coin or bullion. Currencies of other countries may be bought and sold. The Bank may organise a clearing system. It may also act as a correspondent for overseas banks or as agent of other reserve banks.

A trading bank must maintain with the Reserve Bank a balance of not less than 7 per cent. of its demand liabilities in New Zealand and 3 per cent. of its time liabilities in New Zealand. These percentages, however, may be increased by the Governor of the Reserve Bank acting with the authority of the Minister of Finance, and were so increased in August, 1952, to 10 per cent. in respect of demand liabilities and 5 per cent. in respect of time liabilities. This power is one of the important weapons available to the Reserve Bank in exercising effective control of monetary conditions in New Zealand.

Trading banks must submit to the Reserve Bank monthly returns of their assets and liabilities in respect of their New Zealand business. The Reserve Bank has the power to inspect the books of a trading bank. Another safeguard is that the Reserve Bank, with its exclusive right of note-issue, can regulate the supply of notes to a trading bank but, because public confidence in a trading bank would be adversely affected, this overt method of control is unlikely to be used save in exceptional circumstances. The advances made by trading banks are now subject to restrictions imposed by the Reserve Bank in an effort to curb inflation.

The Reserve Bank may buy and sell securities of the New Zealand or United Kingdom Governments or securities guaranteed by the Government of New Zealand or by the Government of the United Kingdom. It may discount, buy, or sell various defined types of Bills providing they mature within the varying periods laid down in the legislation, and advances up to three months may be granted against Bills of this type. Advances up to three months may also be granted against :

(a) gold coin or bullion ;

(b) government local authority or other approved securities readily marketable in New Zealand ;

(c) promissory notes of banks in New Zealand.

Accommodation by way of overdraft may be granted to the Government of New Zealand and to any Department of State or statutory authority having power to carry on any business or to borrow moneys on overdraft.

There is the significant provision that accommodation by way of overdraft may be granted to any authority having statutory powers in relation to the marketing of any New Zealand produce, for the purpose of assisting the purchasing and marketing of any such produce. Moneys may be advanced to the Government of any other country in respect of the purchase of any New Zealand products for export to that country, or the Reserve Bank may guarantee any such advances that may be made by another bank. The amount outstanding in respect of any advances or guarantees in this respect must at no time exceed in the aggregate the sum of £10,000,000.

The Bank is closely concerned with the financial operations of the Government. It holds the public account. By authority of the Governor-General in Council it may underwrite any loan proposed to be raised by the New Zealand Government or by the State Advances Corporation of New Zealand. It may issue and manage loans for the Government or any local authority or public body in New Zealand. It may keep a register of inscribed stock on behalf of a local authority or public body.

In the conduct of its business the Bank is subject to a number of restrictions which cannot be overcome except with the authority of the

Governor-General in Council. It may not engage in trade, or otherwise have a direct interest in any commercial, industrial, or similar undertaking. It may not purchase the shares of any other bank in New Zealand or elsewhere (except shares of the Bank for International Settlements), nor grant loans on the security of any such shares. Unsecured loans or advances cannot be made. The Bank is not permitted to purchase or make advances on the security of real property, except so far as may be required to enable the Bank to conduct its business, but, if any claims of the Bank are endangered, the Bank may secure itself on any real property of the debtor and may acquire such property which must, however, be re-sold as soon as practicable thereafter. Interest may not be paid on the balances that require to be maintained with the Bank by the trading banks, nor is interest payable on any other moneys placed on deposit or on current account with the Bank, except for funds of the New Zealand Government held by the Bank outside New Zealand.

The Bank may not allow the renewal of maturing bills of exchange, promissory notes, or other similar documents, purchased or discounted by, or pledged to the Bank, provided that, in exceptional circumstances, the Board of Directors may by resolution authorise not more than one renewal of any such document. Bills payable otherwise than on demand cannot be drawn or accepted. The Bank is not permitted to grant accommodation, either directly or indirectly, to the Treasury, or to any incorporated Department of State, or to any local authority or public body, by way of discounts, loans, advances, overdrafts, or otherwise, in excess of the revenue or estimated revenue for the year in the case of the Treasury, or one-fourth of their respective revenues or estimated revenues for the year in the case of any other Department of State, or of any local authority or public body.

Formerly, the Reserve Bank was restricted by the provision that its notes in circulation and other demand liabilities had to be backed by a reserve of 25 per cent. in the form of gold coin and bullion and sterling exchange less liabilities in currencies other than New Zealand. Later it was provided that the minimum ratio could be varied or suspended by the Minister of Finance. Since 1950, however, the Bank's duty has been defined as that of maintaining reserves which, in the opinion of the Board of Directors, will provide a reasonable margin for contingencies, after taking into account prospective receipts and disbursements of overseas funds, and having regard to the economic position within New Zealand.

The Reserve Bank must furnish weekly to the Treasury a statement of its assets and liabilities and this statement is published in the Gazette. Within three months after the close of each financial year the Bank must transmit to the Treasury an audited copy of its accounts for the year. The accounts are then published in the Gazette and are also laid before Parliament. The surplus profits are paid to the State if the General

Reserve Fund of the Bank is not less than £1,000,000 but where the Fund is below this figure a statutory formula operates to give the Bank a share in the profits. The amount of any increase in the value of the gold coin and bullion in the unrestricted ownership of the Bank must be credited to the Crown. Any appreciation or depreciation in the assets of the Bank, arising from a variation in the exchange rate between New Zealand and London, is to be credited to or borne by the Consolidated Fund.

Amongst the drastic measures taken in 1938 to check the fall in overseas funds was one to control remittances overseas, and this is still in force and is administered by the Reserve Bank.[4] The statutory obligation of the Bank, on presentation at its head office of notes to any amount not less than £1,000, to give in exchange sterling for immediate delivery in London was suspended. This suspension, which was made on the direction of the Minister of Finance, in terms of the 1936 Amendment Act, is still in force.

We have seen that the Reserve Bank, when originally created, was granted a measure of independence but that it was later brought under close Government control by the Labour Government. The amendment made by the National Government in 1950 does not reverse this development, although the mode in which control may be exercised has been made more public in the requirement that there must be a resolution of the House of Representatives. Although the legal power to alter the rate of exchange is vested in the Reserve Bank, it seems from recent experience that this question has become a political one in the sense that the initiative is taken by the Government of the day with the Reserve Bank moving in harmony to give legal expression to a decision of the Government. This subordination to the political will is not surprising in view of the country's economic structure. Primary producers, who are a powerful political force, have a vital interest in any movement of the exchange rate. Although the capital market has developed in the last twenty years, it does not compare in extent with the capital market that exists in England. Furthermore, there is no Bill market of any consequence. The Reserve Bank must adapt itself to this environment but the legal powers that it has seem sufficient to enable it to fulfil its purpose. However, its control over internal monetary conditions has been made more effective by the concurrent operation of other controls imposed by Government.

[4] The Bank is responsible for the adequacy of foreign exchange to meet imports and through its scheme for the allocation of exchange, it supplements the Government's measures for the control of imports.

CHAPTER 10

CRIMINAL LAW

Transition to a New World

WHEN Godwin wrote his essay on the nature of political justice he declared :

> ' Men who are freed from the injurious institutions of European government, and obliged to begin the world for themselves, are in the direct road to be virtuous.'

Many of those who came to New Zealand in the first half of the nineteenth century did feel that they had been freed from the compulsions of a social system they condemned and looked forward to a life nearer to their ideal. But with them, and preceding them, came men of a very different stamp—hardened wayfarers who knocked about the harbours of the world : ex-convicts from New South Wales ; others bent on amassing a quick fortune and returning to the Old World. Even among the sober settlers conflicts inevitably arose in the scramble for land. Trouble also lay ahead in the divergence of interest between gold-miners and farmers, and in the jostling for power under the early federal system of government. Ere long, sporadic conflict between settlers and Maoris was to develop into war. Life in New Zealand for several generations after serious colonisation began was not only hard but often turbulent. Even if Godwin were right it was not long before the imperative necessity for an adequate administration of justice was impressed upon each scattered community in this newest of British possessions.[1]

To the layman the need was for some branch of government to be armed with sufficient power to preserve the peace and for courts of justice before which malefactors could be tried. To the lawyer (especially to those entrusted with the task of erecting this system out of nothing) the issues were rather different. Should the substance of the criminal law of this new country be the criminal law of England, with a few minor alterations, or should a bold attempt be made to break with tradition ?

---

[1] At Port Nicholson, for example, a Committee of Colonists founded its own Constabulary Force and appointed a magistrate in April, 1840. The committee resolved that the magistrate and constables should respectively possess and exercise within the Colony all the powers which in England belong to the office of a justice of the peace and constables so far as the same were applicable within the Colony. Although the jurisdiction of the magistrate was challenged by the first defendant to appear before him, the court and the constables did exercise their powers until the actions of the Committee of Colonists in appointing them were declared to be an illegal usurpation of authority. *New Zealand Gazette* (newspaper), April 18, 1840.

257

In the administration of law, were English courts and English rules a suitable model ? Did this new community, or group of communities, have so much in common with England that rules and practices evolved there through centuries could be effectively transplanted to this new soil ?

James Stephen, Under-Secretary of the Colonial Office at the time, put the issue broadly in this way :

> ' In the infancy of a colony the choice must be made between the adoption of an old and inapplicable code or of a new and immature code. Both are evils, but in my mind it is much safer to begin with a vigorous effort to lay the foundations of law on a right and durable basis, than to build it on a basis which must be wrong and which can never possess any stability.'[2]

This was also the view of William Swainson, the first Attorney-General, who drafted many of the Ordinances of the period before representative government was granted. Looking back in 1859 at the work of the early years he said :

> ' Not being hampered by any complicated pre-existing system, nor impeded by the opposing influence of a powerful profession, the lawgivers of the Colony were enabled to effect amendments in the law which the British legislature has hardly yet succeeded in accomplishing.'[3]

But it is difficult to find, in the records of those days, much evidence that this reforming zeal was directed to the subject of criminal law. There was ready acceptance of the principle that the efficient and impartial administration of justice is foremost among the essentials of good government.[4] But during the first thirty years of colonisation there appears to have been negligible development in the content and form of the criminal law, and the administration of justice clung tenaciously to English precedents singularly unsuited to the condition of the Colony.

After a variety of enactments which were little more than paper schemes for the constitution of courts and usually followed English practice even to the detail of ' quarter sessions ' and ' petty sessions ', one unified superior court—the Supreme Court—was established, and summary cases were entrusted to magistrates or justices of the peace. English criminal law (both statutory and common law) was made applicable within the Colony. Significant changes in the content of the criminal law were for the time being crowded out while battles were fought over such issues as responsible government, the terms on which land should be made available to settlers, the powers of the provinces, the best site for the seat of the central government, or an improved system of communication with Australia and England.

[2] Minute on Governor's Dispatch of March 29, 1842.
[3] Swainson, *New Zealand and its Colonisation*, p. 94.
[4] A typical remark was that made by the Governor in the Speech from the Throne at the opening of Parliament in 1858 : ' The speedy and certain administration of justice is the most sacred duty of a Government.'

ADOPTION OF ENGLISH CRIMINAL LAW

The adoption of English criminal law, so far as suitable to the circumstances of the Colony, was expressly effected by the English Laws Act, but this merely confirmed the rule of common law applicable to British colonies in general. With the exception of the colonies of New England and New Jersey (which rejected English common law even as a subsidiary law) and one or two others in which English common law was specifically excluded by statute, it was the rule that the plantations and colonies acquired automatically so much of the laws of England as was suitable to their circumstances. While a bold effort was made in New Zealand to devise new and appropriate rules on many subjects (notably property law and conveyancing), English criminal law with all its complexity, its subtle distinctions, its technicalities, was apparently thought appropriate for the utterly different circumstances of New Zealand. Even when the Colony was well established and the question of the suitability of English criminal law came before the Supreme Court no attempt was made to test the matter by comparing the needs and interests of the community with those of the Mother Country. In a case in 1874 the judge said :

> ' As regards a good deal of the English legislation of the last century and a half directed against the practice of gambling, it might no doubt be argued that it is little suited to the necessities or the temper of a colonial population like our own, and that prohibitions openly disregarded and penalties never enforced would be better removed from the Statute-book. These reasons, however, are such as should be addressed to the legislator rather than to the judge ; and they apply with equal, or nearly equal, force to the Mother Country and the Colonies. Regarding the matter from a purely legal point of view, I can see no reason why the statute against lotteries, 10 & 11 Wm. 3, c. 17, should not extend to New Zealand. It has nothing of a local character, but forms part of the general criminal law of England. As such, it is just as much in force here as any other part of English criminal law.'[5]

Two reasons stand out as explaining this marked predisposition to embrace English criminal law as it stood. First, the medieval barbarities which disfigured its history had been almost entirely swept away by 1840. Secondly, the early legislators and judges were drawn from sections of English society in which English institutions were regarded with the deepest veneration. Their views were epitomised in the words of Carleton, speaking in Parliament in 1854 :

> ' I would model New Zealand upon England. I would reproduce, to the extremest verge of possibility, the noble institutions of the Mother Country.'[6]

[5] *Elliott v. Hamilton* (1874) 2 N.Z.Jur. 95.
[6] *New Zealand Parliamentary Debates 1854–1855*, p. 59.

Always the criterion was England. When a Commission was set up in 1861 to consider the proposal to establish a Court of Appeal the Commission reported :

> ' The principle upon which we think our present suggestions ought to be based is simply this, that with respect to the administration of criminal law, on the one hand, Colonial Society has a right to look for as much security to life and limb, liberty, property, and character, as the society of the Mother Country, and on the other hand, the colonial subject accused of breaking the law, is entitled to as much protection in substance and by form as his fellow subject in England.'[7]

The judges of the Supreme Court, who constituted the Commission, expressed the view that we should be slow to recommend any innovations in criminal law not sanctioned by experience or authority in England. It was in conformity with these principles that the Commission saw no occasion to recommend that appeals be allowed in criminal cases, and proposed to confer on the Court of Appeal merely the jurisdiction of a Court for Crown Cases Reserved—a proposal which was adopted, and remained the law until 1945, when the reforms effected in England in 1907 were belatedly adopted.[8]

EARLY PENAL SYSTEM

The penal system in the early years seems by common consent to have been ignored and neglected. There was an extremely crude prison system which those in authority took no pains to improve. Far from venturing into new and untried experiments in penal reform the Governments of those days showed no interest in the existence of those condemned to incarceration, and there was in some respects a retrogression to pre-Howard conditions. Only two questions of criminal administration appear to have caused the early legislators much concern. One was the bitter discovery that transportation—that prime weapon in the penal system of countries too enlightened to put all criminals to death—could not here be used. We had reached a sort of *ultima Thule* : beyond lay no habitable territory to which unwanted criminals could be consigned.[9] Even when the legislature did contrive to enact a practicable measure for a similar purpose the Supreme Court held that the New Zealand Parliament had no power to legislate for deportation involving detention on the high seas, and that the Act was therefore *ultra vires*.[10] The other

---

[7] Report of the judges of the Supreme Court on a Court of Appeal for the Colony (*Appendices to the Journals of the House of Representatives* 1861, D2), para. 65.

[8] Criminal Appeal Act, 1945. With regard to appeals to the Privy Council see *Woolworths (N.Z.) Ltd.* v. *Wynne* [1952] N.Z.L.R. 496 ; [1952] G.L.R. 315.

[9] For a short period criminals were transported to Van Diemen's Land (Tasmania).

[10] *Re Gleich* (1879) O. B. & F. (S.C.) 39.

topic upon which there was a great deal of debate, in and out of the
early legislatures, was capital punishment. But the debate did not
concern the desirability of capital punishment : it turned on the question
whether hangings ought or ought not to be given great publicity. In
1858 a Bill was introduced into the Legislative Council to prevent
executions being carried out in public, on the ground that the practice
had a degrading and demoralising tendency ; but this was opposed,
partly on the ground that ' it would be dangerous in a colony where a
large Native population was found ', but also because it was considered
a salutary practice even for the white population. One honourable
Member said he would have executions witnessed by thousands of men,
as he considered executions were ' shocking affairs, calculated to have a
powerful effect on men's minds '.[11] Similar views probably inspired the
proposal made in 1863 that all Government offices and places of business
be closed for one hour on the day of any execution. It was not until
the twentieth century that there was any strong section of public opinion
opposed to the imposition of the death penalty.

Meanwhile conditions in the gaols of the Colony were unspeakably
bad. Many prisoners, especially dangerous escaped convicts from
Australia, were kept in irons because the gaols were not sufficiently
strong. Youths, old offenders, and those imprisoned for debt were all
herded together, with no system of classification except at Auckland.
There being no institution for the insane, they were simply detained in
the ordinary gaols. An outcry against this state of affairs was voiced in
Parliament in 1858[12] and was reinforced by Chief Justice Arney, who
addressed some strong comments on the subject to the Governor in
1861.[13] Referring to the Auckland gaol, which was known as the Stockade,
he said : ' All ideas of reformation, of moral or religious improvement, of
social development, or of industrial training, will be dispelled from the
mind of the visitor upon merely entering the Stockade.' He complained
of what might euphemistically be called the prison architecture, but he
did not indulge in euphemism in his extraordinary description of the
structure : ' An ingenious scheme has been contrived, by which the cells
are simultaneously volatilised, while the heat and stench of one cell may
be circulated among those around and above it, and the same cell may
be reciprocally compensated through the return of the accumulated heat
and stenches of the whole twenty-four.' He protested at the complete
lack of tools, books, and instruction of any kind. He joined his brother
judges in reporting on the unsatisfactory condition of the gaols in general,
deficiencies in their construction and management, the absence of any
system of classification, and the imprisonment of defaulting debtors with

[11] *New Zealand Parliamentary Debates 1856–1858*, p. 432.
[12] *New Zealand Parliamentary Debates 1858–1860*, p. 154.
[13] Memorandum from the Chief Justice to the Governor, May 21, 1861 (*Appendices
to the Journals of the House of Representatives* 1861, D2A No. 6).

convicted criminals.[14] In particular the judges called attention to ' the present indefensible, inhumane, and probably illegal practice in confining lunatics along with offenders—a practice which they cannot but denounce as utterly inconsistent with the duties of society towards both lunatics and criminals ; as necessarily productive of much useless misery and suffering, and subversive of the objects for which Lunatics and Offenders respectively are committed to custody '.[15]

PROGRESS OF REFORM

From this time onward with steady regularity substantial improvements were effected in every aspect of prison administration. Separate institutions were established for mental defectives ; the conditions under which debtors were detained were improved until ultimately imprisonment for debt was virtually abolished[16] ; and some attempt was made at classification of offenders, although this is still somewhat limited, being restricted partly by the relatively small size of the prison population, and partly by the choice of the prison administrators, to whom segregation (*e.g.*, of sexual offenders) has not always commended itself. Great changes have been effected by the adoption of new techniques for dealing with young offenders and by the use of the highly adaptable system of probation.

The First Offenders Probation Act, 1886, heralded the new outlook on the treatment of criminals. The Act empowered the courts to admit first offenders to probation for a period not exceeding the term for which they might have been sentenced to imprisonment. Provision was made for the appointment of probation officers through whom supervision was to be exercised. Summary offences and a large number of grave indictable offences were excluded from the operation of the Act. This was altered by an amendment in 1903 which defined ' first offender ' as a person convicted of an offence, whose previous character had been good, and against whom a conviction had not previously been recorded for any offence. By the same amendment the maximum period of probation was limited to three years. The legislation was further revised and extended by the Offenders Probation Act, 1920, which is the Act now in force. Under this Act persons convicted of any offence punishable by imprisonment may be admitted to probation for a period not exceeding five years. It is the special duty of the probation officer, if satisfied in any case that the best interests of the public and of the offender would be served by the release of the offender on probation, to recommend accordingly to the court.

[14] Memorandum from the judges to the Governor (*ibid.*, No. 5).
[15] Memorandum from the judges to the Governor, June 3, 1861 (*ibid.*, No. 2).
[16] See now the Imprisonment for Debt Limitation Act, 1908.

The first approach to an indeterminate prison sentence was made in 1906. In the Habitual Criminals and Offenders Act of that year it was provided that certain recidivists might be declared habitual criminals or habitual offenders and detained in a reformatory prison during the pleasure of the Governor. Application for release was made through a Supreme Court judge who, if satisfied after inquiry that the prisoner had sufficiently reformed, could recommend the Governor to grant a discharge. The scheme was broadened in 1910 by the Crimes Amendment Act. A new administrative body, the Prisons Board, was set up, with a Supreme Court judge as President. Persons liable to be sentenced to imprisonment might under this Act be sentenced instead to reformative detention for a period not exceeding ten years. (On summary conviction before a magistrate for an offence punishable by imprisonment for more than three months the offender might be sentenced to reformative detention for a period not exceeding three years.) The court was to have regard to the conduct, character, associations, or mental condition of the offender, the nature of the offence, and any special circumstances. If the court in its discretion decided to order reformative detention this could be made the only sentence or could be made cumulative upon a sentence of imprisonment for the same offence. During the period of reformative detention the offender could apply to the Prisons Board at quarterly or longer intervals for release on probation or discharge. In any event the Board was required to review at least once every year the case of every person undergoing a sentence of reformative detention. Habitual criminals and habitual offenders were brought under the provisions of this Act. The whole purpose of the legislation was to make the date of release of the prisoner depend on his own performance—to require him to comply with ' an active and progressive system of self-improvement' to earn his freedom. The promoters of the measure hoped that he would be induced ' to lift himself, by a sustained effort, from his apathy and moral indifference'. The scheme involved more elaborate classification of criminals, and specific training in agricultural and other pursuits during the period of detention. In substance it was a modified version of the principles of the Elmira reformatory.

The functions of the Prisons Board were later extended until the principle of the legislation of 1910 was carried through almost the whole penal system. In 1920, persons on probation were given the right to apply to the Prisons Board, at the expiration of half of the term of probation, for their discharge. In the same year, by the Crimes Amendment Act, every person undergoing sentence of imprisonment was permitted to apply to the Prisons Board for release on probation or discharge after the expiration of half the term of his sentence.

Borstal institutions were set up for the training of young offenders. The Prevention of Crime (Borstal Institutions Establishment) Act, 1924, empowered the Supreme Court to make orders for detention in Borstal for not less than two nor more than five years where the offender was liable to imprisonment and was not less than fifteen nor more than twenty-one years of age. In special cases an order for Borstal detention could be made although the offender was over twenty-one. Magistrates were given similar but more restricted powers. The court in each case was first to be satisfied that it was expedient that the offender should be subject to detention ' for such term and under instruction and discipline as appear most conducive to his reformation and the repression of crime '. Release from Borstal was to be followed by a year under the supervision of a probation officer. In 1925 a vital change was made in the method of dealing with young delinquents. The Child Welfare Act of that year created special Children's Courts and introduced the system of committing delinquent or neglected children to the care of the Child Welfare Division of the Department of Education.[17] This system is described in Chapter 5.

CODIFICATION

While these transformations were being effected a very significant change occurred in the form and content of the criminal law itself. This was the codification of the law relating to indictable offences in the Criminal Code Act, 1893. New Zealand's readiness to emulate England has already been stressed, but this event showed that New Zealand was no longer prepared to defer all major changes until they had first been adopted and tried in England. The legislature provided another instance (they are now legion) in which schemes mooted elsewhere have been taken over and applied in New Zealand, sometimes with insufficient adaptation to local circumstances but in the present case with entire and unqualified success.

Sir James FitzJames Stephen, the eminent English jurist and criminal historian, had been engaged in the seventies in drafting a Bill to codify the law governing indictable offences. His draft had been revised by some of the most distinguished judges and later by eminent counsel under the direction of the Attorney-General. But although the Bill which resulted from their labours had been brought before the Imperial Parliament over many years it had not been adopted. New Zealand, however, had been watching these proceedings with the keenest interest, as the proposal for codification had the enthusiastic approval of many influential lawyers in this country. At last, despairing of the early adoption

[17] The Child Welfare Act, 1925, confers on the Children's Court exclusive jurisdiction in regard to offences other than murder or manslaughter committed by children under the age of seventeen : *R.* v. *Rix* [1931] N.Z.L.R. 984 ; *sub nom. Re R.* [1931] G.L.R. 582 ; *R.* v. *Swinton* [1946] N.Z.L.R. 43 ; [1946] G.L.R. 44. A person under twenty-one may not be imprisoned for non-payment of a fine unless the court is of opinion that no other method of dealing with him is appropriate : Summary Penalties Act, 1939, s. 5.

of the proposed legislation in England, the Government of New Zealand made a move. Commissioners were appointed to prepare a draft Bill which the Government could present to Parliament. They worked carefully through the reports of the Commissions in England, studied our own legislation and case law, and finally completed a draft Criminal Code Bill. This was introduced into Parliament in 1883. At first it seemed destined for a fate similar to that of the English Bill. But in 1893 it was accepted by Parliament and took its place in the Statute-book as the Criminal Code Act, 1893.

England has since travelled along much of the same road by various enactments such as the Perjury Act, 1911, the Forgery Act, 1913, the Larceny Act, 1916, and the Indictments Act, 1915. But New Zealand, taking over the scheme evolved in England a generation before, simplified and improved the criminal law in a way that even now is the envy of some English lawyers. The distinction between treason, felony and misdemeanour, with the multitude of procedural differences which this distinction once entailed, was abolished at a stroke. Many old common law rules which no longer commanded general acceptance were abolished.[18] In a host of details, rules relating to specific crimes were improved or clarified.[19] Criminal procedure was standardised and simplified, ample powers of amendment (subject to proper safeguards) were conferred, and the scope for purely technical defences founded on procedural irregularities was reduced to insignificant proportions.[20] The Act provided, for example (s. 363), that every count of an indictment should be sufficient if it contained in substance a statement that the accused had committed some crime therein specified. The statement might be made in popular language, without any technical averments, in any words sufficient to give the accused notice of the crime with which he was charged.[21] Every

---

[18] But there was one that got away. In *R. v. McKechie* [1926] N.Z.L.R. 1 ; [1925] G.L.R. 484, the Court of Appeal held by a majority that for the purpose of the crime of conspiracy husband and wife still count as one person and cannot be convicted of conspiring with each other.

[19] For example, theft was defined to include conversion of property in the lawful possession of the accused. Consequently English decisions on the conversion of goods received by mistake are inapplicable, and the question whether *R. v. Hudson* [1943] K.B. 458 ; [1943] 1 All E.R. 642 ; 29 Cr.App.R. 65 was rightly decided is not of direct concern in New Zealand.

[20] Those who drafted the Act might, however, have been surprised had they known that the provisions for amendment would be held to be insufficient to enable an indictment to be amended unless it already charged a crime : *R. v. White* [1938] N.Z.L.R. 610 ; [1938] G.L.R. 362.

[21] The profuse wordiness and flights of fancy which were traditional in criminal indictments were not without their charm (for those not concerned in the proceedings), and one may wistfully recall such indictments as that in *R. v. Spencer and Mayo* (1875) 3 N.Z.C.A. 117, in which a landlord who had wrongfully evicted his tenant was charged in these terms : ' The jurors for our Lady the Queen upon their oath present, that Thomas Spencer and Frederick Mayo, together with divers other persons to the number of six or more, to the jurors aforesaid unknown, on the 28th day of May, in the year of our Lord one thousand eight hundred and seventy five, with force and arms, to wit with pistols, swords, sticks, staves and other offensive weapons,

indictable offence was made statutory, it being provided that the offender must be charged under some provision of the Criminal Code Act or under some other statute not inconsistent therewith. Oddly enough, those who framed the measure did not include contempt of court, but the Supreme Court decided that the legislature could not have intended to deprive the courts of power to punish for contempt, and that this common law offence must be deemed to continue to exist notwithstanding the terms of the Act.[22] All the defences which could be raised at common law in answer to a charge were preserved except where expressly modified or abolished by the Act ; and the common law presumption that criminal liability requires proof of *mens rea* continued to apply.[23]

The value of the results achieved by this Act was clearly considerable. It put an end to the chaotic form in which much of the law then appeared. By the statutory definitions of crimes much doubt and obscurity was removed. The abolition of the felony-misdemeanour classification saved us from ' the exceptional accident and the daily nonsense ' over which A. P. Herbert has made merry. The general revision of the law relating to a number of crimes and defences brought the law in many respects better into line with current opinion.

In some ways it is remarkable that the Act was ever passed. The whole scheme had a savour of doctrinaire reformism, and the politicians of New Zealand in the eighteen-eighties and eighteen-nineties were at the opposite pole from those who look first for principles and then for applications. Their public utterances put them in the direct line of descent from Richmond, the Colonial Treasurer in an earlier administration, who had said : ' The Government feels the English dislike of cut-and-dried principles as strongly as any of its opponents.' On another occasion he remarked : ' It is the duty of a Government rather to look to the practical result of the measures they bring forward than to inquire

into a certain dwellinghouse situate and being at Parawai, in the District of Hauraki, in Queen's County, in the Province of Auckland, in the Colony of New Zealand, and then in the possession of one Frederick Bennett, unlawfully violently, forcibly, injuriously, and with a strong hand did enter. And the said Thomas Spencer and Frederick Mayo, together with the said other evil-disposed persons to the jurors aforesaid unknown, as aforesaid then and there with force and arms, to wit with pistols, swords, sticks, staves, and other offensive weapons, unlawfully, violently, forcibly, injuriously, and with a strong hand the said Frederick Bennett from the said possession of the said dwelling-house did expel, remove, and put out ; the said Frederick Bennett so as aforesaid expelled, removed, and put out from the possession of the said dwellinghouse, then and there with force and arms, to wit with pistols, swords, sticks, staves, and other offensive weapons, unlawfully, violently, forcibly, injuriously, and with a strong hand did keep out, and still do keep out, and other wrongs to the said Frederick Bennett then and there did, to the great damage of the said Frederick Bennett, and against the peace of our Lady the Queen, her crown and dignity.'

[22] *Re Cobb, Nash* v. *Nash* [1924] N.Z.L.R. 495 ; [1924] G.L.R. 229.
[23] See, for example, *R.* v. *Carswell* [1926] N.Z.L.R. 321 ; [1926] G.L.R. 185, in which the Court of Appeal distinguished but adversely commented upon *R.* v. *Wheat*, *R.* v. *Stocks* [1921] 2 K.B. 119 ; 15 Cr.App.R. 134.

too curiously into theoretic points.' This pragmatic approach has, indeed, been one of the most striking features of New Zealand legislation throughout the country's history. But on this occasion the proposed measure appealed to all shades of opinion as it promised substantial practical advantages in addition to its academic attractions. The enormous prestige of those who had drawn up and revised the draft measure in England was probably the greatest single reason for the adoption of the measure, but there were other influences at work. Naturally there was the opposition of those who thought that the existing system worked very well (which was said to be proved by the fact that ' the number of appeals under the present statutes is infinitesimal and is getting smaller every year '). This was offset by the support of others whose naïve ideas on the subject of codification can hardly fail to entertain any reader with some knowledge of law. One honourable Member of the Legislative Council supported the Bill with these observations :

> ' I have always considered it a sort of reproach against our nation that we have not long before this had a codification of the laws of England. Why should we be behindhand in this matter, when the French have had such a thing for nearly a hundred years ? When I used to go among the lawyers at the Palais de Justice I was pleased to see the way in which they carried about their little volume in their hands—the *Codes Français*. They carried all the laws of France, I might say, in the palm of their hands to refer to.' [24]

Codification met with considerable opposition in England on the ground that a statute would lack the elasticity of the common law, and that it would facilitate technical defences based on the particular wording that might be adopted. It can be asserted with confidence that the experience of New Zealand since 1893 lends no support whatever to these fears. Moreover, the legislation embodies the spirit of the maxim *nullum crimen sine lege* and eliminates the risks which attend judicial inventiveness in retrospectively declaring an act to be a crime.[25]

The Act of 1893 did little or nothing to effect reforms in the punishments that might be imposed for various offences.[26] The maximum sentences that might be imposed for crimes against property retained an almost medieval savagery compared with the mild punishments for grave crimes against the person. While the punishment that might be imposed for an aggravated assault on a human being was two years' imprisonment, the miscreant who wounded a goat could get fourteen

---

[24] 79 *New Zealand Parliamentary Debates*, p. 181.
[25] *R.* v. *Manley* [1933] 1 K.B. 529 ; 102 L.J.K.B. 323 ; 24 Cr.App.R. 25, which illustrates the common law doctrine, was the subject of much justifiable criticism in England. In New Zealand a simple statutory amendment was enacted to cover that type of case : Police Offences Amendment Act 1935, s. 4.
[26] Certain types of penal sanction were, however, abolished. Imprisonment with hard labour was substituted for penal servitude ; outlawry was abolished ; and it was provided that attainder, corruption of blood, forfeiture and escheat were not to follow upon conviction. (See now the Crimes Act 1908, ss. 7, 413.)

years. To steal a parcel from a railway station was twice as serious an offence as ' stealing ' a child. A maximum of two years' imprisonment could be imposed for a number of grave sexual offences, and the same punishment could be imposed for damaging a fence round a monument. These comparisons, which could be multiplied, seem to warrant the suggestion that the Act must trace its ancestry not so much to the Victorian era as to the days of feudalism. When the legislation of 1893 was re-enacted and consolidated in the Crimes Act, 1908, these maximum penalties were not altered, but they no longer reflect with accuracy the relative severity of the sentences actually imposed in recent times. The extreme bias in favour of the protection of property is no longer in evidence.

CAPITAL PUNISHMENT

When the Labour Government came to power in 1935 it made a practice for some years of commuting all death sentences to life imprisonment, and in 1941 it carried its policy into legislation in the Crimes Amendment Act. The death penalty was not abolished (being still prescribed for treason and piracy) but it was abolished in regard to murder, which is the only crime for which the death penalty has been imposed in practice in New Zealand. It was made mandatory for the court to sentence any person convicted of murder to life imprisonment. The law was altered only after considerable debate and opposition, and not a year passed without some public expression of opinion that the change was a mistake and that capital punishment should be reintroduced. The available statistics do not show that the incidence of the crime of murder has been materially affected either for better or for worse by the change in the penalty. However, the National Party on becoming the Government reinstated capital punishment for murder.[27] The Capital Punishment Act, 1950, provides that every person convicted of murder shall be sentenced to death. Exceptions are made in the case of persons under eighteen years of age and pregnant women, who are to be detained during Her Majesty's pleasure. The royal prerogative of mercy may still be exercised, but if the sentence is commuted to imprisonment for life the prisoner may not be released on probation or discharged until the approval of the Governor-General in Council has been obtained.

It was also proposed in 1950 that New Zealand should follow England in recognising a separate crime of ' infanticide ' ; but this clause was deleted from the Bill during its passage through Parliament, apparently in the belief that no jury would convict a woman of murder (and that she would be found guilty only of manslaughter) if the circumstances were such as to bring her within the scope of the proposed clause.

[27] In the main this was based on the view that the death penalty must in some cases act as a deterrent even though the available statistics did not clearly establish the fact.

In 1936 it ceased to be lawful for a Children's Court to order whipping, and in 1941 the penalties of whipping and flogging were completely abolished.[28] Occasionally this change, too, has been publicly deplored, and it is doubtful whether the alteration has become generally accepted.

GENERAL PRINCIPLES OF LIABILITY

It can hardly be said that New Zealand has contributed notably to the development of the general principles of criminal liability. It is true that while Sir John Salmond was a member of the Supreme Court Bench there was an important examination of the theory of criminal attempts, but the solution Salmond proposed has not met with universal acceptance.[29] Similarly in the kindred realm of criminal evidence, the decision of the Court of Appeal delivered by Salmond J. in *R. v. Whitta*[30] on the admissibility of evidence of similar acts closely paralleled the later decision in England in *R. v. Sims*,[31] but must now be qualified in the light of more recent decisions of the Privy Council and the House of Lords.[32] The recognition and refinement of the concept of *mens rea* progressed rather limpingly. In *R. v. Fetzer*[33] the Court of Appeal identified ' colour of right ' with ' absence of *mens rea* ', with unhappy consequences in the law relating to theft, arson, and mischief. On the other hand, although it was held in New South Wales in 1876 that drunkenness could not reduce murder to manslaughter[34] this rule was clearly repudiated in New Zealand.[35]

In England the general concept of *mens rea* as a condition of penal liability is becoming progressively restricted and clarified, there being a considerable weight of authority for the view that its very essence is foresight of possible consequences. This brings within the scope of *mens rea* intentional and reckless wrongdoing, but excludes mere negligence (which involves civil but not criminal liability). In New Zealand development has been tardy, and the view which is becoming established may prove to be fundamentally different. In the first place the Crimes Act itself contains (in sections 182, 183) two definitions of murder.

---

[28] Statutes Amendment Act 1936, s. 17; Crimes Amendment Act 1941, s. 3.
[29] In *R. v. Barker* [1924] N.Z.L.R. 865; [1924] G.L.R. 393, it was held that a criminal attempt (as distinct from mere preparation) requires an overt act which unequivocally indicates criminal intent and is inconsistent with innocence. For a critical examination and rejection of this theory see Hall, *Principles of Criminal Law* (1947), p. 106; Glanville Williams, *Criminal Law: The General Part*, p. 145.
[30] [1921] N.Z.L.R. 519; [1921] G.L.R. 353.
[31] [1946] K.B. 531; [1946] 1 All E.R. 697; [1947] L.J.R. 160; 175 L.T. 72.
[32] *Noor Mohamed v. R.* [1949] A.C. 182; [1949] 1 All E.R. 365; *Harris v. D.P.P.* [1952] 1 All E.R. 1044.
[33] (1900) 19 N.Z.L.R. 438; 3 G.L.R. 82. This case may well be reconsidered in the light of *R. v. Bernhard* [1938] 2 K.B. 264; [1938] 2 All E.R. 140; 26 Cr.App.R. 137 and later cases in England.
[34] *R. v. Boon* (1876) 14 S.C.R. (N.S.W.) 483; 2 N.Z. Jur. (journal) N.S. 41.
[35] *R. v. Mathieson* (1906) 25 N.Z.L.R. 879; 8 G.L.R. 649; *R. v. Garr* (1909) 28 N.Z.L.R. 546; 12 G.L.R. 8.

These definitions specify in the most precise manner the extent to which foresight of possible consequences is a prerequisite for a conviction of murder, and include some cases of culpable homicide where the offender did not mean death to ensue and did not know that death was likely to ensue. This has affected the development of the doctrine of *mens rea* in several ways. It has retarded the judicial development of the doctrine by avoiding the necessity of examining it in the sphere in which it would otherwise have been all-important; and it may have fostered the view that *mens rea* may include mental attitudes other than intention or recklessness. Secondly, the Act contains numerous provisions imposing criminal sanctions for mere negligence. Culpable homicide is defined in part as the killing of any person by an omission without lawful excuse to perform or observe any legal duty; and it is provided that persons failing to use reasonable care when doing dangerous acts or while in charge of dangerous things are criminally responsible for the consequences. In *R.* v. *Storey* [36] both Divisions of the Court of Appeal sitting together followed an earlier decision of the Court of Appeal [37] and held that these sections impose criminal liability for mere negligence and do not require proof of gross negligence or recklessness. The court considered the common law doctrine enunciated in *R.* v. *Bateman* [38] and held that it did not apply, as the statute required no more than the breach of a duty to take reasonable care. The case related to alleged negligent driving of a motor-vehicle; but all criminal offences in New Zealand are statutory and it is difficult to believe that a different rule of construction would be applied in the case of other criminal charges based on negligence. The decision therefore tends to establish that there is no distinction in New Zealand between negligence as the foundation of civil liability and negligence as the foundation of criminal liability. What is the effect of this decision on the doctrine of *mens rea* ? If foresight of consequences need not be proved when the charge is negligence is there any reason to require such proof when the charge is one involving *mens rea* ? Will intention, recklessness, and negligence all satisfy the requirement of *mens rea* ? These are questions which have not yet been clearly answered.

The principle of the common law whereby an unintentional homicide in the course of committing another offence may be held to be murder has been materially restricted in scope over a long period, but even today it may perhaps operate more severely than the rules which were embodied in the Criminal Code Act. To regulate the liability of the offender in such circumstances the Act first declared it to be murder if the offender for any unlawful object did an act which he knew or ought to have known

[36] [1931] N.Z.L.R. 417; [1931] G.L.R. 105.
[37] *R.* v. *Dawe* (1911) 30 N.Z.L.R. 673; 13 G.L.R. 574.
[38] (1925) 19 Cr.App.R. 8; 28 Cox 33; 94 L.J.K.B. 791 (subsequently approved by the House of Lords in *Andrews* v. *D.P.P.* [1937] A.C. 576; [1937] 2 All E.R. 552).

to be likely to cause death and thereby killed any person.[39] It then added the provision that culpable homicide is murder if the offender meant to inflict grievous bodily harm, or administered any stupefying or overpowering thing, or wilfully stopped the breath of any person, in order to facilitate the commission of certain specified offences or the flight of the offender upon the commission or attempted commission of the offence, and death ensued.[40] The need for judicial development of the principles of criminal liability through the felony-murder doctrine has virtually been eliminated by these statutory provisions.

In New Zealand, as in England, the courts have proceeded with much hesitation in extending criminal liability to corporate bodies. A forward move was made in 1932 when the Court of Appeal held by a majority that a company could be convicted of a particular offence involving *mens rea* [41]; but the majority supported their decision on the ground that *mens rea*, although an ingredient of the offence charged, was not expressly imported into it by the regulation creating the offence.[42] This limitation, which lacked any adequate basis, has since been removed, not by further decisions in New Zealand but by later English decisions[43] which would, it is thought, be followed in New Zealand.

The McNaghten rules relating to the defence of insanity were incorporated in the Criminal Code Act, 1893, and now form section 43 of the Crimes Act, 1908. The words of the section, however, provided that insanity was a defence if it rendered the accused ' incapable of understanding the nature and quality of the act or omission, and of knowing that such act or omission was wrong '. This was a departure from the terms of the McNaghten rules, under which it was sufficient to show that by reason of insanity the accused was incapable of understanding the nature and quality of the act or omission *or* of knowing that such act or omission was wrong. But the Court of Appeal has now held that in this clause the word ' and ' means ' or '.[44] ' Uncontrollable impulse ' is not a defence to a criminal charge in New Zealand.

The common law presumptions relating to the criminal capacity of children under seven and children under fourteen are embodied in sections 41 and 42 of the Crimes Act, but the incapacity of children under seven has been expressed, not as an irrebuttable presumption, but as a substantive rule of law.[45]

---

[39] Now s. 182 (d) of the Crimes Act, 1908.
[40] Now s. 183 of the Crimes Act, 1908.
[41] *O. F. Nelson & Co. Ltd.* v. *Police* [1932] N.Z.L.R. 337 ; [1932] G.L.R. 109.
[42] Samoa Seditious Organisations Regulations 1930, clause 3.
[43] *D.P.P.* v. *Kent & Sussex Contractors Ltd.* [1944] K.B. 346 ; [1944] 1 All E.R. 119 ; *R.* v. *I.C.R. Haulage Ltd.* [1944] K.B. 551 ; [1944] 1 All E.R. 691 ; 30 Cr.App.R. 31.
[44] *Murdoch* v. *British Israel Federation* [1942] N.Z.L.R. 600 ; [1942] G.L.R. 390.
[45] If the jury find that by reason of insanity a person under the age of fourteen years did not know that the act or omission was wrong they are bound to acquit him under s. 42, and s. 43 relating to the defence of insanity has no

TRIAL BY JURY

Trial by jury has endured through all stages of colonisation as the most favoured procedure for ascertaining guilt consistent with protecting the innocent. An American writer says : ' While some misgivings have been expressed over the fact that the " criminal jury is smouldering to extinction ", there can be little doubt that this trend is a salutary one. It has resulted " in speedier, cheaper, and more efficient trials and the elimination of unwholesome publicity in certain classes of cases ".'[46] The Summary Jurisdiction Act, 1952, which increases substantially the number of indictable cases which may be tried summarily, may be the first indication of the growth of a similar attitude in this country. A person charged with a summary offence which is punishable by imprisonment for a term exceeding three months may claim to be tried by jury.[47] On the other hand most indictable offences may now be tried summarily unless the defendant insists on jury trial.[48]

In 1942 women between the ages of twenty-five and sixty became eligible to have their names added to the jury rolls[49] but very few have elected to avail themselves of the privilege. Maoris are eligible for jury service, and a Maori who is committed for trial for an offence against another Maori is entitled to be tried, if he so wishes, by a jury composed entirely of Maoris.[50]

CRIMINAL LAW AND INDIVIDUAL LIBERTY

In the administration of the criminal law the judiciary has adopted on the whole the standpoint of liberal individualism. The importance of the independence of the courts from political interference or outside pressure was always acknowledged in principle and, it is believed, substantially and emphatically asserted in practice.[51] The judges in their turn almost invariably succeeded in giving a reasonable and effective interpretation to legislation whether or not they were personally in sympathy with it. In the field of criminal law, however, a policy of restrictive interpretation, which might well be open to criticism in other spheres, had long been regarded as justified lest measures enacted to

---

application : *R.* v. *Brooks* [1945] N.Z.L.R. 584 ; [1945] G.L.R. 278. The standard of care required of a person over fourteen but under twenty-one is the same as that required from an adult : *Tauranga Electric Power Board* v. *Karora Kohu* [1939] N.Z.L.R. 1040 ; [1939] G.L.R. 585.

[46] Harno, *Some Significant Developments in Criminal Law and Procedure in the Last Century* (1951), p. 42. J. Crim. L. Criminol. & Police Sc., pp. 427, 453.

[47] Justices of the Peace Act, 1927, s. 124, as amended by Summary Jurisdiction Act, 1952, s. 14.

[48] Summary Jurisdiction Act, 1952.

[49] Women Jurors Act, 1942.

[50] Juries Act, 1908, s. 144.

[51] See, for example, the protest of the judges after the decision of the Privy Council in *Wallis* v. *Solicitor-General* [1903] A.C. 173 ; [1903] N.Z.P.C.C. 23, recorded in N.Z.P.C.C. 730 and referred to in Chap. 1.

protect life and liberty be made fetters upon freedom. New Zealand inherited this liberal tradition from England. In one of the first cases decided by the Court of Appeal the court said :

> ' A particular act which the legislature has failed definitely to prohibit must never, in an English court, be construed a crime by implication on the ground that otherwise some supposed or even some manifest end of public policy will be frustrated. It is our duty, in favour of individual liberty, to maintain this fundamental principle as jealously as if we lived in the days of the Prerogative.'[52]

On this matter there has always been unanimity. The early records reveal only this difference, that in the heyday of *laisser-faire* one could apply these principles in a more thorough-going fashion than is today thought practicable. When criminals from the Australian colonies formed a rather numerous section of our immigrants a Bill was introduced to make it a punishable offence for a criminal to enter New Zealand before his sentence had expired and to impose a penalty on the captain of the vessel by which the offender reached New Zealand. This measure was thrown out because of what was termed ' its arbitrary and discreditable nature '.[53] One of the first actions of the Stafford Government was to disallow a number of provincial enactments, including a measure which required passports. The Premier declared : ' We felt a peculiar pleasure in disallowing an Act based purely on the system of Continental despots.'[54]

Delegated legislation of a regulatory nature, and penal sections of statutes relating to industrial disputes, constitute in modern times a vital part of the criminal law affecting individual liberty, and have already been considered in earlier chapters. The liquor licensing laws and laws relating to gambling are discussed in Chapter 13.

The decision in *Duncan* v. *Jones*,[55] which can be a potent instrument for abrogating freedom of speech and assembly, has been followed in New Zealand in *Burton* v. *Power*.[56] A New Zealand writer, after examining these decisions, has said :

> ' From this example of an unsatisfactory state of one part of our constitutional law, one is led to reflect that in the past we have uncritically accepted too many generalisations concerning our public liberties.'[57]

---

[52] *R.* v. *Harley* (1871) 1 N.Z.C.A. 485, 491. The Acts Interpretation Act, 1924, s. 5 (j), provides inter alia that every Act shall be deemed remedial and shall receive such fair, large, and liberal construction as will best ensure the attainment of the object of the Act. But although the old distinction between penal and remedial statutes has thus largely disappeared the distinction is one which ought not to be erased from the mind of a judge. A case must be brought within the words as well as within the spirit of a penal enactment. See *Combes* v. *Harkness* [1951] N.Z.L.R. 212, 215.

[53] *New Zealand Parliamentary Debates 1861–1863*, p. 1009.

[54] *New Zealand Parliamentary Debates 1858–1860*, p. 115.

[55] [1936] 1 K.B. 218 ; 105 L.J.K.B. 71 ; 52 T.L.R. 26.

[56] [1940] N.Z.L.R. 305 ; [1940] G.L.R. 192.

[57] Brassington, *Constitutional Law : Some Aspects of Change*, in *Liberty and Learning* (reprinted : (1950) 17 N.Z.L.J. 265, 268).

On the other hand the liberal trend of thought which has often predominated is shown by the fact that in the middle of the Second World War a judge in the Court of Appeal could say :

> ' I think that a trial under the Regulations[58] may have a further safeguard if the presiding judge thinks fit to follow the practice of judges in cases of seditious libel of warning the jury that they have become the guardians of bona fide speech and expression, that they should remember that criticism delivered in good faith may be necessary for the safety of the State, and that they should allow for the heat of the moment and not subject the passages complained of to any narrow or jealous review.'[59]

The Maori People

Crime and delinquency among the Maori population have been an exceptionally difficult social problem from the beginning, a problem created by the white immigrants. At an early stage in the development of the Colony a benevolent Government with missionary zeal felt that the problem might be partly solved by making sure that the Maoris knew the white man's rules. In the Speech from the Throne at the opening of Parliament in 1858 the Governor said :

> ' To confirm the reliance of the Natives on the wisdom and justice of our institutions it is important that the principles and to some extent the details also of our civil and criminal law should be made known amongst them in a familiar shape. With this view I have directed the compilation in the Native language of a summary of English law.'[60]

While there was ample justification for this step it was totally inadequate in dealing with an extremely complex problem, and no more likely to prevent crime among the Maoris than the distribution of copies of the Crimes Act would be likely to abolish theft. Culture conflict is not amenable to treatment by this simple device. There is now a more positive approach to the question of Maori welfare and mutual understanding between the two races, as is discussed in Chapter 5. Crime among Maoris is largely an aspect of this broader problem of assimilation or adjustment.

Current Trends

Prison administration has shared in the general trend of increasing the discretionary powers of administrative authorities. There is further expansion of ' public welfare offences ' at a considerable rate, and no sign that this development is thought to require critical examination. The services (and evidence) of psychologists, psychoanalysts, and

[58] The Public Safety Emergency Regulations 1940.
[59] *R.* v. *Barrington* [1942] N.Z.L.R. 502, 518 ; [1942] G.L.R. 324, 331, per Smith J.
[60] *New Zealand Parliamentary Debates 1856–1858*, p. 372.

psychiatrists are regarded, in general, with the deepest distrust. Prevailing opinion is against admitting any new categories of persons with diminished responsibility. There is continued confidence in the deterrent effect of punishment, based on our ' knowledge of human nature ' and firmly established without much inquiry into statistical or other evidence on the subject. Criminal sanctions (or the threat of them) are part of the strategy in dealing with industrial unrest. Amendments on matters of procedure or evidence testify to the desire, never abated, to guarantee to every man on a criminal charge the reality of a fair trial.

Research into the causes of crime and the effectiveness of existing measures of prevention or punishment has in the past been slight. There are signs of new vigour in this direction. But the population is small and the facilities for research are very limited. Reliance must continue to be placed principally on investigations made overseas for any major advances in the understanding of crime and the criminal.

CHAPTER 11

THE HISTORICAL DEVELOPMENT OF THE CIVIL LAW

In this chapter we propose to discuss those subjects which comprise the core of the substantive civil law, namely, property, contracts, and torts. As New Zealand is a common law country these branches of the law in New Zealand are based on, and are in the main, the same as English law. The discussion will therefore be confined to those special developments in the law which have occurred in New Zealand, and accordingly no attempt will be made to expound as a whole the law here under consideration, even in an elementary form, as to do so would involve the compilation of a digest of English private law. In view of their close association with Family Law, certain aspects of the law of property, such as the Family Protection Act, and the Joint Family Homes Act, will, however, for the sake of convenience, be dealt with in the next chapter.

PROPERTY

The law relating to real property and conveyancing in New Zealand has been characterised by two outstanding features. The first has been the statutory simplification and adaptation to New Zealand conditions of the much more technical and complicated system of real property law which prevailed in England. The second was the early introduction into the country of the Torrens or 'Land Transfer' system of registering the title to land.

Statutory Simplification of Real Property Law

Although by the time that European government was established in New Zealand in 1840, the common law of England as a whole had already reached a stage of maturity in its growth and development, there were still large portions of the law, particularly in the sphere of real property, which bore the stamp of their medieval origin and comprised many rules of a highly technical and anomalous character. While other branches of the common law could be readily adapted as they stood to meet the circumstances of the infant Colony, this was not so in the case of that branch of it which was concerned with real property.

Far-reaching changes in the application to New Zealand of the English system of real property and conveyancing were therefore effected by an ordinance which was passed by the Legislative Council of the new Colony in 1842. Subsequently described as ' the Charter of New Zealand

Conveyancing ', this ordinance embodied many of the suggestions contained in the report of the English Commissioners on the law of real property, made in the year 1829. It not only instituted a uniform and simple method of conveyancing in New Zealand in place of the highly technical forms of conveyancing then in use in England, but it also introduced a number of far-reaching reforms in the substantive law affecting real property. Hight and Bamford in their *Constitutional History and Law of New Zealand* pay the following tribute to the draftsman of this ordinance, Swainson, who had become Attorney-General in 1841 :

> ' Many of his ordinances, though now concealed in consolidating acts, still remain both in substance and in letter upon the statute-book, and the Colony owes him a particular debt of gratitude for having, by a single enactment of most technical character, but drawn with lucidity and conciseness, successfully swept away from the conveyancing system a host of awkward survivals of feudal and technical rules.'[1]

Although many enactments have from time to time been passed by the legislature amending and consolidating the law relating to property, this ordinance has remained the framework on which the New Zealand system of real property law is based. Much of the later legislation embodied parallel legislation which had already been enacted in England, *e.g.*, many of the provisions of the Conveyancing Act, which had been passed in England in 1881, were adopted when a general revision of the law took place in New Zealand in 1905 ; but parts of it were peculiar to New Zealand and the reform of the law of real property in New Zealand was so radical in its nature, and so continuous in its process that there was no necessity for the legislature to make the sweeping changes in this branch of the law which were effected by the great property statutes that were passed in England in 1922 and 1925.

The existing legislation has recently been consolidated in the Property Law Act, 1952, which provides a comprehensive code governing the general law relating to property in New Zealand. Part I contains various provisions relating to the execution and construction of deeds and other instruments. In Part II there are set out the different general rules affecting property which have, from time to time, been enacted in New Zealand, many of which abrogate either highly technical or obsolete rules and doctrines. For instance in 1951 estates tail (which had never been of any great practical importance in the country) were abolished in New Zealand. Part III deals with assurances of real and personal property, Part IV with powers and conditions of sale and the protection of purchasers and creditors, Part V with covenants and powers generally, and Part VI with the covenants to be implied in conveyances.

[1] Hight and Bamford, *The Constitutional History and Law of New Zealand*, pp. 156, 157.

Part VII embodies a code of provisions relating to mortgages. An important feature of this branch of the law in New Zealand, dating back to the Conveyancing Ordinance of 1842, is the fact that the mortgagee has no right, as he had according to English law, to foreclose the equity of redemption under the mortgage. Foreclosure is the procedure whereby a mortgagee, or a person claiming an interest in the mortgage under him, can compel the mortgagor upon default being made under the mortgage to elect either to redeem the mortgage security or to suffer the extinguishment of his equity of redemption by order of the court. Instead, machinery is provided whereby a mortgagee, who has become entitled to exercise his power of sale under a mortgage, may apply to the Registrar of the Supreme Court in the appropriate district to sell the mortgaged land by auction. In his application the mortgagee must state the value at which he estimates the land to be sold. At any time before the sale the mortgagor may redeem at the mortgagee's valuation but, if the amount in fact paid by him is less than the amount owing under the mortgage, the mortgagee may recover the balance from him under his personal covenant. The mortgagee is himself entitled to purchase the property but, if he does so, the consideration payable by him must not be less than the amount of his estimate of the value of the mortgaged land. The intention underlying this provision is to preclude the mortgagee from buying in the property at a gross undervalue.

In Part VIII of the Act, there is similarly a general code of provisions relating to leases and tenancies. Section 105 of the 1952 Act re-enacted an interesting and important rule simplifying the law relating to landlord and tenant which was first introduced in a slightly different form in 1885. Under this section it is provided that no tenancy from year to year shall be created or implied by payment of rent ; and that if there is a tenancy it shall be deemed, in the absence of proof to the contrary, to be a tenancy determinable at the will of either of the parties by one calendar month's notice in writing. The object of this provision is to substitute a definite and uniform rule, dealing with the duration of all indefinite tenancies, for the more difficult and complicated rules which prevailed at common law.

Topics dealt with in other parts of the Act include easements, restrictive stipulations, and encroachments, the assignment of debts and things in action, marriage settlements, powers of attorney, the partition of land and the division of chattels, and the rules relating to the apportionment of rents, annuities, dividends and other periodical payments in the nature of income, to the charging of debts on real estate, and to rent charges and other annual sums charged on land.

Registration of Deeds

A system for registering deeds, as distinct from registering the title to land, was in operation in New Zealand from the first beginnings of government in the country. Passed in the same year as the conveyancing ordinance, the Deeds Registration Ordinance of 1842, which was enacted ' for the purpose of rendering titles to real property more secure and facilitating the transfer of the same ', provided for the establishment throughout the country of ' Register Offices ' for the registration of ' deeds, wills and memorials '. It then proceeded to specify in detail what instruments might be registered and the effect and mode of registration and to set out a number of miscellaneous provisions regulating the system of registration which it established.

Under this system registration was not made compulsory, but the purpose underlying the provisions relating to it was to induce purchasers and mortgagees to register their deeds so that subsequent purchasers and mortgagees should be protected against loss by possible fraud on the part of the original owner. The inducement to register was based on the fact that a subsequent deed if registered would take priority over an earlier unregistered instrument.

Land Transfer System

The Land Registry Act of 1860 first introduced into New Zealand the Torrens system providing for the registration of the title to land, but it was not until 1870, when an Act based on the original legislation in South Australia was passed, that this system of registration became really effective. The Act of 1870, under which the legislation introduced in 1860 was repealed and the present Land Transfer Office was established, was followed by the Land Transfer Acts of 1885, 1908 and 1915.

The legislation was enacted in order to facilitate dealings in land and the system of registration established under it was designed to provide security of title in substitution for the costly and troublesome investigation of title with its attendant risks which prevailed under the old Deeds system of registration. The two systems of registration continued to operate side by side in New Zealand for very many years, but the policy of bringing all the land in New Zealand under the Land Transfer system was greatly speeded up by the passing in 1924 of the Land Transfer (Compulsory Registration of Titles) Act. The object of this Act was to enable the Land Transfer Office to take steps on its own initiative to bring compulsorily under the land transfer system all land not already subject to the system, within a period of five years, or so soon thereafter as might be possible. As a result of this Act the older system of registration is now largely obsolete.

The various enactments relating to the land transfer system were consolidated in the Land Transfer Act, 1952. Advantage was taken of this consolidation, which took place at the same time as that relating to the various measures dealing with property law in general, to assimilate the two sets of enactments, and some minor inconsistencies which existed between them were eliminated frcm the law. It is now provided that the Property Law Act shall be read and construed so as not to conflict with the provisions of the Land Transfer Act as regards land under the latter Act; and that, except as otherwise expressly provided, all the provisions of the former Act shall, as far as they are applicable, apply to land under the latter Act, as well as to other land and instruments.

Crown Land Tenures

It is a commonplace with New Zealand historians that from 1840 to 1914 New Zealand politics were dominated by the land question more than by any other issue, and that, during that time, it was over land policy that all the principal changes of government were precipitated. Not only did the central government throughout this period produce an enormous output of legislation relating to land, but during the years when the provincial system of government was in operation, there were many provincial ordinances dealing with this subject.

Mr. W. R. Jourdain, in his book on *Land Legislation and Settlement in New Zealand* published in 1925, distinguishes four phases in the history of the legislation relating to land. The first phase corresponds roughly with the Crown Colony period of government. During this period, apart from fairly extensive areas which had been granted out under the pastoral licence system—a system which was based on Australian experience—the disposal of Crown land was very much restricted. The second phase covers the period of provincial government. During this period the disposal of unoccupied lands belonging to the Crown became the function of the provincial councils and, although there were some divergences between the methods of disposal adopted by the different provinces, a certain measure of uniformity was obtained by reason of the fact that provincial legislation required the assent of the Governor, whilst the Waste Lands Act, 1858, provided for various general principles of land administration. Under this system, very considerable areas of land were alienated.

The third phase was inaugurated by the abolition of the provinces and the passing of the Land Act, 1877, which embodied to a large extent the principle of State leasehold and was the forerunner of much subsequent legislation relating to land under which many different types of Crown tenures were created. Speaking of this legislation Jourdain says:

> ' Although Crown land could still be acquired in freehold, yet between 1877 and 1911 many forms of leasehold were introduced, all of which had for their object the settlement of men of small means upon holdings of land sufficient in size to afford them a livelihood, but not large enough to constitute aggregation of land to an undesirable extent. Moreover, the legislation which authorised the purchase of private freehold land by the Crown, with a view

to its subdivision and closer settlement in smaller areas, tended to reduce the average size of the holdings held by farmers and to increase the productiveness of the Colony. This experiment was watched with interest by persons outside New Zealand, and enhanced the prestige that the Colony had acquired by its readiness to adopt new forms of administration and development in order that the country might progress in the best possible manner.' [2]

One of the most interesting of the many types of tenure which have been in operation under the land legislation was the lease in perpetuity which was first introduced by the Land Act of 1892. This form of tenure was a result of a compromise between the advocates of a freehold form of tenure and those who favoured the State leasehold system. Under it a term of 999 years was granted to the tenant at a fixed annual rental of 4 per cent. of the capital value throughout the term without any provision for revision, although it was subject to a system of graduated land-tax. This type of tenure may have been defensible as a method for encouraging settlement, but it was much criticised as being a bad bargain for the State, and the provisions under which it was granted were repealed in 1907, though without affecting existing leases.

The fourth phase began in 1912 when the Reform Party attained office under the premiership of Mr. W. F. Massey. In accordance with their election pledges this Government proceeded to enact legislation granting the freehold to Crown tenants. Various classes of these tenants were enabled to acquire the fee simple of their holdings, the purchase price being payable either in cash or on deferred payments at the option of the purchaser. Since the commencement of this fourth phase there has been much legislation relating to Crown land, and two important consolidations of the land laws have been brought out, the first in 1924, and the second in 1948. A feature of the consolidating Act of 1948, which sets out the current law on the subject, has been a very substantial reduction in the number of Crown tenures now available.

To promote more intensive settlement of land, successive legislative enactments relating to Crown land have provided for restrictions on the area which any one person might hold. In the latest legislation this principle has of course been retained, but expression has been given to it in a somewhat different form. The restrictions as to the specific area of Crown land which might be held imposed by certain former enactments have been abolished and instead of these restrictions the future limitation on the area which may be acquired is a general limitation on the undue aggregation of land. Section 175 of the Land Act, 1948, provides that no person shall be capable of acquiring any land or interest

[2] Jourdain, *History of Land Legislation and Settlement in New Zealand*, pp. 25, 26.

in land under the Act whether by way of allotment by the Land Settlement Board (which is a central body charged with the general administration of the legislation relating to land) or grant in fee simple, or by transfer or sublease of a lease or licence if :

(i) having regard to the land already held by that person the acquisition of the additional land would, in the opinion of the Board, amount to ' undue aggregation of land ' ; or

(ii) the land is intended, in the opinion of the Board, to be used for speculative or uneconomic purposes.

The Right of Eminent Domain and the Control and Conservation of Land and Natural Resources

The right of eminent domain consists of the power possessed by the State, as an attribute of its sovereignty, to take private property for public purposes. Closely associated with this right are the powers which the Government has assumed from time to time by legislation to deal with the control, conservation, and exploitation of land and natural resources for the more effective promotion of the social and economic welfare of the country.

Shortly after the abolition of the provinces and the vesting of all the powers of government in the central legislature, the Public Works Act, 1876, was passed. This statute provided a comprehensive system of legislation dealing with roads, railways and other public works in substitution for the existing enactments both of the central government and the provinces, which it repealed. Although this Act was concerned primarily with matters of an administrative character, it contained a number of provisions relating to the compulsory taking of private land for public works and other public purposes and to the assessment and payment of compensation for the taking of this land or for injurious affection resulting to other private land from the carrying out of these works and purposes. The statutory provisions regulating this branch of the law are now contained in Parts II, III, and IV of the Public Works Act, 1928, which embodies a vast mass of legislation relating to a number of miscellaneous matters in connection with various works of a public character and which with its amendments has greatly amplified and modified the original legislation of 1876. The provisions for the determination of compensation to be paid to private owners contained in the Public Works Act have also been utilised for the assessment of the compensation payable to them where their land has been taken for or injuriously affected by community purposes under other enactments.

Section 29 of the Finance Act (No. 3), 1944, laid down certain specific principles which are to be observed in the assessment of compensation under the Public Works Act, and in particular it is provided that the special suitability or adaptability of the land in respect of which the compensation is being assessed for any purpose shall not be taken into account if that purpose is a purpose to which it could be applied only in pursuance of statutory powers, or for which there is no market apart from the special needs of a particular purchaser or the requirements of any Government Department or any local or public authority.

As the original Town Planning Act of 1926 proved to be largely ineffective a new Act was passed in 1953. This Act was designed to encourage the production of town and country planning schemes, to secure the integration of schemes for adjoining districts, and to provide machinery which will enable schemes to be effective after they have been produced. Appeals arising under this legislation are dealt with by a special Town and Country Planning Appeal Board.

Although gold had been found elsewhere in New Zealand as early as 1852, it was with the discovery of gold in Otago in 1861, followed by similar discoveries three years later on the west coast of the South Island, that the gold mining era properly began. The exploitation of these discoveries, resulting as they did in gold rush after gold rush, brought in its wake various legal problems which led to the passing by the legislature of a series of enactments which have developed into a fairly comprehensive code of law dealing with the subject of gold mining. At common law the Crown was entitled, by virtue of the royal prerogative, to all mines containing gold and silver, but in New Zealand, instead of the Crown attempting to work such mines itself, a special code of legislation had been enacted providing for the granting of rights to mine to persons desiring to do so, subject to certain conditions. The original Act of 1858 was followed by much subsequent legislation which has now been consolidated and incorporated in the Mining Act of 1926. Many of the provisions contained in this legislation are based on the mining laws of Victoria where extensive discoveries of gold were made prior to the finding of gold in New Zealand.

The Coal Act, 1948, made provision for the acquisition by the Crown of the property in all unworked coal. A global sum, representing the total amount of compensation payable to the owners, was to be determined in accordance with the provisions of the Act by a coal commission established for the purpose. This sum was to be apportioned among the owners in proportion to the values of their respective holdings, but in 1950, after the National Party came into office, this legislation was repealed and the property in the unworked coal was revested in the former private owners.

In 1937 the Petroleum Act was passed for the purpose of encouraging and regulating the mining of petroleum in New Zealand. All petroleum existing in its natural condition on or below the surface of any land within the territorial limits of the country, whether the land had been alienated or not, was declared to be Crown property, but provision was made for the issue of prospecting and mining licences by private individuals and companies to investigate and exploit these petroleum resources. An intensive survey of practically all the potential oil-bearing lands of the Dominion has been conducted by various overseas oil organisations, but the results have proved to be uniformly disappointing.

Under the Atomic Emergency Act, 1945, provision was made for the control in New Zealand of the means of producing atomic energy, for the control of the mining and treatment of uranium ores and other elements which might be used for this purpose, and for the vesting of such substances in the Crown.

From time to time there has been much speculation in engineering and scientific circles in New Zealand as to the possibility of utilising the extensive geothermal resources of the country for economic purposes. About 1950 a serious scientific investigation of these resources was commenced with a view to using them for the generation of electrical power and since then a large amount of drilling for geothermal steam has been carried out at Wairakei, where one of the bores has now reached a depth of 3,000 feet, and at various other places in the well-known thermal area to the north of Lake Taupo. Although the results appear to be promising, the work is still in its exploratory stages.

Recently legislation was enacted to regulate the legal aspects of the utilisation of geothermal energy. Under the Geothermal Energy Act, 1953, the sole right to tap, take, use, and apply geothermal energy for the generation of electricity and any other purposes is vested in the Crown, subject to the qualification that a private person may be granted a licence by the Minister of Works to exercise a right of this nature. Any injury or damage caused to land, whether by the Crown or a private person, gives rise to a claim for compensation on the part of the owners or other persons suffering damage from the exercise of any powers conferred by the Act, or by such a licence.

The Iron and Steel Industry Act, 1937, was passed to make provision for the establishment by the Government in New Zealand of iron and steel works and subsidiary undertakings. As a general principle the sole right to mine for iron-ore is vested in commissioners appointed under the Act, but authority may be given to mine for iron-ore to be used otherwise than in the manufacture of iron and steel for commercial purposes, and mining privileges in respect of iron-ore may be granted on certain conditions with the consent of the Minister of Industries and Commerce. However the exploitation by the State of the iron-ore deposits at Onekaka in the Nelson district of the South Island, which the Government had specifically in mind in enacting this legislation, has so far not been proceeded with.

With a view to conserving the soil resources of the country, preventing damage by erosion, and more adequately protecting property from damage by flood, the Soil Conservation and Rivers Control Act was passed in 1941. Provision was made for the payment of full compensation to private owners whose land was taken or injuriously affected or damaged under the system of control set up under this Act.

A scheme for insuring property against war damage was established under another Act passed in 1941. This Act was repealed by the Earthquake and War Damage Act, 1944, which enlarged the scope of this system of insurance to cover damage arising from earthquake as well as that caused by enemy action. By an amendment to the law made in 1948, power was conferred upon the Governor-General in Council to extend the provisions of this legislation to damage arising from ' tempest, storm, flood, encroachment of the sea, or other natural disaster '. Regulations have since been made under this power dealing with insurance against disasters of this nature.

Married Women's Property Legislation

Although New Zealand was well to the forefront in the movement to give women enhanced political and social status, being the second country in the world to grant them the franchise, the legislature of the country displayed no similar initiative in removing the many disabilities which married women suffered at common law, but merely contented itself with adopting the various measures of law reform which have from time to time been instituted in England on this subject. A New Zealand enactment passed in 1860 and modelled on section 21 of the English Divorce and Matrimonial Causes Act of 1857, enabled a wife who had been deserted by her husband to apply for a court order protecting any money or property she might acquire by her own lawful industry, or which she might become possessed of after being deserted, against her husband or his creditors or any person claiming under him. During the continuance of the order, a wife was regarded as if she were a single woman, both with regard to the ownership and disposition of property of every description which she might acquire or which might come to or devolve upon her, and also for the purposes of contract and wrongs and injuries, and suing and being sued in any civil proceedings. The Married Women's Property Protection Act of 1860 was amplified by an Act with a similar title passed in 1870 which extended the benefits of the former Act to wives who had been the victims of certain other specified forms of matrimonial misbehaviour on the part of their husbands. The two Acts of 1860 and 1870 were consolidated in the Married Women's Property Protection Act, 1880 (later replaced by Part II of the Married Women's Property Act, 1908), the provisions of which continued to remain in force side by side with other legislation which was subsequently enacted revolutionising the law pertaining to married women, until they were repealed by the Destitute Persons Act, 1910.

The common law relating to married women was completely altered by the Married Women's Property Act of 1884 which was based on the English Act of 1882. The great general principle underlying this legislation was the statutory extension of a doctrine which had been developed in the courts of equity—that of the ' separate estate ' of a married woman. Under this doctrine, a married woman had been permitted to alienate and enter into contracts with respect to property held in trust for her separate use independent of her husband, or in respect of which her husband might be compelled to act as her trustee, although at common law he might have been entitled to it by virtue of his marriage to her. As a result of the Married Women's Property Act, 1884, a married woman became capable of (i) acquiring, holding, and disposing by deed, will, or otherwise of any real or personal property as her separate property, in the same manner as if she were a single woman without the intervention of any trustee, and (ii) entering into and rendering herself liable in respect of and to the extent of her separate property on any contract, and of suing and being sued alone, either in contract or in tort, or otherwise in all respects as if she were a single woman.

The Married Women's Property Act, 1884, as amended by the Married Women's Property Act, 1894 (which was a transcript of the English Married Women's Property Act of 1893) was replaced by Part I of the Married Women's Property Act, 1908. This last-mentioned Act is still in force, but has been substantially modified by the various amendments which have been made by Part IV of the Law Reform Act, 1936.

This enactment is founded on Part I of the English Law Reform (Married Women and Tortfeasors) Act, 1935, which in turn comprises one of a series of enactments passed in England in recent years introducing far-reaching changes and improvements in various branches of the common law. These changes and improvements in the law have, for the most part, also been adopted in New Zealand and in doing so the New Zealand legislature has closely followed the language of the English statutes giving effect to them.

Part IV of the Law Reform Act completed the process of assimilating the legal position of a married woman to that of a woman who is not married. Under the new legislation it is provided that a married woman shall :

(a) be capable of acquiring, holding, and disposing of any property ;
(b) be capable of rendering herself, and being rendered, liable in respect of any tort, contract, debt, or obligation ;

(c) be capable of suing and being sued either in contract or in tort or otherwise ; and

(d) be subject to the law relating to the enforcement of judgments and orders

in all respects as if she were a single woman.

One result of these provisions is that, by virtue of paragraph (d), a married woman can now be committed to prison pursuant to the Imprisonment for Debt Limitation Act, 1908 (which was not the case previously) for contumacious default in the payment of a judgment debt. The corresponding English statute also provided that a married woman should be subject to the law relating to bankruptcy, but such a provision was unnecessary in New Zealand where all married women have for many years been subject to the bankruptcy laws and not merely those engaged in trade separately from their husbands as was previously the case in England.

An important innovation introduced by the Law Reform Act was the abolition for the future of another concept inherited from equity—that of ' restraint upon anticipation '. The settlement of property upon a married woman subject to ' restraint upon anticipation ' provided a very effective protection of it against her creditors, as she was entitled only to the current income of such property and could not touch the corpus thereof nor create future rights over the income. It is now provided that the property of a married woman shall belong to her in all respects as if she were a single woman and may be disposed of accordingly. The Act does not, however, interfere with or render inoperative any restriction upon anticipation or alienation attached to the enjoyment of any property and imposed by any previous Act or any instrument executed before January 1, 1937, but any instrument executed on or after that date, in so far as it purports to attach to the enjoyment of any property by a woman any restriction which could not have been attached to the enjoyment of that property by a man, shall be void.

The Law Reform Act also abolished (i) the rule that a husband was liable for all his wife's torts committed during marriage, and (ii) the limited liability to which a husband was subject under the Married Women's Property Act for his wife's ante-nuptial contracts and wrongs to the extent of all property belonging to his wife which he had acquired or become entitled to from or through her.

Tenancy Law

A measure passed in 1916 was to usher in a new era in the evolution of the law of landlord and tenant. Under Part I of the War Legislation Amendment Act, the provisions of the Increase of Rent and Mortgage Interest (War Restrictions) Act which had been passed in England the previous year, were with certain modifications of detail adopted in New Zealand. In general this legislation prohibited landlords from increasing the rent of dwelling-houses from that prevailing at the outbreak of war. Tenants who continued to pay their rent and to perform the other conditions of their tenancy were also protected from being ousted from possession.

The Act of 1916 did not, however, extend to all tenancies but applied only to the case of a house or any part of a house which was let as a separate dwelling and the ' standard rent ' for which, as defined by the Act, did not exceed £104 per annum. The original enactment, as subsequently amended, was continued in force until October 31, 1936, but it did not apply to (i) dwellings first let as such after November 9, 1920, nor to (ii) any dwellings at all after May 1, 1928, unless an order had been obtained from a stipendiary magistrate declaring that the specific dwelling in question should remain subject to this legislation. Subsequent legislation, however, was to extend greatly the area of this new development in the law of landlord and tenant.

Considerable inroads on the ordinary law of landlord and tenant were made by the Fair Rents Act of 1936. This enactment, which was part of the general social and economic programme, introduced by the Labour Party in its first year of office, was designed ' to make temporary provision for the restriction in the rent of certain classes of dwelling-houses ' and ' for the determination of fair rents ' for these dwelling-houses. Originally it did not apply to a dwelling-house let at a rental exceeding £156 a year, or to a dwelling-house let for the first time after the passing of the Act, but later the scope of its provisions was widened to include all dwellings, including flats and apartments, and dwelling-houses used partly for business purposes, irrespective of the amount of the rent or the date on which they were first let. After the outbreak of the war, analogous provisions restricting increases in the rents of other properties were contained in Part III of the Economic Stabilisation Regulations, 1942.

The Fair Rents Act, which was originally regarded as a temporary measure, contained a provision that it should remain in force only until September 30, 1937. It was, however, in fact continued in force from year to year and, after the advent of the war, it was provided that it should terminate on the expiration of one year from the end of the war. Before arrival of the date when the state of war between New Zealand and Germany was legally terminated, *viz.*, July 9, 1951, the Tenancy Act of 1948 had been passed. This measure, which repealed the existing legislation relating to fair rents and revoked Part III of the Economic Stabilisation Regulations, constitutes a general code setting out the various statutory restrictions which have been placed on the common law rights of landlords and the various benefits, rights, and duties which the legislature has seen fit to confer or impose on tenants. Many of its provisions are applicable not only to tenancies of dwelling-houses but also to those of certain other types of real property. Hotels with licences for the sale of liquor which were affected by some of the provisions of the original Act of 1948 have now, by an amending Act of 1950, been entirely excluded from the operation of this legislation.

Fencing Legislation

At common law an occupier of land was under no obligation to fence off his land from that of his neighbours, but in New Zealand there has been a considerable amount of legislation (which does not seem to have had any counterpart in England) dealing with the liability of adjoining owners to contribute towards the cost of erecting and maintaining dividing fences, and providing for the elimination of many of the difficulties and uncertainties that existed under the common law. A comprehensive measure dealing with this matter and repealing a number of former enactments was passed in 1881, but this statute was repealed by a further Act revising this branch of the law in 1895. This latter enactment was consolidated in the Fencing Act of 1908, which with its amendments, sets out the present law with regard to fencing in New Zealand.

Chattels Securities

The year 1856 saw the passing in New Zealand of the first legislation providing for the registration of bills of sale of personal chattels. The primary object of this legislation, which was the forerunner of later and more extensive enactments on this important branch of the law of personal property, was the prevention of frauds on creditors. Under the Wool and Oil Securities Act, 1858, provision was made for the giving by the proprietors of sheep and whaling stations of valid securities over the future produce of wool, oil, and bone.

A consolidating measure passed in 1880 enacted a comprehensive code of law relating to bills of sale in general, leases and mortgages of live stock, liens on crops, and liens on wool and oil, and set out the procedure for registration in an office of the Supreme Court of instruments executed under the Act. This measure was replaced by subsequent legislation and the current law relating to chattel securities in New Zealand is now contained in the Chattels Transfer Act, 1924, and its amendments.

Although the New Zealand legislation relating to chattel securities is similar in principle to the English Bills of Sale Acts of 1878 and 1882, there are differences in detail between the enactments of the two countries and the New Zealand legislation is much more comprehensive in its provisions than the parallel legislation in England. In particular in New

Zealand where the lending of money on stock, crops, and wool plays an important part in the carrying on of the farming industry, special provision has been made in respect of instruments comprising stock and as to securities over crops and over wool. A difference of terminology between the present New Zealand Act and the English statutes is the use in the former of the term ' instrument ', in general, for that of ' bill of sale ', a chattel mortgage or security being known in New Zealand as an ' instrument by way of security '. An important innovation introduced by the 1924 Act was the creation of a special class of instruments known as customary hire purchase agreements which are peculiar to New Zealand. These agreements are limited to specified types of chattels and the usual provisions with regard to registration do not apply to them.

Succession on Intestacy

The passing of the Real Estate Descent Act, 1874 (which came into force on October 1, 1875), resulted in the first divergence of the law in New Zealand relating to intestate succession from that of England. The Real Estate Descent Act, which applied only to the undevised land of a male person dying after the coming into operation of the Act, leaving wife or children or other lineal descendants surviving, provided that such land should go in the first place to his personal representative and be distributed in the same manner as personalty was then distributed.

Under an Act of 1879 (which repealed the Real Estate Descent Act, 1874), the law relating to all persons in respect of succession to real property was completely assimilated to that in respect of personal property, and on an intestacy all property descended in the same manner as personalty descended. An important feature of this Act was the mitigation of the harshness of the common law in respect of the position of illegitimate persons. At common law such a person was regarded *quasi nullius filius* and was consequently incapable of inheriting property from either his ancestors or collaterals, or on his own intestacy of transmitting property except to his own legitimate issue or to his widow. Special provision was therefore made in this Act for the succession to illegitimate persons dying intestate and in certain circumstances for the succession of illegitimate persons to their mother where she died intestate.

The law was further modified by an Act of 1885 which provided for the case of a deceased intestate who left a widow or widower surviving. The Intestates' Estates Act, 1903, further provided for the payment to a widow or widower of £500 in certain cases in addition to any other share of the intestate estate to which such widow or widower was already entitled.

The various enactments then in existence relating to the distribution of intestate estates were consolidated in the Administration Act of 1908 which, together with the English Statutes of Distributions of 1670 and

1685 contained a code for the devolution of real and personal property of persons dying intestate which remained in force until January 1, 1945.

The passing of the Administration Amendment Act, 1944, which came into operation on January 1, 1945, marked a revolutionary change in the law relating to intestate succession in New Zealand. This Act which was largely copied from the Administration of Estates Act, 1925, in England, although there are differences of detail, provided that the English Statutes of Distribution should cease to be in force in New Zealand in respect of deaths occurring after January 1, 1945 and set out a complete code of provisions regulating the succession to real and personal estate on intestacy. This code sets out detailed provisions as to the order and the proportions and shares in which the various persons who are related either by marriage or kinship to a person who dies intestate are entitled to succeed to that person's estate. Apart from a widow or widower, no person can now possibly participate in an intestate estate unless he falls within that class of persons which comprises the grandparents of the deceased and their descendants. This class consists of the deceased's children, parents, brothers and sisters, grandparents, uncles and aunts and the descendants to any degree of such children, brothers, sisters, uncles and aunts. Failing the existence of any such persons, the estate of an intestate belongs to the Crown as *bona vacantia* although the Crown may, out of the whole or any part of the property devolving on it, provide for dependants, whether kindred or not, of the intestate, and other persons for whom the intestate might reasonably have been expected to make provision.

Recently the Amendment Act of 1944, together with a number of other enactments relating to the administration of deceased persons' estates, was replaced by the Administration Act of 1952, a comprehensive measure which consolidated, with some amendments, the various statutory provisions dealing with this branch of the law.

The Taxation of Property and Incomes

An existing *ad valorem* property tax, dating from 1879, was abolished by the Land and Income Assessment Act, 1891, which substituted for it (i) a graduated land tax on the unimproved value of land and on mortgages, and (ii) a progressive income tax on income derived from other sources. In 1916 the land tax on mortgages was abolished, and income from mortgages was at the same time made liable to income tax. The exemption from income tax of income derived from land was abolished in 1915 (as part of a general wartime increase of taxes), was re-introduced in 1923 (by a farmers' Government) and was abolished again in 1939 (by a workers' Government not as a measure of war finance, but as a measure of peace-time tax reform).

The income-tax legislation has been continually amended in detail. It was last consolidated in 1923. The actual rates of land and income tax are fixed by annual legislation. Special taxes on income were imposed during both World Wars, for instance, the Excess Profits Tax introduced in 1940 and abolished in 1946.

It was intended that the graduated land tax should provide an economic inducement to subdivide large estates. One of the most contentious issues in New Zealand economic history is the extent to which the tax achieved this object : certainly considerable subdivision took place, but the taxation system was only one of a number of factors making subdivision profitable. One interesting feature of the 1891 Act was a provision enabling an owner, who was dissatisfied with the value at which his land had been assessed, to fix a lower value and give the Government the option of taxing or purchasing at this figure. A large estate in North Canterbury was acquired by the Government in this way in 1893 and the land was subdivided. A similar provision still exists, but landowners are chary of taking advantage of it. Since the establishment of the Land Valuation Court (referred to in the next paragraph) a parallel provision has enabled the Government, where it considered the land has been assessed by the court at too low a value, to fix a higher value and give the landowner the option of paying land tax or selling to the Government at the higher price.

Land tax implied land valuation. Till 1896 valuations for property tax and land tax, and for local rating and other revenue purposes, were not properly co-ordinated and there were considerable discrepancies between the values fixed by different departments of the central government and different local authorities. In 1896 the Valuation Department was established, to value land for all taxing and rating purposes. Since 1949 there has been provision for appeal by dissatisfied landowners to the Land Valuation Court (which is discussed in the section of Chapter 4 dealing with administrative tribunals).

CONTRACTS AND COMMERCIAL LAW

The law relating to contracts consists of two parts :

(i) the general principles regulating the formation, operation, interpretation and discharge of contracts and the remedies for breach of contract ; and

(ii) the particular rules governing special types of contracts, such as the sale of goods, negotiable instruments, partnership, bills of lading, the carriage of goods, bailment, agency and suretyship.

Most of the general principles of contract are based on judicial precedents and derive their authority from the decisions of the courts, although here and there the law has from time to time been modified by statute, especially by the ' Law Reform ' legislation of recent years.

Commercial law is not one of the traditionally recognised divisions of English law, but when considering the legal system from a functional viewpoint, it is a convenient term to apply to those branches of the law which are concerned with business transactions, with the organisation and machinery of business, and with the remedies available for the enforcement by creditors of their rights against debtors. Commercial law arises primarily from an extension of the law of contracts to commerce, and its central core consists of the law relating to the various special classes of contracts which are nearly always concerned with transactions entered into for mercantile purposes, but it also includes such matters as company law and the law relating to bankruptcy. The foregoing topics belong to the field of private law, as they merely regulate business and economic relationships between individual members of the community as such, but in modern times, as the State has tended to assume a very much increased control over the economic order, industry trade and commerce have come to be regulated and controlled by a great mass of complex legislation, both of a parliamentary and subordinate character which, although belonging to the field of public or administrative law, must also, from a functional point of view, be regarded as falling within the sphere of commercial law. These developments in the law, however, have been discussed in earlier chapters.

Codification of Commercial Law

The law of New Zealand in respect of contracts and commerce, in so far as such law falls within the scope of ordinary private law, has not deviated to any great degree from that of England. Where the law in England has assumed a statutory form, the New Zealand legislature has, in general, been content merely to copy the relevant English legislation which, in any event, has generally served as a model for other common law countries. In 1883 a Bills of Exchange Act codifying the law relating to negotiable instruments and based on the English Act of 1882 was passed in New Zealand. The English Act was the first of a series of important Imperial enactments which codified various branches of commercial law, and which were soon adopted in New Zealand, the Arbitration Act being passed in 1890, the Partnership Act in 1891, and the Sale of Goods Act in 1895.

Similarly two important measures relating to maritime law, both of which were based on parallel statutes in England, were passed in 1903 and 1907 respectively. The Shipping and Seamen Act, 1903 (since replaced by the Shipping and Seamen Act, 1952), which was made under the authority of, and was to a large extent based on the Merchant Shipping Act, 1894 (Imp.), consolidated and amended a number of Acts relating to

shipping and seamen, which had been enacted from time to time in New
Zealand and were still in force. The codification of the law of marine insurance which had been effected in England by the Marine Insurance Act
of 1906 was adopted in New Zealand by a local enactment bearing a similar
title in the following year.

Mercantile Law Legislation

The Mercantile Law Act of 1880 consolidated no fewer than eleven
existing enactments, mainly based on parallel English legislation, modifying the common law in so far as it affected certain aspects of trade and
commerce and covering such matters as the form of acceptance of bills
of exchange, acknowledgments by agents, advances to agents, bills of
lading, carriers, the delivery of goods and liens for freight, guarantees
and sureties, interest on money, the limitation of actions, marine re-
assurance, partnership, the delivery of goods, title to goods before seizure
under executions and unpaid vendors of warehoused goods. Although
most of these provisions still remain in force, there has been a considerable
re-arrangement of them in the Statute-book. The sections relating to
bills of exchange, marine insurance, partnership and the sale of goods
have been incorporated in the later statutory codifications embracing
these branches of the law, while those dealing with acknowledgments
by agents, the limitation of actions and guarantees and sureties were
later embodied in the Judicature Act of 1908. The law relating to the
limitation of actions, however, is now contained in the Limitation Act,
1950.

The provision contained in section 43 of the Mercantile Law Act,
1880, that the laws of England relating to usury existing on or previously
to January 14, 1840, should be deemed not to have extended to New
Zealand at any time, now appears in section 2 of the English Laws
Act, 1908. By section 44 of the Mercantile Law Act, 1880, it was declared
that there should be no limit to the amount of interest which any person
might lawfully contract to pay, but this provision was subsequently
repealed by the Money-lenders Act, 1901 (since replaced by the Moneylenders Act, 1908)—a general enactment regulating the business of
money-lending, which is based on a similar enactment passed in England
in 1900.

The remainder of the provisions of the Mercantile Law Act, 1880
(including those relating to advances to agents which had been amended
in 1890 to bring them into conformity with the Factors Act passed in
England in 1889), were consolidated in the Mercantile Law Act of 1908.
Also included in this Act were the provisions for the protection of
book-purchasers enacted in 1891. The Mercantile Law Act of 1908
still remains in force except that the provisions which relate to the liability

of carriers have been repealed by and incorporated in the Carriers Act of 1948.

The Carriage of Goods and Passengers

The Carriers Act, 1948, deals generally with the liability of carriers under contracts entered into in New Zealand for the carriage of any person or any goods from any place in New Zealand to any other place in New Zealand. It is provided, however, that the Act is to be read subject to other enactments relating to carriers. The carriage of passengers and goods by the Railway Department is dealt with in the Government Railways Act, 1949.

By the Sea Carriage of Goods Act, 1940, New Zealand adopted The Hague Rules relating to Bills of Lading so far as shipping to ports outside New Zealand is concerned, but for the coastwise trade the existing statutory provisions, which were based on the Harter Act, an American enactment of 1893, were retained.

The Carriage by Air Act was enacted in 1940 for the purpose of giving effect to the convention for the unification of the rules relating to international carriage by air which had been signed at Warsaw in 1929 and to which New Zealand became an acceding party.

Secret Commissions

Under the Secret Commissions Act, 1910, the provisions of which are somewhat different from those contained in the corresponding enactment in England, namely the Prevention of Corruption Act, 1906, a number of offences were created with the object of prohibiting secret commissions. Those offences are directed against :

(i) the giving of secret bribes or other considerations to agents by third persons ;

(ii) the receiving of secret bribes or other considerations by agents from third persons ;

(iii) the concealment by an agent of his pecuniary interest in a contract made by him on behalf of his principal ;

(iv) the giving to an agent by a third person of a false or imperfect receipt, invoice, or other document with intent to deceive the principal ;

(v) the giving by an agent to his principal of any such document ; and

(vi) the receiving of secret commissions for advising third persons to enter into contracts with the person paying such commissions.

No prosecution for an offence under this Act can, however, be commenced without the leave of the Attorney-General.

Contracts Protecting Workers and the Weaker Party to Transactions

The legislation passed during the period the Labour Party was in office showed a marked trend to protect what was considered to be the economically weaker party to legal and business transactions. Examples of this are provided by the Fair Rents Act, 1936 (which has already been referred to), by such industrial legislation as the Agricultural Workers Act, 1936, and the Share Milking Agreements Act, 1937, and by the Hire Purchase Agreements Act, 1939.

The Agricultural Workers Act and the Share Milking Agreements Act afford good illustrations of the tendency of the legislature, in the case of contracts of employment, to fix standard terms and conditions which must be adhered to by the parties. Under Part II of the first of these two enactments, it is the duty of every employer to provide such sufficient and suitable accommodation as the Act and any regulations made pursuant to it may require for all agricultural workers employed by him. ' Agricultural worker ' is defined as meaning ' a person employed for any period exceeding one week in agricultural or horticultural or pastoral or flax-milling or saw-milling work of any kind, but does not include a shearer within the meaning of the Shearers' Accommodation Act, 1919 (under which enactment employers were already required to provide suitable accommodation for this class of worker), or any person, who is being trained at any institution established for the training of agricultural workers, or any apprentice who is bound by an indenture of apprenticeship made under the Master and Apprentice Amendment Act, 1920 '. Certain details of the accommodation to be provided are specifically laid down in the Act. Part III of the Act is concerned with special provisions as to employment on dairy farms, but there is power to extend these provisions by Order in Council to other classes of agricultural workers. This power has been exercised, with the modifications as to wages and conditions of employment specified in the relevant Order in Council, in the cases of workers employed in the tobacco industry, in orchards, on farms and stations used for the commercial production of wool, meat, or grain, and in market gardens.

The Share Milking Agreements Act applies to every share milking agreement made between an employer and a share milker, where the dairy herd is owned or provided by the employer. In this case the contract must operate not less favourably to the share milker in any respect than if the standard terms and conditions set out in the Act, as amended by subsequent legislation, were incorporated in the share milking agreement between the parties.

Other enactments passed during the period the Labour Party was in office, which regulate by law the terms and conditions which must be read into contracts of employment, are the Annual Holidays Act, 1944, and the Minimum Wage Act, 1945. The underlying principle of the Annual Holidays Act is that every worker shall, at the end of each year of his employment by any employer, become entitled to an annual holiday of two weeks on ordinary pay. The Minimum Wage Act has for its central feature the provision that :

> ' notwithstanding anything to the contrary in any enactment, award, industrial agreement, or contract of service, every worker of the age of twenty-one years and upwards to whom this Act applies, shall be entitled to receive from his employer payment for his work at not less than the appropriate minimum rate prescribed under (the Act).'

The Hire Purchase Agreements Act, 1939, which forbids the parties from contracting out of its provisions, was designed for the protection of purchasers under hire purchase agreements. It is provided that, if a vendor resumes possession of goods under such an agreement and their value at the time when possession of them is so resumed, together with the total moneys actually paid by the purchaser (including the value of goods traded in) is greater than the price of the goods, then the purchaser is entitled to recover from the vendor the difference between the two amounts. Furthermore, a vendor, after taking possession of goods comprised in a hire purchase agreement, cannot in any circumstances recover an amount which, together with the then value of goods and the moneys already paid, exceeds the price of the goods. The purchaser has also been given a right, on certain conditions, to have the goods returned and the hiring and purchase continued as if it had not been interrupted.

Protection of Workmen's Wages and Contractors' Liens

The Workmen's Wages Act, 1884, which repealed an earlier enactment relating to contractors' debts, was designed to secure more effectually to workmen the payment of their wages. Under this enactment a workman whose wages remained unpaid for twenty-four hours after the time when they should have been paid was enabled, upon taking out a summons for such wages, to secure the attachment of moneys due to his employer in the hands of a third party, by whom his own employer had in turn been employed, and, on being given judgment for such wages he was then entitled to obtain an order satisfying such judgment out of the moneys so attached.

The Act of 1884 was repealed by the Workmen's Wages Act, 1893. This Act enlarged and simplified the remedy given to a workman under the Act of 1884 to attach moneys payable to his employer by a third party and also provided that, in the absence of an agreement in writing to the contrary, the entire amount of wages earned by or payable to any workman engaged or employed in manual labour should be paid to such workman at intervals of not more than one week. It was expressly enacted by the Act of 1893 that it should be read with and be subject to two other measures dealing with allied aspects of industrial law which had been passed in the meantime. These were the Truck Act, 1891, and the Contractors' and Workmen's Lien Act, 1892.

The Truck Act, which had its counterpart in similar legislation passed under the same title in England, provided that all wages were to be payable in money and ' if by agreement, custom, or otherwise a workman is entitled to receive, in anticipation of the regular period of the payment of his wages, an advance as part or on account thereof, it shall not be lawful for the employer to withhold such advance or make any deduction in respect of such advance on account of poundage, discount, or interest, or any similar charge.' Contracts in contravention of this provision were declared to be void. Employers were also prohibited from imposing any terms as to the place or the manner in which or the person with whom a workman might spend his wages. In any action brought by a workman for his wages, an employer was not allowed to make any set off in respect of goods supplied by him to the workman and, subject to certain exceptions expressly provided for in the Act, he was not entitled to maintain against the workman any action for any goods so supplied.

The Contractors' and Workmen's Lien Act, 1892, which seems to have been based on a similar measure which the Queensland legislature had in turn apparently adapted from legislation enacted in the Canadian province of Ontario, provided for a system of statutory liens and charges in favour of contractors, sub-contractors and workmen. Subject to the conditions and limitations imposed by the Act, a contractor, sub-contractor or worker, who did or procured to be done any work upon or in connection with any land or chattels, was entitled to a lien upon his employer's interest in the land or chattels in question.

A sub-contractor was also entitled to a charge for the money due to him under the sub-contract upon any money payable to his contractor, or to any superior contractor, by the employer or by any superior contractor, in respect of the work done or to be done under the sub-contract. Similarly a workman was entitled to a charge for the money due to him for his work upon any money payable to the contractor or sub-contractor by whom he was employed, or payable to any superior contractor in respect of the work done or to be done under the contract of the sub-contractor by whom he was employed.

Under the Threshing-Machine Owners' Lien Act, 1895, a contractor, who had threshed a crop which was subject to a valid and duly registered chattels security and who remained unpaid for such work at the time of the realisation of such security by the grantee, was entitled to a charge on the proceeds of the realisation for the reasonable cost of such work on giving written notice within a specified period to the grantee of his claim. By the Wages Attachment Act, 1895, a workman's wages up to £2 per week were protected from attachment and the Wages Protection Act, 1899, was designed to prohibit a practice which had grown up amongst certain employers of taking out accident insurance policies to insure their workmen against accident and themselves against liability under the Employers' Liability Acts, and of compelling their workmen to contribute, as premiums for such insurance, sums at a rate proportionate to their wages.

The foregoing enactments were consolidated in the Wages Protection and Contractors' Liens Act, 1908, which, with some minor amendments which were made in 1914, remained in force until 1939 when it was repealed by a fresh measure designed to clarify the law and simplify the procedure relating to wages protection and contractors' liens. The present law on the subject is still contained in this Act of 1939.

Statutory Interference with Contractual Relationships in times of War and Economic Depression

During the First and Second World Wars and during the ' depression ' conditions which prevailed in the 1930's, the legislature did not hesitate to interfere with a wide range of contractual relationships with a view to easing the increased burdens which the economic difficulties arising during the periods in question had imposed on persons who were subject to obligations under these contractual relationships. The Mortgages Extension Act, passed on August 14, 1914, placed a ' moratorium ' on the exercise by mortgagees of their powers and rights during the state of war which had broken out ten days earlier, and the scope of its provisions was extended by various amendments which were made from time to time. It was replaced by the Mortgages Extension Act, 1919, which enacted a completely fresh set of provisions limiting the powers and rights of mortgagees under existing mortgages. The Act of 1919 was, in the first instance, to continue in force only until December 31, 1920, but this date was from time to time extended until December 31, 1924. Ultimately the ' moratorium ' was brought to an end by the Mortgages Final Extension Act, 1924, which repealed the Mortgages Extension Act, 1919, as well as a further Act passed in 1921, and provided machinery for the final disposal of the various problems which still remained outstanding. Reference has already been made to the enactment of Part I of the War Legislation Amendment Act, 1916, which first inaugurated a system of rent restriction in New Zealand.

The onset of the great depression in world prices, which commenced in 1930, had considerable repercussions on the economy of New Zealand, and led to a large amount of legislation interfering with contractual relationships.

Early in 1931 the first Mortgagors Relief Act was passed. The preamble to this enactment recited that ' on account of the special economic conditions prevailing, it is desirable to confer jurisdiction to postpone the exercise of powers of sale by mortgagees under existing mortgages in certain cases '. It was deemed to have come into force on March 18, 1931, and there was a provision that it should continue in force ' until a date to be appointed by Proclamation, or until December 31, 1932, whichever date is the earlier '.

An amendment passed later in 1931 extended the scope of the relief provided for by the original legislation (which was to enure for a further period until December 31, 1933) and established Mortgagors' Liabilities Adjustment Commissions to assist the Supreme or a magistrates' court, as the case might be, in the exercise of its jurisdiction under this legislation, and also to encourage voluntary settlements between mortgagees and mortgagors.

Further amendments followed in 1932 which not only enlarged the scope of the relief available to mortgagors but applied an analogous system of relief in favour of lessees. In 1933 all this legislation was consolidated with some amendments in one enactment—the Mortgagors and Tenants Relief Act. It was provided that this Act should continue in force until December 31, 1935, and should then be deemed to be repealed.

In the meantime economic conditions began to improve and in its last year of office the Forbes-Coates Government passed the Rural Mortgagors Final Adjustment Act, 1934–35. The intention underlying this enactment was to effect a final solution to the existing problems of rural indebtedness, but it had been in operation only for a few months when the Labour Party, who had been critical of various details of the measure, came into power as a result of the general election held at the end of 1935.

Under the new Government the Mortgagors and Lessees Rehabilitation Act was enacted in 1936. It repealed both the Mortgagors and Tenants Relief Act, 1933, and the Rural Mortgagors Final Adjustment Act, 1934–35. The general purpose of the 1936 Act, so far as it concerned mortgages and leases of farm properties, was specifically set out in the following terms :

> ' The general purpose of this Act in relation to farmer applicants
> is to retain them in the use and occupation of their farms as efficient
> producers and to make such adjustments of their liabilities as will
> ensure that the liabilities secured on any property do not exceed the
> value of that property, that the rent of any leasehold property does
> not exceed the rental value of that property, and that the total
> amount and terms of payment of all liabilities (whether secured or
> unsecured) are such that, after allowing for all normal current expendi-
> ture, and providing for the maintenance of themselves and their

families in a reasonable standard of comfort, the applicants may reasonably be expected to meet their liabilities as they become due, either out of their own moneys or by borrowing on reasonable terms.'

The Act also dealt with two other categories of applicants, namely, (i) home applicants, who while not being farmers used either exclusively or principally for their own occupation as a dwelling the premises comprised in the mortgage or lease in respect of which the application for relief was made, and (ii) applicants, who were neither farmers nor home applicants. It contained analogous provisions as to its general purposes in so far as they were affected by it.

To provide machinery for giving effect to the provisions of this measure there was established a court of record called the Court of Review (which was identical with a similar court which had been provided for under the Rural Mortgagors Final Adjustment Act, 1934–35) and also such number of adjustment commissions as the Governor-General in Council might think necessary. Under this legislation over 34,500 applications for relief were filed and orders were made adjusting the applicants' liabilities in nearly 24,000 cases while voluntary settlements were arrived at by the parties in approximately a further 2,600 cases. The total amount written off by way of reduction or remission of principal, interest and rent arrears and unsecured debts pursuant to orders made by the adjustment commissions and filed in the Court of Review came to approximately £10,000,000.[3]

Another important enactment which was passed in 1932 to meet the deflationary conditions which were concomitant with the depression years was the National Expenditure Adjustment Act. The purpose of Part III of this Act was to effect a 20 per cent. reduction in the rates of interest payable under mortgages, in rents and in certain other fixed charges. These reductions were commensurate with the reductions in salaries and wages which were made by Part I of that Act combined with those already made by and pursuant to Parts I and II of the Finance Act, 1931. However, the net rate of interest payable under any mortgage of chattels was not to be reduced below $6\frac{1}{2}$ per cent. per annum, and that payable under any other mortgage was not to be reduced below 5 per cent. per annum. Power was also conferred on the Supreme Court in the event of an application being made to it by any trustee or by any person who took any benefit or incurred any obligation under any deed, will or settlement to authorise a reduction of any annuity or other periodical payment which might be payable under the instrument in question. The reductions in interest and rent effected by Part III of the National Expenditure Adjustment Act were, in the first instance, intended to last

---

[3] *N.Z. Official Year Book 1941*, p. 651.

only for a period of three years, but on the enactment of the Mortgagors and Lessees Rehabilitation Act, 1936, they were made permanent.

On the outbreak of the Second World War the Government made use of the powers conferred upon it by an Emergency Regulations Act which was passed on September 14, 1939, to deal with the type of problem here under discussion. Under the Courts Emergency Powers Regulations, 1939, persons were prohibited, without obtaining the leave of the appropriate court, from obtaining the execution of or otherwise enforcing a judgment, from exercising any ' legal remedy ' as defined for the purposes of these regulations, from calling up or demanding payment of the principal moneys or exercising a power of sale under a mortgage, and from taking proceedings for breach of covenant in a mortgage other than a covenant for the payment of interest. These regulations were superseded in 1940 by (i) the Debtors Emergency Regulations which dealt with the limitations imposed on creditors' rights generally and (ii) the Mortgages Extension Emergency Regulations which placed specific restrictions on the exercise of their rights by mortgagees. The following are the two principal changes made by the Debtors Emergency Regulations :

(1) under the earlier regulations the leave of the court was required in every case, but under the later regulations this leave was necessary only in those cases where the debtor was a member of the Armed Forces or the dependant of such a person, or where he had filed a notice claiming the protection of the regulations ;

(2) in the case of an application made under the earlier regulations, the court could refuse leave only if the debtor's inability to pay were attributable, directly or indirectly, to circumstances arising out of the war but under the Debtors Emergency Regulations this was not essential.

Under these regulations the court was empowered to take into account additional factors, including the extent to which his default had been caused by economic or financial conditions affecting trade and industry in New Zealand whether or not they were attributable to the war. Both the Debtors Emergency Regulations and the Mortgages Extension Emergency Regulations were revoked in 1947.

Law Reform Legislation

The Law Reform Act, 1936, was the first of a series of measures, based on similar English enactments which have effected considerable changes in a number of fundamental common law principles, not only so far as contracts are concerned, but also in the spheres of property and tort. Part IV of the Act, which dealt with the capacity, property, and liabilities of married women and the liabilities of their husbands, has been discussed in the section of this chapter referring to the law of property. Part I (relating to the survival of causes of action after death), Part II (relating to deaths by accidents compensation, and since replaced by the Deaths by Accident Compensation Act, 1952), Part V (relating to the liability of tortfeasors) and Part VI (relating to the liability of employers to their servants for injuries caused by the negligence of fellow-servants) belong to the law of torts and will be dealt with in the section in which that branch of the law is discussed.

Under Part III of the Act it is provided that, where a person enters into a contract of insurance by which he is indemnified against liability to pay any damages or compensation, the amount of the liability on the happening of the event giving rise to the claim for damages or compensation, is to be a charge on the insurance moneys payable against that liability. This charge is to take effect notwithstanding the previous insolvency, bankruptcy, or winding up of the person insured.

In Part VII of the Act (since replaced by section 110 of the Property Law Act, 1952) it was declared that in all leases containing a covenant, condition, or agreement against assigning, underletting, charging, or parting with the possession of the demised premises or any part thereof without licence or consent, that licence or consent, notwithstanding any express provision to the contrary, is not to be unreasonably withheld.

Section 3 of the Law Reform Act, 1944, contained a code of rules setting out the circumstances in which the personal representatives of a deceased person are liable to remunerate out of his estate persons who have done work for him under a promise that he would make some testamentary provisions for them, but this section has since been superseded by the Law Reform (Testamentary Promises) Act, 1949.

Section 4 (which has now been replaced by section 13 of the Property Law Act, 1952) provided that the word ' month ' where used in deeds and other instruments means, unless the context otherwise requires, a calendar month. Previously a ' month ' in legal documents meant a lunar month unless the circumstances and the context showed that a calendar month was meant although in a New Zealand statute by virtue of the Acts Interpretation Act 1924 ' month ' had also meant a calendar month.

The Frustrated Contracts Act, 1944, which is based on a similar measure passed in England in 1943, makes provision for the adjustment of the rights and liabilities of the parties where a contract governed by the law of New Zealand has become impossible of performance or has otherwise been frustrated and the parties have for that reason been discharged from the further performance of the contract.

Third Party Motor-Insurance

Since 1928 there has been in force in New Zealand a system of compulsory insurance under which the owners of motor-vehicles are required to insure against their liability to pay damages on account of death or bodily injury arising from or in connection with the use of their vehicles. Under Part V of the Transport Act, 1949 (in which the original enactment of 1928 is now embodied) the owner of a motor-vehicle is required to nominate each year the insurance company with which the contract of insurance is to be made. This contract is deemed to be complete on the payment of the premium which is payable annually to a Deputy Registrar of Motor-vehicles at the same time as the annual licence fee for the vehicle is paid.

The liability of an insurance company under any contract of insurance is limited to £5,000 for any claim made by or in respect of any passenger in the motor-vehicle to which the contract relates and to £50,000 for all claims by or in respect of these passengers. These amounts are inclusive of all costs incidental to the claims in question.

Apart from the limitations just mentioned, the liability of an insurance company under such a contract is unlimited as to amount, but its liability does not extend to indemnify the owner against claims made in respect of death or injury suffered by any of the following classes of persons :

(1) a person living with the owner as a member of the same family or a relative of his not remoter than the fourth degree of relationship ;

(2) A person in service of the owner at the time of the accident ;

(3) a person who, at the time of the accident, was being conveyed as a passenger in the vehicle at the time of the accident if the vehicle is not a motor-vehicle plying for hire or used in the course of the business of carrying passengers for hire ;

(4) a person who at the time of the accident was being conveyed as a passenger but not as a passenger for hire in a motor-vehicle plying for hire or used in the course of carrying passengers for hire.

Company Law

The Joint Stock Companies Act of 1860 was the first legislation dealing with the subject of company law in New Zealand. This Act was based on the English Act of 1856 and as this branch of the law has developed the New Zealand legislation in respect thereof apart from minor details and the regulation of special types of company enterprises such as mining companies and co-operative dairy companies, has continued to follow closely English statute law. The current Act in which the law relating to companies in New Zealand is embodied, is the Companies Act, 1933, and this enactment brought the law of New Zealand into harmony with the English Companies Act of 1929, although modified to some extent so as to meet local requirements. The whole subject of company law in New Zealand was reviewed by a special committee set up in 1950 to deal with the revision of the existing Act, and a consolidating Bill incorporating the changes made by the English legislation of 1948 is at present before Parliament for consideration.

By virtue of legislation dating back as far as 1865, mining companies had been capable of being formed and carrying on business without being obliged to register under the ordinary legislation relating to companies, being regulated by special provisions of their own. In 1904 the legislation in respect of mining companies was revised so as to assimilate the law relating to these companies to that governing companies generally. There still remain, however, certain special provisions (now contained in Part XV of the Companies Act, 1933) which apply to companies of this nature by way of exception to the general law relating to companies.

Co-operative Companies for Processing and Marketing of Primary Products

Under the Co-operative Dairy Companies Act, 1949, a code of rules was enacted regulating the registration and carrying on of co-operative dairy companies. The provisions of this measure which consolidated and amended earlier legislation on the subject embody the recommendations of a representative committee which was set up by the Government in 1948 to investigate the matter. The Act sets out model articles of association, certain of which must be adopted if a company is to continue to enjoy the benefits of registration as a co-operative dairy company. A distinction is drawn between ' supplying shareholders ' (which are specially defined under the Act) and other shareholders. Only the former class are entitled to vote at any meeting of a co-operative dairy company or on any postal ballot conducted by such a company. In accordance with the recommendations of the representative committee a Co-operative Dairy Companies' Tribunal has been established to carry out the functions specified in the Act.

The Co-operative Companies Act, 1933, and the Co-operative Egg Marketing Act, 1950, contain special provisions in respect of companies whose principal object is either (i) the treatment for human consumption of pigs supplied by the shareholders and the marketing of the produce, or (ii) the marketing or the treatment and marketing of eggs supplied by shareholders. In each case not less than three-fifths of the nominal value of the shares issued by the company must be held by the suppliers.

Restrictions on the Raising of Capital

By virtue of the Finance Emergency Regulations, 1940 (No. 2), as subsequently amended, the consent of the Minister of Finance is required to the formation of a company with a capital exceeding £10,000. His consent is likewise required to an increase in the nominal capital of a company, to the making of calls upon company shares, and to the issue of capital or the public sale of securities by a company or any person other than a local authority if the amount involved is in excess of £10,000 in any one year.

Incorporated Societies

The Unclassified Societies Registration Act, 1895, made provision for the protection of the funds and property of societies not registered or incorporated under any other enactment by enabling them to become incorporated by means of the simple and convenient procedure specified in the Act. Under this procedure any such society consisting of not less than fifteen persons associated for any lawful purpose, but not for pecuniary gain, could become a body corporate. The law on this topic was revised in 1908 when the Incorporated Societies Act of that year was passed. The primary object of the original legislation was apparently to provide for the incorporation of such bodies as athletic and sporting associations but, in the course of time, an extensive use of this legislation was made by societies of a much more complex and important character, and as numerous deficiencies in the law had consequently come to light, the Act of 1908 was designed to make more adequate provision for the incorporation, management, control and dissolution of societies to which it was applicable. Many societies of a social, sporting, cultural, and charitable nature have found it more convenient to become incorporated under this legislation than under the alternative machinery for the incorporation of associations of this nature provided for by the Companies Act.

Bankruptcy

Bankruptcy legislation, dating from 1862, and frequently amended during the next thirty years, was placed in substantially its present form in 1892. The two important deviations from English bankruptcy law are : first, that a public servant, designated the Official Assignee, performs the functions that are performed separately in England by the official receiver and the trustee : and, second, that an immediate adjudication in bankruptcy and not merely a receiving order is asked for in the first instance under the New Zealand procedure.

TORTS

A tort is defined by Salmond as a civil wrong for which the remedy is a common law action for unliquidated damages, and which is not exclusively the breach of a contract or the breach of a trust, or other merely equitable obligation. Between this branch of the law and the law of contracts there are many analogies. Together they constitute, subject to minor qualifications, that great division of the legal system which Roman jurists referred to as the law of obligations ; and in English law the historical development of the law of torts is closely associated with that of contracts. Like the law of contracts the law of torts comprises two parts—the general principles of civil liability and the particular rules relating to liability for the various specific types of wrong-doing. As the bulk of the law of torts rests on judicial decisions and has not been affected to any very great extent by statute, the law of New Zealand in this field very closely follows that of England, although as the result of legislation, there are some differences in the laws of the two countries.

Damage Caused by Dogs

By legislation dating back to 1880 and now contained in the Dogs' Registration Act of 1908, a wider liability is imposed in New Zealand than in England on the owners of dogs for injuries caused by them. At common law, in order to render an owner liable for injury caused by his dog, it was necessary to prove *scienter* or previous knowledge on his part that the dog had the propensity to commit the mischief in question. It was as a result of this rule that the saying arose ' that every dog is entitled to one free bite '.

For many years in England there has been a statutory exception to the foregoing rule in respect of injuries caused by dogs to cattle, horses, mules, asses, sheep, goats, swine and poultry and it has not been necessary in these cases for the person suffering damage to prove *scienter* on the part of the owner of the dog ; but in the case of other kinds of injury caused by a dog the position with regard to the owner's liability therefor still remains as it was at common law. In New Zealand, however, the liability of the owner of a dog in the absence of proof of *scienter* is not restricted to injury caused by it to the classes of animals mentioned above, but extends generally to all types of injury caused by it, including injuries done to human beings.

Statutory Modification of Law of Defamation

The amendment made in England to the common law by the Slander of Women Act, 1891, whereby words imputing unchastity to women were made actionable without any special damage requiring to be proved, was adopted in New Zealand by a similar enactment passed in 1898.

The law of defamation was, however, further altered in 1910. By the Law of Libel Amendment Act, passed in that year, a number of changes were made in the law of libel, especially with regard to problems arising out of the publication of defamatory matter by newspapers. The new provisions were copied from legislation in force in Great Britain, Queensland and Victoria, but these provisions did not go so far as the corresponding statutory alterations which have been made to this branch of the common law in England. Under the Act of 1910, as amended by later legislation, the defence of privilege may, in the absence of proof of malice, be raised as a defence in any action or prosecution for a defamatory libel arising out of the publication of certain specified matters. This defence is not available in the case of a publication in any newspaper of a report of certain types of proceedings protected by the Act if it is proved that the defendant has been requested by the person defamed to publish in that newspaper a reasonable letter or statement by way of contradiction or explanation of the defamatory matter and has, without reasonable justification, refused or neglected to publish the same within a reasonable time. With a view to preventing ' chain actions ' against a number of newspapers for what is in effect the same libel, restrictions were also placed on the bringing of actions against different newspapers for the publication of the same or substantially the same defamatory matter and provision was also made for the consolidation of such actions and for the consolidation and apportionment of the damages awarded in those actions. It was further provided that, in an action for defamation, the defendant might prove in mitigation of damages (i) that he made or offered a public apology to the plaintiff for such defamation before the commencement of the action, or, if the action were commenced before there was a reasonable opportunity of making or offering such an apology, as soon afterward as he had a reasonable opportunity of doing so, and (ii) that the plaintiff has already recovered damages or has brought an action for damages, or has received or agreed to receive compensation, in respect of any other publication by the same or any other person of the same or substantially the same defamatory matter. The Act also contained provisions with regard to the proof of the identity of the publisher or printer of a book, printed document or newspaper containing defamatory matter.

Death in Relation to Torts

At common law it was not an actionable civil wrong to cause the death of a human being, but this principle was modified in England by the Fatal Accidents Act, 1846, generally known as Lord Campbell's Act. Under this Act a right of action against the wrongdoer was conferred in favour of the near relatives of a deceased person where (i) they had suffered pecuniary loss in consequence of his death, and (ii) his death had been caused in such circumstances that he himself would have had a right of action had he been merely injured and not killed. This measure was included among the Imperial enactments extended to New Zealand by the English Acts Act, 1854. In 1880 the provisions of the Act of 1846 and of an amending Act passed in England in 1864 were incorporated in a separate enactment of the New Zealand legislature, *viz.*, the Deaths by Accidents Compensation Act, which was subsequently replaced by the Deaths by Accidents Compensation Act, 1908. The Act of 1908 was amended by Part II of the Law Reform Act, 1936, which was founded on section 2 of the Law Reform (Miscellaneous Provisions) Act, 1934 (Imp.). In New Zealand as far back as 1894, when the first Legitimation Act was passed, the benefits of the Deaths by Accidents Compensation Act were extended to illegitimate children, but in the event of the death of such a child his parents had no corresponding rights. Now for the purposes of the Deaths by Accidents Compensation Act a person is deemed to be the parent of a deceased child even though the parent was only related to the deceased child illegitimately; and the meaning of the expressions ' parent ' and ' child ' have been extended to those cases where the relationship arises in consequence of an adoption.

The various enactments relating to actions for damages on behalf of the families of persons killed by accident have recently been consolidated in the Deaths by Accidents Compensation Act, 1952.

A far-reaching change in the law was made by Part I of the Law Reform Act, 1936, in respect to the survival of causes of action after death. The provisions of this enactment which are an adaptation of section 1 of the Law Reform (Miscellaneous Provisions) Act, 1934 (Imp.) abrogate the old common law rule embodied in the maxim *actio personalis moritur cum persona*. Under this rule, which, however, was subject to a number of special exceptions, a personal action died with the parties to the cause of action and an executor or administrator could not sue or be sued for any tort committed against or by the deceased in his lifetime.

It is now provided that :

> ' Subject to the provisions of this part of this Act, on the death of any person after the passing of this Act all causes of action against or vested in him shall survive against or, as the case may be, for the benefit of his estate.'[4]

Actions for defamation, seduction, and inducing one spouse to leave or remain apart from another, and claims for damages for adultery under the divorce legislation are, however, excluded from the operation of this rule.

With regard to the quantum of damages that may be recovered for the benefit of the estate of a deceased person the following provisions are to apply :

(i) exemplary damages are not to be included ;

(ii) in the case of a breach of promise to marry, the damages are to be limited to such damage (if any) to the estate of the deceased person as flows from the breach of promise to marry ;

---

[4] The Law Reform Act, 1936, s. 3 (1).

(iii) where the death of the deceased person has been caused by
the act or omission which gives rise to the cause of action, the
damages are to be calculated without reference to any loss or
gain to his estate consequent on his death, except that a sum in
respect of funeral expenses may be included.

For proceedings to be maintainable in respect of a cause of action in
tort which survives against the estate of a deceased person by virtue of
the Act either (i) the proceedings in question must have been pending
at his death, or (ii) the cause of action must have arisen not earlier than
two years before his death and the proceedings in respect thereof taken
not later than twelve months after his personal representative took out
representation.

Where damage has been suffered by reason of any act or omission
in respect of which a cause of action would have subsisted against a
person if that person had not died before or at the same time as the
damage was suffered, then a cause of action in respect of such act or
omission shall be deemed to have been subsisting against him immediately
before his death as if he had died after the damage was suffered.

The rights conferred by Part I of the Law Reform Act for the benefit
of the estates of deceased persons are in addition to and not in derogation
of those conferred by the Deaths by Accidents Compensation Act. So
much of such part of the former Act as relates to causes of actions against
the estates of deceased persons is to be applicable in relation to causes
of action under the latter Act.

Provision is also made for the enforcement of any liability in respect
of which proceedings are maintainable against an insolvent estate by
treating such liability as a debt provable in the administration of that
estate.

A departure was made in New Zealand from the provisions contained
in section 1 of the Law Reform (Miscellaneous Provisions) Act, 1934, by
section 17 of the Statutes Amendment Act, 1937. This section introduced an important limitation on the scope of the damages which can be
recovered for the benefit of the estate of a deceased person under Part I
of the Law Reform Act by excluding therefrom ' any damages for the
pain or suffering (of such a person) or for any bodily or mental harm
suffered by him, or for the curtailment of his expectation of life '. As
a result of this provision, no action would lie in New Zealand for damages
under any of the heads on which the plaintiff based his claim under
the English Act of 1934 in the case of *Rose* v. *Ford*.[5] In that case a young
woman was seriously injured in a motor accident caused by the defendant's
negligence. Two days after the accident it was necessary to amputate
her leg and four days after the accident she died from the injuries she

---

[5]   [1937] A.C. 826.

had received, after being unconscious throughout the greater part of the four days. Her father brought an action for the benefit of her estate in which he claimed damages for (i) the pain and suffering she had sustained ; (ii) the loss of her leg ; and (iii) the shortening of her expectation of life by the wrongful act of the defendant. It was held : (*a*) that the damages for pain and suffering must be limited to the four days during which the deceased woman had survived the accident and these were fixed at £20 ; (*b*) that, as she survived the amputation for only two days, merely nominal damages, fixed at forty shillings, were recoverable for the loss of her leg ; and (*c*) that the plaintiff was entitled to damages, assessed at £1,000, for the shortening of the deceased's expectation of life.

The extensive changes which have been effected by the foregoing statutory provisions in the legal consequences of death so far as the law of torts is concerned have been largely brought about by the development of transport in modern society. The prototype of the Deaths by Accidents Compensation Act—the English Fatal Accidents Act of 1846—was passed a few years after the advent of the first railways in England. In recent years, the heavy toll of life exacted on the roads by motor traffic has shown up in a glaring fashion the defects and anomalies of the *actio personalis* principle and has been a primary reason for the statutory abrogation of that principle in New Zealand as in England.

Contributory Negligence

A measure which effected important and far-reaching reforms in the law of torts is the Contributory Negligence Act, 1947. Under this Act, which is based on a similar statute passed in England in 1945, it is provided that, where any person suffers damage as the result partly of his own fault and partly of the fault of any other person, a claim in respect of that damage shall not be defeated by reason of the fault of the person suffering damage, but the damages recoverable in respect thereof shall be reduced to such extent as the court thinks just and equitable having regard to the claimant's share in the responsibility for the damage. An amendment passed in 1948 made this enactment binding on the Crown.

Injuries Arising from Mental or Nervous Shock

By section 2 of the Law Reform Act, 1944, a measure which introduced a number of miscellaneous reforms in the law, most of which have now been embodied in other enactments, it was provided that, in any action for injury to the person, whether founded on contract or in tort or otherwise, a party should not be barred from recovering damages merely because the injury complained of arose wholly or in part from mental or nervous shock.

Injury to Employees and Workers' Compensation

Although a master was, as a general rule, liable at common law for any tort committed by his servant in the course of his employment, there was an exception to this rule in the case of injury caused by one of his servants to a fellow-servant engaged in a common employment with him. This limitation on the general liability of a master for the negligent acts of his servants, known as the rule or doctrine of common employment, which was first laid down in 1837, was the subject of much adverse criticism and one eminent New Zealand authority on industrial law stigmatised it as a ' barbarous rule ' which was ' a blot upon the common law of England '.[6]

It has, however, now been completely abolished both in New Zealand[7] and England[8] but even before its final abolition it had been subjected in both countries to a good many statutory inroads. In New Zealand this rule was abrogated so far as mining cases were concerned as long ago as 1874 by the Regulation of Mines Act passed in that year, and the provisions of that enactment on this point were incorporated in later legislation relating to both mining in general and to coal-mines. In 1880 the Employers' Liability Act was passed in England. Under this Act, railway servants and persons engaged in manual labour, other than domestic or menial servants, were enabled to recover compensation against their employers in certain specified cases and subject to the conditions laid down in the Act for personal injuries, notwithstanding the fact that such injuries might have been caused by the negligence of their fellow workmen in the course of their employment. The amount of compensation recoverable, however, was limited to such sum as might be found to be equivalent to the estimated earnings, during the three years preceding the injury, of a person in the same grade employed during those years in the like employment and in the district in which the workman was employed at the time of the injury.

The language of the English Act of 1880 was reproduced with only minor verbal alterations in a similar Act which was passed in New Zealand in 1882, but the provisions of this Act were considerably amended by the Employers' Liability Act Amendment Acts of 1891 and 1892 which together, with the principal Act of 1882, were consolidated in the Employers' Liability Act, 1908.

In the meantime, however, the law with regard to the liability of employers for injuries sustained by their employees in the course of their employment had taken a completely new turn both in England and New Zealand. In 1897 the first Workmen's Compensation Act

---

[6] Mr. P. J. O'Regan (later Mr. Justice O'Regan) in 1936 N.Z. Law Journal 81.
[7] The Law Reform Act, 1936, s. 18.
[8] The Law Reform (Personal Injuries) Act, 1948, s. 1.

was passed in England and this was followed three years later by similar legislation in New Zealand.

The basic principle of both Acts was embodied in the provision that if in any employment to which such Acts applied ' personal injury by accident arising out of and in the course of his employment is caused to a worker ' his employer should be liable to pay compensation in accordance with the terms and conditions specified therein. This principle amounts to the compulsory insurance by an employer of his workers against accidents sustained by them since the liability imposed upon him attaches irrespective of negligence either on his part or on that of the workers.

Since the enactment of the original legislation, the law relating to Workers' Compensation has grown considerably both in complexity and volume for, not only has there been much subsequent legislation, but this branch of statute law is notorious for the amount of litigation which has arisen from it.

The original Act of 1900, together with subsequent amending legislation, was consolidated in the Workers' Compensation for Accidents Act, 1908, but this last mentioned enactment was repealed by a further enactment of the same year—the Workers' Compensation Act, 1908— which effected a number of changes in the law. This Act, after being amended on several occasions, was, with its amendments, reproduced in the Workers' Compensation Act, 1922. The Act of 1922, together with a large number of detailed amendments which have been made thereto, still remains in force.

As fresh legislation has been enacted, the nature and extent of an employer's liability has been considerably widened. The original Act of 1900 applied only to employment by the employer in or about :

(i) any industrial, commercial, or manufacturing work carried on by or on behalf of the employer as part of his trade or business ; or

(ii) any mining, quarrying, engineering, building, or other hazardous work carried on by or on behalf of the employer, whether as part of his trade or business or not ; or

(iii) any work carried on by or on behalf of the Crown or any local authority as the employer, if the work would, in the case of a private employer, be an employment to which the Act applied.

By an amendment passed in 1902, the benefit of the legislation was extended to workers employed in agriculture.

Under the Workers' Compensation Act, 1908, the legislation was extended to apply to a worker employed (i) in and for the purposes of any trade or business carried on by the employer, and (ii) in certain specified occupations, whether carried on for the purposes of the employers' trade or business or not. Under the present law, however, the legislation is to apply to the employment of any worker in any occupation, whether or not the employment is in or for the purposes of any trade or business carried on by the employer and whether or not the employment is of a casual nature.

A departure was made in the Workers' Compensation Act, 1908, from the general principle of the earlier legislation, under which compensation was granted only where death or incapacity for work resulted from injury, by providing for the payment of compensation for certain specified injuries (or 'schedule injuries' as they are commonly called) quite irrespective of whether or not incapacity results or of the quantum of any incapacity which may arise.

The Employers' Liability Act, 1908, was repealed by the Workers' Compensation Act, 1908. This Act contained a provision (which in substance was repeated in the Act of 1922) abolishing the defence of common employment subject to the qualification that in general the damages which could be recovered by a servant from his employer in respect of the negligence of a fellow servant for any one cause of action were to be limited to the sum of £500 (later increased to the sum of £1,000). The rule with regard to common employment, however, has as previously mentioned now been completely swept away by section 18 of the Law Reform Act, 1936. New Zealand was thus a few years in advance of England in this matter as it was not until 1948 that a similar provision completely abolishing this rule was enacted in that country.

Apart from the foregoing matters, the scope of employers' liability under the workers' compensation legislation has been enlarged from time to time in many other respects. For instance, the scope of the term 'worker' for the purposes of such legislation has been considerably widened and has now a very broad and general meaning. A previous provision, which excluded from this term any person employed otherwise than by way of manual labour, whose remuneration exceeded £400, was repealed in 1945.

In 1943 the principle of compulsory insurance on the part of employers against their liability in relation to Workers' Compensation was introduced. A far-reaching change in this aspect of the law was made in 1947 when, under an amendment to the Workers' Compensation Act passed in that year, employers were required to become contributors to a special system of compulsory insurance. Under this insurance scheme they were entitled to an indemnity in respect of all claims for which they might become liable, not only under the Workers' Compensation Act but also under various other statutes or at common law, for compensation or damages or contribution for the death of or personal injury to any worker in their employment which was caused by accident occurring on or after April 1, 1949, to that worker in the course of any employment to which the Workers' Compensation Act applied. The administration of this scheme was originally vested in the sole charge of the State Fire Insurance Office, but in 1950, after the advent to office of the National Party, the law was altered. Employers are now free to effect such insurance, not only through the State Fire Insurance Office, but through any private insurance company which is duly authorised under the 1950 Act to transact this type of business.

As mentioned above, one of the reasons which led to the passing of the original Workmen's Compensation Act in England in 1897 was the fact that employers were able to contract out of the provisions of the earlier legislation in respect of employers' liability. A feature therefore which has always characterised the legislation relating to workers' compensation both in England and New Zealand, is the provision that, as a general principle, there can be no contracting out of the provisions of this legislation. A further feature of the legislation in New Zealand is that it has always been administered by a special court, but this matter is dealt with in Chapter 3.

CONCLUSION

In comparison with the law of England it will be seen that the greatest changes have occurred in the law relating to property and the fewest in that relating to torts. At a very early stage in the history of New Zealand a system of land law had to be evolved which met the needs of a pioneer community ; and this fact has left a deep and lasting impression on the property law of the country.

While the divergences which have occurred between the law of New Zealand and that of England in respect of contracts are not so great as those which have taken place in the law of property, they are more extensive than the changes which have been brought about in the field of torts. It is true that the general principles of contract are still the same in both countries and that New Zealand has been largely content merely to copy English legislation which has been passed from time to time dealing with this branch of the law, but when the occasion has arisen as the result of war or economic depression the legislature has had little hesitation in interfering with the ' sanctity ' of contractual arrangements, and there is a large amount of legislation in New Zealand dealing with types of contracts which are more or less peculiar to the economy of the country, such, for instance, as the Share Milking Agreements Act, 1937. Under legislation of this nature there is a marked tendency to ' standardise ' the terms of the contract which may be entered into by the parties.

In both countries, however, the same general trends may be observed. The law of contracts and of property is being modified and varied to meet the growing pressure of demands for social welfare and economic planning. In his chapter on the ' Institutional Theory ' in *Modern Theories of Law* Jennings made the following comment :

> ' public law . . . is gradually eating up private law. Industrial law is being controlled by administrative organs and is at the same time eating into the law of obligations. Quotas and marketing schemes under administrative control reduce the operation of commercial law. Housing and planning legislation take the law of property under public control.'[9]

These words aptly describe the situation in New Zealand.

---

[9] *Modern Theories of Law*, p. 72.

CHAPTER 12

FAMILY LAW

THE founders of New Zealand as a British possession, those who shaped and influenced its earliest laws, came chiefly from England and Scotland. They had an abiding conviction that the welfare of a community rests fundamentally on religious faith and individual character, and that these in turn are best developed in the family and in the home. Legislation, from the beginnings until today, has been inspired by the desire to promote to the fullest possible extent the welfare of the family. Anthropologists may tell us that the family, the characteristic unit of so many diverse societies over so many centuries of human history, is not likely to be imperilled by changes in the laws and customs of our day; but New Zealanders, by no means convinced of this, have considered it a chief function of law-makers to promote the stability and well-being of the family. In New Zealand the story is one of perseverance and ingenuity in using legislative measures for this purpose, and violent disagreement (especially when changes in divorce law are contemplated) about the means best calculated to attain this end.

MARRIAGE

There have been no unique developments in New Zealand in the law regulating the forms and ceremonies of marriage or capacity to marry. For the European inhabitants English law was substantially suitable from the beginning.[1] In the main, the alterations that have been made have either followed or anticipated similar changes in England. Marriage may be celebrated by an officiating minister at a religious ceremony or by a registrar at the registry office. Special provision for marriage according to the usages of Quakers and Jews was enacted in 1847. This was repealed in 1854, but in regard to Quakers was reinstated in 1891.[2]

It is by no means self-evident, however, that the common law of England with the statutory modifications which had been made by 1840 was substantially suitable for regulating the form or the validity of the marriage of Maoris, or that it would be proper to subject them immediately to English marriage law. Before colonisation the Maori people had

---

[1] But as early as 1858 it was proposed that the ladies be relieved from telling their exact age, an inquiry which the officiating ministers and registrars found some difficulty in making.

[2] Marriage Ordinance, 1847, s. 45 ; Marriage Act, 1854; Marriage Amendment Act, 1891, s. 4.

their own customary practices,[3] and it could not be expected that these would be suddenly abandoned in favour of the ways of Europeans. The period of colonisation, however, discloses on this subject a discreditable history.

The story begins with the Marriage Ordinance of 1842, which on its face had little to do with the validity of a Maori customary marriage. The Ordinance provided that marriages solemnised by a minister of any Christian denomination who had not received episcopal ordination should be as valid as if the minister had received such ordination. This was followed by a Marriage Ordinance in 1847 which regulated the procedure relating to solemnisation of marriages in general. Section 44 of this Ordinance was as follows : ' Nothing herein contained shall apply to any marriage which may be contracted otherwise than according to the provisions of this Ordinance between two persons both of the Native race : Provided that this Ordinance shall come into operation in respect of marriages between persons of the said race in such districts and at such times as the Governor shall by Proclamation from time to time appoint '.[4] This section was re-enacted in the Marriage Act, 1854, with the addition of a proviso that persons of the aboriginal native race might, if they so desired, contract marriage according to the provisions of this Act. No Proclamation was in fact ever issued under these provisions, and it would be reasonable to assume that marriages between Maoris in accordance with Maori custom were thus permitted to continue and were by implication recognised as valid and legal.

But in 1888 the Chief Justice decided otherwise. In *Rira Peti* v. *Ngaraihi Te Paku*[5] he held that marriage between persons of the Maori race is governed by the common law of England as modified by the Marriage Ordinance of 1842 and must be solemnised before a minister of some Christian denomination. The validating Ordinance of 1842 was held to invalidate all customary Maori marriages not celebrated by a minister of a Christian denomination. This remarkable result was achieved by referring to the preamble to the Ordinance. Mention was there made of ' the common law of England (whereby marriages in the Colony are governed) '. On the basis of this phrase in parentheses in a preamble to a validating ordinance, the statutory exemption of customary marriages from the requirements of the Marriage Act was reduced almost to a nullity. The way was now open for holding that customary marriage between Maoris—including the highly formal, public and ceremonious marriage of a Maori chief—was to have no legal consequences, and that

---

[3] For a description of the three types of customary marriage see Elsdon Best, *The Maori*, Vol. I, p. 442.

[4] It was decided in *Parker* v. *Parker* [1921] N.Z.L.R. 732 ; [1921] G.L.R. 522, that the expression ' persons of the Native race ' included all persons of Maori descent, whether pure or mixed.

[5] (1888) 7 N.Z.L.R. 235.

marriage according to Maori usage was no part of the law of New Zealand.

So it may be found that if the ' husband ' under a Maori customary marriage conveyed property to his ' wife ' gratuitously, there was no presumption of a gift, for she was not his wife.[6] If a widow was to forfeit her interest under her husband's will in the event of remarrying, she might contract a customary marriage with impunity, for she would still remain unmarried.[7] If the parties were inadvertently allowed to adopt a child under the Adoption of Children Act the adoption was null and void, since joint adoption was permitted only in favour of husband and wife.[8] If the ' husband ' had sexual intercourse with his ' wife ' and she was under the age of consent he could be convicted of unlawful carnal knowledge, for he was not her husband.[9] If he were charged with a criminal offence she could be compelled to give evidence against him, for she was not his wife.[10] The issue of the customary union were, of course, illegitimate, for it was a mere voluntary cohabitation. ' The so-called marriage according to Maori custom is no marriage in law.'[11]

There were two statutory exceptions to this rule. Customary marriage was equivalent to legal marriage (and the children of the marriage were in the same position as legitimate children) in regard to intestate succession, and the parents though married only in accordance with native custom were able to succeed on the intestacy of their children.[12] The second exception was created by the Maori Purposes Act, 1940, section 3, which provided that customary marriages were to be deemed lawful and valid marriages for the purpose of adoption of children under the Maori Land Act, 1931.

The final stage in the compulsory assimilation of Maori marriages to the ideas and practices of Europeans was reached on April 1, 1952. On that day the Maori Purposes Act, 1951, section 8, came into force.

[6] A.C.M.B. 6/70 (cited by Smith, *Native Custom and Law affecting Native Land*, p. 123).

[7] *Re Wi Tamahau Mahupuku, Thompson* v. *Mahupuku* [1932] N.Z.L.R. 1397; [1933] G.L.R. 85. It was argued in this case that in construing the will it was the duty of the court to endeavour to ascertain the intention of the testator, and that evidence was admissible to show in what sense a Maori would use the word ' marriage '. But this mode of interpretation had already been rejected by the Court of Appeal in *Love* v. *Ihaka te Rou* (1889) 8 N.Z.L.R. 198, 217, where this remarkable rule was laid down : ' A Maori testator using English words must be deemed to mean what an Englishman would mean by the same words ; a Maori testator using his own language must be deemed to mean *what an Englishman would mean by the equivalent English phrase*.' (Italics added.)

[8] *Tutua Teone* v. *Tipene* [1936] N.Z.L.R. 642 ; [1936] G.L.R. 531 (affirmed on another ground : [1937] N.Z.L.R. 1098 ; [1937] G.L.R. 535).

[9] *R.* v. *Kingi* (1909) 29 N.Z.L.R. 371 ; 12 G.L.R. 175.

[10] *Ibid.*

[11] *Rangi* v. *Public Trustee* [1918] N.Z.L.R. 903 ; [1918] G.L.R. 483, 485.

[12] *Re Hura Rapata* [1936] N.Z.L.R. 949 ; [1936] G.L.R. 668.

This section repealed section 231 of the Maori Land Act, 1931, and substituted the following :

> ' Every marriage to which a Maori is a party shall be celebrated in the same manner, and its validity shall be determined by the same law, as if each of the parties was a European ; and all the provisions of the Marriage Act, 1908, shall apply accordingly.'

The Act further provided that customary marriages are not to be recognised for purposes of succession or adoption unless the marriage was celebrated before April 1, 1952 ; and that, subject only to these exceptions, no marriage according to Maori custom shall be considered valid for any purpose.[12a]

Returning now to the general law relating to marriage, the prohibited degrees of consanguinity or affinity as they appeared in the Book of Common Prayer were at first applicable in New Zealand. In 1880 (thirty-seven years ahead of England) New Zealand ' pricked that annual blister, marriage with deceased wife's sister '. Such marriages were validated retrospectively and made legal for the future.[13] Marriage between a woman and her deceased husband's brother became legal in 1900,[14] a change which preceded by twenty-one years a similar reform in England. Marriage with deceased wife's niece or deceased husband's nephew was retrospectively validated by the Marriages Validation Act, 1905, but was not authorised for the future. It was not until the passing of the Marriage Amendment Act, 1929, that the prohibition against such marriages was removed. Finally the list of prohibited degrees was revised and further restricted by the Marriage Amendment Act, 1946. The existing restrictions are set out in a Schedule to that Act. With regard to the prohibited degrees, legal marriages between Maoris have long been governed by the rules applicable to marriages between Europeans.[15]

Marriageable age was at first fourteen years in the case of a male and twelve years in the case of a female. If a person married under age the marriage was voidable by either party when the age of consent was reached, but if the marriage were not then repudiated it was valid. The Marriage Amendment Act, 1933, section 2, raised the age to sixteen for both parties, and provided that if either party were under sixteen the marriage should be void. But this section was repealed by the Statutes Amendment Act, 1939, section 41. The age remains at sixteen, and no certificate of marriage is to be issued if either party is under sixteen. But if, in error, a certificate is issued and the marriage takes place, it is not deemed to have been unduly solemnised by reason only of the

---

[12a] These provisions are re-enacted, with slight modification, in the Maori Affairs Act, 1953, ss. 78, 79.
[13] Deceased Wife's Sister Marriage Act, 1880.
[14] Deceased Husband's Brother Marriage Act, 1900.
[15] See now the Maori Land Act, 1931, s. 231 (as substituted by the Maori Purposes Act, 1951, s. 8).

infringement of this section. Consequently in New Zealand marriages of males under fourteen and of females under twelve are voidable (on reaching the age of fourteen or twelve), while marriages of persons of or over these ages are valid ; but in the ordinary course of events the marriage of persons under sixteen will be prevented.

Under the Marriage Act, 1854, the general rule was that a person under twenty-one years of age could not marry without the consent of his father. At present a person under twenty-one may not marry without the consent of both parents. Detailed provisions setting out the consents required in various circumstances are contained in a Schedule to the Guardianship of Infants Act, 1926. If the person whose consent is required refuses his consent, the Supreme Court or the Magistrates' Court may in its discretion consent to the marriage, and the consent of the court has the same effect as if it had been given by the person who refused consent. A provision of this type first appeared in the Marriage Act, 1854. It enabled a Supreme Court judge to give consent to a ' proper marriage ' when consent was unreasonably or from undue motives withheld. In 1856 a new member of the House of Representatives devoted his maiden speech to an unsuccessful attack on this clause. He urged that to allow an appeal after the father's refusal of consent was to repeal the Fifth Commandment. ' There is already quite sufficient temptation to disobedience without encouragement from our legislation. It certainly does appear to me that in repealing a portion of the Decalogue we have somewhat overstepped the usual limits of Christian legislation, and, in my opinion, the sooner we return to them the better. The amendment has for its object the removal of the blot of irreligion from our Statute-book, and the relief of our judges from a responsibility never before imposed on any court in Christendom.'[16] But the clause was retained, and the discretionary power entrusted to the court is not infrequently exercised.[17]

Marriage does not now automatically affect the nationality or citizenship of a woman who marries a New Zealand citizen, but she may apply for registration as a New Zealand citizen and if so registered becomes also a British subject.[18] The status of a woman as a Maori is not affected by marriage to a European.

[16] *New Zealand Parliamentary Debates 1856*, p. 151.
[17] For example, in *Re A.B.* [1944] N.Z.L.R. 674 ; [1944] G.L.R. 328, a father refused his consent to the marriage of his daughter aged nineteen to a half-caste Maori aged twenty-two, by whom she was pregnant. A magistrate refused his consent to the marriage, but on appeal to the Supreme Court Myers C.J. gave consent, holding that the welfare of the girl and the interests of the unborn child were more important than the parent's refusal, even though from the parent's point of view there were reasonable grounds for withholding his consent.
[18] British Nationality and New Zealand Citizenship Act, 1948, ss. 3, 9. This statute partly re-enacted an Amendment of 1946. Before 1946 the wife of a British subject acquired British nationality by virtue of the marriage.

DIVORCE

Grounds

Jurisdiction to grant decrees of divorce was conferred on the Supreme Court of New Zealand by the Divorce and Matrimonial Causes Act, 1867. This statute was modelled on the Act passed in England ten years before, and like that Act it was the subject of fierce controversy. Hitherto it had been within the competence of Parliament alone to dissolve the matrimonial bond.[19] To confer this power on a court of law was regarded by many as a disastrous measure, undermining the very foundations of a Christian civilisation.

Under the legislation of 1867 the only ground upon which a divorce decree might be made against a wife was adultery. In proceedings against a husband the permitted grounds were : adultery with a woman with whom, if his wife were dead, he could not contract marriage because of consanguinity or affinity ; bigamy with adultery ; rape ; sodomy ; bestiality ; adultery coupled with cruelty sufficient for judicial separation ; or adultery coupled with desertion without reasonable excuse for two years or upwards. The marked distinction drawn in the Act between adultery of the husband and adultery of the wife epitomises the prevailing Victorian idea of marriage. The list of grounds for divorce was an exact replica of the provisions in the Act of 1857 in England. The proponents of the measure in the New Zealand Parliament may possibly have wished to eliminate some of the anomalies in this catalogue, but a more extensive and more balanced statement of grounds for divorce was found to be impracticable. Correspondence with the Colonial Office had revealed that *so long as* the Colonial Act did not go beyond the English Act or provide for divorce for other causes than the English Act did, Her Majesty's assent would not be withheld.[20]

Opposition to the measure echoed the protests that had been raised in England and eloquently portrayed the calamities that would attend its passing. The Government of the day, bold enough on some subjects but pusillanimous on this, was ready to give its support but was not prepared to take the responsibility of bringing forward any measures providing for divorce. The Bill was introduced by a private member. Opponents declared that ' the very foundations of society would be sapped ', and that no man who professed to be a Christian could approve of the measure. As the Bill stood it would not prevent crime : it would only legalise it. In some cases (so it was averred) a married man of bad moral character, having taken a fancy to another woman, might commit a crime in order to obtain a divorce. The House was dealing the fiercest

---

[19] It is still possible to resort to Parliament for a private Act to dissolve a marriage if a divorce cannot be obtained without legislation.

[20] For this and the ensuing quotations from the debates on divorce legislation see 1 *New Zealand Parliamentary Debates*, pp. 684, 1042, 1093.

fatal blow to the family purity of the nation. If it was the general desire that marriage should be a civil contract, and that a wife should be taken on lease for a term of years renewable at will, let it be put on that footing. One member, endowed with vivid imagination, posed the issue : ' Are we to put it in the power of parents to force their children into whirlpools of ruin and infamy, or quicksands of treachery and seduction—in short, into the broad ocean of human misery ? ' He hoped that they would not put it in the power of the future historian of New Zealand to state that in the Second Session of the Fourth Parliament of New Zealand the legislature opened so wide the flood-gates of immorality that time itself had not been able to close them.

In the retrospect of nearly a century the Divorce Act of 1867 scarcely justifies these hysterical predictions. Throughout its history of amendment, compilation, consolidation, and further amendment the legislation has been steadily widened in scope, though always against the bitter opposition of influential groups. Attempts to secure amendments to the Act of 1867 were for a long time defeated. It was the fate of these proposals to be thrown out on the principle that facilities for divorce are the cause of matrimonial strife, and that happy relationships in a family are best secured when there is no remedy for a man's unfaithfulness. Speaking against one of these measures in 1896 a member of the Legislative Council said it was ' an attempt to upset our social and domestic institutions, and to destroy the harmony which has hitherto reigned amongst us '.[21] In the House of Representatives a third of the members did not think that a husband's attempt to murder his wife should give her grounds for divorce.[22] The proposal that adultery of a husband should by itself entitle a wife to petition for divorce was denounced in these terms : ' In practice it is an absurd provision, and contrary to nature and contrary to common sense, contrary to experience, contrary to physiological knowledge, and will amount to very little.' [23] Resolutions in favour of amendment of the divorce law were being passed at women's conventions in various parts of the Colony, and this led a Legislative Councillor to observe that the tendency of a part of the female community had been in the direction of legislation of this kind ' ever since the very great mistake was made of conferring the franchise upon them.'[24]

At last, in 1898, a successful attempt was made to effect substantial alterations in the law. By this measure—the Divorce Act, 1898— adultery by itself was made a ground for divorce against a husband, long before a similar reform was effected in England. At the same time several new grounds were added : desertion for five years ; habitual drunkenness and failure to maintain (or neglect of domestic duties) for

[21] 92 *New Zealand Parliamentary Debates*, p. 268.
[22] 90 *New Zealand Parliamentary Debates*, p. 68.
[23] 92 *New Zealand Parliamentary Debates*, p. 271.
[24] 94 *New Zealand Parliamentary Debates*, p. 274.

four years ; non-compliance with a decree for restitution of conjugal rights ; and sentence of seven years' imprisonment for attempting to take the life of the petitioner. The period of five years for desertion was a compromise between a term of four years originally proposed and seven years, the period advocated by Seddon, the Prime Minister of the day (a famous Liberal !).

No further change was made until 1907, when the grounds for divorce were again extended by including the conviction of the respondent for the murder or attempted murder of a child of the petitioner or the respondent, and confinement as a lunatic for ten years during the preceding twelve (reduced in 1912 to seven years in the previous ten). An amendment in 1919 reduced the necessary period of desertion from five years to three.[25] The provision making non-compliance with a decree for restitution of conjugal rights a ground for divorce was repealed in 1907 but reinstated in 1920. This amendment in 1920 also recognised new grounds for divorce : three years' separation[25] under a decree of judicial separation, a separation order made by a magistrate, a deed or agreement of separation, or separation by mutual consent ; sentence of imprisonment for seven years or upwards for wounding or doing actual bodily harm to the petitioner or any child of the petitioner or the respondent ; and unsoundness of mind for the preceding seven years, with actual confinement as a mental defective for the final three years of the period.

The legislation on divorce was consolidated and amended by the Divorce and Matrimonial Causes Act, 1928, which is the principal Act relating to divorce in New Zealand. In 1930 separation for three years under a decree or order made outside New Zealand was included (removing a restriction introduced in the Act of 1928). In England the Matrimonial Causes Act, 1937,[26] introduced cruelty as a distinct ground for divorce, but this has not yet been followed in New Zealand.

However, a 1953 Amendment, whilst placing a restriction by providing that non-compliance with a decree for restitution of conjugal rights must now continue for three years or more, did broaden some of the grounds for divorce, *e.g.*, any conviction for murder is now sufficient, as is living apart, without prospect of reconciliation, for not less than seven years.

Domicile

The early legislation was silent on the subject of the domicile of the petitioner, but after the decision of the Privy Council in *Le Mesurier* v. *Le Mesurier* [27] the legislature came to devote attention to this question. In the Divorce Act, 1898, a curiously worded provision was introduced

---

[25] The period of three years is temporarily reduced to one year in certain cases by the Matrimonial Causes (War Marriages) Act, 1947, s. 8.
[26] See now the Matrimonial Causes Act, 1950, s. 1 (1).
[27] [1895] A.C. 517.

requiring that the petitioner be a person ' who at the time of the institution
of the suit or other proceeding is domiciled in New Zealand for two years '.
The statute further provided that a deserted wife who was domiciled in
New Zealand at the time of desertion should be deemed for the purposes
of the Act to have retained her New Zealand domicile notwithstanding
that her husband had since the desertion acquired ' any foreign domicile '
(later amended to ' some other domicile ').

Throughout the subsequent legislation on divorce the requirement
of a New Zealand domicile for not less than two years immediately
preceding the filing of the petition was maintained unaltered until 1953,
but the provision enabling the court to make a decree on the basis of a
notional or statutory domicile was gradually extended. The Divorce Act
of 1928 provided that where a wife prays for a divorce on the ground
of three years' separation and the husband was domiciled in New Zealand
when the separation commenced the wife should be deemed to have
retained her New Zealand domicile notwithstanding that her husband has
since acquired some other domicile. Under an amendment in 1930 a wife
who had been living in New Zealand apart from her husband for three
years and intended to reside here permanently could petition for divorce
on any ground as if she were domiciled in New Zealand.

Experience during the Second World War resulted in a temporary
but far-reaching application of the same device.[28]

The latest changes, effected by the Divorce and Matrimonial Causes
Amendment Act, 1953, reduce still further the barrier of foreign domicile.
The requirement of a New Zealand domicile for two preceding years
(formerly applicable to divorce proceedings on any ground) now applies
only to proceedings based on separation or desertion ; and the device of a
notional New Zealand domicile for a wife separated from her husband
is made applicable to the new ground of divorce, separation for seven
years.

The assumption underlying these measures has been that husband
and wife have the same domicile—that of the husband—so long as the
marriage subsists. This doctrine, long disputed, became finally established in New Zealand as a result of the decision of the Privy Council in
Attorney-General for Alberta v. *Cook*.[29]

---

[28] Matrimonial Causes (War Marriages) Act, 1947. Part I of this Act replaced
emergency regulations made in 1946, based on the Matrimonial Causes (War
Marriages) Act, 1944 (U.K.). Most of Part II of the Act reproduced emergency
regulations made in 1947, carrying the principle still further.

[29] [1926] A.C. 444. See *Ellis* v. *Ellis* [1929] G.L.R. 11. It had previously been
held in New Zealand that after a decree of judicial separation had been made
a married woman could acquire a separate domicile from that of her husband :
Hastings v. *Hastings* [1922] N.Z.L.R. 273 ; [1922] G.L.R. 108. The decision
just cited is also notable for adopting the view that the court cannot grant a
decree of divorce against a respondent domiciled outside the jurisdiction. By
necessary implication this is abrogated by the statutory provisions authorising
decrees to be made in favour of petitioners not domiciled in New Zealand.

Until 1953 a decree of divorce granted outside New Zealand was not generally recognised in New Zealand unless made by a court in the husband's domicile, or there recognised as valid. An important, though limited, exception to this rule was made by the Matrimonial Causes (War Marriages) Act, 1947. A proposal that there should be a substantial and permanent modification of the general rule was recently considered.[32] The outcome was the adoption of principles of recognition which involve a revolutionary departure from previous practice. Under the amending Act of 1953 a decree of divorce made in another country is to be recognised as valid in New Zealand if the court exercised jurisdiction on the basis of the domicile of both or either of the parties in that country or the wife's residence there for two years, or if the decree is recognised as valid in the courts of a country in which one of the parties is domiciled or deemed by the law of that country to be domiciled. The doctrine of the unitary domicile of husband and wife under New Zealand law has not been abandoned, but the more disastrous consequences of the doctrine are being avoided.

OTHER MATRIMONIAL CAUSES

The Divorce and Matrimonial Causes Act, 1867, and the Acts which have succeeded it have conferred on the Supreme Court jurisdiction in respect of judicial separation, nullity of marriage, restitution of conjugal rights, and all other matrimonial causes. Subject to the express requirements of the legislation relief is to be given on principles which conform as nearly as may be with the principles on which the ecclesiastical courts in England acted and gave relief.

A decree for judicial separation may be made on proof of adultery or cruelty, desertion without cause for not less than two years, or failure to comply with a decree for restitution of conjugal rights. The grounds upon which a decree of nullity may be made were not defined by statute until 1953. Up to that time the grounds were: bigamy; marriage within the prohibited degrees of relationship; wilfully and knowingly intermarrying without a certificate from the registrar, or in the absence of an officiating minister or registrar; want of consent; lack of marriageable age; and incapacity to consummate the marriage. In the first four cases the marriage was void, in the others voidable. The Divorce and Matrimonial Causes Amendment Act, 1953, embodied these grounds in legislation and added to them the new grounds which were introduced in England in 1937.[33] Particularly important is a new provision,[34] defining the effect of a decree of nullity of a voidable marriage. It directs that the

---

[32] This investigation was a direct result of the paper by Dean Erwin N. Griswold, *Divorce Jurisdiction and Recognition of Divorce Decrees* (1951) 25 A.L.J. 248.

[33] See now Matrimonial Causes Act, 1950, s. 8.

[34] Divorce and Matrimonial Causes Act, 1928, s. 10B (4) (added by Divorce and Matrimonial Causes Amendment Act, 1953, s. 3).

decree shall declare the marriage to be annulled ' on and from the date of
the decree ', and enacts that the marriage shall be deemed to have been
valid from the time of its celebration until the decree of nullity. Under
this provision not only are the children legitimate, but the decree is substantially comparable with a decree of divorce.

Judicial Interpretation

The creation of a separate Divorce Court in England with its own
separate judges, and later the assigning of certain judges to the divorce
work of the Probate Division, has produced a degree of judicial specialisa-
tion which has no counterpart in New Zealand. In this country all the
judges of the Supreme Court hear matrimonial cases, and this constitutes
only part of the work that each of them performs. This distribution of
matrimonial causes has accentuated the reliance which is placed on the
exposition of the law by judges exercising divorce jurisdiction in England.
There has been a faithful adherence to English decisions, so loyal, indeed,
that some decisions may have been followed too uncritically. *Williams* v.
Williams [35] was overruled in 1951 [36] but in the meantime it had been followed in New Zealand in *M.* v. *M.* [37] *Germany* v. *Germany* [38] and *Lloyd*
v. *Lloyd and Leggeri* [39] were accepted without question by members of
the Court of Appeal in New Zealand in *Lewis* v. *Lewis* [40] although these
decisions were to be disapproved a year later. [41] *Wanbon* v. *Wanbon* [42]
was applied without hesitation in *Dempster* v. *Dempster* [43] although shortly
afterwards the Court of Appeal in England was not disposed to follow
it. [44]

This readiness of New Zealand judges to follow English decisions
extends even to decisions of which they may not approve. There is a
very strong desire in this country to maintain uniformity of legal principle
throughout the Commonwealth. On a number of occasions the court
has considered an English decision unsatisfactory but has nevertheless
followed and applied it, to preserve this uniformity. For example, in
Barker v. *Barker* [45] a Full Court of five judges unanimously followed
Jackson v. *Jackson* [46] although some of the judges considered that the
weight of authority in New Zealand supported the opposite conclusion
and that the rule laid down in *Jackson* v. *Jackson* was unsatisfactory.

[35] [1939] P. 365; [1939] 3 All E.R. 825.
[36] *Crowther* v. *Crowther* [1951] A.C. 723; [1951] 1 All E.R. 1131.
[37] [1944] N.Z.L.R. 328; [1944] G.L.R. 57.
[38] [1938] P. 203; [1938] 3 All E.R. 64.
[39] [1938] P. 174; [1938] 2 All E.R. 480.
[40] [1944] N.Z.L.R. 736; [1944] G.L.R. 317.
[41] *Churchman* v. *Churchman* [1945] P. 44; [1945] 2 All E.R. 190.
[42] [1946] 2 All E.R. 366.
[43] [1948] N.Z.L.R. 857; [1948] G.L.R. 387.
[44] *Hopes* v. *Hopes* [1949] P. 227; [1948] 2 All E.R. 920.
[45] [1924] N.Z.L.R. 1078; [1924] G.L.R. 525.
[46] [1924] P. 19; 40 T.L.R. 45.

As Mr. Justice Reed observed : ' This court is not bound by a decision of the Divisional Court, but we are administering the same law, and it has always been the practice of the courts of New Zealand to follow the decisions of that court unless there is some very good reason to the contrary'.

The rule in *Russell* v. *Russell*,[47] being established by a decision of the House of Lords, was of course followed in New Zealand, and so was *Ettenfield* v. *Ettenfield*.[48] The rule was applied even in a criminal case on a charge of incest.[49] But the rule was severely criticised in a number of cases in New Zealand, and was eventually abrogated by statute in 1945.[50]

On the question of the standard of proof required to establish adultery in a divorce case the Supreme Court in *Price* v. *Price*[51] followed *Wright* v. *Wright*[52] in preference to *Ginesi* v. *Ginesi*[53]; but this course was felt to be open only by reason of the criticisms of *Ginesi* v. *Ginesi* that had been voiced in later cases in England.[54] When, in *McDonald* v. *McDonald*[54a] the Supreme Court declined to follow *Price* v. *Price* this change of view was again mainly attributable to the desire to follow English authority.[54b]

SUMMARY PROCEEDINGS

The Destitute Persons Act, 1910, embodies a number of schemes devised stage by stage from the earliest years of settlement in New Zealand in regard to separation, maintenance, custody and affiliation. As early as 1846 an Ordinance had provided for summary proceedings to impose liability on near relatives to support destitute persons and on a deserting husband to support his wife and children. The court was also empowered to adjudge a person the father of an illegitimate child and to require him to contribute to its maintenance. Later, power was given to make a separation order against a husband if he had been convicted of an aggravated assault on his wife. New grounds for a separation order were added in 1896. The Act of 1910 considerably enlarged the existing provisions. The principal jurisdiction which is vested in magistrates by this Act and its amendments may be summarised as follows :

(1) A maintenance order may be made against the parent of a child directing him to pay up to £50 for past maintenance and a

[47] [1924] A.C. 687.
[48] [1940] P. 96 ; [1940] 1 All E.R. 293.
[49] *R.* v. *Seaton* [1933] N.Z.L.R. 548 ; [1933] G.L.R. 451.
[50] Evidence Amendment Act, 1945, s. 15.
[51] [1951] N.Z.L.R. 1097.
[52] (1948) 77 C.L.R. 191.
[53] [1948] P. 179 ; [1948] 1 All E.R. 373.
[54] *Davis* v. *Davis* [1950] P. 125 ; [1950] 1 All E.R. 40 ; *Gower* v. *Gower* [1950] 1 All E.R. 804.
[54a] [1952] N.Z.L.R. 924.
[54b] *Preston Jones* v. *Preston Jones* [1951] A.C. 391 ; *Bater* v. *Bater*, [1951] p. 35.

reasonable sum towards its future maintenance until the child is sixteen. Extensions of the order until the child attains the age of eighteen may be made where the child is engaged in a course of education or training.[55] An order to pay for future maintenance may be made without proof of the present ability of the parent to make this contribution.

(2) A maintenance order may be made against a ' near relative ' (as defined in the Act) to contribute to the support of a destitute person, if the near relative is of sufficient ability to do so. The near relative has a right of reimbursement from the parent or the husband of the destitute person.

(3) Affiliation and maintenance orders may be made against a person alleged to be the father of an illegitimate child.

(4) An order for payment of an allowance from the assets of a deceased estate for the future maintenance of an illegitimate child may be made in certain circumstances where the deceased was the father or mother of the child.

(5) On proof that a husband has failed or intends to fail to provide his wife with adequate maintenance, or that he has been guilty of persistent cruelty to her or to her children, or that he is an habitual inebriate, or that he has within the previous six months been sentenced to imprisonment or to a fine exceeding five pounds for an assault or other offence of violence against her or any of her children, a magistrate may make (*a*) a maintenance order in favour of the wife, (*b*) an order for past maintenance up to £50, (*c*) a separation order, (*d*) a guardianship order giving the wife legal guardianship of children of the marriage under sixteen years of age. No separation order or guardianship order can be made on the sole ground of failure to maintain unless the failure was wilful and without reasonable cause. A guardianship order may include provision giving the husband a right of access to the children.[56]

(6) Any of the orders mentioned in the last paragraph may, with certain modifications, be made in favour of a husband against his wife.[57]

(7) Some fit person may with his consent be appointed to have the custody of a child during the currency of a maintenance order.

---

[55] Destitute Persons Amendment Act, 1951, s. 7 ; and see Destitute Persons Amendment Act, 1953, ss. 2, 3.

[56] On the death of a parent, grandparents may be given a right of access to the grandchildren in the custody of the surviving parent : Guardianship of Infants Amendment Act, 1927, s. 3 ; *Wilkes* v. *Asher* [1951] N.Z.L.R. 27 ; [1951] G.L.R. 66.

[57] Domestic Proceedings Act, 1939, s. 8.

(8) Maintenance orders may be varied or suspended and arrears may
be cancelled.[58]

Since 1939 efforts have been made to secure the reconciliation of husband
and wife where the differences between them have led to proceedings
for separation, maintenance, or guardianship orders. Under the Domestic
Proceedings Act, 1939, the magistrate, unless he considers it inexpedient
to do so, must refer the matter to a conciliator. A probation officer,
maintenance officer, child welfare officer, or any other person may be
appointed as conciliator. The application to the court for an order
cannot proceed unless the conciliator has reported that the attempt to
effect a reconciliation has been unsuccessful. The negotiations are in
the strictest confidence, and all statements made to the conciliator are
absolutely privileged from disclosure. There are no reports or statistics
from which to gauge the success of this scheme, but an official estimate
is that in about 15 per cent. of the cases referred to conciliators the parties
are induced to settle their differences and make a fresh start. The main
obstacles impeding greater success are the absence of sufficient trained
and gifted conciliators, and the fact that the attempt is not made until
court proceedings are commenced, by which time the hope of reconciliation
is slight indeed.

CUSTODY OF CHILDREN

In England the past hundred years have seen the decline and fall of
the doctrine that the father of a family has, as against the mother, the
exclusive right to the custody and control of their children. The legislation by which the mother acquired the right to receive equal consideration
was copied, step by step, in New Zealand.[59] The only significant
difference lay in the fact that the Supreme Court of New Zealand, from
the beginning, has been a court administering common law and equity
concurrently. The equitable doctrines, which modified in favour of
the mother the bias of the common law towards the father, have accordingly
prevailed when custody has been in dispute between father and mother.
Complete equality in the claims of parents to the custody of, and access
to, their children (subject always to the overriding consideration of the
welfare of the children) could be achieved only by statute, but this has
now been attained. The principle of equality is embodied in the Guardianship of Infants Act, 1926, sections 2–5, the Infants Act, 1908, section 2
(as amended by section 20 (1) of the Statutes Amendment Act, 1949),
and the Judicature Act, 1908, section 98.[60]

---

[58] For fuller discussion of the Destitute Persons Act see Birks, *Legal Relationship
of Parent and Child* (1952). For the supplementary provisions of the Social
Security Act see Chap. 5.

[59] For a detailed comparison see the judgment of Williams J. in *Re J. H. and
L. J. Thompson* (1911) 30 N.Z.L.R. 168.

[60] See *Norton* v. *Norton* [1951] N.Z.L.R. 678 ; *Connett* v. *Connett* [1952] N.Z.L.R.
304 ; [1952] G.L.R. 244.

ILLEGITIMATE CHILDREN

The law of England in 1840 relating to illegitimate children, and the social attitudes reflected in that law, were among the least attractive parts of New Zealand's inheritance from England. The illegitimate child, *filius nullius* in the quaint but harsh fiction of the law, was deprived of the rights of legitimate children in the belief that this would be a deterrent to intercourse between persons who were not husband and wife. With the passage of time this policy has appeared less and less defensible on ethical grounds, and its efficacy as a deterrent has been shown by experience to be negligible. New Zealand law has steadily abandoned the earlier doctrine, and is gradually assimilating the position of an illegitimate child to that of a legitimate child. It has been a generation ahead of England in moving in this direction, but has still some distance to go before illegitimacy entails no serious legal disability.

An extremely illuminating illustration of the sentiments formerly entertained is afforded by a Supreme Court decision in 1869. The question to be determined was whether an Englishman who had come to New Zealand as a gold-miner had acquired a New Zealand domicile. Six years after his arrival he had expressed the hope, in a letter to his mother, that he would ' soon be at home with you all once more '. But he was drowned in the Teremakau River later in the same year. The judge held that as he was an illegitimate child the ordinary ties of blood relationship could not be considered as having existed to bind him to the country of his birth.[61]

Legitimation

The most important change was undoubtedly the introduction of legitimation by subsequent marriage of the parents. It is a curious fact that the first enactment in New Zealand permitting legitimation by subsequent marriage applied only to half-caste Maoris. Under the Half-Caste Disability Removal Act, 1860, the children of a European and a Maori who had subsequently married were deemed to be legitimate. The member who introduced this measure in Parliament considered that the reasons which justified the enactment did not apply with equal force to the illegitimate offspring of Europeans, and the privilege was not extended to them.

When an Act was passed in 1881 authorising the adoption of children there was opposition in Parliament on the ground that this would enable the legitimation of illegitimate children. But the change of view which was now taking place is revealed in the fact that some members considered this to be a reason for supporting the measure.[62]

[61] *Re Hardman* (1869) Macassey 983, 989.
[62] 39 *New Zealand Parliamentary Debates*, p. 4.

A Legitimation Act became law in 1894. Under this Act a child born before the marriage of its parents was deemed on registration of the child to have been legitimated from birth, with the rights of a child born in wedlock. But an illegitimate child could not be legitimated if at the time of the birth of the child there was any legal impediment to the marriage of the parents. This prevented the legitimation of an illegitimate child if either of the parents was married when the child was born. The Legitimation Amendment Act, 1921–22, removed this restriction. A child born to a married woman is presumed to be the legitimate child of the woman and her husband, but if this presumption is displaced by evidence establishing that another person is the father, the child can be legitimated if the father marries the mother after her first marriage has been terminated by death or divorce.[63]

The legislation was further revised and amended in 1939. The Legitimation Act of that year (replacing the previous legislation) made the legitimation automatic upon the marriage of the parents instead of being dependent on registration following the marriage.[64] Section 3 provides that every illegitimate person whose parents have intermarried whether before or after the passing of the Act is deemed to have been legitimated by the marriage as from birth. This applies whether or not the illegitimate child was living at the date of the marriage, and whether or not the parents were domiciled in New Zealand at the time of the birth or at the time of the marriage. But the legitimation, though retrospective, is not to affect rights which have already accrued to other persons.[65]

The Legitimacy Act, 1926 (U.K.), is much more restricted in scope and operation. But if by reason of these restrictions an illegitimate child is not legitimated in England by the subsequent marriage of its parents, the child is nevertheless deemed legitimate as from birth for all purposes under the law of New Zealand. The New Zealand statute confers legitimacy retrospectively regardless of domicile and without limitation of any kind, and in any matter governed by the law of New Zealand (such as the interpretation of a bequest by a testator domiciled in New Zealand) the Legitimation Act, 1939, would apply. Similarly, legitimation under the English Act would not be recognised in New Zealand if the father was not alive and domiciled in England or Wales at the date of legitimation [66]; but this is immaterial since the passing of the Act in 1939, as the child is deemed legitimated as from birth, for purposes of New Zealand law, by virtue of the New Zealand statute.

[63] *Taylor* v. *Harley* [1943] N.Z.L.R. 68 ; [1943] G.L.R. 66.
[64] But the parents are under an obligation to re-register the child's birth : s. 5.
[65] Legitimation Act, 1939, s. 4 (2), reversing the effect of the decision in *Public Trustee* v. *A.* [1925] N.Z.L.R. 744 ; [1925] G.L.R. 468.
[66] *Re Davey, Public Trustee* v. *Wheeler* [1937] N.Z.L.R. 56 ; [1937] G.L.R. 39.

Statutory Provision for Illegitimate Children

Apart from the provision for legitimation by subsequent marriage and legitimation by adoption, the legislature during the past seventy years has been conferring on illegitimate children many of the rights formerly enjoyed only by legitimate children. Provisions at present in force include the following :

(1) On the death of either of its parents an illegitimate child is treated as a legitimate child for the purpose of any claim on behalf of the child under the Deaths by Accidents Compensation Act, 1952.[67]

(2) An illegitimate child is a ' relative ' of both his parents, and of any other child of the same parents, for the purposes of the Workers' Compensation Act, 1922.

(3) Any illegitimate relationship is treated as legitimate relationship for the purpose of a claim under the Carriage by Air Act, 1940.

(4) In determining rights of succession on intestacy the relationship of an illegitimate child to its mother is deemed legitimate unless the child has been adopted by another person.[68]

(5) For the purpose of claims under the Family Protection Act, 1908, ' children ' includes illegitimate children, provided that the court is satisfied that the paternity or maternity of the testator has been admitted by or established against the deceased during his or her lifetime.[69]

(6) Illegitimate children and grandchildren of Maoris are in the same position as legitimate issue in regard to succession to the estate of a Maori.[70]

(7) Illegitimate children are included in the term ' children ' in the War Pensions Act, 1943.

(8) For the purposes of the War Pensions and Allowances (Mercantile Marine) Act, 1940, an illegitimate child is a ' child ' of a member if born before the expiry of ten months after the death, disablement, or commencement of detention of the member.

(9) For the purposes of succession duty illegitimate relationship is recognised as equivalent to legitimate relationship in all cases in which proof is given to the satisfaction of the commissioner of the illegitimate relationship of the successor to the deceased.[71]

Similarly the legislature has in a number of instances given rights to the mother and even to the father of an illegitimate child. For example,

---

[67] This has been the law since 1880.
[68] Statutes Amendment Act, 1946, s. 2.
[69] Statutes Amendment Act, 1936, s. 26 (1).
[70] Maori Affairs Act, 1953, s. 116.
[71] Death Duties Act, 1921, s. 19, as amended by the Finance Act (No. 2), 1944, s. 13.

both the mother and the father of an illegitimate child have been given the rights of parents of legitimate children under the Deaths by Accidents Compensation Act, 1952, the Carriage by Air Act, 1940, the War Pensions Act, 1943, the War Pensions and Allowances (Mercantile Marine) Act, 1940, the Family Protection Act, 1908, and section 116 of the Maori Affairs Act, 1953. The mother (but not the father) has been given similar rights under the Administration Act, 1952 (governing intestate succession) and under the Workers' Compensation Act, 1922. Her consent is required for the marriage of the child while under twenty-one, or for the adoption of the child.[72]

ADOPTION

New Zealand was the first British country to make statutory provision for the adoption of children. The Adoption of Children Act, 1881, partly modelled on earlier legislation in Massachusetts, authorised the making of orders of adoption of children under twelve. The age was raised to fifteen years in 1895, and to twenty-one years in 1939. Adoption is now governed by the Infants Act, 1908, Part III. Married persons may jointly adopt a child, or one of them may do so with the spouse's consent. An unmarried person may adopt a child of the same sex if there is an age difference of eighteen years, and may adopt a person of the opposite sex if the difference in age is forty years. If the child is illegitimate, it becomes on adoption the legitimate child of the adopter, being deemed in law to be the child born in lawful wedlock of the adopting parent.

Until 1950 the adopted child retained rights of succession to its natural relatives, but acquired in addition the right to succeed on the intestacy of his adopting parents. The natural parents lost the right to succeed on the intestacy of the adopted child, this right being vested in the adopting parents instead. By judicial interpretation of the relevant provisions (contained in section 21 of the Infants Act, 1908), it was established that the adopted child continued to be related to all his natural relatives other than his natural parents, and that although he became the child of the adopters he did not become related to any of the relatives of the adopters.[73]

Fundamental alterations were made by the Infants Amendment Act, 1950, which repealed section 21 of the Act of 1908 and inserted a new section in its place. On adoption, the child ceases to be related to any of his natural relatives (except for the purpose of capacity to marry and

---

[72] A magistrate may also require the consent of the father of an illegitimate child before making an adoption order : Statutes Amendment Act, 1947, s. 26 (2).

[73] *Re Taylor, Public Trustee* v. *Lambert* [1932] N.Z.L.R. 1077 ; [1932] G.L.R. 656. *Trustees Executors and Agency Co. of New Zealand Ltd.* v. *Rowley* [1939] N.Z.L.R. 146. *Re Carter, Carter* v. *Carter* [1941] N.Z.L.R. 33 ; [1940] G.L.R. 587. *Re C.K., M.* v. *L.* [1950] G.L.R. 296.

the crime of incest) and becomes related to the adopters and all the adopters' relatives. Rights of succession are based on the new relationships so constituted. An adopted child can take under a gift by will to the children or issue of the adopter (whether the will was made before or after the date of the adoption) provided that the adoption took place in the lifetime of the testator. Adoption does not affect the nationality or citizenship of the child.

Adoption of children by Maoris is governed by the Maori Affairs Act, 1953, Part IX, and differs in many respects from adoption under the Infants Act. Maoris may adopt Maori children (including half-castes) under fifteen years of age, but may not adopt European children.[74]

FAMILY PROTECTION ACT

Among the most widely known measures pioneered in New Zealand is the legislation initiated in 1900 under the title of the Testator's Family Maintenance Act, which became Part II of the Family Protection Act, 1908.[75] In enabling the Supreme Court to make orders which took precedence over the terms of a man's will in the distribution of his estate this Act made a revolutionary departure from the principle of English law that a man might do what he wished with his own. By implication it rejected the view that every man is the best judge of the disposition that he should make of his own estate. The Act empowers the Supreme Court to make provision for certain members of the family of a deceased person, from the estate which he leaves at his death, where adequate provision has not been made for their proper maintenance and support. The restriction on testamentary power is not imposed directly. A testator may still frame his will as he pleases, and if he fails to make adequate provision for his family he does not thereby commit a breach of any legal duty.[76] But in substance though not in form the Act does restrict testamentary power by giving the court power to override the terms of the will. ' It may not be a statute limiting the testamentary freedom of the individual, but it is a statute by which the results of the exercise of that freedom are subject to peremptory control by the court. To this extent it is a limitation on the freedom of the individual to do what he likes with his own.'[77] The exercise of the jurisdiction conferred

---

[74] For further details of the law relating to adoption see Campbell, *Law of Adoption in New Zealand* (1952).

[75] Similar statutes have now been passed in most British countries. There was no corresponding enactment in England for nearly forty years. See now the Inheritance (Family Provision) Act, 1938.

[76] *Dillon* v. *Public Trustee* [1941] A.C. 294; [1941] 2 All E.R. 284; [1941] N.Z.L.R. 557; [1941] G.L.R. 227. The Privy Council in this case rejected the view, which had frequently been expressed in New Zealand, that testamentary power is limited by the Act and that it imposes a duty to include proper provision for dependants.

[77] *Re Kensington* [1949] N.Z.L.R. 382, 397; [1949] G.L.R. 185, 192.

by the Act necessarily alters and may completely abrogate the dispositions which the testator sought to make by his will.

The acceptance of this drastic innovation was assisted by the modest claims of its promoters. They pointed out that a man might be ordered during his lifetime to make payments for the maintenance of his wife and children. Why should he be able to leave them penniless at his death? The Act was needed, so it was said, ' merely to supply after death what the Destitute Persons Act supplies before death '.[78] It is not surprising that the Act was at first construed on this analogy, and that the persons eligible and the amount to be awarded were determined by reference to the rights available to destitute persons.[79] But the terms of the Act did not demand so narrow a construction, and this analogy was soon rejected. In *Allardice* v. *Allardice*[80] the Privy Council affirmed the decision of the Court of Appeal in New Zealand that the Act was much wider in scope than a mere extension post mortem of the liability to support destitute persons. It was an Act which, in the case of large estates, enabled an order to be made even in favour of persons already possessed of considerable means.[81]

What constituted ' adequate provision for proper maintenance and support' has been the subject of consideration in a mass of cases. Probably the most significant single decision was that of Salmond J. in *Allen* v. *Manchester*[82] in which he said :

> ' The Act is designed to enforce the moral obligation of a testator to use his testamentary powers for the purpose of making proper and adequate provision after his death for the support of his wife and children, having regard to his means, to the means and deserts of the claimants, and to the relative urgency of the various moral claims upon his bounty. The provision which the court may properly make in default of testamentary provision is that which a just and wise father would have thought it his moral duty to make in the interests of his widow and children had he been fully aware of all the relevant circumstances.'[83]

It is provided by section 33 (2) that the court may refuse to make an order in favour of any person whose character or conduct is such as in the opinion of the court to disentitle him or her to the benefits of an order under the Act.[84] In addition to investigating the financial position of

---

[78] 111 *New Zealand Parliamentary Debates*, p. 503.

[79] *Re Rush* (1901) 20 N.Z.L.R. 249.

[80] [1911] A.C. 730 ; (1911) N.Z.P.C.C. 156.

[81] This principle was re-affirmed by the Privy Council in *Bosch* v. *Perpetual Trustee Co. Ltd.* [1938] A.C. 463 ; [1938] 2 All E.R. 14, on appeal from New South Wales.

[82] [1922] N.Z.L.R. 218 ; [1921] G.L.R. 613.

[83] This passage was quoted with approval by the Privy Council in *Bosch* v. *Perpetual Trustee Co. Ltd. (supra)*.

[84] If the testator in his will states his reasons for not making any provision for the applicant this does not alter the burden of proof or exclude the making of an order. There is a primary onus on the applicant to satisfy the court

the testator and members of his family the court must therefore attempt the extremely difficult task of discovering all the relevant circumstances in the family history, and must consider on moral grounds the conduct of the applicants.

Although the problem before the court is of such delicacy and complexity, the administration of the Act has been so successful that its scope has been continually widened. The greatest extension was made in 1939. In that year it was provided that with the necessary modifications the Act should apply with respect to every person who dies without leaving a will in the same manner as if he had died leaving a will providing for the distribution of his estate as on intestacy.[85] Other important changes have widened the class of persons eligible to apply for an order. Originally confined to the testator's wife, husband, or children, the class of potential claimants has now been extended to include illegitimate children,[86] adopted children,[87] and grandchildren (including grandchildren by adoption)[87]; and if a person dies without leaving wife, husband, children or grandchildren, his father or mother may apply.[88]

The advent of social security legislation has raised the interesting question of the distribution of the burden of maintenance as between the estate of a deceased person and the Social Security Fund. The Supreme Court evolved the principle that a testator might properly reduce his benefactions by the amount of any social security benefit to which a person would be entitled as of right without a means test; but that he should, if possible, wholly relieve the fund of the necessity of providing other benefits for members of his family.[89] This principle has now been embodied in an amendment to the Social Security Act. In making any order under the Family Protection Act, the court is to disregard any social security benefit which is, or may become, payable to the applicant, other than a superannuation benefit, miner's benefit, or family benefit; and benefits other than those just specified may be

that there has been a failure of moral duty on the part of the testator. The reasons given by the testator concentrate attention on the question whether the character or conduct of the applicant negative the moral obligation. But if on investigation the court is unable to determine whether the testator's allegations are true or false s. 33 (2) does not apply and the court will not refuse an order on this ground: *Re Green* [1951] N.Z.L.R. 135 ; [1951] G.L.R. 50.

[85] Statutes Amendment Act, 1939, s. 22.

[86] Statutes Amendment Act, 1936, s. 26 (1). The court must be satisfied that the paternity or maternity of the testator has been admitted by or established against the deceased during his or her lifetime.

[87] Statutes Amendment Act, 1947, s. 15.

[88] Statutes Amendment Act, 1943, s. 14.

[89] *Re Wood, Wood* v. *Leighton* [1944] N.Z.L.R. 567 ; [1944] G.L.R. 254. *Higgs* v. *Perpetual Trustee Co. Ltd.* [1943] N.Z.L.R. 290. *Re Calder, Calder* v. *Public Trustee* [1950] G.L.R. 465.

reduced where the applicant is entitled to apply for an order under the
Family Protection Act.[90]

In general, an order cannot be made under the Act unless the deceased
left immovable property in New Zealand or was domiciled in New
Zealand.[91] But important exceptions exist in the case of married women
and infants dying after 1948. If a married woman would have been
domiciled in New Zealand if she could retain and acquire a domicile
distinct from that of her husband, the succession to her estate, so far as
it consists of movable property in New Zealand, is determined as if she
had died domiciled in New Zealand. A similar rule applies where the
child of such a woman dies under twenty-one.[92]

FAMILY HOMES

Part I of the Family Protection Act, 1908, re-enacted the provisions of
the Family Homes Protection Act, 1895. The general purpose of this
legislation was to enable the owner of a dwelling-house to settle it as a
' family home ' immune from claims of creditors so long as he was alive,
or any of his children was under twenty-one. This has recently been
supplemented by provisions wider in scope and much more satisfactory
in detail. Under the Joint Family Homes Act, 1950, as amended in
1951, husband and wife or either of them may settle as a joint family
home a house and land used principally for their residence and not
exceeding £5,000 in value. It is immaterial that the property may be
mortgaged. While settled as a joint family home the property (to the
extent of £2,000) is, in general, completely protected from the claims of
creditors other than mortgagees. It vests in the husband and wife
jointly, and the protection continues until the death of the survivor
provided that the property is being used as the residence of one or both
of the owners or members of their household. No gift duty is payable
when the settlement is made, and no succession duty or estate duty is
payable on the value of the property (up to £2,000) when the husband
or the wife dies and the property vests in the survivor. This legislation
is characteristic of New Zealand, where it is the accepted social pattern
for each family to set out to acquire the ownership of its home, normally
in a dwelling which may assert some independence as it stands in its
own ground.

---

[90] Social Security Amendment Act, 1950, s. 18. *Oakey* v. *Thompson* [1951]
N.Z.L.R. 580; [1951] G.L.R. 291.
[91] *Re Butchart, Butchart* v. *Butchart* [1932] N.Z.L.R. 125; [1931] G.L.R. 498.
Re Terry [1951] N.Z.L.R. 30; [1951] G.L.R. 18.
[92] Administration Act, 1952, s. 41.

CHAPTER 13

LEGAL TRENDS WITHIN NEW ZEALAND

NEW ZEALAND may be insular in outlook and far removed from the Western world, but at stages in her history she has responded quickly to ideas which have reached her shores. It is this willingness to embody in legislation an idea derived from elsewhere that distinguishes New Zealand rather than her originality. New Zealand of course has made her own distinctive contribution in such things as the family protection legislation, but the fact remains that in matters of legislation she has gained far more from the common law world than she has given.

As it is the settled policy of the New Zealand courts to follow English decisions, there is unlikely to be any significant deviation from English decisions in the realm of the common law. So it is to legislation that we must turn to find the differences between common law countries. Differences, of course, are to be expected when legislation is a matter for the discretion of individual legislatures, and under this system it is possible for common law countries to have widely differing statutes dealing with the same subject-matter.

In fact, however, the actual differences are far less than might be imagined. It is true that the formal expression of an idea may vary and that different machinery may be created for its fulfilment. But to emphasise such differences is to distort the general picture.

Liberalism, radicalism, and policies of State controls have moved or are moving like waves through the countries of the common law world. There is ample evidence of this in the legislative history of these countries. Comprehensive provisions for dealing with public health came to New Zealand on an early wave. The welfare and protection of the worker has been the subject of special legislation in many countries over the last sixty years. Social security has been introduced in a number of countries. Marketing schemes are a common feature. Central banking has spread widely.

The South Australian system of land transfer is now to be found in other jurisdictions. There is wide application of the principle of protecting trustees who invest trust funds in securities authorised by statute. The status of married women has been improved by legislation in many common law countries.

It will be obvious from these illustrations that any discussion of legal trends within New Zealand would be meaningless if we did not endeavour to see New Zealand in the wider perspective of at least the common law world. Free trade in ideas is one of the strong characteristics of the countries adhering to common law principles. It tends to promote a broad similarity in legislation and to impede any movement towards legislative self-sufficiency. The legislative acceptance of pervasive ideas is of course far from being an even process, but it is remarkable how within a relatively short period many countries within the common law world embody the same ideas in their legislation.

The Growth of Status

So much of modern legislation is protective in character and undermines *laisser-faire* concepts that we come face to face with the growth of status in legal relationships. The trend in New Zealand towards status was early evident in relations between worker and employer. As early as 1900, Sir Robert Stout had this to say :

> ' No doubt the Statute [Industrial Conciliation and Arbitration Act 1894], by abolishing " contract " and restoring " status ", may be a reversal to a state of things that existed before our industrial era, as Maine and other jurists have pointed out. The power of the legislature is sufficient to cause a reversion of this prior state, though jurists may say that from " status " to " contract " marks the path of progress.'[1]

We have already seen how subsequent legislation governing the Court of Arbitration has been a confirmation of the trend noted by Sir Robert Stout. In particular, the provisions made in 1936 for compulsory unionism were a long step in the same direction. But where a relationship of this kind has been created by legislation, efforts have been made as a rule to ensure that its incidents and consequences are, and remain, equitable. Within the framework of the status is usually to be found elaborate machinery designed to achieve fairness in the treatment of those affected.

Although the individual worker cannot be heard in the Court of Arbitration on the question of what is a proper award for an industry, there is provision for his union to be heard, and the court includes a representative of the workers.

We discussed in Chapter 11 the measures that were taken to assist farmers in the depression that began in 1930. Mortgagees and landlords were subject to a measure of restraint in the exercise of their powers. A farmer could be placed under a ' pooling scheme ', which meant that his farming practices could be supervised, his expenditure controlled, and his farming profits shared equitably among the farmer, the mortgagee of his stock and the mortgagee or lessor of his land. In 1936 the newly elected Labour Government placed greater stress on the rehabilitation

---

[1] *Taylor and Oakley* v. *Edwards* [1900] 18 N.Z.L.R. 876, 885.

of the farmer. Farms were valued according to their productivity in the hands of a fictitious 'reasonably efficient farmer', not necessarily the incumbent of the farm, and all fixed charges in excess of the value so found, together with all unsecured debts, were written off. Rents, where payable, were based on the same productive values. The special tribunals that functioned to give effect to the legislation were so recruited as to ensure that the interests of both the farmer and his creditors were considered and that the least possible hardship was inflicted.

We have seen a similar trend in the treatment of the dairy farmer. The disposal of his produce is regulated and in return, he receives a guaranteed price. Efforts are made to safeguard his interests by ensuring that his organisations are represented at crucial points in the machinery which markets his produce and fixes the guaranteed price.

The concept of status that has been adopted by legislation of the type discussed, is a malleable one, and does not suffer from the rigidity of those types that prevailed in ancient communities. First, the relative ease with which legislation is passed in these times means that the framework can be quickly modified from time to time, and there are ample illustrations of this process in our recent legislative history. Second, even within the framework itself, we have seen that there is representation of the interests affected. What is more significant, is that those entrusted with the making of decisions, for example, administrative tribunals, are not required to follow rigid rules ; the areas of discretion are wide. The word 'reasonable' or its equivalent, is frequently used in statutory formulæ.

Legislation and the Common Law

We have already traversed in this and preceding chapters the variety and scope of the legislation that has been enacted in New Zealand. Economic life is now regulated by a complex system of statutory relationships, and it is clear that much of the legislation has encroached upon the common law. Freedom of contract has been restricted in the relations between employer and employee. The title to property has gradually been subjected to a number of restrictions, among the most significant being the Land Sales legislation passed during the last war. Freedom to dispose of property by will, is, in effect restricted by the Family Protection Act. The right to engage in business is hedged in by a number of restrictions such as import control. Freedom of person is restricted by such Acts as the Public Safety Conservation Act, 1932, which on the proclamation of an emergency confers sweeping powers on the Executive, and the Police Offences Amendment Act, 1951, which deals with the suppression of seditious enterprises, and with violence, picketing and demonstrations during periods of industrial unrest.

The manner in which legislation of this kind is interpreted by the courts is significant. It is almost a truism that although a case may be decided on the logical application of legal rules, there is not infrequently, a discretion in the choice of a starting point. If there is not a choice of main paths, there is more often a choice of subsidiary paths, and where there is a choice, there is room for a judge to make his contribution to legal development. Admittedly the doctrine of precedent imposes a restraint on judges and reduces the scope for creative effort, but it is clear that prevailing ideas permeate and affect the decisions of judges. We have already stressed the broad unifying effect of ideas on legislative programmes, but we should not overlook that these same ideas are quietly influencing the development of case law. Some words of Lord Wright are apt here when he says that English law has reacted to the moral, social, and political ideas of the time, which have profoundly and persistently affected not merely the legislature but the judges.[2]

The judicial interpretation of legislation regulating economic activity has quite often showed a conflict between two competing rules of construction. On the one hand there has been in New Zealand since 1888 a statutory rule of construction that all legislation should be given such fair, large and liberal interpretation as will best ensure the attainment of its object. The courts, however, do not seem to have regarded this statutory rule as something alien to the common law and calling for a radical departure. In fact the Privy Council on one occasion remarked that the provision expresses what is meant by the old legal maxim *Qui haeret in littera haeret in cortice*.[3] Chapman J. thought that the provision might not make any material alteration in the law but that it at least acted as a caution to the courts not to allow an Act intended to remedy a known evil to fail of its object through an over-refined construction if it is sufficiently expressed to carry out that object.[4]

An illustration of this rule is provided by a recent case dealing with the Price Tribunal. Here the court said:

> ' It would be strange if in those circumstances the court were to find itself compelled to say that the non-appointment of associate members invalidated all the proceedings of the tribunal since the Act came into force. Any such conclusion would mean that regard was to be paid more to form than to substance and would involve a contradiction of a principle that every Act is to receive such fair, large and liberal construction and interpretation as will best ensure the attainment of its object.'[5]

We have already seen how this rule has been applied in the case of marketing legislation.

[2] L.J. (Eng.) Vol. LXXXV, p. 416.
[3] *Smith* v. *McArthur* [1904] A.C. 389, 398.
[4] *Hutton* v. *Hutton* (1910) 13 G.L.R. 201.
[5] *Jackson and Co. Ltd.* v. *Price Tribunal* [1950] N.Z.L.R. 180, 183, 184.

On the other hand, there is the long-established rule that penal liability cannot be extended unless a statute does so in clear and unambiguous language. So much of public legislation is given teeth in the shape of penal provisions that the balance struck between the competing rules is of material importance. The *Crown Milling Case* of 1925, which is discussed in detail in Chapter 7, shows how finely balanced this question was ; on a counting of heads the judge in the Supreme Court and the judges in the Court of Appeal were equally divided, and the Privy Council finally decided in favour of the subject. For penal liability to be imposed, the statutory provisions need to be meticulously clear, but to allow for every contingency would need a draftsman gifted with prophetic insight.

However, it cannot be said that the courts have not substantially responded to social needs. We have already seen clear evidence of this in their treatment of the legislation governing industrial relations, monopolies, marketing, and export and import controls. In their interpretation of this legislation they have, for the most part, been sympathetic to the attainment of its objects. There has been less tendency to emphasise procedural requirements, although the late Chief Justice, Sir Michael Myers, was zealous in seeing that procedural requirements were met. The decision of another judge who held the Import Control Regulations to be invalid, was a severe reverse for the Government.[6] But whether we look at it on legal or political grounds, it is impossible to deny the cogency of the argument that the foundation for measures so drastic should have been expressed in clearer language. Sir Michael Myers went further in an earlier case[7] when he deprecated the use to which regulations were put. In holding certain regulations to be *ultra vires* he confessed that he was not sorry at being forced to the conclusion at which he had arrived. In his view, if it were thought necessary to interfere with either the personal liberty of the subject or his freedom in exercising a lawful trade or business and particularly in the sale of his own goods in the market of his own choice, then it could scarcely be doubted that such a matter should be the subject of direct legislation by Parliament itself in appropriate, clear and unequivocal language, rather than be left to the discretion of a delegated authority. The only exception he envisaged to this general statement was the existence of emergency conditions which required otherwise in the interests of public safety. Parliament by using the appropriate language can of course confer on a delegated authority power to make regulations of a drastic character, but it was the wisdom of such a step that was being discussed by Sir Michael Myers.

[6] *Jackson and Co. Ltd.* v. *Collector of Customs* [1939] N.Z.L.R. 682.
[7] *Carroll* v. *The Attorney-General* [1933] N.Z.L.R 1461, 1474.

LEGISLATION AND LIMITING FACTORS

We have noted in the preceding pages the extensive use that has been made of legislation, but it would be idle to suggest that legislation has been the panacea for all social and economic ills. Some legislation may be criticised for its lack of harmony with the moral standard of large sections of the community, and some for its pathetic faith in the ability of the Executive to carry it out. Illustrations of legislation of this type will now be discussed.

Betting

One of the most glaring illustrations of the flouting of the law is to be found in the realm of betting. In 1920 an Act declared the business of a bookmaker to be unlawful and betting with a bookmaker became an offence. Despite these provisions bookmaking has flourished to such an extent that the amount now handled by bookmakers is reliably estimated to exceed the amount handled by the totalisator. This was the tenor of evidence given to the Royal Commission on Gaming and Racing which was appointed in 1946. The commission rejected a proposal that bookmakers should be licensed:

> ' We reprobate the suggestion that the State should surrender to the difficulty of suppressing illegal bookmaking and embark upon a policy of appeasement by licensing it.'[8]

Licensing had been tried for a short period between 1907 and 1910 but in the words of the commission the results of the licensing system were disastrous:

> ' The country was invaded by men of criminal tendencies and the whole position became a scandal ; in fact, it became so scandalous that, despite all precedent to the contrary, reference was made to it in emphatic terms by Mr. Justice Chapman from the Supreme Court bench. After referring to the fact that it was unusual for a judge to criticise the law of the land, he said that he nevertheless felt it was his duty to say that recent legislation passed by the New Zealand Parliament had produced a very degrading effect on a certain section of the population of the country. He felt it incumbent upon him, he said, to openly condemn a law which legalised the operations of a section who came very close to the criminal class.'[9]

The commission recommended the introduction of a system of off-course betting which would ensure that moneys staked went through the totalisator. Such a system has since been introduced with the sanction of the Government but as it is still in the process of development it is

---

[8] Report of Royal Commission on Gaming and Racing (Appendices to the Journals of the House of Representatives 1948, H.23) para. 90.
[9] *Ibid.*, para. 43.

too soon to say whether it has led to any substantial reduction in the business of illegal bookmaking.

The Sale of Liquor

The illegal sale of liquor by hotels provides us with another illustration of widespread contempt for the law. The Sale of Liquor Restriction Act, 1917, substantially reduced the hours for the sale of liquor. Hitherto the hours had been from six in the morning until ten at night, with provision for an extension to eleven at night in certain circumstances. The hours now are from nine in the morning until six in the evening. It is an offence for any person who, during the time at which licensed premises are required to be closed, sells any liquor in licensed premises or allows any liquor, although purchased before the hours of closing, to be consumed in licensed premises. Any person found on licensed premises during closing hours is liable to a fine unless he satisfies the court that he was an inmate, servant, or lodger on the premises or a bona fide traveller. The extent to which this legislation is observed was reviewed by the Royal Commission on Licensing which presented its report in 1946. In its majority report the commission said :

> ' The evidence which we took shows clearly that large numbers of people in New Zealand have no hesitation in breaking these laws. . . . It is plain that many people who would regard, say, theft as a crime, have no scruple in demanding a drink after hours from a publican.'[10]

The commission thought that after-hours trading would be diminished if opening hours in the evening were permitted, but their recommendation in this direction was decisively rejected at a referendum on the question and was not adopted by the Government. There is nothing to suggest that after-hours trading has diminished and it remains one of the evils which brings the law into contempt.

Both the Commission on Gaming and Racing and the one on Licensing were concerned with the contempt being shown towards the law. The line taken was that moderate gambling or drinking was not a social evil. Both commissions made constructive recommendations, which were designed to bring the law closer to the current of public opinion. Not all of the recommendations of the two commissions were adopted by Parliament but the legislation that has been passed does reflect broadly the attitude of the two commissions.

Illegal Abortions

The incidence of illegal abortions raises the question whether the current social attitude is in accord with the standard imposed by the

[10] Report of Royal Commission on Licensing (Appendices to the Journals of the House of Representatives 1946, H.-38), paras. 466, 468.

criminal law. The problem of illegal abortions was considered in 1937 by a Committee of Inquiry appointed by the Minister of Health. The committee reported that it was convinced that the induction of abortion was then exceedingly common in New Zealand. They ascribed the main causes to economic and domestic hardship, changes in social and moral outlook, pregnancy amongst the unmarried, and to fear of childbirth in a small proportion of cases. Detailed recommendations were made in an endeavour to meet these causes. What interests us here is the committee's comment on the attitude of juries. The committee was seriously concerned at the failure of juries to convict even in cases where the guilt seemed beyond all doubt. However, it concluded that it could only bring before the public its moral responsibility for the way in which its members as jurors virtually encouraged the evil.

Almost a decade later, the problem was reviewed by a Parliamentary Select Committee.[11] In the words of the Committee's report, the general tenor of the evidence was to emphasise the seriousness of the problem of induced abortion. Statistics showed that the number of prosecutions in any one year was relatively very small. Frequently the police had difficulty in obtaining sufficient evidence to justify a prosecution. Furthermore, there appeared to be an obvious reluctance on the part of juries to convict. It was also generally agreed that, despite the fact that strenuous endeavours had been made to check this crime, it still continued to be a serious evil. The committee endorsed the conclusions of the earlier committee and recorded the progress made in carrying out the detailed recommendations of that committee. However, the committee emphasised that basically the problem was one of the moral standard of the community. There was no thought that the standard imposed by the criminal law should be relaxed. On the other hand, emphasis was placed on the lifting of the moral standard of the community by means of an educational programme.

Industrial Relations

The melancholy truth is that awards made in judicial form by the Court of Arbitration are occasionally flouted. In Chapter 6 we discussed the penal provisions for dealing with unlawful strikes and noted that the occasions were few when proceedings had been instituted to recover penalties. However, when penalties are imposed on workers or their unions, it seems that group solidarity precludes their feeling a sense of moral guilt for breaches of the law. Although most unions turn naturally to the Court of Arbitration for the redress of their grievances, it cannot be said that the court has been markedly successful in dealing with the especially militant union. If on occasions the court has seemed to have

[11] Report of Dominion Population Committee (Appendices to the Journals of the House of Representatives 1946, I.-17).

been a vessel tossed about by the angry waves of industrial strife, it has at least managed to keep afloat. The comparison with the ordinary courts should not be taken too far. It is too much to expect judicial methods and procedure to be the solvent for every industrial dispute of any size, particularly when political issues are involved.

Regulation of Sales of Land

We have noted how the Land Sales legislation of 1943 severely tested the moral standard of the property owner, large or small. War legislation, even if drastic in character, can usually rely on the patriotic support of the citizen, but the Land Sales legislation lost a good deal of this support particularly in respect of the sale of urban property and it was not long before illegal transactions became numerous. The State, in its desire to enforce the legislation, made it possible for the purchaser to recover a portion or all of the excess consideration. The provision was objectionable and in effect tended to encourage wrongdoing. It is doubtful whether the results achieved by this provision offset the further deterioration produced in the moral attitude of vendors towards the control imposed by the legislation.

Tax Evasion

Taxation is a field where there has been extensive evasion of the law. The heavy rates of taxation provide a strong temptation for the evasion of the payment of tax, and the temptation is the greater because the Department of Inland Revenue is short of inspectors. The Land and Income Tax Act provides heavy penalties for those who evade tax, giving power to the Commissioner of Inland Revenue to impose penal tax up to three times the amount of the tax evaded. These provisions, however, have not been a sufficient deterrent. There is also provision for the publication in the Gazette of the names of those who have been convicted of furnishing false returns of income, or who have been charged with penal tax in respect of such offences. Prior to 1948, the commissioner was required to publish the names of all offenders in the Gazette, but he now has authority to omit from that list the names of those taxpayers who have voluntarily disclosed the fact that returns as furnished by them were false. This reliance on a more positive incentive has been productive of results.

Administrative Difficulties

Repeatedly in the recent history of New Zealand legislation there have been instances of legislation which for administrative reasons has failed to achieve its purpose adequately. Either the legislation has expected too much of large sections of the community and enforcement has thus been correspondingly more difficult, or the current administrative resources have not been sufficient to ensure that the provisions of an Act are administered efficiently. We have discussed in this chapter examples of legislation falling into each of these two categories and several of the examples are common to both categories. Betting and the sale of liquor are illustrations belonging to the first category. The Land Sales legislation was common to both categories. Not only did it test the moral standard of the vendor but in the early stages there were long delays in the hearing of applications because of a shortage of valuers. Price control suffered because there was not an adequate expert staff available to police it. We have seen that the evasion of tax has been made easier because of a lack of inspectors. It is clear that however sound the ideas expressed in legislation may be there is no escape from the conclusion that far more attention must be paid by Governments and Parliament to the administrative implications and practicability of proposed legislation.

The Respect of the Executive for the Law

There is a natural tendency for the energetic administrator to regard the law with impatience when it stands in his way, and it would be naïve to suggest that the bureaucrat is meticulous in his observance of the law. His position is rather akin to that of Birrell's trustee whose job was defined as that of making judicious breaches of trust. We also recall the remark of an irate English judge who complained that 'you can never beat into the heads of people exercising bureaucratic authority that they must exercise their power singly and not for collateral objects '.[12] It would not be difficult for a New Zealand judge to find an occasion to express a similar sentiment. Although the courts proceed upon the assumption that the legislature is an ideal person,[13] they do not make the same charitable assumption for the Executive.

However, the ease with which the law is amended makes it less likely that the law will be flouted, but the illegal acts of an administrator may escape challenge through their existence being unknown to members of the public. In these cases, the remedy lies in the efficacy of self-imposed internal control, particularly where the rights of individual citizens are affected. Where, however, there is no specific infringement of the rights of a particular citizen, it is difficult to see what harm is done. It is known in administrative circles that on one occasion, Sir John Salmond as Solicitor-General interpreted an Act by studying its history as a Bill. He was careful to point out that the history of a Bill before it becomes an Act is not legally relevant in the interpretation of that Act, but he decided to depart from this rule, because the question was purely an

[12] *Marshall Shipping Co.* v. *The King*, 41 T.L.R. 285.
[13] *Commissioners of Income Tax* v. *Pemsel* [1891] A.C. 531, 549.

administrative one, not affecting the rights or obligations of private persons.

Remission of Penalties

The Governor-General exercises the royal prerogative of mercy, and is also specially empowered by the Penalties Remission Act, 1908, to remit penalties, fines and forfeitures whether or not they are payable to the Crown. The extent to which the Governor-General exercises these powers must affect the respect accorded to the law by the citizen. In recent years the question has been debated in relation to convictions involving the cancellation of motor drivers' licences. Unless there are special reasons, which must be related to the offence and not to such matters as hardship on the offender, a person convicted of driving or attempting to drive a motor-vehicle while under the influence of drink or a drug to such an extent as to be incapable of having proper control of the vehicle, is required to be automatically disqualified from holding a motor driver's licence for a minimum period of twelve months. The complaint was that the royal prerogative had been used too generously in restoring a driver's licence before the expiration of the period of disqualification. In February, 1950, the Minister of Justice announced that he proposed to be very sparing indeed in making recommendations for the remission of orders disqualifying convicted motor-drivers from holding drivers' licences. He added that the prerogative power of mercy had always been exercised sparingly; that it was there to meet special cases of grave hardship, where circumstances existed which had not been brought to the notice of the court, or which had come to light since the conviction. Under the Transport Amendment Act, 1950, the court now has power to review the cancellation of a driver's licence after the expiration of six months. The statutory provision for review means in practice that only an exceptional case would be considered for the exercise of the royal prerogative.

When a general appeal lay from the decision of a magistrate in a summary criminal case only where the sentence exceeded a month's imprisonment or a fine of £5, penalties were sometimes increased at the express request of the defendant to enable an appeal to be brought. If the appeal failed, application was made for remission or reduction of the penalty, and often it was reduced to the penalty originally imposed. The farce has been ended by an amendment removing this limitation on the right of general appeal against summary conviction.

The Summary Penalties Act, 1939, provides a procedure for the review by a magistrate of the financial circumstances of a person who is unable to pay the penalty imposed by a court.

These various statutory provisions have resulted in a substantial drop in the number of applications for the exercise of the royal

prerogative.   It is a trend in the right direction.   There is little evidence
to suggest that the exercise of the royal prerogative has been abused in
the past but it has the disadvantage of being an administrative process
not open to the public gaze and thus the more likely to attract criticism,
as it has done from early days.

Retrospective and Validating Legislation

It remains to consider the nature and extent of legislation which has
been made retrospective in operation, or which has validated illegal
acts.   It is sometimes urged that legislation of this type is unfair and
tends to lower the respect of the citizen for the law.   The device of
retrospective legislation has been used occasionally from the early days
of the Colony, and it is proposed to discuss here some of the illustrations
to be found within the last twenty years.

The wills of testators have been varied by private Acts of Parliament.
In one instance in 1945 the party benefited by the private Act [14] had failed
in proceedings under the Family Protection Act.   He had been brought
up in the household of a testatrix and her husband as if he were their
lawful son.   However, he was never legally adopted.   Under the will
he received a small legacy but the residue was held for a charitable
purpose.   His application under the Family Protection Act failed because
he was not the legal child of the testatrix.   The private Act, however,
authorised the trustees to pay him a substantial sum, which of course
was at the expense of the gift to charity.   Another private Act [15] was
passed in 1945 to enable a party who was otherwise out of time to make
an application under the Family Protection Act.   This right was granted
at the expense of charitable bequests made under the will.

A most interesting illustration is the Morris Divorce and Marriage
Validation Act, 1943.   Although a decree nisi of dissolution of a marriage
had not been made absolute, the Act dissolved the marriage as at a date
three months and one day from the decree nisi and then validated a subsequent ' marriage '.   Finally, the limitation period under the Deaths by
Accident Compensation Act was extended to enable the ' widow ' of the
subsequent ' marriage ' to take proceedings under that Act.   Another
illustration of Parliament extending the limitation period to enable a
person to claim damages is to be found in the Finance Act (No. 3), 1943,
section 15.

Section 10 of the Marriage Amendment Act, 1946, validates certain
marriages hitherto forbidden, but it does not affect any interest in
property to which any person became absolutely entitled before the
passing of the Act, or affect any proceedings commenced in any court
before the passing of the Act.

[14] Marianne Caughey Preston Estate Act, 1945.
[15] John Duncan McGruer Estate Act, 1945.

In 1948 a private Act [16] was passed to validate in New Zealand an adoption that had been arranged by the adopting parents in California in 1921. The parents had treated the child as their own lawful one. The adoption in California, however, could not be recognised under New Zealand law. This meant that for the purposes of succession duty the child would have been treated as a stranger-in-blood. No one appears to have been adversely affected by the private Act except the State which lost some revenue.

It is in the field of taxation that we see more use made of retrospective legislation. In 1937 a gold-mining company was expressly named and made liable for taxation on income that had been earned by another company with which it was linked and which had ceased to carry on business in New Zealand.[17] Provisions governing gift duty were amended in 1944 and made retrospective to 1942.[18] In 1947 an amendment was made to an Act of 1939 dealing with proprietary income, and this amendment was made retrospective to 1939.[19] In 1949 the definition of a proprietary company was amended and made retrospective to 1939.[20]

Retrospective legislation in matters of taxation does not appear to have drawn much fire. Little public sympathy is extended to those whose ingenious schemes for avoiding tax are defeated by retrospective legislation. The use of retrospective legislation in other fields is infrequent, and it cannot be said that it has had any significant adverse effect on the respect of the citizen for the law.

The passing of validating legislation is a far more frequent happening. Modern administration in some of its phases demands speed, and it is inevitable that the practice should continue of passing legislation to validate a prior administrative step which would otherwise be unlawful. It is frequently used to validate the transactions of local authorities.

Steps taken in an emergency caused by war or a serious strike have been the subject of validating legislation. The Emergency Regulations Act of September, 1939, validated any acts which had been done before the commencement of any emergency regulations and which by virtue of those regulations would have been valid and lawful if the regulations had been in force when the acts were done. A similar provision was inserted in the Supply Regulations Act, 1947, which was enacted to authorise the making of regulations for purposes connected with the maintenance, control and regulation of supplies and services. Although in some ways the practice is objectionable, it would be the counsel of perfection to expect strict compliance with the rule of law. The Government of the day normally has a majority in Parliament and can ensure

[16] Sutton Adoption Act, 1948.
[17] Finance Act, 1937, s. 21.
[18] Finance Act (No. 2), 1944, s. 14.
[19] Finance Act, 1947, s. 10.
[20] Land and Income Tax Amendment Act, 1949, s. 3.

the passage of validating legislation. On the other hand it cannot afford to ride roughshod over public opinion and therein lies the check to any substantial abuse.

LAW REFORM

No system of law based on precedent and requiring of its courts that they administer the law as they find it could survive unless it kept pace with changing times. Occasions arise where the law, by its adherence to precedent, cannot reflect adequately the thought of the day, and these occasions demand the intervention of Parliament. The courts themselves perform a very useful part in the system of law reform in such instances. While recognising their paramount obligation to administer the law as they find it, they occasionally do so with expressed reluctance and are not slow to point out in appropriate cases where the law they are bound to apply is failing to do justice or is otherwise deficient or oppressive according to enlightened thought.

Unfortunately, measures for the reform of private law are seldom vote-catching legislation. The Dominion's policy of law reform has therefore depended for its success on the vigour, enthusiasm and sense of public duty of the Minister or Ministers of the Crown (generally the Minister of Justice or the Attorney-General—portfolios which are usually though not necessarily combined) whose lot it is ultimately to pilot through Parliament legislation which is unlikely to gain any material recognition at the triennial polls. Until comparatively recent years, there was no organised system of law reform and the results which were achieved depended on those to whom the machinery of justice was entrusted, and upon assistance rendered from time to time by individuals and committees in carrying out research in specialised branches of the law. The result was a somewhat piecemeal revision ; while considerable advances were made in some branches, notably in the criminal law, the law of property, and family law, other branches, which did not for the moment command attention, tended to remain static.

Although for many years previously the need had been felt to revitalise the whole body of the law, it was not until 1936 that any organised system materialised. It was in that year decided to establish a Law Revision Committee of men of legal standing to whom could be assigned the task of keeping the law abreast of the times. The idea of the committee was conceived out of the appointment in England of Lord Hanworth's Law Revision Committee, though it was designed to function on very different lines. It has been said that the achievements of the New Zealand Law Revision Committee appointed in the year last mentioned have accelerated law reform in a way that had not previously been experienced in the Dominion.

The Law Revision Committee has no formal constitution, and is unrestricted in its scope. The inaugural meeting, held in August, 1937, was attended on the invitation of the Attorney-General by the Chief Justice, the Solicitor-General, two representatives appointed by the New Zealand Law Society, one representative from the public teachers of law from the Law Faculty of the University of New Zealand, the Under-Secretary of Justice, and the Parliamentary Law Draftsman. Although desiring to be included as a member, the Chief Justice thought that, being a judge, he ought not to take part in the committee's actual discussions and deliberations, though he offered his services in an advisory capacity if they should be so required. Later additions to the committee have been the Chairman of the Statutes Revision Committee of the House of Representatives and a lawyer nominated from the Parliamentary Opposition. Except that the place of the Chief Justice has been given to a puisne judge, who does not attend meetings, the committee's membership comprises those who were originally convened, plus the two additional members who were later invited. The Attorney-General is chairman, and the Department of Justice, which provides the secretariat, is the co-ordinating authority responsible for marshalling matters to be considered, and for the due presentation for legislative action of the committee's recommendations.

Meetings of the committee are convened twice or thrice annually and, although no rigid procedure is followed, business is as far as possible organised in such a way that a general scheme will first be considered on its merits, and, if necessary further considered in detail by a subcommittee. If finally approved, and time permits, a draft bill containing the details of the scheme will then be prepared and reviewed, and recommended for legislative action ; but where the details of the scheme can be finally settled and urgency is desired, the final review of a draft bill may be dispensed with. Suggestions and representations are received from many different organisations and societies, as well as from individual members of the lay public. As is to be expected, however, its most regular contributors are the New Zealand Law Society, the Department of Justice, its own individual members, and individual members of the legal profession. It frequently co-opts the assistance of lawyers and teachers of law in the preparation of reports or to comment on proposals. All work performed by and for the committee is done gratuitously from a sense of public duty, a fact which has several times attracted special tributes from both parties in Parliament.

A major difficulty has been to get the public to take an interest in questions of law reform. There is a great contrast between the apathy of the general public towards such matters and the resentment of the individual member of the public at the effect upon his own concerns of some anomalous rule of substantive law or some cumbrous method of procedure. The small amount of publicity which the Law Revision Committee has received from time to time has, however, served to stimulate public interest in its important functions, with the result that it is becoming a medium of approach to an increasing number of persons and organisations having amendments of the law to advocate.

During the Second World War, the committee went into recess, but otherwise it has functioned continuously since its inception. It has during its brief eleven years of active existence promoted or influenced a long list of improvements in the law. Although it draws freely upon other countries for legislative precedent, it never shirks the difficulties which attend the breaking of new ground. Thus it is to the credit of the committee that a person who has done work under a promise of reward in the employer's will is no longer prevented from recovering where the employer dies with his promise unfulfilled.[21] Through its offices a wider class of dependants has been admitted to the benefits of the Family Protection legislation.[22] It promoted a new table of succession on intestacy.[23] There remains little or no distinction between an adopted child and a legitimate child of marriage.[24] It redesigned the legislation relating to legitimation by subsequent marriage.[25] It has been responsible for the substitution of a more practical procedure than the archaic habeas corpus machinery for obtaining custody of children.[26] It promoted the practical legislation[27] which facilitated divorce proceedings by women who had been deserted by their allied servicemen husbands. Parties to frustrated contracts can thank the committee for the statutory adjustment of their relationships.[28] The improvements in the law for the protection of wages and the amounts payable to sub-contractors[29] passed through its hands. In the sphere of evidence and procedure the committee has done much valuable work. The law relating to the competency and compellability of accused persons, and their spouses, to give evidence has been codified and reformed[30]; induced confessions may be admitted where the court is satisfied that the inducement was not likely to cause an untrue admission of guilt to be made[31]; the rule in *Russell* v. *Russell*,[32] which prevented a spouse from giving evidence of lack of opportunity of sexual relations with the other party to the marriage, has been abolished,[33]

[21] Law Reform (Testamentary Promises) Act 1949.
[22] Statutes Amendment Act 1936, s. 26 ; Statutes Amendment Act 1943, s. 14 ; Statutes Amendment Act 1947, s. 15.
[23] Administration Amendment Act, 1944.
[24] Infants Amendment Act, 1950.
[25] Legitimation Act, 1939.
[26] Statutes Amendment Act, 1949, s. 20.
[27] Matrimonial Causes (War Marriages) Act, 1947.
[28] Frustrated Contracts Act, 1944.
[29] Wages Protection and Contractors' Liens Act, 1939.
[30] Evidence Amendment Act, 1952, s. 2.
[31] Evidence Amendment Act, 1950, s. 3.
[32] [1924] A.C. 687.
[33] Evidence Amendment Act, 1945, s. 3.

and much other work in this branch of the law is at present under review. These are only a few of the legal topics which have engaged the attention of the Law Revision Committee. Of the more important statutes inspired by it, mention might be made of the Magistrates' Courts Act, 1947, the Crown Proceedings Act, 1950, and the Limitation Act, 1950.

Since it holds a great respect for the existing law, the committee has to be thoroughly satisfied that any proposed change submitted to it would be beneficial to the community at large. Although the Statute-book bears the visual testimony to its energy, it has to be remembered that many representations reach it which require the closest scrutiny although they may not in the end receive its support. The committee is never deterred by the magnitude of any undertaking, and indeed one of its great advantages over the system of law reform, such as it was, which preceded its establishment is that changes of government need not interrupt the continuity of its work, some branches of which necessarily entail years of preparation and research. The committee has amply proved its worth.

For the most part the committee has been concerned with the revision of private law. Important though this work is, it is clear that the lawyer should not shrink from taking a close interest in the vast amount of social and economic legislation that has been passed in recent times. It is true that most of this legislation is administered by Government Departments who are responsible for seeing that it is adapted from time to time to meet changing conditions. There is room, however, for an examination performed in an atmosphere of detachment and disinterestedness.

It is fashionable in some circles to deride the public servant as one who thirsts for power. The allegation that he seeks power for its own sake can be readily dismissed, but there still remains the departmental enthusiast who, convinced of the soundness of his views presses hard for the passage of legislation. Enthusiasm does not necessarily embrace wisdom, but a Minister, even if competent, may have neither the time nor the particular knowledge necessary in order to pass judgment on legislative proposals. However, it is only fair to say that some departments make a point of securing the best advice they can, and it matters not that the persons who can give that advice are to be found elsewhere in the community.

Whether or not there is danger from enthusiasts, it remains true that there are some proposals which, because of their intrinsic importance or special difficulty, lend themselves to study by a committee working outside the framework of the departments which have initiated the proposals. A similar function is successfully performed for the French Government and Executive by the administrative sections of the Conseil D'Etat. The committee that is contemplated would be an advisory one and would be specially recruited to bring in laymen of acumen, administrators, and lawyers.

The Government in its discretion could refer to such a committee legislative proposals that raise exceptional difficulties. There are also some phases of social and economic legislation that could be examined by the committee, either on its own initiative or on invitation from Government. It is not contemplated that the committee should take the place of the occasional Royal Commission to deal with a contentious social question such as drinking or gambling, but it could be within the scope of the committee to recommend matters for such treatment. The committee could review the provisions and operation of subordinate legislation. Likewise it could examine the provisions governing administrative tribunals and their operation.

By the very nature of the questions that would be considered, a committee of this kind could not expect to work in the same placid atmosphere as does the Law Revision Committee in the field of private law. The questions would tend to be more contentious, and for this reason it is necessary to consider what would be the committee's place in the scheme of democratic government. We have already mentioned that the committee would be an advisory one. It could function effectively, and yet in harmony with the principle of ultimate ministerial responsibility. Its reports could be made to the individual Ministers concerned, or to the Prime Minister. The extent to which a report on a given subject should be published, and at what stage, would be a matter for the Government of the day. It may be argued that, if New Zealand returned to a second chamber, there would be little justification for a committee of this kind. We have already stressed that what is sought is an atmosphere of detachment and disinterestedness. There has been nothing in the proposals for a resuscitation of the second chamber to suggest that party politics would not be a significant factor.

A committee as envisaged here could make a contribution to the smoother working of New Zealand's democracy. In the last analysis its success would depend upon the standing of its members and the quality of its reports. Too much, however, should not be expected of such a committee for the reason that its members would normally be people already busy in their own walks of life. The time they could devote to study and deliberation would be limited and this would necessarily restrict the number of topics that could be handled.

It remains then to consider whether there are forces at work which will contribute to the desired end. Fortunately there are. Today there is more ' scrutiny and dissection of social facts '. Many Government Departments have research sections which enable them to be better informed on the social impact of legislation and on comparable situations overseas. Research has been encouraged by the establishment of university schools in Social Science and Public Administration. Amongst law students there is evidence of a desire to go beyond the study of the law as it is, to consider what it should be. There is also evidence of a more informed and a maturer attitude within the community.

In these pages we have seen ample evidence of the quantity and variety of New Zealand's legislation. We quoted in the preface Sir Joshua Williams's remark that the changes political, social, and material that took place in New Zealand during the latter half of the nineteenth century were greater than those that had taken place in England from the time of the Tudors. The speed with which these changes have been made has involved some loss. A more leisurely evolution would have produced wiser legislation, and the task now is to make good what has been lost through haste, immaturity, and inexperience. There is also need for greater precision in determining what the social wants of the day are, and how those wants should be met. Although predictions are hazardous, it seems clear that the forces now at work will be productive of worthwhile results.

BIBLIOGRAPHY

ADMINISTRATIVE LAW

CURRIE, A. E. *Crown and Subject.* Legal Publications, 1953.
HEWITT, D. J. *The Control of Delegated Legislation.* Butterworth & Co., 1953.
McGECHAN, R. O. Journals of Public Administration (N.Z.), periodical surveys since 1942.

COMPANY LAW

ANDERSON and DALGLISH. *The Law Relating to Companies in New Zealand.* H. H. Tombs & John Friend, 1934.
MORISON and SPRATT. *Morison's Company Law in New Zealand.* Butterworth & Co., 2nd Edition, 1934.
NORTHEY, J. F. *Company Law in New Zealand.* Butterworth & Co., 1954.

CONSTITUTIONAL HISTORY AND LAW

BEAGLEHOLE, J. C. (Ed.). *New Zealand and the Statute of Westminster.* Victoria University College, 1944.
BRASSINGTON, A. C. *Constitutional Law: Some Aspects of Change,* in *Liberty and Learning.* (Reprinted : (1950) 17 N.Z.L.J. 265, 268.)
CURRIE, A. E. *New Zealand and the Statute of Westminster 1931.* Butterworth & Co., 1944.
CURRIE, A. E. *Crown and Subject.* Legal Publications, 1953.
FODEN, N. A. *The Constitutional Development of New Zealand in the First Decade (1839-1849).* L. T. Watkins, 1938.
HIGHT and BAMFORD. *The Constitutional History and Law of New Zealand.* Whitcombe & Tombs, 1914.
KEITH, A. B. (Ed.). *Speeches and Documents on the British Dominions 1918-1931.* Oxford University Press, 1932, reprinted 1938.
KEITH, A. B. *Responsible Government in the Dominions.* Clarendon Press, Oxford, 2nd Edition, Vol. 1, 1928.
KEITH, A. B. *The Dominions as Sovereign States.* Macmillan & Co., 1938.
RUTHERFORD, J. *The Treaty of Waitangi and the acquisition of British Sovereignty in New Zealand, 1840.* Auckland University College, 1949.
SIMPSON, F. A. *Parliament in New Zealand.* A. H. & A. W. Reed, 1947.
WHEARE, K. C. *The Statute of Westminster and Dominion Status.* Oxford University Press, 5th Edition, 1953.

CRIMINAL LAW

GARROW, J. M. E. *Criminal Law in New Zealand.* Butterworth & Co., 3rd Edition, 1950.
GARROW and WILLIS. *Law of Evidence in New Zealand.* Butterworth & Co., 3rd Edition, 1949.
LUXFORD, J. H. *Police Law in New Zealand.* Butterworth & Co., 2nd Edition, 1950.
LUXFORD, J. H. *Liquor Laws of New Zealand.* Butterworth & Co., 2nd Edition, 1953.
MAUNSELL, T. E. *New Zealand Justice of the Peace and Police Court Practice.* Butterworth & Co., 1935.
PHILIPP, E. *Juvenile Delinquency in New Zealand.* New Zealand Council for Educational Research, 1946.
WILY, H. J. *New Zealand Justices of the Peace and Police Court Practice.* Butterworth & Co., 2nd Edition, 1953.

359

ECONOMIC CONTROLS

HASLAM, A. L. *The Law Relating to Trade Combinations.* George Allen & Unwin, 1931.

PARKER, R. S. (Ed.). *Economic Stability in New Zealand.* N.Z. Institute of Public Administration, 1953.

PLUMPTRE, A. F. W. *Central Banking in the British Dominions.* University of Toronto Press, 1940.

EXECUTORS, ADMINISTRATORS AND TRUSTEES

ANDERSON, A. E. J. *Executorship Law and Accounts in New Zealand.* Butterworth & Co., 2nd Edition, 1946.

DOBBIE, A. E. *Probate and Administration Practice in New Zealand.* Butterworth & Co., 1951.

GARROW, J. M. E. *Laws of Wills and Administration and Succession on Intestacy.* Butterworth & Co., 2nd Edition, 1949.

GARROW and HENDERSON. *Law of Trusts and Trustees.* Butterworth & Co., 2nd Edition, 1953.

ROBSON, J. L. *Comparative Study of Law affecting Corporate Trustees in the United States of America, New Zealand and England,* 1939. Unpublished thesis, copy deposited University College Library, University of London.

FAMILY LAW

BIRKS, W. R. *Legal Relationship of Parent and Child.* Legal Publications, 1952.

CAMPBELL, I. D. *Law of Adoption in New Zealand.* Butterworth & Co., 1952.

MASON, TUTHILL and LENNARD. *Testator's Family Maintenance in Australia and New Zealand.* Law Book Co. of Australasia, 1929.

SIM, W. J. *Divorce Law and Practice in New Zealand.* Butterworth & Co., 5th Edition, 1943.

STEPHENS, A. C. *Testator's Family Maintenance in New Zealand.* Butterworth & Co., 1934.

HISTORY

BEAGLEHOLE, J. C. *New Zealand—a short history.* George Allen & Unwin, 1936.

BELSHAW, H. (Ed.). *New Zealand.* University of California Press, 1947.

BEST, E. *The Maori.* Board of Maori Ethnological Research, 1924.

BRYCE, J. B. *Modern Democracies.* Macmillan & Co., 1931.

CONDLIFFE, J. B. *New Zealand in the Making.* George Allen & Unwin, 1930.

HANLON, A. C. *Random Recollections.* Otago Daily Times and Witness Newspapers Co., 1939.

LIPSON, L. *The Politics of Equality.* University of Chicago Press, 1948.

MILLER, H. G. *New Zealand.* Hutchinson's University Library, 1950.

MORRELL, W. P. *The Provincial System of Government in New Zealand (1852-76).* Longmans, Green & Co., 1932.

MORRELL, W. P. *New Zealand.* Ernest Benn, 1935.

REEVES, W. P. *The Long White Cloud.* George Allen & Unwin, 4th Edition, 1950.

SHRIMPTON and MULGAN. *Maori and Pakeha.* Whitcombe & Tombs, 2nd Edition, 1930.

SIEGFRIED, A. *Democracy in New Zealand (1904).* G. Bell & Sons, translation 1914.

STEWART, W. D. *Portrait of a Judge: Sir Joshua Strange Williams.* Whitcombe & Tombs, 1945.

STEWART, W. D. *Sir Francis H. D. Bell—His Life and Times.* Butterworth & Co., 1937.

WEBB, L. *Government in New Zealand.* N. Z. Department of Internal Affairs, 1940.

WOOD, F. L. W. *Understanding New Zealand (1944),* republished as *This New Zealand.* Paul's Book Arcade, 1946. Revised Edition 1952.

SEWELL, H. *Journals.* Vols. 1 and 2 (not printed, but typewritten copy in Turnbull Library, Wellington).

INDUSTRIAL LAW

HARE, A. E. C. *Industrial Relations in New Zealand.* Whitcombe & Tombs, 1946.

MACDONALD, J. W. *The Law Relating to Workers Compensation in New Zealand.* Butterworth & Co., 2nd Edition, 1934.

MAZENGARB. A. J. *The Industrial Laws of New Zealand.* Butterworth & Co., 2nd Edition, 1947.

LAND LAW (including Landlord and Tenant)

BAIRD, R. F. *Real Property.* Whitcombe & Tombs, 1926.

BALL, C. E. H. *The Law of Mortgages of Land in New Zealand.* Butterworth & Co., 1935.

GARROW and GOODALL. *Law of Real Property in New Zealand.* Butterworth & Co., 3rd Edition, 1936.

GOODALL, S. I. *Law and Practice relating to Conveyancing in New Zealand.* Butterworth & Co., 2nd Edition, 1951.

HUTCHEN, D. *The Land Transfer Act.* Whitcombe & Tombs, 2nd Edition, 1925.

JOURDAIN, W. R. *Digest of the Land Laws of New Zealand.* New Zealand Government Publication, 2nd Edition, 1928.

JOURDAIN, W. R. *Land Legislation and Settlement in New Zealand.* New Zealand Government Publication, 1925.

MARTIN, T. F. *Conveyancing in New Zealand.* Whitcombe & Tombs, 1906.

PAGE, E. F. *Tenancy Legislation in New Zealand.* Legal Publications, 2nd Edition, 1953.

SALMOND, J. W. *Notes on the History of Native Land Legislation,* see extract from introduction to the Native Land Act, 1909; The Public Acts of New Zealand (reprint), Vol. 6, p. 87.

SMITH, N. W. *Native Custom and Law affecting Native Land.* Maori Purposes Fund Board, 1942.

WILY, H. J. *Tenancy Act.* Butterworth & Co., 3rd Edition, 1953.

MERCANTILE LAW

BALL, C. E. H. *The Law Relating to Chattels Transfer and the Hire-purchase Agreements Act* 1939. Butterworth & Co., 1940.

GARROW, J. M. E. *Law of Personal Property in New Zealand.* Ferguson & Osborn, 3rd Edition, 1947.

HOLLINGS, P. L. *The New Zealand Sale of Goods Act and Mercantile Law Act.* Abel Dykes, 1929.

SPRATT, F. C. *Law and Practice of Bankruptcy in New Zealand.* Butterworth & Co., 1930, with Supplement No. 1, 1953.

WADDY, P. R. *Mercantile Law in New Zealand.* Whitcombe & Tombs, 3rd Edition, 1934.

WARD and WILD. *Mercantile Law in New Zealand.* Whitcombe & Tombs, 2nd Edition, 1953.

PRACTICE AND PROCEDURE

RHODES, E. G. *Practice Precedents and Statements of Claim.* Butterworth & Co., 1936.

RHODES, E. G. *Practice Precedents and Statements of Defence.* 2nd series. Butterworth & Co., 1944.

STEPHENS, J. C. *Supreme Court Forms.* Whitcombe & Tombs, 1933.

SIM, W. J. *Divorce Law and Practice in New Zealand.* Butterworth & Co., 5th Edition, 1943.

STOUT and SIM. *The Practice of the Supreme Court and Court of Appeal of New Zealand.* Whitcombe & Tombs, 8th Edition, 1940.

WILY, H. J. *Magistrates' Courts Practice.* Butterworth & Co., 3rd Edition, 1949.

PUBLIC ADMINISTRATION

LIPSON, L.   *The Politics of Equality.*   University of Chicago Press, 1948.
STEPHENS, F. B. (Ed.).   *Local Government in New Zealand.*   N.Z. Department of
    Internal Affairs, 1949.
WEBB, L.   *Government in New Zealand.*   N.Z. Department of Internal Affairs,
    1940.
Journal of Public Administration, New Zealand (half-yearly from 1938).

SOCIAL LEGISLATION

BELSHAW, H. (Ed.).   *New Zealand* (United Nations Series).   University of
    California Press, 1947.
SMITH, N. W.   *The Maori People and Us.*   A. H. & A. W. Reed, 1948.
SUTCH, W. B.   *Poverty and Progress in New Zealand.*   Modern Books, 1941.
SUTCH, W. B.   *The Quest for Security in New Zealand.*   Penguin Books, 1942.
SOCIAL SECURITY AND HEALTH DEPARTMENTS.   *The Growth and Development of
    Social Security in New Zealand.*   Government Printer, 1950.

TORTS

CHALMERS and DIXON.   *Road Traffic Laws in New Zealand.*   Butterworth & Co.,
    2nd Edition, 1952.
DAVIS, A. G.   *Law of Torts in New Zealand.*   Butterworth & Co., 1951.
MAZENGARB, O. C.   *Negligence on the Highway.*   Butterworth & Co., 1952.
McELROY and GRESSON.   *The Law Reform Act* 1936.   Butterworth & Co., 1937.

MISCELLANEOUS

New Zealand Privy Council Cases: 1840-1932.   Butterworth & Co.
Macassey's Reports of Cases: 1861-1872.   Wise & Co.
Colonial Law Journal: Vol. 1, Part 1, 1865-1875.
Reports of the Court of Appeal of New Zealand: 1867–1877.   Government Printer.
New Zealand Jurist: 1873-1879.   Wilkie & Co.
Ollivier, Bell and Fitzgerald's Reports of Cases: 1878-80.   Lyon & Blair.
New Zealand Law Reports: 1883-.   New Zealand Council of Law Reporting.
Gazette Law Reports: 1898-1953.   Trade Auxiliary Co. of New Zealand.
Magistrates Court Reports: 1906-1953.   Trade Auxiliary Co. of New Zealand.
Magistrates Court Decisions: 1939-.   Butterworth & Co.
New Zealand Law Journal.   Fortnightly from 1925.   Butterworth & Co.
New Zealand Pilot to 3rd Edition, Halsbury's Laws of England.   Butterworth &
    Co., Vol. 1, 1953.

TABLE OF STATUTES

British and Imperial Statutes

1368—None put to answer without due process (42 Edw. 3, c. 3) . . 75
1640—Habeas Corpus Act (16 Car. 1, c. 10) 75
1670—Statute of Distributions (22 & 23 Car. 2, c. 10) . . . 290-291
1685—Administration of Intestates Estates (1 Jac. 2, c. 17) . . . 290-291
1698—An Act for Suppressing of Lotteries (10 Will, 3, c. 17) . . . 259
1817—Murders Abroad Act (57 Geo. 3, c. 53) 2
1831—Truck Act (1 & 2 Will. 4, c. 37) 298
1840—New South Wales Continuance Act (3 & 4 Vict. c. 62) . . . 3
1846—Fatal Accidents Act (9 & 10 Vict. c. 93) 308, 311
Constitution of Government in the New Zealand Islands (9 & 10
Vict. c. 103) 6
1848—Suspension of constitution of Government in New Zealand (11 & 12
Vict. c. 5) 6
Justices Protection Act (11 & 12 Vict. c. 44) 78n
1852—New Zealand Constitution Act (15 & 16 Vict. c. 72)
1, 5, 30, 31, 33-37, 40-50, 76, 85, 93, 211
1856—Joint Stock Companies Act (19 & 20 Vict. c. 47) . . . 304
1857—New Zealand Constitution (Amendment) Act (20 & 21 Vict. c. 53) 41-44, 47
Court of Probate Act (20 & 21 Vict. c. 77) 61
Matrimonial Causes Act (20 & 21 Vict. c. 85) . . . 285, 322
1862—Amendment to Constitution Act (25 & 26 Vict. c. 48) . . 42-43
1864—Fatal Accidents Act (27 & 28 Vict. c. 95) 308
1865—Dogs Act (28 & 29 Vict. c. 60) 307
Colonial Laws Validity Act (28 & 29 Vict. c. 63) . . . 42-45, 49
1868—New Zealand Legislative Council (31 & 32 Vict. c. 57) . . 37, 43
New Zealand Assembly's Powers (31 & 32 Vict. c. 92) . . 43
1878—Bills of Sale Act (41 & 42 Vict. c. 31) 289
1880—Employers' Liability Act (43 & 44 Vict. c. 42) . . . 312
1881—Conveyancing Act (44 & 45 Vict. c. 41) 277
1882—Bills of Sale Act (1878) Amendment Act (45 & 46 Vict. c. 43) . 289
Bills of Exchange Act (45 & 46 Vict. c. 61) . . . 293-294
Married Women's Property Act (45 & 46 Vict. c. 75) . . 286
1889—Factors Act (52 & 53 Vict. c. 45) 294
1890—Colonial Courts of Admiralty Act (53 & 54 Vict. c. 27) . . 46-48
Foreign Jurisdiction Act (53 & 54 Vict. c. 37) . . . 92
1891—Slander of Women Act (54 & 55 Vict. c. 51) . . . 307
1893—Married Women's Property Act (56 & 57 Vict. c. 63) . . 286
1894—Merchant Shipping Act (57 & 58 Vict. c. 60) . . 46-48, 92, 293
1896—Truck Act (59 & 60 Vict. c. 44) 298
1897—Workmen's Compensation Act (60 & 61 Vict. c. 37) . 312-313, 315
1900—Moneylenders' Act (63 & 64 Vict. c. 51) 294
Colonial Stock Act (63 & 64 Vict. c. 62) 49
1906—Prevention of Corruption Act (6 Edw. 7, c. 34) . . . 295
Marine Assurance Act (6 Edw. 7, c. 41) 294
1907—Criminal Appeal Act (7 Edw. 7, c. 23) 260
1911—Perjury Act (1 & 2 Geo. 5, c. 6) 265
1913—Forgery Act (3 & 4 Geo. 5, c. 27) 265
1915—Indictments Act (5 & 6 Geo. 5, c. 90) 265
Increase of Rent and Mortgage Interest (War Restrictions) Act (5 & 6
Geo. 5, c. 97) 287-288

1916—Larceny Act (6 & 7 Geo. 5, c. 59) 265
1925—Administration of Estates Act (15 Geo. 5, c. 23) 291
1926—Legitimacy Act (16 & 17 Geo. 5, c. 60) 332
1929—Companies Act (19 & 20 Geo. 5, c. 23) 304
1931—Statute of Westminster (22 & 23 Geo. 5, c. 4) . 41, 43-45, 48, 50, 92
1934—Law Reform (Miscellaneous Provisions) Act (24 & 25 Geo. 5, c. 41)
309, 310
      Colonial Stock Act (24 & 25 Geo. 5, c. 47) 49
      Whaling Industry (Regulation) Act (24 & 25 Geo. 5, c. 49) . . 45
1935—Law Reform (Married Women and Tortfeasors) Act, (25 & 26 Geo. 5, c. 30) 286-287
1937—Matrimonial Causes Act (1 Edw. 8 & 1 Geo. 6, c. 57) . . 324
1938—Inheritance (Family Provisions) Act (1 & 2 Geo. 6, c. 45) . 335n
1939—Emergency Powers (Defence) Act (2 & 3 Geo. 6, c. 62) . ' . 45
1940—Truck Act (3 & 4 Geo. 6, c. 38) 298
1943—Law Reform (Frustrated Contracts) Act (6 & 7 Geo. 6, c. 40) . 303
1944—Matrimonial Causes (War Marriages) Act (7 & 8 Geo. 6, c. 43) . 325
1945—Supplies and Services (Transitional Powers) Act (9 & 10 Geo. 6, c. 10) 95
      Law Reform (Contributory Negligence) Act (8 & 9 Geo. 6, c. 28) . 311
1947—New Zealand Constitution (Amendment) Act (11 & 12 Geo. 6, c. 4)
41, 44, 46, 48, 50
      Crown Proceedings Act (10 & 11 Geo. 6, c. 44) . . . 132
1948—Law Reform (Personal Injuries) Act (11 & 12 Geo. 6, c. 41) . 312
1950—Matrimonial Causes Act (14 Geo. 6, c. 25) . . . 324n, 326n

NEW ZEALAND

Ordinances

1841—(Session 1, No. 2) Land Claims Ordinance 5
      (Session 1, No. 4) General and Quarter Sessions Ordinance . 52, 258
      (Session 1, No. 6) Courts of Requests Ordinance . . . 53
1841-42—(Session II, No. 1) Supreme Court Ordinance . . 60, 79, 258
      (Session II, No. 2) County Courts Ordinance . . . 53
      (Session II, No. 4) Police Magistrates Ordinance . 53, 54, 55
      (Session II, No. 5) Summary Proceedings Ordinance . 54, 258
      (Session II, No. 9) Deeds Registration Ordinance 22, 92-93, 259, 279
      (Session II, No. 10) Property Law Ordinance . 22, 259, 276-277
      (Session II, No. 11) Marriage Validation Ordinance . . 318
      (Session II, No. 15) Harbours Ordinance . . . 93
1844—(Session III, No. 1) Supreme Court Ordinance . . . 60
      (Session III, No. 8) Courts of Request Ordinance . . 53, 54
      (Session III, No. 18) Natives' Exemption Ordinance . . 17
1846—(Session VII, No. 2) Armed Constabulary Ordinance . . 17
      (Session VII, No. 9) Destitute Persons Ordinance . . . 328
      (Session VII, No. 15) Ordinances Repeal Ordinance . . 54
      (Session VII, No. 16) Resident Magistrates Courts Ordinance 17, 54
      (Session VII, No. 18) Arms Ordinance 17
      (Session VII, No. 20) Sessions of the Peace Ordinance . . 55
1847—(Session VIII, No. 2) Gunpowder Ordinance . . . 17
      (Session VIII, No. 7) Marriage Ordinance . . . 317-318
1848—(Session IX, No. 3) Supreme Court Ordinance . . . 60
1853—(Session XII, No. 5) Legal Practitioners Ordinance . . 80

Statutes

Abolition of Provinces Act, 1875 . . . . 31, 42
Acts Interpretation Act, 1924 . . . . 273n
Administration Act, 1879 . . . . 25, 290

Administration Act, 1908 290
Administration Act, 1952 . . . . . . 64, 291, 334, 338
Administration Act, 1879, Amendment Act, 1885 290
Administration Amendment Act, 1944 . . . . . . 291, 354
Adoption of Children Act, 1881 . . . . . . 23, 332, 334
Adoption of Children Act, 1895 334
Aged and Infirm Persons' Protection Act, 1912 64
Agriculture (Emergency Powers) Act, 1934 . . . 100-101, 231
Agricultural Implement Manufacture, Importation and Sale Act, 1905 . 197
Agricultural Workers Act, 1936 296
Annual Holidays Act, 1944 296-297
Arbitration Act, 1890 293-294
Atomic Energy Act, 1945 284
Auckland Metropolitan Milk Act, 1933 101
Banking Act, 1908 . . . . 96, 249
Bankruptcy Act, 1892 306
Bankruptcy Act, 1908 . . . . 64, 306
Bills of Exchange Act, 1883 293
Bills of Exchange Act, 1908 293-294
Bills of Sale Registration Act, 1856 289
Board of Trade Act, 1919 . . . 199, 203, 206, 207, 214, 215
Board of Trade Amendment Act, 1923 199
Book-purchasers Protection Act, 1891 294
British Investors in New Zealand Government Securities Act, 1900 . 49-50
British Nationality and New Zealand Citizenship Act, 1948 . . 321
Capital Punishment Act, 1950 268
Carriage by Air Act, 1940 . . . . . . 295, 333-334
Carriers Act, 1948 295
Cemeteries Act, 1908 146
Chattels Securities Act, 1880 289
Chattels Transfer Act, 1924 . . . . 289, 290
Child Welfare Act, 1925 . . . 72, 153, 154, 155, 157, 158, 159, 264
Child Welfare Amendment Act, 1927 158
Children's Protection Act, 1890 25
Cinematograph Films Act, 1928 123
Civil Aviation Act, 1948 . . . . 96, 98
Civil List Act, 1950 10
Clerks of Works Act, 1944 97
Coal Act, 1948 283
Coal-mines Act, 1925 74
Commercial Trusts Act, 1910 . . . 197, 198, 200, 201, 202-209
Commissions of Inquiry Act, 1908 . . . . . 75, 111, 220
Companies Act, 1933 . . . . 64, 304-306
Contractors' and Workmen's Lien Act, 1892 298
Contractors Debts Act, 1871 297
Contributory Negligence Act, 1947 311
Control of Prices Act, 1947 . . . . . . 105, 218, 342
Control of Prices Amendment Act, 1953 218
Co-operative Companies Act, 1933 305
Co-operative Dairy Companies Act, 1949 305
Co-operative Egg Marketing Act, 1950 305
Coroners Act, 1908 71
Coroners Act, 1951 . . . . 71, 72
Corrupt Practices Prevention Act, 1858 34
Court of Appeal Act, 1862 . . . . 67, 260
Court of Appeal Act, 1882 67
Crimes Act, 1908 . . 63, 68, 94, 196, 267, 268, 269, 270, 271, 274
Crimes Amendment Act, 1910 . . . . 94, 263

Crimes Amendment Act, 1920 263
Crimes Amendment Act, 1941 . . . . 268, 269
Criminal Appeal Act, 1945 . . . . . . 68, 69, 260
Criminal Code Act, 1893 . . . . 63, 264, 265, 266, 267, 270, 271
Crown Proceedings Act, 1950 . . . . . . 130, 132, 355
Crown Redress Act, 1871 130
Crown Suits Act, 1881 130
Crown Suits Amendment Act, 1910 131
Customs Act, 1913 . . . . 210, 211, 212, 226, 228, 245, 246, 247
Customs Acts, Amendment Act, 1939 247
Customs Amendment Act, 1921 . . . . 127, 128
Dairy Board Act, 1953 . . . . 233*n*
Dairy Industry Act, 1908 305
Dairy-Produce Export Control Act, 1923 . . . . 228, 229, 230
Dairy Products Marketing Commission Act, 1947 232-235
Dairy Products Marketing Commission Amendment Act, 1948 . . . 233
Deaths by Accidents Compensation Act, 1880 309
Deaths by Accidents Compensation Act, 1908 350
Deaths by Accidents Compensation Act, 1952 . . 303, 309-310, 333-334
Death Duties Act, 1921 333
Debtors and Creditors Act, 1862 306
Deceased Husband's Brother Marriage Act, 1900 320
Deceased Wife's Sister Marriage Act, 1880 320
Destitute Persons Act, 1910 . . . . . 154, 160, 286, 328-329
Destitute Persons Amendment Act, 1951 . . . . . . 329*n*
Destitute Persons Amendment Act, 1953 . . . . . . 329*n*
Distillation Act, 1908 123
District Courts Abolition Act, 1925 55
District Courts Act, 1858 . . . . 54, 55, 59
District Courts Criminal Jurisdiction Extension Act, 1870 . . . 55
District Courts Jurisdiction Extension Act, 1866 55
District Courts Jurisdiction Extension Act, 1893 55
Divorce Act, 1898 323-324
Divorce and Matrimonial Causes Act, 1867 . . . 63, 322-323, 326
Divorce and Matrimonial Causes Act Amendment Act, 1907 . . 324
Divorce and Matrimonial Causes Act Amendment Act, 1920 . . 324
Divorce and Matrimonial Causes Act, 1928 . . . 64, 324-327
Divorce and Matrimonial Causes Amendment Act, 1930 . . 324, 325
Divorce and Matrimonial Causes Amendment Act, 1953 . . 324-327
Dog Registration Act, 1880 307
Dogs Registration Act, 1908 307
Domestic Proceedings Act, 1939 330
Earthquake and War Damage Act, 1944 285
Education Act, 1877 . . . . 135, 147
Education Act, 1908 151
Education Act, 1914 . . . . 96, 147, 148, 149, 150, 151, 152
Education Amendment Act, 1953 . . . . 149*n*
Electoral Act, 1893 . . . . 30, 31, 36
Electoral Act, 1902 . . . . 30, 42
Electoral Act, 1927 36
Electoral Amendment Act, 1934 36
Electoral Amendment Act, 1945 . . . . 31, 32
Electoral Amendment Act, 1950 31
Electoral Amendment Act, 1953 36
Electoral Law Amendment Act, 1896 30-31
Electoral Petitions Act, 1880 34
Emergency Forces Act, 1950 96

Emergency Regulations Act, 1939 . . . 93-95, 97-101, 302, 351
Emergency Regulations Continuance Act, 1947 . . . . 95, 100
Employers' Liability Act, 1882 . . . . . . 299, 312
Employers' Liability Act, 1908 . . . . . . 312, 314
Employers' Liability Act Amendment Act, 1891 . . . . 26, 312
Employers' Liability Acts, Amendment Act, 1892 312
English Acts Act, 1854 . . . . 259, 308
English Laws Act, 1858 5
English Laws Act, 1908 294
Evidence Amendment Act, 1945 . . . . . . 328n, 354n
Evidence Amendment Act, 1950 . . . . 354n
Evidence Amendment Act, 1952 . . . . 354n
Excess Profits Tax Act, 1940 292
Factories Act, 1891 173
Factories Act ,1946 96
Fair Rents Act, 1936 . . . . 288, 296
Family Allowances Act, 1926 159
Family Homes Protection Act, 1895 338
Family Protection Act, 1908 . . . 64, 276, 333-338, 341, 350
Fencing Act, 1881 289
Fencing Act, 1895 289
Fencing Act, 1908 . . . . 71, 289
Finance Act, 1915 291
Finance Act, 1918 36
Finance Act, 1931 . . . . 189, 301
Finance Act, 1937 351
Finance Act (No. 3), 1943 131
Finance Act (No. 2), 1944 . . . . 333, 351
Finance Act (No. 3), 1944 282-283
Finance Act, 1947 351
Finance Act (No. 2), 1948 285
Finance Act, 1950 288
First Offenders Probation Act, 1886 262
First Offenders Probation Amendment Act, 1903 262
Fisheries Amendment Act, 1945 106
Flour and other Products Monopoly Prevention Act, 1907 . . . 197
Foreign Offenders' Apprehension Act, 1863 260
Fruit Control Act, 1924 . . . . 230, 231
Frustrated Contracts Act, 1944 . . . . . . 303, 354
Gaming Amendment Act, 1910 344
Gaming Amendment Act, 1920 344
Gaming Amendment (No. 2) Act, 1920 344
Gaming and Lotteries Act Amendment Act, 1907 344
Geothermal Energy Act, 1953 284
Gold Fields Act, 1858 283
Government Annuities Act, 1869 24
Government Railways Act, 1926 98
Government Railways Act, 1949 . . . . . . 98, 295
Government Service Tribunal Act, 1948 75
Government Valuation of Land Act, 1896 292
Guardianship of Infants Act, 1908 321
Guardianship of Infants Act, 1926 . . . . . 321, 330
Guardianship of Infants Amendment Act, 1927 . . . . 329n
Habitual Criminal and Offenders Act, 1906 263
Half-caste Disability Removal Act, 1860 331
Health Act, 1920 . . . . . 136, 137, 138, 139, 142
Hire Purchase Agreements Act, 1939 . . . . . 296, 315
Hospitals Act, 1926 140

Hospitals Amendment Act, 1948 140
Hospitals Amendment Act, 1951 141
Hospitals and Charitable Institutions Act, 1885 140
Housing Improvement Act, 1945 139
Imprisonment for Debt Limitation Act, 1908 . . . . . 262, 287
Incorporated Societies Act, 1908 306
Indemnity Act, 1867 (disallowed) 49
Industrial Conciliation and Arbitration Act, 1894 . . 172, 173, 174, 340
Industrial Conciliation and Arbitration Act, 1908 185
Industrial Conciliation and Arbitration Act, 1925
                72, 124, 174, 175, 176, 185, 186, 187, 195*n*
Industrial Conciliation and Arbitration Amendment Act, 1932 . . . 177
Industrial Conciliation and Arbitration Amendment Act, 1936
                174, 177, 188, 189, 190, 193, 340
Industrial Conciliation and Arbitration Amendment Act, 1937 . . . 193
Industrial Conciliation and Arbitration Amendment Act, 1939 . . 183, 195
Industrial Conciliation and Arbitration Amendment Act, 1947 . . . 183
Industrial Conciliation and Arbitration Amendment Act, 1951
                174, 175, 180, 190, 195
Industrial Efficiency Act, 1936 . . . . . . 106, 219-224
Industrial Relations Act, 1949 . . . . . . 183, 196
Industrial Schools Act, 1882 . . . . 152, 153
Infants Act, 1908 . . . . . . 156, 157, 330-334
Infants Amendment Act, 1950 . . . . . . 334, 354
Infants Guardianship and Contracts Act, 1887 25
Interpretation Act, 1888 342
Intestates Estates Act, 1903 290
Iron and Steel Industry Act, 1937 284-285
John Duncan McGruer Estate Act, 1945 350
Joint Family Homes Act, 1950 . . . . 276, 338
Joint Family Homes Amendment Act, 1951 338
Joint Stock Companies Act, 1860 304
Judicature Act, 1908 . . . . . 60, 63, 67, 68, 76, 97, 294, 330
Juries Act, 1908 . . . . 67, 272
Juries Act, Amendment Act, 1898 66
Justices of the Peace Act, 1866 56
Justices of the Peace Act, 1882 . . . . 56, 57
Justices of the Peace Act, 1908 57
Justices of the Peace Act, 1927 . . . . 54, 56, 57, 78*n*, 272*n*
Labour Disputes Investigation Act, 1913 185-187
Land Act, 1877 280
Land Act, 1892 281
Land Act, 1924 281
Land Act, 1948 281
Land Act, 1877 Amendment Act, 1882 38
Land and Income Assessment Act, 1891 291
Land and Income Tax Act, 1916 291
Land and Income Tax Act, 1923 . . . . . . 291-292, 347
Land and Income Tax Amendment Act, 1939 291
Land and Income Tax Amendment Act, 1946 292
Land and Income Tax Amendment Act, 1949 351
Land Registry Act, 1860 . . . . 22, 279
Land Settlement Promotion Act, 1952 . . . . 105, 106, 106*n*
Land-tax Collection Act, 1879 26
Land Transfer Act, 1870 279
Land Transfer Act, 1885 279
Land Transfer Act, 1908 279
Land Transfer Act, 1915 279

Land Transfer Act, 1952 . . . . 279, 280
Land Transfer (Compulsory Registration of Titles) Act, 1924 . . . 279
Land Valuation Court Act, 1948 . . . . 105, 292
Law Amendment Act, 1878 62
Law Amendment Act, 1882 62
Law of Libel Amendment Act, 1910 307-308
Law Practitioners Act, 1861 80
Law Practitioners Act, 1908 80
Law Practitioners Act, 1931 . . . . 80, 82
Law Practitioners Act Amendment Act, 1865 80
Law Practitioners Amendment Act, 1935 82
Law Reform Act, 1936 . . 286, 287, 293, 302-303, 309, 310, 312, 314
Law Reform Act, 1944 . . . . 303, 311
Law Reform (Testamentary Promises) Act, 1949 . . . 341, 354
Legal Aid Act, 1939 82
Legislative Council Act, 1891 . . . . . 37-38, 40, 42
Legislative Council Act, 1914 . . . . . . 38, 96-97
Legislative Council Abolition Act, 1950 . . . 37-39, 42, 97
Legislature Amendment Act, 1910 36
Legislature Amendment Act, 1912 33-34
Legislature Amendment Act, 1924 34
Legitimation Act, 1894 . . . . . . 26, 309, 332
Legitimation Act, 1939 332
Legitimation Amendment Act, 1921-1922 332
Licensing Amendment Act, 1948 75
Limitation Act, 1950 . . . . 294, 355
Local Government Commission Act, 1946 75
Lunacy Act, 1866 262
Magistrates' Courts Act, 1893 . . . . . . 58, 59
Magistrates' Courts Act, 1947 . . . . 54n, 56, 59, 72, 355
Magistrates' Courts Amendment Act, 1913 59
Maori Affairs Act, 1953 . . . . . 70, 320n, 333-335
Maori Councils Act, 1900 166-167
Maori Land Act, 1931 319-320
Maori Purposes Act, 1940 319
Maori Purposes Act, 1951 . . . . 319, 320
Maori Representation Act, 1867 30
Maori Social and Economic Advancement Act, 1945 . . . 166-169
Marianne Caughey Preston Estate Act, 1945 350
Marine Insurance Act, 1907 294
Marketing Amendment Act, 1953 238
Marriage Act, 1854 . . . . 317-318, 321
Marriage Act, 1908 320
Marriage Act Amendment Act, 1858 . . . . . . 317n
Marriage Amendment Act, 1891 317
Marriage Amendment Act, 1929 320
Marriage Amendment Act, 1933 320
Marriage Amendment Act, 1946 . . . . . . 320, 350
Marriages Validation Act, 1905 320
Married Persons Summary Separation Act, 1896 328
Married Women's Property Act, 1884 286
Married Women's Property Act, 1894 286
Married Women's Property Act, 1908 286
Married Women's Property Protection Act, 1860 285
Married Women's Property Protection Act, 1870 285
Married Women's Property Protection Act, 1880 . . . 285-286
Master and Apprentice Amendment Act, 1920 . . . 296, 315

Matrimonial Causes (War Marriages) Act, 1947 . . 324*n*, 325-326, 354
Meat Export Control Act, 1921-1922 . . . . . . 225, 229
Medical Advertisements Act, 1942 . . . . . . 144, 145
Mental Defectives Act, 1911 160
Mercantile Agents Act, 1890 294
Mercantile Law Act, 1880 294
Mercantile Law Act, 1908 294
Military Service Act, 1916 38
Military Training Act, 1949 190
Milk Act, 1944 . . . . 233*n*
Milk Amendment Act, 1951 . . . . 233*n*
Minimum Wage Act, 1945 297
Mining Act, 1926 . . . . 73, 74
Mining Companies Act, 1904 305
Mining Companies' Limited Liability Act, 1865 305
Moneylenders Act, 1901 294
Moneylenders Act, 1908 294
Monopoly Prevention Act, 1908 197
Morris Divorce and Marriage Validation Act, 1943 350
Mortgages Extension Act, 1914 299
Mortgages Extension Act, 1919 299
Mortgages Final Extension Act, 1924 299
Mortgagors and Lessees Rehabilitation Act, 1936 . . . 300-302
Mortgagors and Tenants Relief Act, 1933 300
Mortgagors Relief Act, 1931 299
Motor-vehicles Insurance (Third-party Risks) Act, 1928 . . 303-304
Municipal Corporations Act, 1900 101
National Expenditure Adjustment Act, 1932 . . . 301-302
Native Land Act, 1873 42
Native Lands Act, 1862 70
Native Rights Act, 1865 5
Neglected and Criminal Children Act, 1867 . . . . 135, 152
New Zealand Army Act, 1950 97
New Zealand Constitution (Request and Consent) Act, 1947 . . 44
New Zealand Council of Law Reporting Act, 1938 . . . 82*n*, 83
New Zealand Law Society's Act, 1869 82
New Zealand Loans Act, 1932 50
New Zealand Loans Amendment Act, 1947 49-50
New Zealand National Airways Act, 1945 98
New Zealand National Airways Act, 1948 . . . . 89*n*
Offenders Probation Act, 1920 . . . . . . 262, 263
Old-age Pensions Act, 1898 . . . . . . 28, 38, 135
Parliamentary Elections Postponement Act, 1916 36
Parliamentary Privileges Act, 1865 39
Partnership Act, 1891 293-294
Partnership Act, 1908 294
Penalties Remission Act, 1908 349
Petroleum Act, 1937 283-284
Petty Sessions Act, 1858 258
Petty Sessions Act, 1865 56
Police Offences Act, 1927 . . . . 57*n*
Police Offences Amendment Act, 1935 . . . . . 267*n*
Police Offences Amendment Act, 1951 . . . . 196, 341
Political Disabilities Removal Act, 1936 194
Poor Prisoners' Defence Act, 1933 82
Prevention of Crime (Borstal Institutions Establishment) Act, 1924 . 263
Prevention of Profiteering Act, 1936 . . . . 213, 214, 215
Primary Products Act, 1953 . . . . . 100, 102, 238, 239

Primary Products Marketing Act, 1936 . . . . . . 231, 232
Primary Products Marketing Amendment Act, 1937 . . 96, 236-238
Private Industrial Schools Regulation and Industrial Schools Act Amend-
        ment Act, 1900 153
Privileges Act, 1856 39
Prolongation of Parliament Act, 1941 36
Property Law Act, 1905 277
Property Law Act, 1952 . . . . . . 277-278, 303
Property-tax Act, 1879 291
Public Health Act, 1872 . . . . 135, 136
Public Health Act, 1900 136
Public Revenues Act, 1953 88
Public Safety Conservation Act, 1932 . . . 93-94, 99, 101, 195, 341
Public Service Act, 1912 98
Public Service Amendment Act, 1927 . . . . . 120, 121, 125
Public Trust Office Act, 1872 24
Public Works Act, 1876 282
Public Works Act, 1928 282
Qualification of Electors Act, 1879 . . . . . . 30, 31
Rating Act, 1925 76
Real Estate Descent Act, 1874 290
Registration of Electors Act, 1858 34
Regulation of Elections Act, 1870 30
Regulation of Elections Act, 1881 42
Regulation of Mines Act, 1874 312
Regulation of Trade and Commerce Act, 1914 . . . 27, 209-212
Regulations Act, 1936 99
Rent Restriction Act, 1935 288
Repeals Act, 1878 42
Repeals Act, 1891 56
Representation Act, 1881 . . . . 31-33, 35
Representation Act, 1887 . . . . 31, 32
Representation Act, 1900 35
Representation Act Amendment Act, 1889 . . . . 32, 33
Representation Acts Amendment Act, 1887 35
Reserve Bank of New Zealand Act, 1933 . . . . 248, 250-256
Reserve Bank of New Zealand Amendment Act, 1936
                        245, 246, 247, 251-253, 256
Reserve Bank of New Zealand Amendment Act, 1939 . . . 253
Reserve Bank of New Zealand Amendment Act, 1950 . . 253, 255
Resident Magistrates' Act, 1867 58
Resident Magistrates' Courts Extension of Jurisdiction Act, 1856 . 54, 59
Resident Magistrates' Jurisdiction Extension Act, 1862 . . . 54
Royal Titles Act, 1947 . . . . 97, 99
Rural Mortgagors Final Adjustment Act, 1934-1935 . . 300-301
Sale of Goods Act, 1895 293-294
Sale of Goods Act, 1908 294
Sale of Liquor Restriction Act, 1917 345
Scotch Law Practitioners Act, 1856 80
Sea Carriage of Goods Act, 1922 295
Sea Carriage of Goods Act, 1940 295
Second Ballot Act, 1908 33-34
Secret Commissions Act, 1910 295
Servicemen's Settlement and Land Sales Act, 1943 114, 116, 118, 126, 347-348
Servicemen's Settlement and Land Sales Amendment Act, 1946 . . 113
Sharemilking Agreements Act, 1937 . . . . . 296, 315
Shearers' Accommodation Act, 1919 . . . . . 296, 315
Shipping and Seamen Act, 1903 293-294

Shipping and Seamen Act, 1952 . . . . . . 75, 293-294
Shipping and Seamen Amendment Act, 1909 47-48
Shipping and Seamen Amendment Act, 1911 47-48
Shops and Offices Act, 1921-1922 . . . . 102*n*
Slander of Women Act, 1898 307
Social Hygiene Act, 1917 142
Social Security Act, 1938 . . . 75, 135, 141, 146, 147, 159-165
Social Security Amendment Act, 1950 . . . . 338*n*
Soil Conservation and Rivers Control Act, 1941 . . . . 75, 285
Statute of Westminster Adoption Act, 1947 . . . . 41, 44, 46, 92
Statutes Amendment Act, 1936 . . . 66, 269*n*, 333, 337, 354*n*
Statutes Amendment Act, 1937 310
Statutes Amendment Act, 1939 . . . . 66, 320, 334, 337*n*
Statutes Amendment Act, 1941 . . . . . 38, 124, 193
Statutes Amendment Act, 1942 . . . . . . 106, 106*n*
Statutes Amendment Act, 1943 . . . . . . 337*n*, 354
Statutes Amendment Act, 1946 333
Statutes Amendment Act, 1947 . . . . . 334, 337*n*, 354
Statutes Amendment Act, 1948 311
Statutes Amendment Act, 1949 . . . . . . 331, 354
Summary Jurisdiction Act, 1952 . . . . . 58, 63*n*, 272
Summary Penalties Act, 1939 . . . . . 264*n*, 272, 349
Supply Regulations Act, 1947 . . . . 93, 95, 97-101, 351
Supreme Court Act, 1860 . . . . 60, 61
Supreme Court Act, 1882 . . . . 25, 60
Supreme Court Procedure Act, 1856 60
Sutton Adoption Act, 1948 350
Tenancy Act, 1908 289
Tenancy Act, 1948 288
Tenancy Amendment Act, 1950 289
Testator's Family Maintenance Act, 1900 . . . . . 29, 335
Threshing-machine Owners' Liens Act, 1895 298-299
Town and Country Planning Act, 1953 283
Town Planning Act, 1926 283
Trade Union Act, 1878 . . . . . 172, 173, 174, 175
Transport Act, 1949 . . . . 106, 303-304
Transport Act Amendment Act, 1950 349
Transport Law Amendment Act, 1948 105
Triennial Parliaments Act, 1879 35
Truck Act, 1891 . . . . 26, 298
Trustee Act, 1908 64
Tuberculosis Act, 1948 . . . . 142, 143
Unclassified Societies Registration Act, 1895 306
Valuation of Land Act, 1951 292
Wages Attachment Act, 1895 299
Wages Protection Act, 1899 299
Wages Protection and Contractors' Liens Act, 1908 . . . 299
Wages Protection and Contractors' Liens Act, 1939 . . 299, 354
Wages Protection and Contractors' Liens Amendment Act, 1914 . . 299
War Damage Act, 1941 285
War Legislation Amendment Act, 1916 287-288
War Pensions Act, 1943 . . . . . . 107, 333-334
War Pensions and Allowances (Mercantile Marine) Act, 1940 . 333-334
War Regulations Act, 1914 . . . . . . 93-94, 99-101
War Regulations Continuance Act, 1920 93-94
Waste Lands Act, 1856 (disallowed) 49
Waste Lands Act, 1858 280
Waterfront Industry Act, 1953 . . . . 195*n*

Whaling Industry Act, 1935 45
Women Jurors Act, 1942 272
Women's Parliamentary Rights Act, 1919 34
Workers' Compensation Act, 1922 . . . 72, 313-315, 333-334
Workers' Compensation Amendment Act, 1943 314
Workers' Compensation Amendment Act, 1945 314
Workers' Compensation Amendment Act, 1947 314
Workers' Compensation Amendment Act, 1950 315
Workers' Compensation Amendment Act, 1952 72
Workers' Compensation for Accidents Act, 1900 . . . . 72, 313
Workers' Compensation for Accidents Act, 1908 313
Workers' Compensation for Accidents Act Amendment Act, 1902 . 313
Workmen's Wages Act, 1884 297
Workmen's Wages Act, 1893 297-298

TABLE OF CASES

A.B., *Re* 321
A.C.M.B... 319
Allardice *v.* Allardice 336
Allen *v.* Manchester 336
Andrews *v.* D.P.P. 270
Att.-Gen. for Alberta *v.* Cook .. 325
Att.-Gen. (N.S.W.) *v.* Trethowan 50, 51

Barker *v.* Barker 327
Bater *v.* Bater 328*n*
Blackball Miners *v.* Judge of
    Court of Arbitration 191
Bosch *v.* Perpetual Trustee Co.
    Ltd. 336*n*
Boyes *v.* Carlyon 119, 120, 121, 125
Broad *v.* R. 132
Burton *v.* Power 273
Butchart *Re*, Butchart *v.* Butc-
    hart 338
Butt *v.* Frazer 190

Calder *Re*, Calder *v.* Public Trus-
    tee 337*n*
Campbell *v.* Frerichs 101
Carroll *v.* Att.-Gen. 343*n*
Carter *Re*, Carter *v.* Carter .. 334*n*
Chapman *v.* Tooth 62
Christie *v.* Hastie, Bull & Picker-
    ing Ltd. .. 215, 216, 217
Churchman *v.* Churchman .. 327*n*
C.K. *Re*, M. *v.* L. 334*n*
Clarke *v.* Att.-Gen. & Pritchard.. 28
Cobb *Re*, Nash *v.* Nash .. 266
Cock *v.* Att.-Gen. 74
Commissioners of Income Tax *v.*
    Pemsel 348*n*
Connett *v.* Connett, ... 330*n*
Coombes *v.* Harkness 273
Croft *v.* Dunphy 45
Crown Milling Company Limited
    v. R. .. 198, 202, 203, 204, 205,
      206, 207, 208, 209, 213, 343
Crowther *v.* Crowther 327*n*

Davis *v.* Davis 328*n*
Davy *Re*, Public Trustee *v.* Wheeler 332*n*
Dempster *v.* Dempster 327
Dillon *v.* Public Trustee .. 335*n*
D.P.P. *v.* Kent & Sussex Contrac-
    tors Ltd. 271
Duncan *v.* Jones 273

Eagle *v.* Booth 62
Elliott *v.* Hamilton 259
Ellis *v.* Ellis 325*n*
Ettenfield *v.* Ettenfield 328

Fairbairn Wright & Co. *v.* Levin
    & Co. 23

Germany *v.* Germany 327
Giles to Burns, *Re* a proposed sale 125
Gillies & Davidson 62
Ginesi *v.* Ginesi 328
Gleich, *Re* 260
Gower *v.* Gower 328*n*
Green, *Re* 337*n*
Griffin *v.* Police 94

Hardman, *Re* 331*n*
Harris *v.* D.P.P. 269
Harris *v.* Minister of the Interior 51
Hastings *v.* Hastings 325*n*
Heyting, *Re* 81
Higgs *v.* Perpetual Trustee Co.
    Ltd. 337*n*
Hopes *v.* Hopes 327*n*
Hura Rapata, *Re* 319
Hutton *v.* Hutton 342*n*

Jackson *v.* Jackson 327
Jackson & Co. Ltd. *v.* Collector of
    Customs 101, 243, 244, 245, 246,
      247, 251, 252, 253, 343*n*
Jackson & Co. Ltd. *v.* Price Tri-
    bunal 342*n*
Jackson (F. E.) & Co. Ltd. *v.* Price
    Tribunal (No. 2) 218
Jaffrey *v.* Mulgan 152
Jensen *v.* Wellington Woollen Co. 101
Jorgensen *v.* Minister of Customs 122

Kensington, *Re* 335*n*
Kerridge *v.* Girling-Butcher .. 123
King *v.* Frazer 123

Le Mesurier *v.* Le Mesurier .. 324
Lewis *v.* Lewis 327
Liversidge *v.* Anderson .. 102
Lloyd *v.* Lloyd and Leggeri .. 327
Love *v.* Ihaka te Rou 319

McDonald *v.* McDonald .. 328
McKellar *v.* Otago Land Board 123
M. *v.* M. 327
Magner *v.* Gohns 192
Manawatu Flaxmillers' Award, *Re* 181
Marshall Shipping Co. *v.* The
    King 348*n*
Merchants' Association of New
    Zealand *v.* R. 201, 202
Murdoch *v.* British Israel Federa-
    tion 271

Nelson & Co. Ltd. *v.* Police .. 271
New Zealand Dairy Control
 Board *v.* Att.-Gen. 229
New Zealand Educational Insti-
 tute *v.* The Marlborough Educa-
 tion Board 151
New Zealand Meat-producers
 Board *v.* Att.-Gen. 229
New Zealand Waterside Workers'
 Federation *v.* Frazer
  118, 119, 122, 124, 125, 178, 192
Noor Mohamed *v.* R. 269
Norton *v.* Norton 330*n*

Oakey *v.* Thompson 338
Otago Clerical Workers' Award,
 Re 125, 190

Palmer *v.* Crone 78
Park *v.* Minister of Education
  123, 151, 152
Parker *v.* Parker 318
Preston-Jones *v.* Preston-Jones .. 328*n*
Price *v.* Price 328
Public Trustee *v.* A. 332*n*

R., *Re* 264
— *v.* Barker 269
— *v.* Barrington 274
— *v.* Bateman 270
— *v.* Bernhard 269
— *v.* Boon 269
— *v.* Carswell 266
— *v.* Crown Milling Co. Ltd. 23, 202,
  203, 207, 208, 209, 213, 343
— *v.* Dawe 270
— *v.* Fetzer 269
— *v.* Garr 269
— *v.* Harley 273
— *v.* Hudson 265
— *v.* I.C.R. Haulage Ltd. .. 271
— *v.* Kingi 319
— *v.* Lander 44
— *v.* McKechie 265
— *v.* Manley 267
— *v.* Mathieson 269
— *v.* Mayor, Councillors and Citizens of City of Wellington .. 132
— *v.* Merchants' Association of
 New Zealand 200, 201
— *v.* Rix 264
— *v.* Seaton 328*n*
— *v.* Sims 269
— *v.* Spencer and Mayo .. 265*n*
— *v.* Stocks 266
— *v.* Storey 270
— *v.* Swinton 264
— *v.* Wheat 266
— *v.* White 265
— *v.* Whitta 269

Rangi *v.* Public Trustee .. 319
Rayner *v.* R. 132
Rayner *Re*, Daniell *v.* Rayner .. 79
Redpath, J. A. & Sons Ltd. *v.*
 New Zealand Fruit - export
 Control Board 230, 231
Reynolds *v.* Att.-Gen. .. 121, 122
Riddell *v.* Dodds 172
Rira Peti *v.* Ngaraihi Te Paku .. 318
Rose *v.* Ford 310-11
Rush, *Re* 336*n*
Russell *v.* Russell .. 328, 354
Ryan *v.* Evans 119, 126

Scott *v.* Empire Printing & Box
 Manufacturing Co. Ltd. .. 193
Seed *v.* Somerville .. 110,180
Sheehan *v.* Russell 61
Smerle *v.* Minister of Customs 123
Smith *v.* McArthur 342*n*
Southland Dairy Co. Ltd. *v.* New
 Zealand Dairy-Produce Con-
 trol Board 229, 230

Tagaloa *v.* Inspector of Police .. 44
Taratahi Dairy Co. and Mangorei
 Dairy Co. *v.* Att.-Gen.
  23, 27, 210, 211, 212, 213
Taylor *Re*, Public Trustee *v.*
 Lambert 334*n*
Taylor *v.* Harley 332*n*
Taylor and Oakley *v.* Edwards
  191, 340*n*
Terry, *Re* 338
Thompson, J. H. and L. J., *Re*.. 330*n*
Thompson *v.* Auckland Metro-
 politan Milk Council .. 101
Trustees Executors and Agency
 Co. of New Zealand *v.* Rowley 334*n*
Tutua Teone *v.* Tipene .. 319

Waitaki Dairy Co. *v.* New Zea-
 land Dairy-Produce Control
 Board 230
Wallis *v.* Solicitor-General 20, 21, 272
Wanbon *v.* Wanbon 327
Wilkes *v.* Asher 329*n*
Wilkinson *v.* Associated Chemists
 Ltd. 102
Wilkinson *v.* The Education
 Board of Otago 151
Williams *v.* Williams 327
Wi Tamahau Mahupuku, Thomp-
 son *v.* Mahupuku 319
Wood *Re*, Wood *v.* Leighton .. 337*n*
Woolworths (N.Z.) Ltd. *v.*
 Wynne 45, 260
Wright *v.* Wright 328

INDEX

abortions, illegal, 345-6
administration of justice, problems facing, 1, 16-21, 257-8
administrative law :
  administrative tribunals, 103-29, 342, 356
  appeals to ordinary courts, 127-8
  appraisal, 126-9
  classification, 103-5
  contribution to legal development, 117-18
  extent of independence, 112-17
  final administrative court, 128
  functions, 105-7
  hearings in public, 111
  introductory, 103
  judicial control 118-26
  judicial remedies, 119
  lawyers as members of, 126-7
  legislative, administrative, and adjudicative powers of, 107-8
  Lewis case, the, 114-17
  ministerial control 113-17
  numerical strength of, 108
  procedure, 110-11
  qualifications for appointment, 109-10
  quorum and decision making, 111, 112
  reasons for decisions, 129
  representation of parties, 111
  standards, formulation of, 117-18
  Supreme Court, attempts to limit its controlling power, 123-6
  tenure of office, 108-9
  trends, 126
  See also Social Legislation
  Crown, proceedings against the, 129-34, 355
  legislative history, 129-32
  present remedies, 132-4
  general, 89-134
  subordinate legislation, 91-103, 273, 356
  amending statutes, 96
  amplifying policies, 96
  appraisal of, 102-3
  confirmation by Parliament, 99, 100
  delegate of legislative authority, 97, 98
  drafting of, 98
  emergency statutes, 93-6
  judicial controls, 101-2
  laying before Parliament, 99
  New Zealand Executive, 92-103
  Organisation for National Security, 94

administrative law—*cont.*
  subordinate legislation—*cont.*
    Parliamentary debate, 100, 101
    phraseology of clauses, 98
    political prosecution, 94
    powers delegated by statute, 91
    practice of National Government, 100
    prerogative powers, 91-2
    publication of, 99
    retrospective, 97
    Select Committee, 1947-8, 100
    United Kingdom Executive, 92
    variety of designation, 98
administrative tribunals : *see* Administrative Law
adoption, 334-5, 351, 354
airways, main civil, 87, 89
Aliens Appeal Tribunal, 107, 108, 109, 112, 113
Aliens Authority, 107, 108, 109, 112, 113
Alpers, J., 208
American influence, 22-3, 198, 295
Anglican Church, 23
annexation, 2-4, 4n, 5
Arbitration, Court of, 26, 29, 69, 72, 104, 109, 122, 124, 125, 219, 340, 346-7
  see also Industrial Relations
Armed Forces Appeal Boards, 106, 108, 109, 111, 112
Arney, C. J., 261
Audit Office : see Public Administration
Australia, 28, 43, 45, 188, 198, 250, 261, 273

ballot, the second, 33-4
banking :
  commercial banking, 247-9
  general, 86, 87, 247-56, 339
  Reserve Bank, 240-2, 245-7, 247-56
    directorate, 251
    functions, 250-1, 253
    monetary policy of government, 251-3
    overseas remittances, 256
    powers of, 253-4
    restrictions on, 254-5
  state bank, 247
Bar, the New Zealand, 19-20
Bell, Sir Francis, 38
betting, 259, 344-5, 348, 356
bookmakers, 344-5
Boothby, J., 42
broadcasting, 40, 87
Browne, Sir Thomas Gore, 9-10

Bureau of Industry, 87, 106, 219-22
Busby, James, 2

Canada, 8, 11, 21, 43, 185
Capital punishment, 261, 268-9
Carleton, 259
cession, 2-5
Chadwick, 136
Chapman (F.R.) J., 23, 344
charitable aid, 25, 140
children, 23, 25, 26, 137, 173, 290, 309, 319, 327, 328-38, 354
  see also Social Legislation
Children's Courts : see Social Legislation
coal, 26, 283
Cockburn, Lord, 22
codification, 264-7, 293-4
commercial law, 292-306
  see also Contracts
commission of inquiry, 111, 220
  see also Judicial System
Commissions, Royal, see Judicial System
company law, 304-5
conciliation : see Industrial Relations
Conseil D'Etat, 129, 355
constitution :
  British sovereignty, extension to New Zealand of, 1
  conventions, 9
  early developments, 1-7
  proclamation of New Zealand as separate colony, 3
  representative, of 1846, 6
  whether federal, 7
  see also Parliament
contempt of Court, 20, 266
contract, freedom of, 26, 342
contracts, 276, 292-306, 315-16
  annual holidays, 296-7
  bankruptcy, 306
  carriage of goods and passengers, 295
  contractors' liens, 297-9, 354
  co-operative companies (primary products), 305
  Co-operative Dairy Companies' Tribunal, 305
  frustrated contracts, 303, 354
  hire purchase agreements, 297
  incorporated societies, 306
  mercantile law, 294-5
  minimum wage, 297
  Mortgagors' Liabilities Adjustment Commissions, 300
  protecting worker and weaker party, 296-7
  restrictions on raising capital, 305-6
  secret commissions, 295
  statutory interference with contractual relationships, 299-302, 341-2
  third party motor insurance, 303-4
  workmen's wages, 297-9, 354
Controller and Auditor-General : see Public Administration

conveyancing, 22, 277
  see also Property Law
Cook, Captain James, 1
Cook Islands, 237
corporations, public : see Public Administration
country quota, 31-2
Court of Appeal : see Judicial System
Court of Arbitration : see Judicial System, Industrial Relations
courts, system of : see Judicial System
criminal law, 257-75, 352
Crown Lands, Commissioner of, 74
Crown Milling Case, 202-9, 213, 343
Crown, proceedings against : see Administrative Law

Dairy Board, New Zealand : see Marketing (primary produce)
Dairy - Products Marketing Commission : see Marketing (primary produce)
defamation, 307-8
delegated legislation : see Administrative Law
Denmark, 29
destitute persons, 328-30
disallowance : see Parliament
Disputes Committee, Emergency, 106, 108, 109, 112
  See also Industrial Relations
divorce, 317, 322-6, 354
domicile, 324-6, 331, 338

easements, 22
education : see Social Legislation
elections, 33-5
electoral boundaries, 31-2
Electoral Courts, 34-5
employment, 26
English law, reception of, 5, 17, 258-9
entrenched sections : see Parliament
estates of deceased persons, administration, 25
evidence, 354-5
exchange control :
  export control, 240-2
  general, 87, 240-7
  import control, 242-7
  Monetary Committee, New Zealand, 242, 248, 250
  Reserve Bank, 240-2, 245-7, 247-56
  types of licence, 241-2
Executive Commission of Agriculture : see Marketing (primary produce)
Executive Council, 8-9, 10, 20
Executive, respect for law, 348-9
export control, 209-13, 343
Export Licences Regulations, 87, 240-2, 246
External Affairs, 87
extraterritorial legislation : see Parliament

factory code, 26, 173
family homes, 338-9
family law, 276, 317-39, 352
family protection, 335-8, 339, 341, 350, 354
Fenton, Francis D., 18
fidelity fund : *see* Judicial System
fire insurance, 26, 86
Fitzroy, Governor, 85, 117
forty-hour week, 28, 187
franchise :
  Maoris, 30-4
  parliamentary, 30-1
  women, 31
Frazer, Sir Francis, 106*n*, 127, 189

Game, Sir Philip, 15
General Assembly, 6, 8, 93
  See also Parliament
Godwin, 257
gold, discovered, 21, 283
Goods Services Charges Tribunal, 105, 107, 108, 110, 111, 112, 113, 127
Gorst, John, 18
government departments, 84-9
Government Railways Industrial Tribunal, 106, 107, 108, 109, 110, 111, 112
Government Service Tribunal, 75
Governor-General (Governor) :
  amended instructions, 9, 10
  change in system for appointment of, 12
  constitutional conventions, 9
  dismissal of ministry, 14, 15
  dissolution of parliament, 14, 15
  formation of new ministry, 15, 16
  general, 8-16
  imperial interests, 9, 10, 11
  naval escort of troops, 11
  New South Wales and Pacific, 1
  power to appoint executive council, 9
  power to reject advice, 12, 13, 14
  prerogative of pardon, 9, 10, 11
  relations with New Zealand Company 16
  to whom responsible, 8, 11
Great Britain, legislative borrowing, 28
Gresson (H. B.), J., 19
Grey, Earl, 6, 37
Grey, Sir George, 6, 10, 40

Hanworth, Lord, 352
Hawke's Bay, 18
health : *see* Social Legislation
Herdman, J., 208
High Commissioner for United Kingdom, first appointment of, 12
highways, 22
Hobson, Captain William, 2-4, 84
Holmes, Allan, 62
hospitals, 28, 140, 141
House of Representatives : *see* Parliament, General Assembly
housing : *see* Social Legislation

illegitimacy : *see* Children
immigration, 25, 85
imperial interests, 10-11, 13
import control, 342, 343
Import Control Regulations (1938), 87, 210, 240, 242-7, 343
India, 28
industrial efficiency : *see* Monopolies
Industrial Efficiency Appeal Authority 106, 108, 109, 110, 112, 127, 222-224
industrial relations :
  Arbitration, Court of, 177-8, 187-95, 198
    see also Judicial System
  awards, 178-80
  compulsory unionism, 190, 192, 194, 340
  conciliation and arbitration, 173-5
  conciliation procedure, 175-7
  conscientious objectors, 190
  disputes committees, 179-80
  evidence and procedure, 180-1
  general, 172-96, 343, 346-7
  general orders of Court of Arbitration, 188
  health of unions, 193-5
  industrial unrest, prevention of, 196, 341
  intimidation, 196
  introductory, 172-3
  ordinary Courts, attitude of, 191-3
  penalties, 181-5, 187, 191-2, 275
  picketing, 196
  preference for unionists, 190-1
  problems facing Court of Arbitration, 191
  profit-sharing schemes, 190
  registration, cancellation or suspension of unions, 183-4
  secret ballot, 183-6
  sedition, 196
  special provisions, 184-5
  strikes, 195-6
  tribunals, ad hoc, 194-5
  unions beyond jurisdiction of Court of Arbitration, 185-7
  victimisation, 181
internal defence, ministerial control of, 10
intestacy, succession on, 290-1, 354

Jennings, 316
Jourdain, W. R., 280-1
judges, difficulties of, in early years, 19
judicial system :
  administrative tribunals, 75
  Assessment Courts, 76
  Children's Courts, 69
    see also Social Legislation
  commissions of inquiry, 75
  Compensation Court, 72
  Cook Islands Native Appellate Court, 70

judicial system—*cont.*
  Coroners' Courts, 71-2
  County Courts, 53, 54, 55
  Court of Appeal, 19, 20, 67, 68, 69,
    260
  Court of Arbitration, 69, 72
  Court of Review, 72, 301
  District Courts, 54, 55, 59, 63
  general, 52-83, 258
  general and quarter sessions, 53, 55,
    63, 258
  grand jury, 63, 64, 65, 67
  jury lists, 64, 272
  Justices of the Peace, criminal juris-
    diction of, 57, 58
  Land Valuation tribunals, 72
  Magistrates' Courts, 53-60, 257*n*, 355
  Maori Appellate Court, 69, 70, 71
  Maori Land Court, 19, 69, 71, 169
  miscellaneous tribunals, 76
  petty sessions, 53, 56, 258
  Police Magistrate, 53-54
  Privy Council 20, 21, 68, 70
  procedure commissioners, English, 62
  procedure commissioners, New Zea-
    land, 61, 62
  Requests, Courts of, 53, 54, 55
  Resident Magistrates' Courts, 54, 55,
    56, 58
  royal commissions, 74-5
  Sessions of the Peace, Courts of, 55
  shipping tribunals, 75-6
  special jury, 64, 66, 67
  Stipendiary Magistrates, 55-60, 63,
    72, 73
  Supreme Court, 19, 20, 54, 55, 57, 58,
    59, 60-7, 75, 258
  Vice-Admiralty Court, 60
  Wardens' Courts, 73-4
  women jurors, 64, 272
Judiciary and Magistracy:
  burden of proof, 78
  conduct of judicial proceedings, 78
  constitutional position and duties
    of, 76-9
  immunities, 77, 78
  independence and impartiality, 76,
    78
  judge and jury, province of, 78, 272
  judicial precedents, 78-9
  legal profession, 79-82, 258
  barrister and solicitor, amalgama-
    tion of professions of, 79, 81
  Council of Legal Education, 80, 90
  fidelity fund, 80
  law reporting, 19, 82, 83
  legal aid, poor persons, 82
  New Zealand Law Society, 80, 82,
    83, 353
  qualifications for admission, 79-82
Judiciary : *see* Judicial System
juries : *see* Judicial System
Jurist, The New Zealand, 23
justice, problems facing the administration of, 1, 16-21, 257-8

Katatore, 18
Kororareka Vigilants' Association, 52

Labour, Department of, 86, 87
labour unionism, 25
land, 5, 20, 22, 26, 84, 86
  See also Property Law
Land Registrar, District, 104
Land, Registrar-General of, 104
Land Sales Committees, 104, 105, 107,
  108, 109, 109*n*, 110, 111, 113,
  114-17, 118, 119, 120, 124, 125,
  126
Land Sales Court, 104, 105, 107, 108,
  109, 111, 112, 113, 114-17, 118,
  119, 120, 124, 125
land sales legislation, 341, 347, 348
Land Settlement Board, 282
land transfer system, 22, 28, 279-80, 339
  See also Property Law
Land Valuation Committees, 105, 106,
  106*n*, 109*n*, 112
Land Valuation Court, 69, 105, 106,
  106*n*, 111, 112, 128, 292
law reform, 302-3, 352-7
Law Reporting, New Zealand Council
  of : *see* Judicial System
Law Revision Committee, 353-6
Law Society, New Zealand : *see* Judicial
  System
legal aid, poor persons : *see* Judicial
  System
Legal Education, Council of : *see* Judicial System
legal profession : *see* Judicial System
legal representation of parties, 111, 150
  176, 180-1
legal trends, 339-57
legislation, historical sketch of, 21-9
  administrative difficulties, 347-8
  judicial interpretation, 272-3, 341-3
  limiting factors, 344-51
  retrospective, 350-1
  validating, 350-1
Legislative Council : *see* Parliament
legislatures, provincial, 6
legitimation, 331-3, 354
Lewis, the case of, 114-17
Licensing Control Commission, 75
Life Insurance Department, Government, 24, 86
limitation periods, 355
liquor, sale of, 345, 348, 356
local government, 25, 87, 89, 171
  See also Social Legislation
Local Government Commission, 75

McCleverty, Lt. Col., 85
McNaghten rules, 271
MacGregor, John, 26
MacGregor, (W. C.), J., 23, 207
Magistrates' Courts: *see* Judicial System
Maine, Sir Henry, 65
Manpower Committees, Industrial, 107,
  108, 109, 111, 112, 113, 114

Manpower Officers, District, 107
Maori Land Board, 169
Maori Land Court, 19, 69-71, 169
Maoris, 2, 3, 4, 5, 6, 10, 16-19, 21, 23,
    26, 30, 31, 34, 84, 85, 257, 274,
    317-20, 321, 331
    See also Social Legislation
marketing (primary produce):
    Agriculture, Department of, 86, 238
    consumer, the, 237-8
    co-operative companies, 230
    courts, marketing boards and the,
        229-31
    Dairy Board, New Zealand, 226, 231,
        232, 233, 234, 236
    Dairy-Produce Control Board, 228-
        230, 231
    Dairy-Products Marketing Commis-
        sion, 232-6, 238
    Executive Commission of Agricul-
        ture, 86, 231, 235
    Fruit-export Control Board, 230-1
    general, 27, 28, 86, 87, 96, 209, 225-
        239, 339, 341, 342, 343
    internal marketing, 236-8
    marketing authorities, 238-9
    Marketing Department, 87, 232, 235-
        238
    Meat Producers' Board, 225-8
    producer, more control to, 238
    proprietary companies, 230
    Reserve Bank, 234, 254
    state guarantee of prices of dairy-
        produce, 232-4
    trade policy of government, 234, 236,
        239
marriage, 317-21
Massachusetts, 23, 334
Meat Producers' Board : *see* Market-
    ing (primary produce)
mercantile law : *see* Contracts
mercy, prerogative of, 9, 10, 11, 69, 268,
    349
mines and mining, 22, 86
ministers' powers (U.K.), report of
    committee on, 96
missionaries, 1, 16
monopolies :
    commercial profit, 215-16
    Crown Milling case, 202-9, 213
    export control and internal prices,
        209-13
    general, 23, 197-209, 343
    industrial efficiency, 219-24
        Bureau of Industry, 219-22
        Industrial Efficiency Appeal Auth-
            ority, 222-4
        industrial plans, 219-20
        legislative scheme, 219-20
        registration and licensing, 220-2
    judicial inquiries, 199-200
    price control, 215-18
    price orders, 218
    Price Tribunal, 215-18
    profiteering, 213-15

monopolies—*cont.*
    prosecutions, 217
    regulations, 200
    special approvals, 218
    standards, 217, 220
    statutory formula, 218
    subsequent trends, 213
    subsidies, 217
    sugar, 200-2
municipal corporations, 6, 7
    See also Local Government
Myers, Sir Michael, 90, 118, 151, 214,
    343

natives : *see* Maoris
negligence : *see* Torts
New Munster, 6
New Plymouth, 3
New South Wales, 1-5, 53, 84, 257, 269
New Ulster, 6
New Zealand Association, 4
New Zealand Company, 3, 5, 16, 84
New Zealand Law Society, 80, 82, 83
North Island, sovereignty, 3
Norway, 29
Nova Scotia, 8
nursing services, 26

Ontario, 298

Pacific, the, 1, 2
Pakington, Sir John, 37
pardon : *see* Prerogative of Pardon
Parliament :
    assent to bills, 40, 41
    broadcasting, 40
    caucus, 40
    disallowance, 41, 49-50
        stockholders, 49-50
    entrenched sections, 41-4
        colonial judiciary, 43
        elections, 41
        electoral machinery, 41
        General Assembly, 42
        Legislative Council, 42, 43
        legislature, 43
        plenary powers, 1, 42
        privileges, 41
        provinces, powers of, 41
        repugnancy, 42-43, 45-6
    extraterritorial legislation, 44-5
        Pacific, war in, 45
        Western Samoa, 45
        whaling, 45
    flexibility of constitution, 50-1
    general, 30-51
    House of Representatives, 8, 35
        disputed elections, 34, 35
        life, 35, 36, 37
        Maori members of, 35
        size of House, 35
        women candidates, 34

Parliament—*cont.*
　Legislative Council, 5, 6, 8, 11, 31,
　　34, 37, 38, 39, 54, 92
　　abolition, 1, 38, 39, 356
　　Constitutional Reform Committee
　　　(2), 39
　　Maori members, 38
　　senate, 39
　limitations on powers of, 41-50
　money bills, 39, 40
　organization, ceremonial and proce-
　　dure, 40
　repugnancy, 45-6
　　United Kingdom Parliament, su-
　　　premacy of, 46
　reservation, 41, 47-9
　　advice of ministers, 47-8
　　Colonial Courts of Admiralty, 48
　　competence of General Assembly,
　　　48-9
　　imperial interests, 47-8
　　instructions to Governor, 47
　　shipping and seamen, 47-8
　time limits on speeches, 40
　veto by Governor, 40, 41
　written constitution, 50-1
　　See also Governor-General
pastoral age, 21
Patents, Commissioner of, 103
penal system, 260-2
penalties, remission of, 350-1
pensions, 26, 28, 38, 86, 87
　See also Social Legislation
pleading, 25
poor persons, legal aid : *see* Judicial
　System
population in early years, 2, 16
prerogative of pardon, 9, 10, 11, 69, 268,
　349-50
price control : *see* Monopolies
Price Tribunal, formerly Price Investi-
　gation Tribunal, 105, 107, 108,
　109, 110, 111, 112, 113, 342
　See also Monopolies
Prince Edward Island, 8
Prisons Board, 263
Privy Council, judicial committee of :
　see Judicial System
Procedure Commissioners, English, 62
Procedure Commissioners, New Zea-
　land, 61, 62
profiteering : *see* Monopolies
prohibition (licensing), 31
property law, 276-92, 315-16, 352
　atomic energy, 284
　bills of exchange, 293
　chattels securities, 289-90
　coal, 283
　crown land tenures, 280-2
　customary hire purchase agreements,
　　290
　eminent domain, 282-5
　erosion, 285
　fencing, 289
　geothermal energy, 284

property law—*cont.*
　illegitimate persons, 290
　iron and steel, 284-5
　land and natural resources, conserva-
　　tion, 282-5
　land tax, 281
　married women, 285-7
　natural disasters, 285
　petroleum, 283-4
　registration of deeds, 278-9
　statutory simplification, 276-8
　undue aggregation, 281-2
　war damage, 285
proportional representation, 33, 34
Protector of the Aborigines, 17
provinces, New Zealand divided into, 7
provinces abolished, 7, 86
provincial government, 7
provincial councils, 24, 37, 85, 273
Provincial Council for Canterbury, 24
public administration :
　Agriculture, 86
　Bank of New Zealand, 87
　Broadcasting, 87
　Controller & Auditor-General, 88-9
　Crown Lands, 86
　Education, 86
　exchange control, 87
　export control, 87
　External Affairs, 87
　Forestry, 86
　general, 84-9, 357
　Health, 86
　historical sketch, 84-7
　Housing, 87
　Immigration, 85
　import control ,87
　Industries and Commerce, 86, 87
　Labour, 86, 87
　legal status, 88
　linen flax industry, 87
　local government, 87, 89
　main civil airways, 87, 89
　Maori affairs, 84, 85
　Marketing, 86, 87
　Mines, 86
　mode of control, 88
　Mortgage Corporation, 87
　national employment, 87
　Pensions, 86, 87
　Prime Minister, 86
　public corporations, 87, 88, 89
　Public Service, 84, 85, 86, 87, 88, 89,
　　104, 120, 121, 122, 125
　Railways, 87, 295
　Reserve Bank, 87, 89
　Scientific and Industrial Research,
　　86
　secondary industries, 87
　Social Security, 87
　State Advances, 86
　State Fire Insurance, 86
　State Hydro-Electricity, 87
　Tourist, 86
　Transport, 86

public administration—*cont.*
  Treasury, 88
  Valuation, 86, 292
  Wheat Committee, 88, 89
  Works, 85, 87
public corporations, 87, 88, 89
Public Service, 84, 85, 86, 87, 88, 89,
    104, 120, 121, 122, 125
Public Service Commission, 86, 88, 89,
    104, 120, 121, 125
Public Trustee, 24, 28, 86, 169
public works, 25

Queensland, 28, 298, 307

Rawiri, 18
reception of laws of England, 5, 17
Reed, J., 207-8
refrigeration, 22, 26
Representation Commission, 31, 32
representative government, 8
repugnancy : *see* Parliament
reservation : *see* Parliament
Reserve Bank, 87, 89, 234
    See also Exchange Control, Banking
resident magistrates, 19
    See also Judicial System
responsible government, 7, 8, 9, 10, 24
Revenue, Commissioner of Inland, 347
Revision Authorities, 106, 108, 109, 111,
    124
Richmond, 266-7
riparian rights, 22
Rules Committee, 97
Russell, Lord John, government of, 37

Salmond, Sir John, 88, 90, 211, 269,
    348-9
Scottish law, 26
Sea-Fisheries Licensing Appeal Auth-
    ority, 106, 108, 112, 127
secondary industry, 28, 87
Selwyn, Bishop, 20, 23
settled colony, New Zealand, at law a, 4
Sewell, Henry, 18, 20, 24
social legislation :
  age benefit, 160
  appeal tribunals (teachers), 150
  central administration (health), 136,
    137
  character, 163
  child welfare, 152-9
  Children's Courts, 154-5, 157-9, 170,
    264, 269
  dentists, 143-4
  education, 25, 86, 147-52, 170, 171
  education boards, 148-9
  Education, Department of, 149-50
  emergency benefit, 162
  family benefit, 160-1
  financing of social security scheme,
    165
  foster-homes, 156-7

social legislation—*cont.*
  general, 25, 26, 135-71, 315-16
  health, 86, 136-47, 170, 171, 339
  health benefits, 146-7
  Health, Department of, 141-2
  health education, 146
  health services, 146
  hospital boards, 140-1
  housing, 87, 135, 138, 139, 169
  illegitimate births, 157
  introduction, 135-6
  infirm and neglected persons, 143
  invalid's benefit, 161, 170
  judicial control, 151-2
  legislative history of child welfare,
    152-3
  local authorities, 138-9
  Maori welfare, 165-9, 171
  masseurs, 143-4
  means test, 164
  medical advertisements, 144-5
  medical practitioners, 143-4
  midwives, 143-4
  miner's benefit, 161, 170
  miscellaneous regulatory functions,
    145-6
  nurses, 143-4
  opticians, 143-4
  orphan's benefit, 160
  pharmaceutical chemists, 144
  plumbers, 143-4
  post-primary schools, 149
  private or public institutions, control
    of, 155-6
  rates of benefits, 163-4
  reciprocity with other countries, 164-
    165
  reform in social legislation, 169-71
  residential qualifications, 162-3
  school committees, 147-8
  sickness benefit, 162
  social security, 28, 75, 87, 159-65,
    170, 171, 337-8, 339
  standards, professional, vocational and
    technical, 143-4
  superannuation benefit, 160
  tuberculosis, 142-3
  tribal committee, 166-9
  tribal executive, 166-9
  unemployment benefit, 161-2
  widow's benefit, 160
social security : *see* Social Legislation
social science, 357
Soil Conservation and Rivers Control
    Council, 75
Solicitor-General, 20
South Australia, 22, 28, 42, 43, 279
South Island, sovereignty, 2, 3
sovereignty,
  denial, 2
  establishment, 2, 5
  South Island, 2, 3
Spain, William, 84, 85, 117
Special Tribunal, 106, 108, 109, 111,
    124